I0832479

A HISTORY OF THE STRUGGLE FOR SLAVERY EXTENSION OR RESTRICTION IN THE UNITED STATES, FROM THE DECLARATION OF INDEPENDENCE TO THE PRESENT DAY.

MAINLY

COMPILED AND CONDENSED FROM THE JOURNALS OF CONGRESS AND OTHER OFFICIAL RECORDS, AND SHOWING THE VOTE BY YEAS AND NAYS ON THE MOST IMPORTANT DIVISIONS IN EITHER HOUSE.

BY HORACE GREELEY.

NEW YORK:
DIX, EDWARDS & CO., 321 BROADWAY.
1856.

MILLER & HOLMAN,
Printers and Stereotypers, N. Y.

CONTENTS.

THE

HISTORY OF THE QUESTION

OF

SLAVERY EXTENSION OR RESTRICTION.

MAINLY BY DOCUMENTS.

I.

SLAVERY IN THE COLONIES.

HUMAN Slavery, as it existed in the pagan world, and especially in the infancy, vigor, and decline of Greek and Roman civilization, gradually died out in the advancing light of Christianity. When Columbus opened the New World to European enterprise and settlement, the serfdom of Russia and Hungary, and the mild bondage of Turkey —each rather an Asiatic or Scythian than a European power—were the last remaining vestiges of a system which had pervaded, and mastered, and ruined, the vast empires of Alexander and the Cæsars. The few ignorant and feeble dependents elsewhere held in virtual bondage by force rather of custom than of positive law, serve rather to establish than disprove this general statement.

Lust of gold and power was the main impulse of Spanish migration to the marvelous regions beyond the Atlantic. And the soft and timid Aborigines of tropical America, especially of its islands, were first compelled to surrender whatever they possessed of the precious metals to the imperious and grasping strangers; next forced to disclose to those strangers the sources whence they were most readily obtained; and finally driven to toil and delve for more, wherever power and greed supposed they might most readily be obtained. From this point, the transition to general enslavement was ready and rapid. The gentle and indolent natives, unaccustomed to rugged, persistent toil, and revolting at the harsh and brutal severity of their Christian masters, had but one unfailing resource—death. Through privation, hardship, exposure, fatigue and despair, they drooped and died, until millions were reduced to a few miserable thousands within the first century of Spanish rule in America.

A humane and observant priest (Las Casas,) witnessing these cruelties and sufferings, was moved by pity to devise a plan for their termination. He suggested and urged the policy of substituting for these feeble and perishing "Indians" the hardier natives of Western Africa, whom their eternal wars and marauding invasions were constantly exposing to captivity and sale as prisoners of war, and who, as a race, might be said to be inured to the hardships and degradations of Slavery by an immemorial experience. The suggestion was unhappily approved, and the woes and miseries of the few remaining Aborigines of the islands known to us as "West Indies," were inconsiderably prolonged by exposing the whole continent for unnumbered generations to the evils and horrors of African slavery. The author lived to perceive and deplore the consequences of his expedient.

The sanction of the Pope having been obtained for the African slave-trade by representations which invested it with a look of philanthropy, Spanish and Portuguese mercantile avarice was readily enlisted in its prosecution, and the whole continent, north and south of the tropics, became a slave-mart before the close of the sixteenth century.

Holland, a comparatively new and Protestant state, unable to shelter itself from the reproaches of conscience and humanity behind a Papal bull, entered upon the new traffic more tardily; but its profits soon overbore all scruples, and British merchants were not proof against the glittering evidences of their success. But, the first slave-ship that ever entered a North American port for the sale of its human merchandise, was a Dutch trading-vessel which landed twenty negro bondmen at Jamestown, the nucleus of Virginia, almost simultaneously with the landing of the Pilgrims of the Mayflower on Plymouth rock, Dec. 22d, 1620.

The Dutch slaver had chosen his market with sagacity. Virginia was settled by CAVALIERS—gentlemen-adventurers aspiring to live by their own wits and other men's labor —with the necessary complement of followers and servitors. Few of her pioneers cherished any earnest liking for downright, persistent, muscular exertion; yet some exertion was urgently required to clear away the heavy forest which all but covered the soil of the infant colony, and grow the Tobacco which easily became its staple export, by means of which nearly everything required by its people but food was to be paid for in England. The slaves, therefore, found ready purchasers at satisfactory prices, and the success of the first venture induced others; until not only Virginia but every part of British America was supplied with African slaves.

This traffic, with the bondage it involved, had no justification in British nor in the early colonial laws; but it proceeded nevertheless, much as an importation of dromedaries to replace with presumed economy our horses and oxen might now do. Georgia was the first among the colonies to resist and remand it in her original charter under the lead of her noble founder-Governor, General Oglethorpe; but the evil was too formidable and inveterate for local extirpation, and a few years saw it established, even in Georgia; first evading or defying, and at length molding and transforming the law.

It is very common at this day to speak of our revolutionary struggle as commenced and hurried forward by a union of free and slave colonies; but such is not the fact. However slender and dubious its legal basis, Slavery existed in each and all of the colonies that united to declare and maintain their independence. Slaves were proportionately more numerous in certain portions of the South; but they were held with impunity throughout the North, advertised like dogs or horses, and sold at auction, or otherwise, as chattels. Vermont, then a territory in dispute between New-Hampshire and New-York, and with very few civilized inhabitants, mainly on its southern and eastern borders, is probably the only portion of the revolutionary confederation never polluted by the tread of a slave.

The spirit of liberty, aroused or intensified by the protracted struggle of the colonists against usurped and abused power in the mother country, soon found itself engaged in natural antagonism against the current form of domestic despotism. "How shall we complain of arbitrary or unlimited power exerted over us, while we exert a still more despotic and inexcusable power over a dependent and benighted race?" was very fairly asked. Several suits were brought in Massachusetts—where the fires of liberty burnt earliest and brightest—to test the legal right of slaveholding; and the leading Whigs gave their money and their legal services to support these actions, which were generally, on one ground or another, successful. Efforts for an express law of emancipation, however, failed even in Massachusetts; the Legislature, doubtless, apprehending that such a measure, by alienating the slaveholders, would increase the number and power of the Tories; but in 1777, a privateer having brought a lot of captured slaves into Jamaica, and advertised them for sale, the General Court, as the legislative assembly was called, interfered and had them set at liberty. The first Continental Congress which resolved to resist the usurpations and oppressions of Great Britain by force, had already declared that our struggle would be "for the cause of human nature," which the Congress of 1776, under the lead of Thomas Jefferson, expanded into the noble affirmation of the right of "all men to life, liberty, and the pursuit of happiness" contained in the immortal preamble to the Declaration of Independence. A like averment that 'all men are born free and equal.' was in 1780 inserted in the Massachusetts Bill of Rights; and the Supreme Court of that State, in 1783, on an indictment of a master for assault and battery, held this declaration a bar to slaveholding henceforth in the state.

A similar clause in the second Constitution of New-Hampshire, was held by the courts of that State to secure freedom to every child, born therein after its adoption. Pennsylvania, in 1780, passed an act prohibiting the further introduction of slaves and securing freedom to all persons born in that State thereafter. Connecticut and Rhode Island passed similar acts in 1784. Virginia, 1778, on motion of Mr. Jefferson, prohibited the further importation of slaves; and in 1782, removed all legal restrictions on emancipation: Maryland adopted both of these in 1783. North Carolina, in 1786, declared the introduction of Slaves into that state "of evil consequences and highly impolitic," and imposed a duty of £5 per head thereon. New-York and New-Jersey followed the example of Virginia and Maryland, including the domestic in the same interdict with the foreign slave trade. Neither of these States, however, declared a general emancipation until many years thereafter, and Slavery did not wholly cease in New-York until about 1830, nor in New-Jersey till a much later date. The distinction of free and slave States, with the kindred assumption of a natural antagonism between the North and South, was utterly unknown to the men of the Revolution.

Before the Declaration of Independence, but during the intense ferment which preceded it, and distracted public attention from everything else, Lord Mansfield had rendered his judgment from the King's Bench, which expelled Slavery from England, and ought to have destroyed it in the colonies as well. The plaintiff in this famous case was James Somerset, a native of Africa, carried to Virginia as a slave, taken thence by his master to England, and there incited to resist the claim of his master to his services, and assert his right to liberty. In the first recorded case, involving the legality of modern slavery in England, it was held (1697) that negroes, "being usually bought and sold among merchants as merchandise, and *also being infidels*, there might be a property in them sufficient to maintain trover." But this was overruled by Chief Justice Holt from the King's Bench (1697,) ruling that "so soon as a negro lands in England he is free;" and again, (1702) that "there is no such thing as a slave by the law of England." This judgment proving exceedingly troublesome to planters and merchants from slave-holding colonies visiting the mother country with their servants, the merchants concerned in the American trade, in 1729, procured from Yorke and Talbot, the Attorney General and Solicitor General of the Crown, a written opinion that negroes, legally enslaved elsewhere, might be held as slaves in England, and that even baptism was no bar to the master's claim. This opinion was, in 1749, held to be sound law by Yorke (now Lord Hardwicke), sitting as Judge, on the ground that, if the contrary ruling of Lord Holt were upheld, it would abolish slavery in Jamaica or Virginia as well as in England; British law being paramount in each. Thus the law stood until Lord Mansfield, in Somerset's case, reversed it with evident reluctance, and after having vainly endeavored to bring about an accommodation between the parties. When delay would serve no longer, and a judgment must be rendered, Mansfield declared it in these memorable words:

> "We cannot direct the law; the law must direct us. * * * The state of Slavery is of such a nature that it is incapable of being introduced on any reasons, moral or political, but only by positive law. which preserves its force long after the reasons, occasion, and time itself whence it was created, is erased from the memory. It is so odious that nothing can be sufficient to support it but positive law. Whatever inconveniences, therefore, may follow from the decision, I cannot say this case is allowed or approved by the law of England, and therefore the black must be discharged."

The natural, if not necessary, effect of this decision on Slavery in these colonies, had their connection with the mother country been continued, is sufficiently obvious.

II.

SLAVERY UNDER THE CONFEDERATION.

THE disposition or management of unpeopled territories, pertaining to the thirteen recent colonies now confederated as independent States, early became a subject of solicitude and of bickering among those States, and in Congress. By the terms of their charters, some of the colonies had an indefinite extension westwardly, and were only limited by the power of the grantor. Many of these charters conflicted with each other—the same territory being included within the limits of two or more totally distinct colonies. As the expenses of the Revolutionary struggle began to bear heavily on the resources of the States, it was keenly felt by some that their share in the advantages of the expected triumph, would be less than that of others. Massachusetts, Connecticut, New-York, Virginia, North Carolina, and Georgia, laid claim to spacious dominions outside of their proper boundaries; while New-Hampshire (save in Vermont), Rhode Island, New-Jersey, Maryland, Delaware, and South Carolina, possessed no such boasted resources to meet the war-debts constantly augmenting. They urged, therefore, with obvious justice, that these unequal advantages ought to be surrendered, and all the lands included within the territorial limits of the Union, but outside of the proper and natural boundaries of the several States, respectively, should be ceded to, and held by, Congress, in trust for the common benefit of all the States, and their proceeds employed in satisfaction of the debts and liabilities of the Confederation. This reasonable requisition was ultimately, but with some reservations, responded to. Virginia reserved a sufficiency beyond the Ohio to furnish the bounties promised to her revolutionary officers and soldiers. Connecticut, a western reserve, since largely settled from the parent State. Massachusetts reserved five millions of acres, located in Western New York, which she claimed to be entitled by her charter to own. In either of these cases, the fee only was reserved, the sovereignty being surrendered.

The cessions were severally made during, or directly after, the close of the Revolutionary War. And one of the most obvious duties devolved on the Continental Congress, which held its sessions in Philadelphia directly after the close of that exhausting struggle, was the framing of an act or ordinance for the government of the vast domain thus committed to its care and disposal.

The responsible duty of framing this ordinance was devolved by Congress on a Select Committee, consisting of Mr. Jefferson of Va. (Chairman), Chase of Md., and Howell of R. I.; who in due time reported a plan for the government of the Western Territory, contemplating the whole region included within our boundaries west of the old thirteen States, and as far south as our 31st degree of North latitude; territory as yet partially ceded to the Confederation, but which was expected to be so, and embracing several of our present Slave States. This plan contemplated the ultimate division of this territory into seventeen States, eight of them situated below the parallel of the Falls of the Ohio (now Louisville), and nine above it. Among other rules reported from this Committee by Mr. Jefferson, for the government of this vast region, was the following:

> "That after the year 1800, of the Christian era, there shall be neither Slavery nor involuntary servitude in any of the said *States*, otherwise than in punishment of crimes, whereof the party shall have been convicted to be personally guilty."

April 19th, 1784.—Congress having the aforesaid Report under consideration, Mr. Spaight, of N. C., moved the striking out of the above paragraph. Mr. Read, of S. C., seconded the motion The ayes and nays, being required by Mr. Howell, were ordered, and put in this form—"Shall the words moved to be stricken out stand?"—and decided as follows:

N.-Hampshire	Mr. Foster	ay	Ay.
	" Blanchard	ay	
Massachusetts	" Gerry	ay	Ay.
	" Partridge	ay	
Rhode Island	" Ellery	ay	Ay.
	" Howell	ay	
Connecticut	" Sherman	ay	Ay.
	" Wadsworth	ay	
New-York	" De Witt	ay	Ay.
	" Paine	ay	
New-Jersey	" Dick	ay	*
Pennsylvania	" Mifflin	ay	Ay.
	" Montgomery	ay	
	" Hand	ay	
Maryland	" McHenry	no	No.
	" Stone	no	
Virginia	" Jefferson	ay	No.
	" Hardy	no	
	" Mercer	no	
N. Carolina	" Williamson	ay	Divided.
	" Spaight	no	
S. Carolina	" Read	no	No.
	" Beresford	no	

* No quorum.

So the question was lost, and the words were struck out.

Lost—although six States voted ay to only three nay; and though of the members present, sixteen voted for, to seven against, Mr. Jefferson's proposition. But the Articles of Confederation required a vote of nine States to carry a proposition; and, failing to receive so many, this comprehensive exclusion of Slavery from the Federal Territories was defeated.

The Ordinance, thus depleted, after undergoing some further amendments, was finally approved April 23rd—all the delegates, but those from South Carolina, voting in the affirmative.

In 1787 the last Continental Congress, sitting in New York simultaneously with the Convention at Philadelphia which framed our Federal Constitution, took up the subject of the government of the Western Territory, raising a Committee thereon, of which Nathan Dane, of Massachusetts, was Chairman. That Committee reported (July 11th), "An Ordinance for the government of the Territory of the United States, *Northwest of the Ohio*"—the larger area contemplated by Mr. Jefferson's bill not having been ceded by the Southern States claiming dominion over it. This bill embodied many of the provisions originally drafted and reported by Mr. Jefferson, but with some modifications, and concludes with six unalterable articles of perpetual compact, the last of them as follows:

"There shall be neither slavery nor involuntary servitude, in the said territory, otherwise than in punishment of crimes, whereof the parties shall be duly convicted."

To this was added, prior to its passage, the stipulation for the delivery of fugitives from labor or service, soon after embodied in the Federal Constitution; and in this shape, the entire ordinance was adopted (July 13th) by a unanimous vote, Georgia and the Carolinas concurring.

III.

UNDER THE CONSTITUTION.

The old Articles of Confederation having proved inadequate to the creation and maintenance of a capable and efficient national or central authority, a Convention of Delegates from the several States, was legally assembled in Philadelphia, in 1787—George Washington President; and the result of its labors was our present Federal Constitution, though some amendments, mainly of the nature of restrictions on Federal power, were proposed by the several State Conventions assembled, to pass upon that Constitution, and adopted. The following are all the provisions of that instrument, which are presumed to bear upon the subject of Slavery:

(Preamble): "We, the people of the United States, in order to form a more perfect Union, establish justice, insure domestic tranquillity, provide for the common defense, promote the general welfare, and secure the blessings of liberty to ourselves and our posterity do ordain and establish this Constitution for the United States of America.

"Art. I. § 1. All legislative powers herein granted, shall be vested in a Congress of the United States, which shall consist of a Senate and House of Representatives.

"§ 2. * * * Representatives and direct taxes shall be apportioned among the several States which may be included within this Union, according to their respective numbers, which shall be determined, by adding to the whole number of free persons, including those bound to servitude for a term of years, and excluding Indians not taxed, three-fifths of all other persons.

"§ 9. The migration or importation of such persons as any of the States now existing, shall think proper to admit, shall not be prohibited by the Congress prior to the year 1808; but a tax or duty may be imposed, not exceeding ten dollars on each person.

"The privilege of the writ of *habeas corpus* shall not be suspended, unless when, in cases of rebellion or invasion, the public safety may require it.

"No bill of attainder, or *ex post facto* laws shall be passed.

"Art. III. § 3. Treason against the United States, shall consist only in levying war against them, or in adhering to their enemies, giving them aid and comfort.

"Art. IV. § 2. The citizens of each State shall be entitled to all the privileges of citizens, in the several States.

"No person held to service or labor in one State, under the laws thereof, escaping into another, shall, in consequence of any law or regulation therein, be discharged from such service or labor, but shall be delivered up on claim of the party to whom such service or labor may be due.

"§ 3. New States may be admitted by the Congress into this Union; but no new State shall be formed or erected within the jurisdiction of any other State; nor any State be formed by the junction of two or more States, or parts of States, without the consent of the legislatures of the States concerned, as well as of the Congress.

"The Congress shall have power to dispose of, and make all needful rules and regulations respecting the territory or other property, belonging to the United States; and nothing in this Constitution shall be so construed as to prejudice any claims of the United States, or of any particular State.

"§ 4. The United States shall guarantee to every State in this Union, a republican form of government, and shall protect each of them against invasion; and on application of the legislature, or of the executive when the legislature cannot be convened, against domestic violence.

"Art. VI. This Constitution, and the laws of the United States, which shall be made in pursuance thereof, and all the treaties made, or which shall be made, under the authority of the United States, shall be the supreme law of the land; and the judges in every State shall be bound thereby, anything in the Constitution or laws of any State to the contrary notwithstanding."

The above are all—and perhaps more than all—the clauses of the Constitution, that have been quoted on one side or the other as bearing upon the subject of Slavery.

It will be noted that the word "slave," or "slavery" does not appear therein. Mr. Madison, who was a leading and observant member of the Convention, and who took notes of its daily proceedings, affirms that this silence was designed—the Convention being unwilling that the Constitution of the United States should recognize property in human beings. In passages where slaves are presumed to be contemplated, they are uniformly designated as "persons," never as property. Contemporary history proves that it was the belief of at least a large portion of the delegates that Slavery could not long survive the final stoppage of the slave-trade, which was expected to (and did) occur in 1808. And, were Slavery this day banished forever from the country, there might, indeed, be some superfluous stipulations in the Federal compact or charter; but there are none which need be repealed, or essentially modified.

A direct provision for the restoration of fugitive slaves to their masters was, at least once, voted down by the Convention. Finally, the clause respecting persons "held at service or labor," was proposed by Mr. Butler, of South Carolina, and adopted, with little or no opposition.

The following, among the amendments to the Constitution proposed by the ratifying conventions of one or more States, and adopted, are supposed by some to bear on the questions now agitated relative to Slavery:

"Art. I. Congress shall make no law respecting an establishment of religion, or prohibiting the free exercise thereof; or abridging the freedom of speech, or of the press; or of the rights of the people peacefully to assemble, and to petition the Government for a redress of grievances.

"Art. II. A well-regulated militia being necessary to the security of a free State, the right of the people to keep and bear arms shall not be infringed.

"Art. V. No person shall be * * * deprived of life, liberty, or property, without due process of law; nor shall private property be taken for public use without just compensation."

IV.

CESSIONS OF SOUTHERN TERRITORY.

THE State of KENTUCKY was set off from the State of Virginia in 1790, by mutual agreement, and admitted into the Union by act of Congress, passed February 4th, 1791; to take effect June 1st, 1792. It was never a territory of the United States, nor under Federal jurisdiction, except as a State, and inherited Slavery from the 'Old Dominion.'

The State of North Carolina, like several others, claimed, during and after the Revolution, that her territory extended westward to the Mississippi. The settlers west of the Alleganies resisted this claim, and a portion of them assumed to establish (1784–5) the State of Frankland, in what is now East Tennessee; but North Carolina forcibly resisted and subverted this, and a considerable portion of the people of the embryo State derided its authority, and continued to act and vote as citizens of North Carolina. A delegate (William Cocke) was sent from Frankland to the Continental Congress, but was not received by that body. On the 22nd of December, 1789, however—one month after her ratification of the Federal Constitution—North Carolina passed an act, ceding, on certain conditions, all her territory west of her present limits to the United States. Among the conditions exacted by her, and agreed to, by Congress, (Act approved April 2nd, 1790) is the following:

"*Provided always*, that no regulations made, or to be made, by Congress shall tend to emancipate slaves."

Georgia, in like manner, ceded (April 2nd, 1802) the territories lying west of her present limits, now forming the States of Alabama and Mississippi. Among the conditions exacted by her, and accepted by the United States, is the following:

"Fifthly. That the territory thus ceded shall become a State, and be admitted into the Union as soon as it shall contain sixty thousand free inhabitants, or, at an earlier period, if Congress shall think it expedient, on the same conditions and restrictions, with the same privileges, and in the same manner, as is provided in the ordinance of Congress of the 13th day of July, 1787, for the government of the Western territory of the United States; which ordinance shall, in all its parts, extend to the territory contained in the present act of Cession, the article only excepted which forbids slavery."

V.

EARLY ATTEMPTS TO OVERRIDE THE ORDINANCE.

WHEN Ohio (1802–3) was made a State, the residue of the vast regions originally conveyed by the ordinance of '87, was continued under Federal pupilage, by the name of "Indiana Territory," whereof Wm. Henry Harrison (since President) was appointed Governor. An earnest though quiet effort was made by the Virginia element, which the location of her military bounty warrants on the soil of Ohio had infused into that embryo State, to have Slavery for a limited term authorized in her first Constitution; but it was strenuously resisted by the New England element, which was far more considerable, and defeated. The Virginians either had or professed to have the countenance of President Jefferson, though his hostility to Slavery, as a permanent social state, was undoubted. It was quite commonly argued that, though Slavery was injurious in the long run, yet, as an expedient while clearing away the heavy forests, opening settlements in the wilderness, and surmounting the inevitable hardships and privations of border life, it might be tolerated, and even regarded with favor. Accordingly, the new Territory of Indiana made repeated efforts to procure a relaxation in her favor of the restrictive clause of the Ordinance of '87, one of them through the instrumentality of a Convention assembled in 1802–3, and presided over by the Territorial Governor; so he, with the great body of his fellow-delegates, memorialized Congress, among other things, to suspend temporarily the operation of the sixth article of the Ordinance aforesaid. This memorial was referred in the House to a select committee of three, two of them from Slave States, with the since celebrated John Randolph as chairman. On the 2nd of March, 1803, Mr. Randolph made what appears to have been a unanimous report from this Committee, of which we give so much as relates to Slavery—as follows:

"The rapid population of the State of Ohio sufficiently evinces, in the opinion of your committee, that the labor of slaves is not necessary to promote the growth and settlement of colonies in that region. That this labor—demonstrably the dearest of any—can only be employed in the cultivation of products more valuable than any known to that quarter of the United States; that the Committee deem it highly dangerous and inexpedient to impair a provision wisely calculated to promote the happiness and prosperity of the northwestern country, and to give strength and security to that extensive frontier. In the salutary operation of this sagacious and benevolent restraint, it is believed that the inhabitants of Indiana will, at no very distant day, find ample remuneration for a temporary privation of labor, and of emigration."

The Committee proceed to discuss other subjects set forth in the prayer of the memorial, and conclude with eight resolves, whereof the only one relating to Slavery is as follows:

"*Resolved*, That it is inexpedient to suspend, for a limited time, the operation of the sixth article of the compact between the original States and the people and States west of the river Ohio."

This Report, having been made at the close of the Session, was referred at the next to a new Committee, whereof Cæsar Rodney, a new Representative from Delaware, was Chairman. Mr. Rodney from this Committee reported (February 17th, 1804),

"That, taking into their consideration the facts stated in the said memorial and petition, they are induced to believe that a qualified suspension, for a limited time, of the sixth article of compact between the original States and the people and States west of the river Ohio, might be productive of benefit and advantage to said Territory.",

The Report goes on to discuss the other topics embraced in the Indiana memorial, and concludes with eight resolves, of which the first (and only one relative to Slavery) is as follows:

"*Resolved*, That the sixth article of the Ordinance of 1787, which prohibited Slavery within the said Territory, be suspended in a qualified manner, for ten years, so as to permit the introduction of slaves, born within the United States, from any of the individual States; *provided*, that such individual State does not permit the importation of slaves from foreign countries: *and provided, further*, that the descendants of all such slaves shall, if males, be free at the age of twenty-five years, and, if females, at the age of twenty-one years."

The House took no action on this Report. The original memorial from Indiana, with several additional memorials of like purport, was again, in 1805–6, referred by the House to a select committee, whereof Mr. Garnett of Virginia was chairman, who, on the 14th of February, 1806, made a report in favor of the prayer of the petitioners—as follows:

That, having attentively considered the facts stated in the said petitions and memorials, they are of opinion that a qualified suspension, for a limited time, of the sixth article of compact between the original States, and the people and States west of the river Ohio, would be beneficial to the people of the Indiana Territory. The suspension of this article is an object almost universally desired in that Territory.

It appears to your committee to be a question entirely different from that between Slavery and Freedom; inasmuch as it would merely occasion the removal of persons, already slaves, from one part of the country to another. The good effects of this suspension, in the present instance, would be to accelerate the population of that Territory, hitherto retarded by the operation of that article of compact, as slave-holders emigrating into the Western country might then indulge any preference which they might feel for a settlement in the Indiana Territory, instead of seeking, as they are now compelled to do, settlements in other States or countries permitting the introduction of slaves. The condition of the slaves themselves would be much ameliorated by it, as it is evident, from experience, that the more they are separated and diffused, the more care and attention are bestowed on them by their masters—each proprietor having it in his power to increase their comforts and conveniences, in proportion to the smallness of their numbers. The dangers, too, (if any are to be apprehended) from too large a black population existing in any one section of country, would certainly be very much diminished, if not entirely removed. But, whether dangers are to be feared from this source or not, it is certainly an obvious dictate of sound policy to guard against them, as far as possible. If this danger does exist, or there is any cause to apprehend it, and our Western brethren are not only willing but desirous to aid us in taking precautions against it, would it not be wise to accept their assistance?

We should benefit ourselves, without injuring them, as their population must always so far exceed any black population which can ever exist in that country, as to render the idea of danger from that source chimerical.

After discussing other subjects embodied in the Indiana memorial, the committee close with a series of Resolves, which they commend to the adoption of the House. The first and only one germane to our subject is as follows:

Resolved, That the sixth article of the Ordinance of 1787, which prohibits Slavery within the Indiana Territory, be suspended for ten years, so as to permit the introduction of slaves, born within the United States, from any of the individual States.

This report and resolve were committed and made a special order on the Monday following, but were never taken into consideration.

At the next session, a fresh letter from Gov. William Henry Harrison, inclosing resolves of the Legislative Council and House of Representatives in favor of suspending, for a limited period, the sixth article of compact aforesaid, was received (Jan. 21st, 1807) and referred to a Select Committee, whereof Mr. B. Parke, delegate from said Territory, was made chairman. The entire Committee (Mr. Nathaniel Macon of N. C. being now Speaker) consisted of

Messrs. Alston of N. C.	Rhea of Tenn.
Masters of N. Y.	Sandford of Ky.
Morrow of Ohio.	Trigg of Va.
Parke of Ind.	

Mr. Parke, from this Committee, made (Feb. 12th,) a *third* Report to the House in favor of granting the prayer of the memorialists. It is as follows:

"The resolutions of the Legislative Council and House of Representatives of the Indiana Territory, relate to a suspension, for the term of ten years, of the sixth article of compact between the United States and the Territories and States northwest of the river Ohio, passed the 13th July, 1787. That article declares that there shall be neither Slavery nor involuntary servitude in the said Territory.

"The suspension of the said article would operate an immediate and essential benefit to the Territory, as emigration to it will be inconsiderable for many years, except from those States where Slavery is tolerated.

"And although it is not considered expedient to force the population of the Territory, yet it is desirable to connect its scattered settlements, and, in admitted political rights, to place it on an equal footing with the different States. From the interior situation of the Territory, it is not believed that slaves could ever become so numerous as to endanger the internal peace or future prosperity of the country. The current of emigration flowing to the Western country, the Territories should all be opened to their introduction. The abstract question of Liberty and Slavery is not involved in the proposed measure, as Slavery now exists to a considerable extent in different parts of the Union; it would not augment the number of slaves, but merely authorize the removal to Indiana of such as are held in bondage in the United States. If Slavery is an evil, means ought to be devised to render it least dangerous to the community, and by which the hapless situation of the slaves would be most ameliorated; and to accomplish these objects, no measure would be so effectual as the one proposed. The Committee, therefore, respectfully submit to the House the following resolution:

"*Resolved*, That it is expedient to suspend, from and after the 1st day of January, 1808, the sixth article of compact between the United States and the Territories and States northwest of the Ohio, passed the 13th day of July, 1787, for the term of ten years."

This report, with its predecessors, was committed, and made a special order, but never taken into consideration.

The same letter of Gen. Harrison, and resolves of the Indiana Legislature, were submitted to the Senate, Jan. 21st, 1807. They were laid on the table "for consideration," and do not appear to have even been referred at that session; but at the next, or first session of the fourth Congress, which convened Oct. 26th, 1807, the President (Nov. 7th) submitted a letter from Gen. Harrison and his Legislature—whether a new or the old one does not appear—and it was now referred to a select committee, consisting of Messrs. J. Franklin of N. C., Kitchel of N. J., and Tiffin of Ohio.

Nov. 13th, Mr. Franklin, from said committee, reported as follows:

"The Legislative Council and House of Representatives, in their resolutions, express their sense of the propriety of introducing Slavery into their Territory, and solicit the Congress of the United States to suspend, for a given number of years, the sixth article of compact, in the ordinance for the government of the Territory northwest of the Ohio, passed the 13th day of July, 1787. That article declares: 'There shall be neither Slavery nor involuntary servitude within the said Territory.'

"The citizens of Clark County, in their remonstrance, express their sense of the impropriety of the measure, and solicit the Congress of the United States not to act on the subject, so as to permit the introduction of slaves into the Territory; at least, until their population shall entitle them to form a constitution and State government.

"Your Committee, after duly considering the matter, respectfully submit the following resolution:

"*Resolved*, That it is not expedient at this time to suspend the sixth article of compact for the government of the Territory of the United States northwest of the River Ohio."

And here ended, so far as we have been able to discover, the effort, so long and earnestly persisted in, to procure a suspension of the restriction in the Ordinance of 1787, so as to admit Slavery, for a limited term, into the Terrritory lying between the Ohio and Mississippi rivers, now forming the States of Ohio, Indiana, Illinois, Michigan, and Wisconsin.

VI.

THE FIRST MISSOURI STRUGGLE.

THE vast and indefinite territory known as Louisiana, was ceded by France to the United States in the year 1803, for the sum of $15,000,000, of which $3,750,000 was devoted to the payment of American claims on France. This territory had just before been ceded by Spain to France without pecuniary consideration. Slaveholding had long been legal therein, alike under Spanish and French rule, and the Treaty of Cession contained the following stipulation:

"Art. III. The inhabitants of the ceded territory shall be incorporated into the Union of the United States, and admitted as soon as possible, according to the principles of the Federal Constitution, to the enjoyment of all the rights, advantages and immunities of citizens of the United States; and in the mean time they shall be maintained and protected in the free enjoyment of their liberty, property, and the religion which they profess."

The State of Louisiana, embodying the southern portion of this acquired territory, was recognized by Congress in 1811, and fully admitted in 1812, with a State Constitution. Those who chose to dwell among the inhabitants of the residue of the Louisiana purchase, henceforth called Missouri Territory, continued to hold slaves in its sparse and small, but increasing settlements, mainly in its southeastern quarter, and a pro-slavery court—perhaps any court—would undoubtedly have pronounced Slavery legal anywhere on its vast expanse, from the Mississippi to the crests of the Rocky Mountains, if not beyond them, and from the Red River of Louisiana to the Lake of the Woods.

The XVth Congress assembled at Washington, on Monday, Dec. 1st, 1817. Henry Clay was chosen Speaker of the House. Mr. John Scott appeared on the 8th, as delegate from Missouri Territory, and was admitted to a seat as such. On the 16th of March following, he presented petitions of sundry inhabitants of Missouri, in addition to similar petitions already presented by him, praying for the admission of Missouri into the Union as a State, which were, on motion, referred to a Select Committee, consisting of

Messrs. Scott of Mo. Poindexter of Miss. Robertson of Ky. Hendricks of Ind. Livermore of N. H. Mills of Mass. Baldwin of Pa.

April 3rd, Mr. Scott, from this Committee, reported a bill to authorize the People of Missouri Territory to form a Constitution and State Government, and for the admission of such State into the Union on an equal footing with the original States; which bill was read the first and second time, and sent to the Committee of the Whole, where it slept for the remainder of the session.

That Congress convened at Washington for its second session, on the 16th of November, 1818. Feb. 13th, the House went into Committee of the Whole—Gen. Smith, of Md., in the chair—and took up the Missouri bill aforesaid, which was considered through that sitting, as also that of the 15th, when several amendments were adopted, the most important of which was the following, moved in Committee by Gen. James Tallmadge, of Dutchess County, New York, (lately deceased:)

"*And provided also*, That the further introduction of Slavery or involuntary servitude be prohibited, except for the punishment of crimes, whereof the party shall be duly convicted; and that all children of slaves, born within the said State, after the admission thereof into the Union, shall be free, but may be held to service until the age of twenty-five years."

On coming out of Committee, the Yeas and Nays were called on the question of agreeing to this amendment, which was sustained by the following vote: [taken first on agreeing to so much of it as precedes and includes the word "convicted."]

YEAS—For the Restriction:

NEW HAMPSHIRE.—Clifton Clagett, Samuel Hale, Arthur Livermore, Nathaniel Upham—4.

MASSACHUSETTS—(then including Maine).—Benjamin Adams, Samuel C. Allen, Walter Folger, jr., Timothy Fuller, Joshua Gage, Enoch Lincoln, Elijah H. Mills, Marcus Morton, Jeremiah Nelson, Benjamin Orr, Thomas Rice, Nathaniel Ruggles, Zabdiel Sampson, Nathaniel Silsbee, John Wilson—15.

RHODE ISLAND.—James B. Mason—1.

CONNECTICUT.—Sylvester Gilbert, Ebenezer Huntington, Jonathan O. Moseley, Timothy Pitkin, Samuel B. Sherwood, Nathaniel Terry, Thomas S. Williams—7.

VERMONT.—Samuel C. Crafts, William Hunter, Orsamus C. Merrill, Charles Rich, Mark Richards—5.

NEW-YORK.—Oliver C. Comstock, John P. Cushman, John R. Drake, Benjamin Ellicott Josiah Hasbrouck, John Herkimer, Thomas H. Hubbard, William Irving, Dorrance Kirtland, Thomas Lawyer, John Palmer, John Savage, Philip J. Schuyler, John C. Spencer, Treadwell Scudder, James Tallmadge, John W. Taylor, Caleb Tompkins, Geo. Townsend, Peter H. Wendover, Rensselaer Westerlo, James W. Wilkin, Isaac Williams—23.

NEW-JERSEY.—Ephraim Bateman, Benjamin Bennett, Charles Kinsey, John Linn, Henry Southard—5.

PENNSYLVANIA.—William Anderson, Andrew Boden, Isaac Darlington, Joseph Heister, Joseph Hopkinson, Jacob Hostetter, William Maclay, William P. Maclay, David Marchand, Robert Moore, Samuel Moore, John Murray, Alexander Ogle, Thomas Patterson, Levi Pawling, Thomas J. Rogers, John Sergeant, James M. Wallace, John Whiteside, William Wilson—20.

OHIO.—Levi Barber, Philemon Beecher, John W. Campbell, Samuel Herrick, Peter Hitchcock —5.

INDIANA.—William Hendricks—1.

DELAWARE.—Willard Hall—1.

Total Yeas 87—only one (the last named) from a Slave State.

NAYS—Against the Restriction:

MASSACHUSETTS.—John Holmes, Jonathan Mason, Henry Shaw—3.

NEW-YORK.—Daniel Cruger, David A. Ogden, Henry R. Storrs—3.

NEW-JERSEY.—Joseph Bloomfield—1,

NEW-HAMPSHIRE.—John F. Parrott—1.

OHIO.—William Henry Harrison—1.

ILLINOIS.—John McLean—1. [10 from Free States.]

DELAWARE.—Louis McLane—1.

MARYLAND.—Archibald Austin, Thomas Bayly; Thomas Culbreth, Peter Little, George Peter, Philip Reed, Samuel Ringgold, Samuel Smith, Philip Stuart—9.

VIRGINIA.—William Lee Ball, Philip P. Barbour, Burwell Bassett, William A. Burwell, Edward Colston, Robert S. Garnett, James Johnson, William J. Lewis, William McCoy, Hugh Nelson, Thomas M. Nelson, John Pegram, James Pindall, James Pleasants, Ballard Smith, Alexander Smyth, Henry St. George Tucker, John Tyler—18.

NORTH CAROLINA.—Joseph H. Bryan, William Davidson, Weldon N. Edwards, Charles Fisher, Thomas H. Hall, James Owen, Lemuel Sawyer, Thomas Little, Jesse Slocumb, James G. Smith, James Stewart, Felix Walker, Lewis Williams—13.

SOUTH CAROLINA.—James Ervin, William Lowndes, Henry Middleton, Wilson Nesbitt, Elbert Simkins, Sterling Tucker—6.

GEORGIA.—Joel Abbot, Thomas W. Cobb, Zadoc Cook, William Terrell—4.

KENTUCKY.—Richard C. Anderson, jr., Joseph Desha, Richard M. Johnson, Anthony New, Thomas Newton, George Robertson, Thomas Speed, David Trimble, David Walker—9.

TENNESSEE.—William G. Blount, Francis Jones, George W. L Marr, John Rhea—4.

MISSISSIPPI.—George Poindexter—1.

LOUISIANA.—Thomas Butler—1.

Total Nays, 76—10 from Free States, 66 from Slave States.

The House now proceeded to vote on the residue of the reported amendment [from the word "convicted" above], which was likewise sustained.—Yeas 82; Nays 78.

Messrs. Barber and Campbell of Ohio, Linn of N. J., and Mason of R. I., who on the former division voted Yea, now voted Nay.

Messrs. Schuyler and Westerlo of N. Y. (Yeas before) did not vote now. Gen. Smith of Md. changed from Nay before to Yea now.

So the whole amendment—as moved by Gen. Tallmadge in Committee of the Whole, and there carried—was sustained when reported to the House.

Mr. Storrs of New-York (opposed to the Restriction), now moved the striking out of so much of the bill as provides that the new State shall be admitted into the Union "on an equal footing with the original States"—which, he contended, was nullified by the votes just taken. The House negatived the motion.

Messrs Desha of Ky., Cobb of Ga., and Rhea of Tenn., declared against the bill as amended.

Messrs. Scott of Mo., and Anderson of Ky., preferred the bill as amended to none.

The House ordered the bill, as amended, to a third reading; Yeas 98; Nays 56. The bill thus passed the House next day, and was sent to the Senate.

The following sketch of the debate on this question (Feb. 15th) appears in the Appendix to *Niles's Register*, vol. xvi.

HOUSE OF REPRESENTATIVES, FEB. 15, 1819.

Mr. Tallmadge, of New York, having moved the following amendment, on the Saturday preceding—

"*And provided that the introduction of Slavery, or involuntary servitude, be prohibited, except for the punishment of crimes, whereof the party has been duly convicted, and that all children born within the said State, after the admission thereof into the Union, shall be declared free at the age of* 25 *years.*"

Mr. FULLER, of Massachusetts, said, that in the admission of new States into the Union, he considered that Congress had a discretionary power. By the 4th article and 3d section of the Constitution, Congress are *authorized* to admit them; but nothing in that section, or in any part of the Constitution, enjoins the admission as imperative, under any circumstances. If it were otherwise, he would request gentlemen to point out what were the circumstances or *conditions precedent*, which being found to exist, Congress *must* admit the new State. All discretion would, in such case, be taken from Congress, Mr. F. said, and deliberation would be useless. The hon. speaker (Mr. Clay) has said that Congress has no right to prescribe any condition whatever to the newly-organized States, but must admit them by a simple act, leaving their sovereignty unrestricted. [Here the speaker explained—he did not intend to be understood in so broad a sense as Mr. F. stated.] With the explanation of the honorable gentleman, Mr. F. said, I still think his ground as untenable as before. We certainly have a right, and our duty to the nation requires, that we should examine the actual state of things in the proposed State; and, above all, the Constitution expressly makes a REPUBLICAN *form of government* in the several States a fundamental principle, to be preserved under the sacred guarantee of the national legislature.—[Art. 4, sec. 4.] It clearly, therefore, is the duty of Congress, before admitting a new sister into the Union, to ascertain that her constitution or form of government is republican. Now, sir, the amendment proposed by the gentleman from New York, Mr. Tallmadge, merely requires that Slavery shall be prohibited in Missouri. Does this imply anything more than that its constitution shall be republican? The existence of Slavery in any State is, *so far*, a departure from republican principles. The Declaration of Independence, penned by the illustrious statesman then, and at this time, a citizen of a State which admits Slavery, defines the principle on which our national and state constitutions are all professedly founded. The second paragraph of that instrument begins thus: "We hold these truths to be self-evident—that *all men are created equal*—that they are endowed by their Creator with certain unalienable rights; that among these are life, LIBERTY, and the pursuit of happiness." Since, then, it cannot be denied that slaves are *men*, it follows that they are, in a *purely* republican government, born *free*, and are entitled to *liberty* and the pursuit of happiness. [Mr. Fuller was here interrupted by several gentlemen, who thought it improper to question in debate the republican character of the slave-holding States, which had also a tendency, as one gentleman (Mr. Colston, of Virginia) said, to deprive those States of the right to hold slaves as property, and he adverted to the probability that there might be slaves in the gallery, listening to the debate.] Mr. F. assured the gentleman that nothing was farther from his thoughts, than to question on that floor, the right of Virginia and other States, which held slaves when the Constitution was established, to continue to hold them. With that subject the National Legislature could not interfere, and ought not to attempt it. But, Mr. F. continued, if gentlemen will be patient, they will see that my remarks will neither derogate from the constitutional rights of the States, nor from a due respect to their several forms of government. Sir, it is my wish to *allay*, and not to excite local animosities, but I shall never refrain from advancing such arguments in debate as my duty requires, nor do I believe that the reading of our Declaration of Independence, or a discussion of republican principles on any occasion, can endanger the rights, or merit the disapprobation of any porton of the Union.

My reason, Mr. Chairman, for recurring to the Declaration of our Independence, was to draw from an authority admitted in all parts of the Union, a definition of the basis of republican government. If, then, all men have equal rights, it can no more comport with the principles of a free government to exclude men of a certain color from the enjoyment of "liberty and the pursuit of happiness," than to exclude those who have not attained a certain portion of wealth, or a certain stature of body, or to found the exclusion on any other capricious or accidental circumstance. Suppose Missouri, before her admission as a State, were to submit to us her Constitution, by which no person could elect, or be elected to any office, unless he possessed a clear annual income of twenty thousand dollars; and suppose we had ascertained that *only five*, or a very small number of persons had such an estate, would this be anything more or less than a *real aristocracy*, under a form nominally republican? Election and representation, which some contend are the only essential principles of republics, would exist only in name—a shadow without substance, a body without a soul. But if all the other inhabitants were to be made slaves, and mere property of the favored few, the outrage on principle would be still more palpable. Yet, sir, it is demonstrable, that the exclusion of the black population from all political freedom, and making them the property of the whites, is an equally palpable invasion of right, and abandonment of principle. If we do this in the admission of *new States*, we violate the Constitution, and we have not now the excuse which existed when our National Constitution was established. Then, to effect a concert of interests, it was proper to make concessions. The States where Slavery existed not only claimed the right to continue it, but it was manifest that a general emancipation of slaves could not be asked of them. Their political existence would have been in jeopardy; both masters and slaves must have been involved in the most fatal consequences.

To guard against such intolerable evils, it is provided in the Constitution, "that the migration or importation of such persons, as any of the *existing* States think proper to admit, shall not be prohibited till 1808."—Art. 1, sec. 9. And it is provided elsewhere, that persons held to service by the laws of any State, shall be given up by other States, to which they may have escaped, etc.—Art. 4, sec. 2.

These provisions effectually recognized the right in the States, which, at the time of framing the Constitution, held the blacks in Slavery, to *continue* so to hold them until they should think proper to meliorate their condition. The Constitution is a compact among all the States then existing, by which certain principles of government are established for the whole, and for each individual State. The *predominant* principle in both respects is, that ALL MEN are FREE, and have an EQUAL RIGHT TO LIBERTY, and all other privileges; or, in other words, the predominant principle is REPUBLICANISM, in its largest sense. But, then, the same compact contains certain exceptions. The States then holding slaves are *permitted*, from the necessity of the case, and for the sake of union, to exclude the republican principle so far, and *only* so far, as to retain their slaves in servitude, and also their progeny, as had been the usage, until they should think it proper or safe to conform to the pure principle, by abolishing Slavery. The compact contains on its face the *general* principle and the *exceptions*. But the attempt to extend Slavery to the *new States*, is in direct violation of the clause, which guarantees a republican form of government to all the States. This clause, indeed, must be construed in connection with the exceptions before mentioned; but it cannot, without violence, be applied to any other States than those in which Slavery was allowed at the formation of the Constitution.

The honorable speaker cites the first clause in the 2d section of the 4th article—"The citizens of each State shall be entitled to all the privileges and immunities of citizens of the several States," which he thinks would be violated by the condition proposed in the Constitution of Missouri. To keep slaves—to make one portion of the population the property of another, hardly deserves to be called a *privilege*, since what is gained by the masters must be lost by the slaves. But, independently of this consideration, I think the observations already offered to the committee, showing that holding the black population in servitude is an exception to the general principles of the Constitution, and cannot be allowed to extend beyond the fair import of the terms by which that exception is provided, are a sufficient answer to the objection. The gentleman proceeds in the same train of reasoning, and asks, if Congress can require one condition, how many more can be required, and where these conditions will end? With regard to a republican constitution, Congress are *obliged* to require that condition, and that is enough for the present question; but I contend, further, that Congress has a right, at their discretion, to require any other reasonable condition. Several others were required of Ohio, Indiana, Illinois and Mississippi. The State of Louisiana, which was a part of the territory ceded to us at the same time with Missouri, was required to provide in her Constitution for trials by jury, the writ of habeas corpus, the principles of civil and religious liberty, with several others, peculiar to that State. These, certainly, are none of them more indispensable ingredients in a republican form of government than the equality of privileges of all the population; yet these have not been denied to be reasonable, and warranted by the National Constitution in the admission of new States. Nor need gentlemen apprehend that Congress will set no reasonable limits to the conditions of admission. In the exercise of their constitutional discretion on this subject, they are, as in all other cases, responsible to the people. Their power to levy direct taxes is not limited by the Constitution. They may lay a tax of one million of dollars, or of a hundred millions, without violating the letter of the Constitution; but if the latter enormous and unreasonable sum were levied, or even the former, without evident necessity, the people have the power in their own hands—a speedy corrective is found in the return of the elections. This remedy is so certain, that the representatives of the people can never lose sight of it; and, consequently, an abuse of their powers to any considerable extent can never be apprehended. The same reasoning applies to the exercise of *all* the powers entrusted to Congress, and the admission of new States into the Union is in no respect an exception.

One gentleman, however, has contended against the amendment, because it abridges the rights of the slaveholding States to transport their slaves to the new States, for sale or otherwise. This argument is attempted to be enforced in various ways, and particularly by the clause in the Constitution last cited. It admits, however, of a very clear answer, by recurring to the 9th section of article 1st, which provides that "the *migration* or importation of such persons as any of the States then existing shall admit, shall not be prohibited by Congress till 1808." This clearly implies, that the *migration* and importation may be prohibited *after* that year. The importation has been prohibited, but the migration has not hitherto been restrained; Congress, however, may restrain it, when it may be judged expedient. It is, indeed, contended by some gentlemen, that migration is either synonymous with importation, or that it means something different from the transportation of slaves from one State to another. It certainly is not synonymous with *importation*, and would not have been used if it had been so. It cannot mean *exportation*, which is also a definite and precise term. It cannot mean the reception of *free* blacks from foreign countries, as is alleged by some, because no possible reason existed for regulating their admission by the Constitution; no free blacks ever came from Africa, or any other country, to this; and to introduce the provision by the side of that for the importation of slaves, would have been absurd in the highest degree. What alternative remains but to apply the term "migration" to the transportation of slaves from those States, where they are admitted to be held, to other States. Such a provision might have in view a very natural object. The price of slaves might be affected so far by a sudden prohibition to transport slaves from State to State, that it was as reasonable to guard against that inconvenience as against the sudden interdiction of the importation. Hitherto it has not been found necessary for Congress to prohibit migration or transportation from State to State. But now it becomes the right and duty of Congress to guard against the further extension of the intolerable evil and the crying enormity of Slavery.

The expediency of this measure is very apparent. The opening of an extensive slave market will tempt the cupidity of those who, otherwise, perhaps, might gradually emancipate their slaves. We have heard much, Mr. Chairman, of the Colonization Society; an institution which is the favorite of the humane gentlemen in the slaveholding States. They have long been lamenting the miseries of Slavery, and earnestly seeking for a remedy compatible with their own safety, and the happiness of their slaves. At last the great desideratum is found—a colony in Africa for the emancipated blacks. How will the generous intentions of these humane persons be frustrated, if the price of slaves is to be doubled by a new and boundless market! Instead of emancipation of the slaves, it is much to be feared, that unprincipled wretches will be found kidnapping those who are already free, and transporting and selling the hapless victims into hopeless bondage. Sir, I really hope that Congress will not contribute to discountenance and render abortive the generous and philanthropic views of this most worthy and laudable society. Rather let us hope, that the time is not very remote, when the shores of Africa, which have so long been a scene of barbarous rapacity and savage cruelty, shall exhibit a race of free and enlightened people—the offspring, indeed, of cannibals or of slaves; but displaying the virtues of civilization and the energies of independent freemen. America may then hope to see the developement of a germ, now scarcely visible, cherished and matured under the genial warmth of our country's protection, till the fruit shall appear in the regeneration and happiness of a boundless continent.

One argument still remains to be noticed. It is said, that we are bound, by the treaty of cession with France, to admit the ceded territory into the Union, "as soon as possible." It is obvious that the President and Senate, the treaty-making power, cannot make a stipulation with any foreign nation in derogation of the constitutional powers and duties of this House, by making it imperative on us to admit the new territory according to the literal tenor of the phrase; but the additional words in the treaty, "according to the principles of the Constitution," put it beyond all doubt that no such compulsory admission was intended, and that the republican principles of our Constitution are to govern us in the admission of this, as well as all the new States, in the national family.

Mr. Tallmadge, of New York, rose—

Sir, said he, it has been my desire and my intention to avoid any debate on the present painful and unpleasant subject. When I had the honor to submit to this House the amendment now under consideration, I accompanied it with a declaration that it was intended to confine its operation to the newly acquired territory across the Mississippi; and I then expressly declared, that I would in no manner intermeddle with the slaveholding States, nor attempt manumission in any one of the original States in the Union. Sir, I even went further, and stated that I was aware of the delicacy of the subject—and, that I had learned from southern gentlemen the difficulties and the dangers of having free blacks intermingling with slaves; and, on that account, and with a view to the safety of the white population of the adjoining States, I would not even advocate the prohibition of Slavery in the Alabama territory; because, surrounded as it was by slaveholding States, and with only imaginary lines of division, the intercourse between slaves and free blacks could not be prevented, and a servile war might be the result. While we deprecate and mourn over the evil of Slavery, humanity and good morals require us to wish its abolition, under circumstances consistent with the safety of the white population. Willingly, therefore, will I submit to an evil which we cannot safely remedy. I admitted all that had been said of the danger of having free blacks visible to slaves, and, therefore, did not hesitate to pledge myself that I would neither advise nor attempt coercive manumission. But, sir, all these reasons cease when we cross the banks of the Mississippi, into a territory separated by a natural boundary—a newly acquired territory, never contemplated in the formation of our government; not included within the compromise or mutual pledge in the adoption of our Constitution—a new territory acquired by our common fund, and ought justly to be subject to our common legislation.

Sir, when I submitted the amendment now under consideration, accompanied with these explanations, and with these avowals of my intentions and of my motives—I did expect that gentlemen who might differ from me in opinion would appreciate the liberality of my views, and would meet me with moderation, as upon a fair subject for general legislation. I did expect, at least, that the frank declaration of my views would protect me from harsh expressions, and from the unfriendly imputations which have been cast out on this occasion. But, sir, such has been the character and the violence of this debate, and expressions of so much intemperance, and of an aspect so threatening have been used, that continued silence on my part would ill become me, who had submitted to this house the original proposition. While this subject was under debate before the Committee of the whole, I did not take the floor, and I avail myself of this occasion to acknowledge my obligations to my friends (Mr. Taylor and Mr. Mills) for the manner in which they supported my amendment, at a time when I was unable to partake in the debate. I had only on that day returned from a journey, long in its extent and painful in its occasion; and from an affection of my breast I could not then speak. I cannot yet hope to do justice to the subject; but I do hope to say enough to assure my friends that I have not left them in the controversy, and to convince the opponents of the measure, that their violence has not driven me from the debate.

Sir, the hon. gentleman from Missouri (Mr. Scott, who has just resumed his seat, has told us of the ides of March, and has cautioned us to "beware of the fate of Cæsar and of Rome." Another gentleman (Mr. Cobb) from Georgia, in addition to other expressions of great warmth, has said, that if we persist, the Union will be dissolved; and with a look fixed on me, has told us, "we have kindled a fire which all the waters of the ocean cannot put out, which seas of blood can only extinguish."

Language of this sort has no effect on me; my purpose is fixed, it is interwoven with my existence; its durability is limited with my life; it is a great and glorious cause, setting bounds to a slavery the most cruel and debasing the world has ever witnessed; it is the freedom of man; it is the cause of unredeemed and unregenerated human beings.

If a dissolution of the Union must take place, let it be so! If civil war, which gentlemen so much threaten, must come, I can only say, let it come! My hold on life is probably as frail as that of any man who now hears me; but while that hold lasts, it shall be devoted to the service of my country—to the freedom of man. If blood is necessary to extinguish any fire which I have assisted to kindle, I can assure gentlemen, while I regret the necessity, I shall not forbear to contribute my mite. Sir, the violence to which gentlemen have resorted on this subject will not move my purpose, nor drive me from my place. I have the fortune and the honor to stand here as the representative of freemen, who possess intelligence to know their rights; who have the spirit to maintain them. Whatever might be my own private sentiments on this subject, standing here as the representative of others, no choice is left me. I know the will of my constituents, and, regardless of consequences, I will avow it—as their representative, I will proclaim their hatred to Slavery in every shape—as their representative here will I hold my stand, till this floor, with the Constitution of my country which supports it, shall sink beneath me—if I am doomed to fall, I shall, at least, have the painful consolation to believe that I fall, as a fragment, in the ruins of my country.

Sir, the gentleman from Virginia (Mr. Colston) has accused my honorable friend from New Hampshire (Mr. Livermore) of "speaking to the galleries," and by his "language endeavoring to excite a servile war;" and has ended by saying, "he is no better than Arbuthnot and Ambrister, and deserves no better fate." When I hear such language uttered upon this floor, and within this house, I am constrained to consider it as hasty and unintended language, resulting from the vehemence of debate, and not really intending the personal indecorum the expressions would seem to indicate. [Mr. Colston asked to explain, and said he had not distinctly understood Mr. T. Mr. Livermore called on Mr. C. to state the expressions he had used. Mr. C. then said he had no explanation to give.] Mr. T. said he had none to ask—he continued to say, he would not believe any gentleman on this floor would commit so great an indecorum against any member, or against the dignity of this house, as to use such expressions, really intending the meaning which the words seem to import, and which had been uttered against the gentleman from New Hampshire. [Mr. Nelson, of Virginia, in the Chair, called to order, and said no personal remarks would be allowed.] Mr. T. said he rejoiced the Chair was at length aroused to a sense of its duties. The debate had, for several days, progressed with unequaled violence, and all was in order; but now, when at length this violence on one side is to be resisted, the Chair discovered it is out of order. I rejoice, said Mr. T., at the discovery, I approve of the admonition, while I am proud to say it has no relevancy to me. It is my boast that I have never uttered an unfriendly personal remark on this floor; but I wish it distinctly understood, that the immutable laws of self-defense will justify going to great lengths, and that, in the future progress of this debate, the rights of defense would be regarded.

Sir, has it already come to this: that in the Congress of the United States—that, in the legislative councils of republican America, the subject of Slavery has become a subject of so much feeling—of such delicacy—of such danger, that it cannot safely be discussed? Are members who venture to express their sentiments on this subject, to be accused of talking to the galleries, with intention to excite a servile war; and of meriting the fate of Arbuthnot and Ambrister? Are we to be told of the dissolution of the Union, of civil war, and of seas of blood? And yet, with such awful threatenings before us, do gentlemen, in the same breath, insist upon the encouragement of this evil; upon the extension of this monstrous scourge of the human race? An evil so fraught with such dire calamities to us as individuals, and to our nation, and threatening, in its progress, to overwhelm the civil and religious institutions of the country, with the liberties of the nation, ought at once to be met, and to be controlled. If its power, its influence, and its impending dangers, have already arrived at such a point, that it is not safe to discuss it on this floor, and it cannot now pass under consideration as a proper subject for general legislation, what will be the result when it is spread through your widely-extended domain? Its present threatening aspect, and the violence of its supporters, so far from inducing me to yield to its progress, prompt me to resist its march. Now is the time. It must now be met, and the extension of the evil must now be prevented, or the occasion is irrecoverably lost, and the evil can never be controlled.

Sir, extend your view across the Mississippi, over your newly-acquired territory—a territory so far surpassing, in extent, the limits of your present country, that that country which gave birth to your nation—which achieved your Revolution—consolidated your Union—formed your Constitution, and has subsequently acquired so much glory, hangs but as an appendage to the extended empire over which your republican government is now called to bear sway. Look down the long vista of futurity; see your empire, in extent unequaled, in advantageous situation without a parallel, and occupying all the valuable part of one continent. Behold this extended empire, inhabited by the hardy sons of American freemen, knowing their rights, and inheriting the will to protect them—owners of the soil on which they live, and interested in the institutions which they labor to defend; with two oceans laving your shores, and tributary to your purposes, bearing on their bosoms the commerce of our people; compared to yours, the governments of Europe dwindle into insignificance, and the whole world is without a parallel. But, sir, reverse this scene; people this fair domain with the slaves of your planters; extend *Slavery*, this bane of man, this abomination of heaven, over your extended empire, and you prepare its dissolution; you turn its accumulated strength into positive weakness; you cherish a canker in your breast; you put poison in your bosom; you place a vulture preying on your heart—nay, you whet the dagger and place it in the hands of a portion of your population, stimulated to use it, by every tie, human and divine. The envious contrast between your happiness and their misery, between your liberty and their slavery, must constantly prompt them to accomplish your destruction. Your enemies will learn the source and the cause of your weakness. As often as external dangers shall threaten, or internal commotions await you, you will then realize, that by your own procurement, you have placed amidst your families, and in the bosom of your country, a population producing at once the greatest cause of individual danger, and of national weakness. With this defect, your government must crumble to pieces, and your people become the scoff of the world.

Sir, we have been told, with apparent confidence, that we have no right to annex conditions to a State, on its admission into the Union; and it has been urged that the proposed amendment, prohibiting the further introduction of Slavery, is unconstitutional. This position, asserted with so much confidence, remains unsupported by any argument, or by any authority derived from the Constitution itself. The Constitution strongly indicates an opposite conclusion, and seems to contemplate a difference between the old and the new States. The practice of the government has sanctioned this difference in many respects.

The third section of the fourth article of the Constitution says, "*new States may be admitted by the Congress into this Union*," and it is silent as to the terms and conditions upon which the new States may be so admitted. The fair inference from this is, that the Congress which might admit, should prescribe the time and the terms of such admission. The tenth section of the first article of the Constitution says, "*the migration or importation of such persons as any of the States* NOW EXISTING *shall think proper to admit, shall not be prohibited by the Congress prior to the year* 1808." The words "*now existing*" clearly show the distinction for which we contend. The word *slave* is nowhere mentioned in the Constitution; but this section has always been considered as applicable to them, and unquestionably reserved the right to prevent their importation into any *new State* before the year 1808.

Congress, therefore, have power over the subject, probably as a matter of legislation, but more certainly as a right, to prescribe the time and the condition upon which any new State may be admitted into the family of the Union. Sir, the bill now before us proves the correctness of my argument. It is filled with conditions and limitations. The territory is required to take a census, and is to be admitted only on condition that it have 40,000 inhabitants. I have already submitted amendments preventing the State from taxing the lands of the United States, and declaring that all navigable waters shall remain open to the other States, and be exempt from any tolls or duties. And my friend (Mr. Taylor) has also submitted amendments prohibiting the State from taxing soldiers' lands for the period of five years. And to all these amendments we have heard no objection—they have passed unanimously. But now, when an amendment, prohibiting the further introduction of Slavery is proposed, the whole house is put in agitation, and we are confidently told it is unconstitutional to annex conditions to the admission of a new State into the Union. The result of all this is, that all amendments and conditions are proper, which suit a certain class of gentlemen, but whatever amendment is proposed, which does not comport with their interests or their views, is unconstitutional, and a flagrant violation of this sacred charter of our rights. In order to be consistent, gentlemen must go back and strike out the various amendments to which they have already agreed. The Constitution applies equally to all, or to none.

Sir, we have been told that this is a new principle for which we contend, never before adopted, or thought of. So far from this being correct, it is due to the memory of our ancestors to say, it is an old principle, adopted by them, as the policy of our country. Whenever the United States have had the right and the power, they have heretofore prevented the extension of Slavery. The States of Kentucky and Tennessee were taken off from other States, and were admitted into the Union without condition, because their lands were never owned by the United States. The Territory northwest of the Ohio is all the land which ever belonged to them. Shortly after the cession of those lands to the Union, Congress passed, in 1787, a compact, which was declared to be unalterable, the sixth article of which provides that "*there shall be neither Slavery nor involuntary servitude in the said Territory, otherwise than in the punishment for crimes, whereof the parties shall have been duly convicted.*" In pursuance of this compact, all the States formed from that Territory have been admitted into the Union upon various conditions, and, amongst which, the sixth article of this compact is included as one.

Let gentlemen also advert to the law for the admission of the State of Louisiana into the Union: they will find it filled with conditions. It was required not only to form a Constitution upon the principles of a republican government, but it was required to contain the "fundamental principles of civil and religious liberty." It was even required as a condition of its admission, to keep its records, and its judicial and its legislative procedings in the English language; and also to secure the trial by jury, and to surrender all claim to unappropriated lands in the Territory, with the prohibition to tax any of the United States' lands.

After this long practice and constant usage to annex conditions to the admission of a State into the Union, will gentlemen yet tell us it is unconstitutional, and talk of our principles being novel and extraordinary? It has been said, that, if this amendment prevails, we shall have an union of States possessing unequal rights. And we have been asked, whether we wished to see such a "*chequered union?*" Sir, we have such a union already. If the prohibition of Slavery is the denial of a right, and constitutes a chequered union, gladly would I behold such rights denied, and such a chequer spread over every State in the Union. It is now spread over the States northwest of the Ohio, and forms the glory and the strength of those States. I hope it will be extended from the Mississippi to the Pacific Ocean.

Sir, we have been told that the proposed amendment cannot be received, because it is contrary to the treaty and cession of Louisiana. "Article 3. The inhabitants of the ceded territory shall be incorporated in the Union of the United States, and admitted as soon as possible, according to the principles of the Federal Constitution, to the enjoyment of all the rights advantages, and immunities of citizens of the United States. and in the mean time they shall be maintained and protected in the free enjoyment of their liberty, their property, and the religion which they profess." I find nothing, said Mr. T., in this article of the treaty, incompatible with the proposed amendment. The rights, advantages, and immunities of citizens of the United States are guaranteed to the inhabitants of Louisiana. If one of them should choose to remove into Virginia, he could take his slaves with him: but if he removes to Indiana, or any of the States northwest of the Ohio, he cannot take his slaves with him. If the proposed amendment prevail, the inhabitants of Louisiana, or the citizens of the United States, can neither of them take slaves into the State of Missouri. All, therefore, may enjoy equal privileges. It is a disability, or what I call a blessing, annexed to the particular district of country, and in no manner attached to the individual. But, while I have no doubt that the treaty contains no solid objection against the proposed amendment, if it did, it would not alter my determination on the subject. The Senate, or the treaty-making power of our government, have neither the right, nor the power to stipulate by a treaty, the terms upon which a people shall be admitted into the Union. This House have a right to be heard on the subject. The admission of a State into the Union is a Legislative act, which requires the concurrence of all the departments of Legislative power. It is an important prerogative of this House, which I hope will never be surrendered.

The zeal and the ardor of gentlemen, in the course of this debate, have induced them to announce to this house, that, if we persist and force the state of Missouri to accede to the proposed amendment, as the condition of her admission into the Union, she will not regard it, and, as soon as admitted, will alter her constitution, and introduce Slavery into her territory. Sir, I am not prepared, nor is it necessary to determine, what would be the consequence of such a violation of faith—of such a departure from the fundamental condition of her admission into the Union. I would not cast upon a people so foul an imputation, as to believe they would be guilty of such fraudulent duplicity. The States northwest of the Ohio have all regarded the faith and the conditions of their admission: and there is no reason to believe the people of Missouri will not also regard theirs. But, sir, whenever a State admitted into the Union shall disregard and set at naught the fundamental conditions of its admission, and shall, in violation of all faith, undertake to levy a tax upon lands of the United States, or a toll upon their navigable waters, or introduce Slavery, where Congress have prohibited it, then it will be in time to determine the consequence. But, if the threatened consequence were known to be the certain result, yet would I insist upon the proposed amendment. The declaration of this house, the declared will of the nation to prohibit Slavery, would produce its moral effect, and stand as one of the brightest ornaments of our country.

Sir, it has been urged with great plausibility, that we should spread the slaves now in our country, and thus spread the evil, rather than confine it to its present districts. It has been said, we should thereby diminish the dangers from them, while we increase the means of their living, and augment their comforts. But, you may rest assured, that this reasoning is fallacious, and that, while Slavery is admitted, the market will be supplied. Our coast, and its contiguity to the West Indies and the Spanish possessions, render easy the introduction of slaves into our country. Our laws are already highly penal against their introduction, and yet, it is a well-known fact, that about fourteen thousand slaves have been brought into our country this last year.

Since we have been engaged in this debate, we have witnessed an elucidation of this argument, of bettering the conditions of slaves, by spreading them over the country. A slave-driver, a trafficker in human flesh, as if sent by Providence, has passed the door of your capitol, on his way to the West, driving before him about fifteen of these wretched victims of his power collected in the course of his traffic, and by their removal, torn from every relation and from every tie which the human heart can hold dear. The males, who might raise the arm of vengeance, and retaliate for their wrongs, were hand-cuffed and chained to each other, while the females and children were marched in their rear, under the guidance of the driver's whip! Yes, sir, such has been the scene witnessed from the windows of Congress Hall, and viewed by members who compose the legislative councils of republican America!

In the course of the debate on this subject, we have been told that, from the long habit of the southern and western people, the possession of slaves has become necessary to them, and an essential requisite in their living. It has been urged, from the nature of the climate and soil of the southern countries, that the lands cannot be occupied or cultivated without slaves. It has been said that the slaves prosper in those places, and that they are much better off there than in their own native country. We have ever been told that if we succeed and prevent Slavery across the Mississippi, we shall greatly lessen the value of property there, and shall retard, for a long series of years, the settlement of that country.

Sir, said Mr. T., if the western country cannot be settled without slaves, gladly would I prevent its settlement till time shall be no more. If this class of arguments is to prevail, it sets all morals at defiance, and we are called to legislate on this subject as a matter of mere personal interest. If this is to be the case, repeal all your laws prohibiting the slave-trade; throw open this traffic to the commercial States of the East; and if it better the condition of these wretched beings, invite the dark population of benighted Africa to be translated to the shores of republican America. But I will not cast upon this or upon that gentleman an imputation so ungracious as the conclusion to which their arguments would necessarily tend. I do not believe any gentleman on this floor would here advocate the slave-trade; or maintain in the abstract the principles of Slavery. I will not outrage the decorum, nor insult the dignity of this house, by attempting to argue in this place, as an abstract proposition, the moral right of Slavery. How gladly would the "*legitimates of Europé chuckle*," to find an American Congress in debate on such a question!

As an evil brought upon us without our own fault, before the formation of our government, and as one of the sins of that nation from which we have revolted, we must of necessity legislate upon this subject. It is our business so to legislate as never to encourage, but always to control, this evil; and, while we strive to eradicate it, we ought to fix its limits, and render it subordinate to the safety of the white population, and the good order of civil society.

Sir, on this subject the eyes of Europe are turned upon you. You boast of the freedom of your constitution and your laws, you have proclaimed, in the Declaration of Independence, "*That all men are created equal; that they are endowed by their Creator with certain unalienable rights—that amongst these are life, liberty, and the pursuit of happiness*;" and yet you have slaves in your country. The enemies of your government, and the legitimates of Europe, point to your inconsistencies, and blazon your supposed defects. If you allow Slavery to pass into territories where you have the lawful power to exclude it, you will justly take upon yourself all the charges of inconsistency; but confine it to the original slaveholding States, where you found it at the formation of your government, and you stand acquitted of all imputation.

This is a subject upon which I have great feeling for the honor of my country. In a former debate upon the Illinois constitution, I mentioned that our enemies had drawn a picture of our country, as holding in one hand the Declaration of Independence, and with the other brandishing a whip over our affrighted slaves. I then made it my boast that we could cast back upon England the accusation—that she had committed the *original sin* of bringing slaves into our country. I have since received, through the post-office, a letter post marked in South Carolina, and signed "*A native of England*," desiring that, when I had occasion to repeat my boast against England, I would also state that she had atoned for her original sin, by establishing in her slave-colonies a system of humane laws, meliorating their condition, and providing for their safety, while America had committed the secondary sin of disregarding their condition, and had even provided laws, by which it was not murder to kill a slave. Sir, I felt the severity of the reproof; I felt for my country. I have inquired on the subject, and I find such were formerly the laws in some of the slaveholding States; and that even now, in the State of South Carolina, by law, the penalty of death is provided for stealing a slave, while the murder of a slave is punished with a trivial fine. Such is the contrast and the relative value which is placed, in the opinion of a slaveholding State, between the property of the master and the life of a slave.

Sir, gentlemen have undertaken to criminate, and to draw odious contrasts between different sections of our country—I shall not combat such arguments; I have made no pretense to exclusive morality on this subject, either for myself or my constituents; nor have I cast any imputations on others. On the contrary, I hold that mankind under like circumstances are alike, the world over. The vicious and unprincipled are confined to no district of country; and it is for this portion of the community we are bound to legislate. When honorable gentlemen inform us we overrate the cruelty and the dangers of Slavery, and tell us that their slaves are happy, and contented, and would even contribute to their safety, they tell us but very little; they do not tell us, that, while their slaves are happy, the slaves of some depraved and cruel wretch in their neighborhood may not be stimulated to revenge, and thus involve the country in ruin. If we had to legislate only for such gentlemen as are now embraced within my view, a law against robbing the mail would be a disgrace upon the nation; and, as useless, I would tear it from the pages of your statute book; yet sad experience has taught us the necessity of such laws—and honor, justice, and policy teach us the wisdom of legislating to limit the extension of Slavery.

In the zeal to draw sectional contrasts, we have been told by one gentleman, that gentlemen from one district of country talk of their morality, while those of another practice it. And the superior liberality has been asserted of Southern gentlemen over those of the North, in all contributions to moral institutions, for bible and missionary societies. Sir, I understand too well the pursuit of my purpose, to be decoyed and drawn off into the discussion of a collateral subject. I have no inclination to controvert these assertions of comparative liberality. Although I have no idea they are founded in fact, yet, because it better suits the object of my present argument, I will, on this occasion, admit them to the fullest extent. And what is the result? Southern gentlemen, by their superor liberality in contributions to moral institutions, justly stand in the first rank, and hold the first place in the brightest page in the history of our country. But, turn over this page, and what do you behold? You behold them contributing to teach the doctrines of Christianity in every quarter of the globe. You behold them legislating to secure the ignorance and stupidity of their own slaves! You behold them, prescribing, by law, penalties against the man that dares teach a negro to read. Such is the statute law of the State of Virginia. [Mr. Bassett and Mr. Tyler said that there was no such law in Virginia.]

No, said Mr. T., I have mis-spoken myself; I ought to have said, such is the statute law of the State of Georgia. Yes, while we hear of a liberality which civilizes the savages of all countries, and carries the gospel alike to the *Hottentot* and the *Hindoo*, it has been reserved for the republican State of Georgia, not content with the care of its overseers, to legislate to secure the oppression and the ignorance of their slaves. The man who there teaches a negro to read, is liable to a criminal prosecution. The dark, benighted beings of all creation profit by our liberality—save those of our own plantations. Where is the missionary who possesses sufficient hardihood to venture a residence to teach the slaves of a plantation? Here is the stain! Here is the stigma! which fastens upon the character of our country; and which, in the appropriate language of the gentleman from Georgia, (Mr. Cobb,) *all the waters of the ocean cannot wash out; which seas of blood can only take away.*

Sir, there is yet another, and an important point of view, in which this subject ought to be considered. We have been told by those who advocate the extension of Slavery into the Missouri, that any attempt to control this subject by legislation, is a violation of that faith and mutual confidence upon which our Union was formed, and our Constitution adopted. This argument might be considered plausible, if the restriction was attempted to be enforced against any of the slaveholding States, which had been a party in the adoption of the Constitution. But it can have no reference or application to a new district of country recently acquired, and never contemplated in the formation of government, and not embraced in the mutual concessions and declared faith upon which the Constitution was adopted. The Constitution provides, that the Representatives of the several States to this House shall be according to their number, including *three-fifths* of the slaves in the respective States. This is an important benefit yielded to the slaveholding States, as one of the mutual sacrifices for the Union. On this subject, I consider the faith of the Union pledged, and I never would attempt coercive manumission in a slaveholding State.

But none of the causes which induced the sacrifice of this principle, and which now produce such an unequal representation on this floor, of the free population of the country, exist as between us and the newly-acquired Territory across the Mississippi. That portion of country has no claims to such an unequal representation, unjust in its results upon the other States. Are the numerous slaves in extensive countries, which we may acquire by purchase, and admit as States into the Union, at once to be represented on this floor, under a clause of the Constitution, granted as a compromise and a benefit to the southern States which had borne part in the Revolution? Such an extension of that clause in the Constitution would be unjust in its operations, unequal in its results, and a violation of its original intention. Abstract from the moral effects of Slavery, its political consequence in the representation under this clause of the Constitution, demonstrate the importance of the proposed amendment.

Sir, I shall bow in silence to the will of the majority, on whichever side it shall be expressed: yet I confidently hope that majority will be found on the side of an amendment, so replete with moral consequences, so pregnant with important political results.

Mr. SCOTT, of Missouri, said, he trusted that his conduct, during the whole of the time in which he had the honor of a seat in the House, had convinced gentlemen of his disposition not to obtrude his sentiments on any other subjects than those on which the interest of his constituents, and of the Territory he represented, were immediately concerned. But when a question such as the amendments proposed by the gentlemen from New York (Messrs. Tallmadge and Taylor), was presented for consideration, involving constitutional principles to a vast amount, pregnant with the future fate of the Territory, portending destruction to the liberties of that people, directly bearing on their rights of property, their state rights, their all, he should consider it as a dereliction of his duty, as retreating from his post, nay, double criminality, did he not raise his voice against their adoption. After the many able and luminous views that had been taken of this subject, by the speaker of the House, and other honorable gentlemen, he had not the vanity to suppose that any additional views which he could offer or any new dress in which he could clothe those already advanced, would have the happy tendency of inducing any gentleman to change his vote. But, if he stood single on the question, and there was no man to help him, yet, while the laws of the land and the rules of the House guaranteed to him the privilege of speech, he would redeem his conscience from the imputation of having silently witnessed a violation of the Constitution of his country, and an infringement on the liberties of the people who had intrusted to his feeble abilities the advocation of their rights. He desired, at this early stage of his remarks, in the name of the citizens of Missouri Territory, whose rights on other subjects had been too long neglected and shamefully disregarded, to enter his solemn protest against the introduction, under the insidious form of amendment, of any principle in this bill, the obvious tendency of which would be to sow the seeds of discord in, and perhaps eventually endanger the Union.

Mr. S. entertained the opinion, that, under the Constitution, Congress had not the power to impose this, or any other restriction, or to require of the people of Missouri their assent to this condition, as a pre-requisite to their admission into the Union. He contended this from the language of the Constitution itself, from the practice in the admission of new States under that instrument, and from the express terms of the treaty of cession. The short view he intended to take of those points would, he trusted, be satisfactory to all those who were not so anxious to usurp power as to sacrifice to its attainment the principles of our government, or who were not desirous of prostrating the rights and independence of a State to chimerical views of policy or expediency. The authority to admit new States into the Union was granted in the third section of the fourth article of the Constitution, which declared that "new States my be admitted by the Congress into the Union." The only power given to the Congress by this section appeared to him to be, that of passing a law for the admission of the new State, leaving it in possession of all the rights, privileges, and immunities, enjoyed by the other States; the most valuable and prominent of which was that of forming and modifying their own State Constitution, and over which Congress had no superintending control, other than that expressly given in the fourth section of the same article, which read, "the United States shall guarantee to every State in this Union a republican form of government." This end accomplished, the guardianship of the United States over the Constitutions of the several States was fulfilled; and all restrictions, limitations and conditions beyond this, was so much power unwarrantably assumed. In illustration of this position, he would read an extract from one of the essays written by the late President Madison, contemporaneously with the Constitution of the United States, and from a very celebrated work: "In a confederacy founded on republican principles, and composed of republican members, the superintending government ought clearly to possess authority to defend the system against aristocratic or monarchical innovations. The more intimate the nature of such an Union may be, the greater interest have the members in the political institutions of each other, and the greater right to insist that the forms of government under which the compact was entered into, should be substantially maintained. But this authority extends no further than to a *guarantee of a republican form* of government, which supposes a pre-existing government of the form which is to be guaranteed. As long, therefore, as the existing republican forms are continued by the States, they are guaranteed by the Federal Constitution. Whenever the States may choose to substitute other republican forms, they have a right to do so, and to claim the Federal guarantee for the latter. The *only restriction* imposed on them is, that they shall not exchange republican for anti-republican Constitutions; a restriction which, it is presumed, will hardly be considered as a grievance."

Mr. S. thought that those two clauses, when supported by such high authority, had they been the only ones in the Constitution which related to the powers of the general government over the States, and particularly at their formation and adoption into the Union, could not but be deemed satisfactory to a reasonable extent; but there were other provisions in the Constitution, to which he would refer, that beyond all doubt, to his mind, settled the question. One of those was the tenth article in the amendments, which said that "the powers not delegated to the United States by the Constitution, nor prohibited by it to the States, are reserved to the States respectively or to the people." He believed that, by common law, and common usage, all grants giving certain defined and specific privileges, or powers, were to be so construed as that no others should be intended to be given but such as were particularly enumerated in the instruments themselves, or indispensably necessary to carry into effect those designated. In no part of the Constitution was the power proposed to be exercised, of imposing conditions on a new State, given, either in so many words, or by any justifiable or fair inference; nor in any portion of the Constitution was the right prohibited to the respective States, to regulate their own internal police, of admitting such citizens as they pleased, or of introducing any description of property, that they should consider as essential or necessary to their prosperity; and the framers of that instrument seem to have been zealous lest, by implication or by inference, powers might be assumed by the general government over the states and people, other than those expressly given: hence they reserve in so many terms to the states, and the people, all powers not delegated to the federal government. The ninth article of the amendments to the Constitution still further illustrated the position he had taken; it read, that "the enumeration in the Constitution of certain rights shall not be construed to deny or disparage others retained by the people." Mr. S. believed it to be a just rule of interpretation, that the enumeration of powers delegated to Congress weakened their authority in all cases not enumerated; and that beyond those powers enumerated they had none, except they were essentially necessary to carry into effect those that were given. The second section of the fourth article of the Constitution, which declared that "the citizens of each State shall be entitled to all the privileges and immunities of citizens in the several States," was satisfactory, to his judgment, that it was intended the citizens of each State, forming a part of one harmonious whole, should have, in all things, *equal privileges;* the necessary consequences of which was, that every man, in his own State, should have the same rights, privileges, and powers, that any other citizen of the United States had in his own State; otherwise discontent and murmurings would prevail against the general government who had deprived him of this equality.

For example, if the citizens of Pennsylvania, or Virginia, enjoyed the right, in their own State, to decide the question whether they would have Slavery or not, the citizens of Missouri, to give them the same privileges, must have the same right to decide whether they would or would not tolerate Slavery in their State; if it were otherwise, then the citizens of Pennsylvania and Virginia would have more rights, privileges, and powers in their respective States, than the citizens of Missouri would have in theirs. Mr. S. said he would make another quotation from the same work he had before been indebted to, which he believed had considerable bearing on this question. "The powers delegated by the proposed constitution, to the federal government, are few and defined; those which are to remain in the State Governments, are numerous and indefinite; the former will be exercised principally on external objects, as war, peace, negotiation, and foreign commerce, with which last the powers of taxation will, for the most part, be connected. The powers reserved to the several States will extend to all the objects, which in the ordinary course of affairs concern the lives, liberties, and properties of the people, and the internal order, improvement, and prosperity of the State." The applicability of this doctrine to the question under consideration was so obvious, that he would not detain the House to give examples, but leave it for gentlemen to make the application. He would, however, make one other reference to the Constitution, before he proceeded to speak of the practice under it; in the second section of that instrument it was provided, that "representatives, and direct taxes, shall be apportioned among the several States which may be included within this Union, according to their respective numbers, which shall be determined by adding to the whole number of free persons, including those bound to service for a term of years, and excluding Indians not taxed, three-fifths of all other persons." This provision was not restricted to the States then formed, and about to adopt the Constitution; but to all those States which *might* be included within this Union, clearly contemplating the admission of new States thereafter, and providing, that to them, also, should this principle of representation and taxation equally apply. Nor could he subscribe to the construction, that as this part of the Constitution was matter of compromise, it was to be limited in its application to the original States only, and not to be extended to all those States that might after its adoption become members of the Federal Union; and a practical exposition had been made by Congress of this part of the Constitution, in the admission of Kentucky, Louisiana, and Mississippi States, all of whom were slaveholding States, and to each of them this principle had been extended.

Mr. S. believed, that the practice under the Constitution had been different from that now contended for by gentlemen; he was unapprised of any similar provision having ever been made, or attempted to be made, in relation to any other new State heretofore admitted. The argument drawn from the States formed out of the Territory northwest of the river Ohio, he did not consider as analogous; that restriction, if any, was imposed in pursuance of a compact, and only, so far as Congress could do, carried into effect the disposition of Virginia in reference to a part of her own original Territory, and was, in every respect, more just, because that provision was made and published to the world at a time when but few, if any, settlements were formed within that tract of country; and the children of those people of color belonging to the inhabitants then there have been, and still were, held in bondage, and were not free at a given age, as was contemplated by the amendment under consideration, nor did he doubt but that it was competent for any of those States admitted in pursuance of the ordinance of '87, to call a convention, and so to alter their constitution as to allow the introduction of Slaves, if they thought proper to do so. To those gentlemen who had in their argument, in support of the amendments, adverted to the instance where Congress had, by the law authorizing the people of Louisiana to form a constitution and State government, exercised the power of imposing the terms and conditions on which they should be permitted to do so, he would recommend a careful examination and comparison of those terms with the Constitution of the United States, when, he doubted not, they would be convinced that these restrictions were only such as were in express and positive language defined in the latter instrument, and would have been equally binding on the people of Louisiana had they not been enumerated in the law giving them authority to form a constitution for themselves.

Mr. S. said, he considered the contemplated conditions and restrictions, contained in the proposed amendments, to be unconstitutional and unwarrantable, from the provisions of the treaty of cession, by the third article of which it was stipulated, that "the inhabitants of the ceded Territory shall be incorporated in the Union of the United States, and admitted, as soon as possible, according to the principles of the Federal Constitution, to the enjoyment of all the rights, advantages, and immunities of citizens of the United States, and, in the mean time, they shall be maintained and protected in the free enjoyment of their liberty, property, and the religion which they profess."

This treaty having been made by the competent authority of government, ratified by the Senate, and emphatically sanctioned by Congress in the acts making appropriations to carry it into effect, became a part of the supreme law of the land, and its bearings on the rights of the people had received a practical exposition by the admission of the State of Louisiana, part of the same Territory, and acquired by the same treaty of cession, into the Union. It was in vain for gentlemen to tell him that, by the terms of the treaty of cession, the United States were not bound to admit any part of the ceded Territory into the Union as a State; the evidence of the obligation Congress considered they were under, to adopt States formed out of that Territory, is clearly deducible from the fact, that they had done so in the instance of Louisiana. But, had no State been admitted, formed of a part of the Territory acquired by that treaty, the obligation of the government to do so would not be the less apparent to him. "The inhabitants of the ceded Territory shall be incorporated in the Union of the United States." The people were not left to the wayward discretion of this, or any other government, by saying that they *may be incorporated* in the Union. The language was different and imperative: "*they shall be incorporated.*" Mr. Scott understood by the term *incorporated*, that they were to form a constituent part of this republic; that they were to become joint partners in the character and councils of the country, and in the national losses and national gains; as a Territory they were not an essential part of the government; they were a mere province, subject to the acts and regulations of the general government in all cases whatsoever. As a Territory they had not all the *rights, advantages and immunities*, of citizens of the United States. Mr. S. himself furnished an example, that, in their present condition, they had not all the rights of the other citizens of the Union. Had he a vote in this House? and yet these people were, during the war, subject to certain taxes imposed by Congress. Had those people any voice to give in the imposition of taxes to which they were subject, or in the disposition of the funds of the nation, and particularly those arising from the sales of the public lands to which they already had, and still would largely contribute? Had they a voice to give in selecting the officers of this government, or many of their own? In short, in what had they equal *rights, advantages, and immunities* with the other citizens of the United States, but in the privilege to submit to a procrastination of their rights, and in the advantage to subscribe to your laws, your rules, your taxes, and your powers, even without a hearing? Those people were also "to be admitted into the Union as soon as possible." Mr. Scott would infer from this expression, that it was the understanding of the parties, that so soon as any portion of the Territory, of sufficient extent to form a State, should contain the number of inhabitants required by law to entitle them to a representative on the floor of this House, that they then had the right to make the call for admission, and this admission, when made, was to be, not on conditions that gentlemen might deem expedient, not on conditions referable to future political views, not on conditions that the constitution the people should form should contain a clause that would particularly open the door for emigration from the North or from the South, not on condition that the future population of the State should come from a slaveholding or non-slaveholding State, "*but according to the principles of the Federal Constitution*," and none other. The people of Missouri were, by solemn treaty stipulation, when admitted, to enjoy all the rights, advantages, and immunities of citizens of the United States. Can any gentleman contend, that, laboring under the proposed restriction, the citizens of Missouri would have all the rights, advantages, and immunities of other citizens of the Union? Have not other new States, in their admission, and have not all the States in the Union, now, privileges and rights beyond what was contemplated to be allowed to the citizens of Missouri? Have not all other States in this government the right to alter, modify, amend, and change their state constitutions, having regard alone to a republican form? And was there any existing law, or any clause in the Federal Constitution, that prohibited a total change from a slaveholding to a non-slaveholding State, or from a non-slaveholding to a slaveholding State? Mr. Scott thought, that if this provision was proper, or within the powers of Congress, they also had the correlative right to say, that the people of Missouri should not be admitted as a state, unless they provided, in the formation of their state constitution, that Slavery should be tolerated. Would not those conscientious gentlemen startle at this, and exclaim, *what*, impose on those people slaves, when they do not want them? This would be said to be a direct attack on the State independence. Was it in the power of Congress to annex the present condition, Mr. Scott deemed it equally within the scope of their authority to say, what color the inhabitants of the proposed state should be, what description of property, other than slaves, those people should or should not possess, and the quantity of property each man should retain, going upon the agrarian principle. He would even go further, and say, that Congress had an equal power to enact to what religion the people should subscribe; that none other should be professed, and to provide for the excommunication of all those who did not submit.

The people of Missouri were, if admitted into the Union, to come in on an equal footing with the original States. That the people of the other States had the right to regulate their own internal police, to prescribe the rules of their own conduct, and, in the formation of their constitutions, to say whether Slavery was or was not admissible, he believed was a point conceded by all. How, then, were the citizens of Missouri placed on an equal footing with the other members of the Union? Equal in some respects—a shameful discrimination in others. A discrimination not warranted by the Constitution, nor justified by the treaty of cession, but founded on mistaken zeal, or erroneous policy. They were to be bound down by onerous conditions, limitations, and restrictions to which he knew they would not submit. That people were brave and independent in spirit, they were intelligent, and knew their own rights; they were competent to self-government, and willing to risk their own happiness and future prosperity on the legitimate exercise of their own judgment and free will. Mr. Scott protested against such a guardianship as was contemplated now to be assumed over his constituents. The spirit of freedom burned in the bosoms of the freemen of Missouri, and if admitted into the national family, they would be equal, or not come in at all. With what an anxious eye have they looked to the east, since the commencement of this session of Congress, for the good tidings, that on them you had conferred the glorious privilege of self-government, and independence. What seeds of discord will you sow, when they read this suspicious, shameful, unconstitutional inhibition in their charter? Will they not compare it with the terms of the treaty of cession, that bill of their rights, emphatically their magna charta? And will not the result of that comparison be a stigma on the faith of this government? It had been admitted by some gentlemen, in debate, that, were the people of Missouri to form a constitution conforming to this provision, so soon as they were adopted into the Union it would be competent for them to call a convention and alter their constitution on this subject. Why, then, he would ask gentlemen, would they legislate, when they could produce no permanent, practical effect? Why expose the imbecility of the general government, to tie up the hands of the State, and induce the people to an act of chicanery, which he knew from principle they abhorred, to get clear of an odious restriction on their rights? Mr. Scott had trusted that gentlemen who professed to be actuated by motives of humanity and principle would not encourage a course of dissimulation, or, by any vote of theirs, render it necessary for the citizens of Missouri to act equivocally to obtain their rights. He was unwilling to believe, that political views alone led gentlemen on this or any other occasion; but, from the language of the member from New-York (Mr. Taylor), he was compelled to suspect that they had their influence upon him. That gentleman has told us, that if ever he left his present residence, it would be for Illinois or Missouri; at all events, he wished to send out his brothers and his sons. Mr. Scott begged that gentleman to relieve him from the awful apprehension excited by the prospect of this accession of population. He hoped the House would excuse him while he stated, that he did not desire that gentleman, his sons, or his brothers, in that land of brave, noble, and independent freemen. The member says that the latitude is too far north to admit of Slavery there. Would the gentleman cast his eye on the map before him, he would there see, that a part of Kentucky, Virginia, and Maryland, were as far north as the northern boundary of the proposed State of Missouri. Mr. Scott would thank the gentleman if he would condescend to tell him what precise line of latitude suited his conscience, his humanity, or his political views, on this subject. Could that member be serious, when he made the parallel of latitude the measure of his good-will to those unfortunate blacks? Or was he trying how far he could go in fallacious argument and absurdity, without creating one blush even on his own cheek, for inconsistency? What, starve the negroes out, pen them up in the swamps and morasses, confine them to southern latitudes, to long, scorching days of labor and fatigue, until the race becomes extinct, that the fair land of Missouri may be tenanted by that gentleman, his brothers, and sons? He expected from the majority of the House a more liberal policy, and better evidence that they really were actuated by humane motives.

Mr. S. said, he would trouble the House no longer; he thanked them for the attention and indulgence already bestowed; but he desired to apprise gentlemen, before he sat down, that they were sowing the seeds of discord in this Union, by attempting to admit states with unequal privileges and unequal rights; that they were signing, sealing, and delivering their own death-warrant; that the weapon they were so unjustly wielding against the people of Missouri, was a two-edged sword. From the cumulative nature of power, the day might come when the general government might, in turn, undertake to dictate to *them* on questions of internal policy; Missouri, now weak and feeble, whose fate and murmurs would excite but little alarm or sensibility, might become an easy victim to motives of policy, party zeal, or mistaken ideas of power; but other times and other men would succeed; a future Congress might come, who, under the sanctified forms of constitutional power, would dictate to *them* odious conditions; nay, inflict on their internal independence a wound more deep and dreadful than even this to Missouri. The House had seen the force of precedent, in the mistaken application of the conditions imposed on the people of Louisiana anterior to their admission into the Union. And, whatever might be the ultimate determination of the House, Mr. S. considered this question big with the fate of Cæsar and of Rome.

Mr. Cobb, of Georgia, observed that he did not rise for the purpose of detaining the attention of the House for any length of time. He was too sensible of the importance of each moment which yet remained of the session to obtrude many remarks upon their patience. But, upon a measure involving the important consequences that this did, he felt it to be an imperious duty to express his sentiments, and to enter his most solemn protest against the principle proposed for adoption by the amendment. Were gentlemen aware of what they were about to do? Did they foresee no evil consequences likely to result out of the measure if adopted? Could they suppose that the southern States would submit with patience to a measure the effect of which would be to exclude them from all enjoyment of the vast region purchased by the United States beyond the Mississippi, and which belonged equally to them as to the northern States? He ventured to assure them that they would not. The people of the *slaveholding States*, as they are called, *know* their rights, *and will insist* upon the enjoyment of them. He should not now attempt to go over ground already occupied by others, with much more ability, and attempt to show that, by the treaty with France, the people of that Territory were secured in the enjoyment of the property which they held in their slaves. That the proposed amendment was an infraction of this treaty, had been most clearly shown. Nor would he attempt to rescue from slander the character of the people of the southern States, in their conduct towards, and treatment of, their black population. That had also been done with a degree of force and eloquence, to which he could pretend no claim, by the gentleman from Virginia (Mr. Barbour), and the honorable speaker. He was, however, clearly of opinion that *Congress possessed no power under the Constitution* to adopt the principle proposed in the amendment. He called upon the advocates of it to point out, and lay their finger upon that clause of the Constitution of the United States, which gives to this body the *right* to legislate upon the subject. Could they show in what clause or section this right was *expressly given*, or from which it could be inferred? Unless this authority could be shown, Congress would be *assuming* a power, if the amendment prevailed, not delegated to them, and most dangerous in its exercise. What is the end and tendency of the measure proposed? It is to impose on the State of Missouri conditions not imposed upon any other State. It is to deprive her of one branch of sovereignty not surrendered by any other State in the Union, not even those beyond the Ohio; for all of them had legislated upon this subject; all of them had decided for themselves whether Slavery should be tolerated, at the time they framed their several constitutions. He would not now discuss the propriety of admitting Slavery. It is not now a question whether it is politic or impolitic to tolerate Slavery in the United States, or in a particular State. It was a discussion into which he would not *permit himself* to be dragged. Admit, however, its *moral impropriety*: yet there was a vast difference between moral impropriety and political sovereignty. The people of New York or Pennsylvania may deem it highly immoral and politically *improper* to permit Slavery, but yet they possess the *sovereign right and, power* to permit it, if they *choose*. They can to-morrow so alter their constitutions and laws as to admit it, if they were so disposed. It is a branch of sovereignty which the old Thirteen States never surrender in the adoption of the Federal Constitution. Now, the bill proposes that the new State shall be admitted upon an *equal footing* with the other states of the Union. It is in this way only that she can be admitted under the Constitution. These words can have no other meaning than that she shall be required *to surrender no more* of her rights of sovereignty than the other States, into a union with which she is about to be admitted, *have* surrendered. But if the proposed amendment is adopted, will not this new State be *shorn of one* branch of her sovereignty, *one right*, which the other States *may and have* exercised, (whether properly or not, is immaterial,) and *do now* exercise whenever they think fit?

Mr. C. observed, that he did conceive the principle involved in the amendment pregnant with danger. It was one, he repeated, to which he believed the people of the region of country which he represented *would not* quietly submit. He might, perhaps, subject himself to ridicule, for attempting the display of a spirit of prophecy which he did not possess, or of zeal and enthusiasm for which he was entitled to little credit. But he *warned* the advocates of this measure against the certain effects which it must produce. Effects destructive of the peace and harmony of the Union. He believed that they were kindling a fire which all the waters of the ocean could not extinguish. It could be extinguished only in *blood !*

Mr. Livermore, of N. H., said, I am in favor of the proposed amendment. The object of it is to prevent the extension of Slavery over the Territory ceded to the United States by France. It accords with the dictates of reason, and the best feelings of the human heart; and is not calculated to interrupt any legitimate right arising either from the Constitution or any other compact. I propose to show what Slavery is, and to mention a few of the many evils which follow in its train; and I hope to evince that we are not bound to tolerate the existence of so disgraceful a state of things beyond its present extent, and that it would be impolitic and very unjust, to let it spread over the whole face of our Western Territory. Slavery in the United States, is the condition of man subjected to the will of a master, who can make any disposition of him short of taking away his life. In those States where it is tolerated, laws are enacted, making it penal to instruct slaves in the art of reading, and they are not permitted to attend public worship, or to hear the gospel preached. Thus, the light of science and of religion is utterly excluded from the mind, that the body may be more easily bowed down to servitude. The bodies of slaves may, with impunity, be prostituted to any purpose, and deformed in any manner by their owners. The sympathies of nature in slaves are disregarded: mothers and children are sold and separated; the children wring their little hands, and expire in agonies of grief, while the bereft mothers commit suicide, in despair. How long will the desire of wealth render us blind to the sin of holding both the bodies and souls of our fellow-men in chains! But, sir, I am admonished of the Constitution, and told we cannot emancipate slaves. I know we may not infringe that instrument, and therefore do not propose to emancipate slaves. The proposition before us goes only to prevent our citizens from making slaves of such as have a right to freedom. In the present slaveholding States let Slavery continue, for our boasted Constitution connives at it; but do not, for the sake of cotton and tobacco, let it be told to future ages that, while pretending to love liberty, we have purchased an extensive country, to disgrace it with the foulest reproach of nations. Our Constitution requires no such thing of us. The ends for which that supreme law was made, are succinctly stated in its preface. They are first to form a more perfect Union, and insure domestic tranquillity. Will Slavery effect this? Can we, sir, by mingling bond with free, black spirits with white, like Shakespeare's witches in Macbeth, form a more perfect Union, and insure domestic tranquillity? Secondly, to establish justice. Is justice to be established by subjecting half mankind to the will of the other half? Justice, sir, is blind to colors, and weighs in equal scales the rights of all men, whether white or black. Thirdly, to provide for the common defense, and secure the blessings of liberty. Does Slavery add anything to the common defense? Sir, the strength of a republic is in the arm of freedom. But, above all things, do the blessings of liberty consist in Slavery? If there is any sincerity in our profession, that Slavery is an ill, tolerated only from necessity, let us not, while we feel that ill, shun the cure, which consists only in an honest avowal that liberty and equal rights are the end and aim of all our institutions, and that to tolerate Slavery beyond the narrowest limits prescribed for it by the Constitution, is a perversion of them all.

Slavery, sir, I repeat, is not established by our Constitution; but a part of the States are indulged in the commission of a sin from which they could not at once be restrained, and which they would not consent to abandon. But, sir, if we could, by any process of reasoning, be brought to believe it justifiable to hold others to involuntary servitude, policy forbids that we should increase it. Even the present slaveholding States have an interest, I think, in limiting the extent of involuntary servitude; for, should slaves become much more numerous, and, conscious of their strength, draw the sword against their masters, it will be to the free States the masters must resort for an efficient power to suppress servile insurrection. But we have made a treaty with France, which, we are told, can only be preserved by the charms of Slavery.

Sir, said Mr L., until the ceded Territory shall have been made into States, and the new States admitted into the Union, we can do what we will with it. We can govern it as a province, or sell it to any other nation. A part of it is probably at this time sold to Spain, and the inhabitants of it may soon not only enjoy the comforts of Slavery, but the blessings of the holy inquisition along with them. The question is on the admission of Missouri, as a State, into the Union. Surely it will not be contended that we are bound by the treaty to admit it. The treaty-making power does not extend so far. Can the President and Senate, by a treaty with Great Britain, make the province of Lower Canada a State of this Union? To be received as a State into this Union, is a privilege which no country can claim as a right. It is a favor to be granted or not, as the United States may choose. When the United States think proper to grant a favor, they may annex just and reasonable terms: and what can be more reasonable than for these States to insist that a new Territory, wishing to have the benefits of freedom extended to it, should renounce a principle that militates with justice, morality, religion, and every essential right of mankind? Louisiana was admitted into the Union on terms. The conditions, I admit, were not very important, but still they recognize the principles for which I contend.

An opportunity is now presented, if not to diminish, at least to prevent the growth of a sin which sits heavily on the soul of every one of us. By embracing this opportunity, we may retrieve the national character, and, in some degree, our own. But if we suffer it to pass unimproved, let us at least be consistent, and declare that our Constitution was made to impose Slavery, and not to establish liberty. Let us no longer tell idle tales about the gradual abolition of Slavery; away with colonization societies, if their design is only to rid us of free blacks and turbulent slaves; have done also with bible societies, whose views are extended to Africa and the East Indies, while they overlook the deplorable condition of their sable brethren within our own borders; make no more laws to prohibit the importation of slaves, for the world must see that the object of such laws is alone to prevent the glutting of a prodigious market for the flesh and blood of man, which we are about to establish in the West, and to enhance the price of sturdy wretches, reared, like black cattle and horses, for sale on our own plantations.

The House bill thus passed, reached the Senate, Feb. 17th, when it was read twice and sent to a Select Committee already raised on a like application from Alabama, consisting of

Messrs. Tait of Ga., Morrow of Ohio, Williams of Miss., Edwards of Ill., Williams of Tenn.

On the 22nd, Mr. Tait, from this Committee, reported the bill with amendments, strikout the anti-slavery restrictions inserted by the House. This bill was taken up in Committee of the Whole on the 27th, when Mr. Wilson of N. J. moved its postponement to the 5th of March—that is, to the end of the session—negatived: Yeas 14; Nays 23.

The Senate then proceeded to vote on agreeing to the amendments reported by the Select Committee, viz.: 1. to strike out of the House bill the following:

"And that all children of slaves born within the said State, after the admission thereof into the Union, shall be free, but may be held to service until the age of twenty-one years."

Which was stricken out by the following vote:

YEAS—Against the Restriction:

Messrs. Barbour of Va — Leake of Miss.
Crittenden of Ky. — Macon of N. C.
Daggett of Conn. — Otis of Mass.
Eaton of Tenn. — Palmer of Vt.
Edwards of Ill. — Roberts of Penn.
Eppes of Va. — Sanford of N. Y.
Fromentin of La. — Tait, of Ga.
Gaillard of S. C. — Talbort of Ky.
Goldsborough Md. — Taylor of Ind.
Horsey of Del. — Thomas of Ill.
Johnson of La. — Trichenor of Vt.
King of N. Y. — Van Dyke of Del.
Lacock of Pa. — Williams of Miss.
Williams of Tenn.—27.

NAYS—For the Restriction:

Messrs. Burrill of R. I. — Morrill of N. H.
Dickerson of N. J. — Noble of Ind.
Mellen of Mass. — Ruggles of Ohio.
Wilson of N. J.—7

The Senate then proceeded to vote on the residue of the House Restriction, as follows:

"*And provided also*, That the further introduction of slavery or involuntary servitude be prohibited, except for the punishment of crimes, whereof the party shall have been duly convicted."

The vote on this clause was as follows:

YEAS—For striking out the Restriction:

Messrs. Barbour of Va. — Leake of Miss.
Crittenden of Ky. — Macon of N. C.
Eaton of Tenn. — Otis of Mass.
Edwards of Ill. — Palmer of Vt.
Eppes of Va. — Stokes of N. C.
Fromentin of La. — Talbot of Ga.
Gaillard of S. C. — Tait of Ga.
Goldsborough Md. — Thomas of Ill.
Horsey of Del. — Van Dyke of Del.
Johnson La. — Williams of Miss.
Lacock of Pa. — Williams of Tenn.—22.

NAYS—Against striking out:

Messrs. Burrill of R. I. — Noble of Ind.
Daggett of Conn. — Roberts of Pa.
Dana of do. — Ruggles of Ohio,
Dickerson of N. J. — Sanford of N. Y.
King of N. Y. — Storer of N. H.
Mellen of Mass. — Taylor of Ind.
Morrill of N. H. — Tichenor of Vt
Morrow of Ohio, — Wilson of N. J.—16

The bill thus amended was ordered to be engrossed, and was (March 2nd—last day but one of the Session) read a third time, and passed without a division. The bill was on that day returned to the House, and the amendments of the Senate read: whereupon, Mr. Tallmadge of N. Y. moved that the bill be postponed indefinitely. Yeas 69; Nays 74.

[The record shows hardly a vote changed from Yea, on the original passage of the Restriction, to Nay now, but many members who voted then were now absent or silent.]

The vote was then taken on concurring in the Senate's amendments, as aforesaid, and the House refused to concur: Yeas 76; Nays 78.

[Hardly a vote changed; but more Members voting than on the previous division, and less than when the Restriction was carried.]

The bill was now returned to the Senate, with a message of non-concurrence; when Mr. Tait moved that the Senate adhere to its amendment, which was carried without a division. The bill being thus remanded to the House, Mr. Taylor of N. Y. moved that the House adhere to its disagreement, which prevailed. Yeas 78; Nays 66. So the bill fell between the two Houses, and was lost.

The southern portion of the then Territory of Missouri (organized by separation from Louisiana in 1812) was excluded from the proposed State of Missouri, and organized as a separate Territory, entitled Arkansas.

The bill being under consideration, Mr. Taylor of N.Y. moved that the foregoing restriction be applied to it also; and the clause, proposing that slaves born therein after the passage of this act be free at twenty-five years of age, was carried (Feb. 17th) by 75 Yeas to 73 Nays; but that providing against the farther introduction of slaves was lost: Yeas 70; Nays 71. The next day, the clause just adopted was stricken out, and the bill ultimately passed without any allusion to Slavery. Arkansas of course became a Slave Territory and ultimately (1836) a Slave State.

VII.

THE SECOND MISSOURI STRUGGLE.

A new Congress assembled on the 6th of December, 1819. Mr. Clay was again chosen Speaker. On the 8th, Mr. Scott, delegate from Missouri, moved that the memorial of her Territorial Legislature, as also of several citizens, praying her admission into the Union as a State, be referred to a select committee; carried, and Messrs. Scott of Mo., Robertson of Ky., Terrell of

Ga., Strother of Va., and De Witt of N. Y. (all but the last from the slave region), were appointed said committee.

Mr. Strong of N. Y. that day gave notice of a bill "To prohibit the further extension of Slavery in the United States."

On the 14th, Mr. Taylor of N. Y. moved a select committee on this subject, which was granted; and the mover, with Messrs. Livermore of N. H., Barbour (P. P.) of Va., Lowndes of S. C., Fuller of Mass., Hardin of Ky., and Cuthbert of Ga., were appointed such committee. A majority of this committee being Pro-Slavery, Mr. Taylor could do nothing; and on the 28th the Committee was, on motion, discharged from the further consideration of the subject.

On the same day Mr. Taylor moved:

"That a Committee be appointed with instructions to report a bill prohibiting the further admission of Slaves into the Territories of the United States west of the river Mississippi."

On motion of Mr. Smith, of Md., this resolve was sent to the Committee of the Whole, and made a special order for Jan. 10th; but it was not taken up, and appears to have slept the sleep of death.

In the Senate, the memorial of the Missouri Territorial Legislature, asking admission as a State, was presented by Mr. Smith of S. C., Dec. 29th, and referred to the Judiciary Committee, which consisted of,

Messrs. Smith of S. C., Leake of Miss., Burrill of R. I., Logan of Ky., Otis of Mass.

DANIEL WEBSTER ON SLAVERY EXTENSION.

The following "Memorial to the Congress of the United States, on the subject of restraining the increase of Slavery in New *States* to be admitted into the Union," in pursuance of a vote of the inhabitants of Boston and its vicinity, assembled at the State House on the 3rd of December, 1819, was drawn up by Daniel Webster, and signed by himself, George Blake, Josiah Quincy, James T. Austin, etc. It is inserted here instead of the resolves of the various New England Legislatures, as a fuller and clearer statement of the views of the great body of the people of that section during the pendency of the Missouri question:

"MEMORIAL

"*To the Senate and House of Representatives of the United States, in Congress assembled:*

"The undersigned, inhabitants of Boston and its vicinity, beg leave most respectfully and humbly to represent: That the question of the introduction of Slavery into the new States to be formed on the west side of the Mississippi River, appears to them to be a question of the last importance to the future welfare of the United States. If the progress of this great evil is ever to be arrested, it seems to the undersigned that this is the time to arrest it. A false step taken now, cannot be retraced; and it appears to us that the happiness of unborn millions rests on the measure which Congress on this occasion may adopt. Considering this as no local question, nor a question to be decided by a temporary expediency, but as involving great interests of the whole United States, and affecting deeply and essentially those objects of common defense, general welfare, and the perpetuation of the blessings of liberty, for which the Constitution itself was formed, we have presumed, in this way, to offer our sentiments and express our wishes to the National Legislature. And as various reasons have been suggested against prohibiting Slavery in the new States, it may perhaps be permitted to us to state our reasons, both for believing that Congress possesses the constitutional power to make such prohibition a condition, on the admission of a new State into the Union, and that it is just and proper that they should exercise that power.

"And in the first place, as to the constitutional authority of Congress. The Constitution of the United States has declared that 'Congress shall have power to dispose of and make all needful rules and regulations respecting the territory or other property belonging to the United States: and nothing in this Constitution shall be so construed as to prejudice the claims of the United States or of any particular State.' It is very well known, that the saving in this clause of the claims of any particular State, was designed to apply to claims by the then existing States, of territory which was also claimed by the United States as their own property. It has, therefore, no bearing on the present question. The power, then, of Congress over its own territories, is, by the very terms of the Constitution, unlimited. It may make all 'needful rules and regulations,' which of course include all such regulations as its own views of policy or expediency shall, from time to time, dictate. If, therefore, in its judgment it be needful for the benefit of a territory to enact a prohibition of Slavery, it would seem to be as much within its power of legislation as any other act of local policy. Its sovereignty being complete and universal as to the territory, it may exercise over it the most ample jurisdiction in every respect. It possesses, in this view, all the authority which any State Legislature possesses over its own territory; and if any State Legislature may, in its discretion, abolish or prohibit Slavery within its own limits, in virtue of its general legislative authority, for the same reason Congress also may exercise the like authority over its own territories. And that a State Legislature, unless restrained by some constitutional provision, may so do, is unquestionable, and has been established by general practice. * * * * *

"The creation of a new State, is, in effect, a compact between Congress and the inhabitants of the proposed State. Congress would not probably claim the power of compelling the inhabitants of Missouri to form a Constitution of their own, and come into the Union as a State. It is as plain, that the inhabitants of that territory have no right of admission into the Union, as a State, without the consent of Congress. Neither party is bound to form this connection. It can be formed only by the consent of both. What, then, prevents Congress, as one of the stipulating parties, to propose its terms? And if the other party assents to these terms, why do they not effectually bind both parties? Or if the inhabitants of the Territory do not choose to accept the proposed terms, but prefer to remain under a Territorial Government, has Congress deprived them of any right, or subjected them to any restraint, which, in its discretion, it had no authority to do? If the admission of new States be not the discretionary exercise of a constitutional power, but in all cases an imperative duty, how is it to be performed? If the Constitution means that Congress *shall* admit new States, does it mean that Congress shall do this on every application and under all circumstances? Or if this construction cannot be admitted, and if it must be conceded that Congress must in some respects exercise its discretion on the admission of new States, how is it to be shown that that discretion may not be exercised in regard to this subject as well as in regard to others?

"The Constitution declares, 'that the migration or importation of such persons as any of the States *now existing*, shall think proper to admit, shall not be prohibited by the Congress, prior to the year 1808.' It is most manifest that the Constitution does contemplate, in the very terms of this clause, that Congress possesses the authority to prohibit the migration or importation of slaves; for it limits the exercise of this authority for a specific period of time, leaving it to its full operation ever afterward. And this power seems necessarily included in the authority which belongs to Congress, 'to regulate commerce with foreign nations *and among the several States*.' No person has ever doubted that the prohibition of the foreign slave trade was completely within the authority of Congress since the year 1808. And why? Certainly only because it is embraced in the regulation of *foreign commerce*; and if so, it may for the like reason be prohibited since that period between the States. Commerce in slaves, since the year 1808, being as much subject to the regulation of Congress as any other commerce, if it should see fit to enact that no slave should ever be sold from one State to another, it is not perceived how its constitutional right to make such provision could be questioned. It would seem to be too plain to be questioned, that Congress did possess the power, before the year 1808, to prohibit the migration or importation of slaves into the territories (and in point of fact it exercised that power) as well as into any *new States*; and that its authority, after that year, might be as fully exercised to prevent the migration or importation of slaves into any of the old States. And if it may prohibit new States from importing slaves, it may surely, as we humbly submit, make it a condition of the admission of such States into the Union, that they shall never import them. In relation, too, to its own Territories, Congress possesses a more extensive authority, and may, in various other ways, effect the object. It might, for example, make it an express condition of its grants of the soil, that its owners shall never hold slaves; and thus prevent the possession of slaves from ever being connected with the ownership of the soil.

"As corroborative of the views which have been already suggested, the memorialists would respectfully call the attention of Congress to the history of the national legislation, under the Confederation as well as under the present Constitution, on this interfering subject. Unless the memorialists greatly mistake, it will demonstrate the sense of the nation, at every period of its legislation, to have been, that the prohibition of Slavery was no infringement of any just rights belonging to free States, and was not incompatible with the enjoyments of all the rights and immunities which an admission into the Union was supposed to confer.

"The memorialists, after this general survey, would respectfully ask the attention of Congress to the state of the question of the right of Congress to prohibit Slavery in that part of the former Territory of Louisiana which now forms the Missouri Territory. Louisiana was purchased of France by the Treaty of the 30th April, 1803. The third article of that Treaty is as follows: 'The inhabitants of the ceded Territory shall be incorporated into the Union of the United States, and admitted as soon as possible, *according to the principles of the Federal Constitution*, to the enjoyment of all the *rights, advantages*, and *immunities* of *citizens of the United States*; and in the mean time they shall be maintained and protected in the free enjoyment of their liberty, property, and the religion which they profess.'

"Although the language of this article is not very precise or accurate, the memorialists conceive that its real import and intent cannot be mistaken. The first clause provides for the admission of the ceded territory into the Union, and the succeeding clause shows this must be *according to the principles of the Federal Constitution; and this very qualification necessarily excludes the idea that Congress were not to be at liberty to impose any conditions upon such admission which were consistent with the principles of that Constitution, and which had been, or might justly be, applied to other new States.* The language is not by any means so pointed as that of the Resolve of 1780; and yet it has been seen that that Resolve was never supposed to inhibit the authority of Congress, as to the introduction of slavery. And it is clear, upon the plainest rule of construction, that in the absence of all restrictive language, a clause, merely providing for the admission of a territory into the Union, must be construed to authorize an admission in the manner, and upon the terms, which the Constitution itself would justify. This construction derives additional support from the next clause. The inhabitants 'shall be admitted as soon as possible, according to the principles of the Federal Constitution, to the enjoyment of all the *rights, advantages*, and *immunities* of *citizens of the United States*.' The rights, advantages, and immunities here spoken of, must, from the very force of the terms of the clause, be such as are recognized or communicated by the Constitution of the United States; such as are common to all citizens, and are uniform throughout the Unifed States. The clause cannot be referred to rights, advantages, and immunities derived exclusively from the State Government, for these do not depend upon the Federal Constitution. Besides, it would be impossible that all the rights, advantages, and immunities of citizens of the different States, could be at the same time enjoyed by the same persons. These rights are different in different States; a right exists in one State which is denied in others, or is repugnant to other rights enjoyed in others. In some of the States, a freeholder alone is entitled to vote in elections; in some a qualification of personal property is sufficient; and in others, age and freedom are the sole qualifications of electors. In some States, no citizen is permitted to hold slaves: in others, he possesses that power absolutely; in others, it is limited. The obvious meaning, therefore, of the clause is, that the rights derived under the Federal Constitution, shall be enjoyed by the inhabitant of Louisiana in the same manner as by the citizens of other States. The United States, by the Constitution, are bound to guarantee to every State in the Union a republican form of government; and the inhabitants of Louisiana are entitled, when a State, to this guarantee. Each State has a right to two Senators, and to Representatives according to a certain enumeration of population, pointed out in the Constitution. The inhabitants of Louisiana, upon their admission into the Union, are also entitled to these privileges. The Constitution further declares, 'that the citizens of each State shall be entitled to all the privileges and immunities of citizens *in* the several States.' It would seem as if the meaning of this clause could not well be misinterpreted. It obviously applies to the case of the removal of a citizen of one State to another State; and in such a case it secures to the migrating citizen all the privileges and immunities of citizens *in* the State to which he removes. It cannot surely be contended, upon any rational interpretation, that it gives to the citizens of each State all the privileges and immunities of the citizens of every other State, at the same time, and under all circumstances. Such a construction would lead to the most extraordinary consequences. It would at once destroy all the fundamental limitations of the State constitutions upon the rights of their own citizens; and leave all those rights to the mercy of the citizens of any other State, which should adopt different limitations. According to this construction, if all the State constitutions, save one, prohibited slavery, it would be in the power of that single State, by the admission of the right of its citizens to hold slaves, to communicate the same right to the citizens of all the other States within their own exclusive limits, in defiance of their own constitutional prohibitions; and to render the absurdity still more apparent, the same construction would communicate the most opposite and irreconcilable rights to the citizens of different States at the same time. It seems, therefore, to be undeniable, upon any rational interpretation, that this clause of the Constitution communicated no rights in any State which its own citizens do not enjoy; and that the citizens of Louisiana, upon their admission into the Union, in receiving the benefit of this clause, would not enjoy higher or more extensive rights than the citizens of Ohio. It would communicate to the former no right of holding slaves except in States where the citizens already possessed the same right under their own State Constitutions and laws. * * * * *

"Upon the whole, the memorialists would most respectfully submit that the terms of the Constitution, as well as the practice of the Governments under it, must, as they humbly conceive, entirely justify the conclusion that Congress may prohibit the further introduction of Slavery into its own territories, and also make such prohibition a condition of the admission of any new State into the Union.

"If the constitutional power of Congress to make the proposed prohibition be satisfactorily shown, the justice and policy of such prohibition seem to the undersigned to be supported by plain and strong reasons. The permission of Slavery in a new State, necessarily draws after it an extension of that inequality of representation, which already exists in regard to the original States. It cannot be expected that those of the original States, which do not hold slaves, can look on such an extension as being politically just. As between the original States the representation rests on compact and plighted faith; and your memorialists have no wish that that compact should be disturbed, or that plighted faith in the slightest degree violated. But the subject assumes an entirely different character, when a new State proposes to be admitted. With her, there is no compact, and no faith plighted; and where is the reason that she should come into the Union with more than an equal share of political importance and political power? Already the ratio of representation, established by the Constitution, has given to the States holding slaves twenty members of the House of Representatives more than they would have been entitled to, except under the particular provision of the Constitution. In all probability, this number will be doubled in thirty years. Under these circumstances, we deem it not an unreasonable expectation that the inhabitants of Missouri should propose to come into the Union, renouncing the right in question, and establishing a constitution prohibiting it for ever. Without dwelling on this topic, we have still thought it our duty to present it to the consideration of Congress. We present it with a deep and earnest feeling of its importance, and we respectfully solicit for it the full consideration of the National Legislature.

"Your memorialists were not without the hope that the time had at length arrived when the inconvenience and the danger of this description of population had become apparent in all parts of this country, and in all parts of the civilized world. It might have been hoped that the new States themselves would have had such a view of their own permanent interests and prosperity as would have led them to prohibit its extension and increase. The wonderful increase and prosperity of the States north of the Ohio is unquestionably to be ascribed, in a great measure, to the consequences of the ordinance of 1787; and few, indeed, are the occasions, in the history of nations, in which so much can be done, by a single act, for the benefit of future generations, as was done by that ordinance, and as may now be done by the Congress of the United States. We appeal to the justice and to the wisdom of the National Councils to prevent the further progress of a great and serious evil. We appeal to those who look forward to the remote consequences of their measures, and who cannot balance a temporary or trifling convenience, if there were such, against a permanent, growing, and desolating evil. We cannot forbear to remind the two Houses of Congress that the early and decisive measures adopted by the American Government for the abolition of the slave-trade, are among the proudest memorials of our nation's glory. That Slavery was ever tolerated in the Republic is, as yet, to be attributed to the policy of another Government. No imputation, thus far, rests on any portion of the American Confederacy. The Missouri Territory is a new country. If its extensive and fertile field shall be opened as a market for slaves, the Government will seem to become a party to a traffic which, in so many acts, through so many years, it has denounced as impolitic, unchristian, inhuman. To enact laws to punish the traffic, and, at the same time, to tempt cupidity and avarice by the allurements of an insatiable market, is inconsistent and irreconcilable. Government, by such a course, would only defeat its own purposes, and render nugatory its own measures. Nor can the laws derive support from the manners of the people, if the power of moral sentiment be weakened by enjoying, under the permission of Government, great facilities to commit offenses. The laws of the United States have denounced heavy penalties against the traffic in slaves, because such traffic is deemed unjust and inhuman. We appeal to the spirit of these laws: We appeal to this justice and humanity: We ask whether they ought not to operate, on the present occasion, with all their force? We have a strong feeling of the injustice of any toleration of Slavery. Circumstances have entailed it on a portion of our community, which cannot be immediately relieved from it without consequences more injurious than the suffering of the evil. But to permit it in a new country, where yet no habits are formed which render it indispensable, what is it, but to encourage that rapacity, and fraud, and violence, against which we have so long pointed the denunciations of our penal code? What is it, but to tarnish the proud fame of the country? What is it, but to throw suspicion on its good faith, and to render questionable all its professions of regard for the right of humanity and the liberties of mankind?

"As inhabitants of a free country—as citizens of a great and rising Republic—as members of a Christian community—as living in a liberal and enlightened age, and as feeling ourselves called upon by the dictates of religion and humanity, we have presumed to offer our sentiments to Congress on this question, with a solicitude for the event far beyond what a common occasion could inspire."

Instead of reprinting the Speeches elicited by this fruitful theme, which must necessarily, to a great extent, be a mere reproduction of ideas expressed in the debate of the last session, already given, we here insert the Resolves of the Legislatures of New-York, New-Jersey, Pennsylvania, Delaware, and Kentucky—the first three being unanimous expressions in favor of Slavery Restriction; the fourth, from a Slave State, also in favor of such Restriction, though probably not unanimously agreed to by the Legislature; the last against Restriction, and also (we presume) unanimous. The Legislatures of the Free States were generally unanimous for Restriction; those of the Slave States (Delaware excepted) unanimous against it. It is not deemed necessary to print more than the following:

NEW YORK.

"State of New-York, in Assembly, Jan. 17, 1820:

"*Whereas*, The inhibiting the further extension of Slavery in these United States is a subject of deep concern among the people of this State; and whereas we consider Slavery as an evil much to be deplored; and that every constitutional barrier should be interposed to prevent its further extension; and that the Constitution of the United States clearly gives Congress the right to require of new States, not comprised with the original boundaries of these United States, the prohibition of Slavery, as a condition of its admission into the Union: Therefore,

"*Resolved* (if the honorable the Senate concur herein), That our Senators be instructed, and our Representatives in Congress be requested, to oppose the admission as a State into the Union, any territory not comprised as aforesaid, without making the prohibition of Slavery therein an indispensable condition of admission: therefore,

"*Resolved*, That measures be taken by the clerks of the Senate and Assembly of this State, to transmit copies of the preceding resolutions to each of our Senators and Representatives in Congress."

[Unanimously concurred in by the Senate.]

NEW JERSEY.

HOUSE OF REPRESENTATIVES,
January 24th, 1820.

Mr. Wilson of N. J. communicated the following Resolutions of the Legislature of the State of New-Jersey, which were read:

"*Whereas*, A Bill is now depending in the Congress of the United States, on the application of the people in the Territory of Missouri for the admission of that Territory as a State into the Union, not containing provisions against Slavery in such proposed State, and a question is made upon the right and expediency of such provision.

"The representatives of the people of New-Jersey, in the Legislative Council and General Assembly of the said State, now in session, deem it a duty they owe to themselves, to their constituents, and posterity, to declare and make known the opinions they hold upon this momentous subject; and,

"1. *They do resolve and declare*, That the further admission of Territories into the Union, without restriction of Slavery, would, in their opinion, essentially impair the right of this and other existing States to equal representation in Congress (a right at the foundation of the political compact), inasmuch as such newly-admitted slaveholding State would be represented on the basis of their slave population; a concession made at the formation of the Constitution in favor of the then existing States, but never stipulated for new States, nor to be inferred from any article or clause in that instrument.

"2. *Resolved*, That to admit the Territory of Missouri as a State into the Union, without prohibiting Slavery there, would, in the opinion of the representatives of the people of New-Jersey aforesaid, be no less than to sanction this great political and moral evil, furnish the ready means of peopling a vast Territory with Slaves, and perpetuate all the dangers, crimes, and pernicious effects of domestic bondage.

"3. *Resolved*, As the opinion of the Representatives aforesaid, That inasmuch as no Territory has a right to be admitted into the Union, but on the principles of the Federal Constitution, and only by a law of Congress, consenting thereto on the part of the existing States, Congress may rightfully, and ought to refuse such law, unless upon the reasonable and just conditions, assented to on the part of the people applying to become one of the States.

"4. *Resolved*, In the opinion of the Representatives aforesaid, That the article of the Constitution which restrains Congress from prohibiting the migration or importation of Slaves, until after the year 1808, does, by necessary implication, admit the general power of Congress over the subject of Slavery, and concedes to them the right to regulate and restrain such migration and importation after that time, into the existing, or any newly-to-be-created State.

"5. *Resolved*, As the opinion of the Representatives of the people of New-Jersey aforesaid, That inasmuch as Congress have a clear right to refuse the admission of a Territory into the Union, by the terms of the Constitution, they ought in the present case to exercise that absolute discretion in order to preserve the political rights of the several existing States, and prevent the great national disgrace and multiplied mischiefs, which must ensue from conceding it, as a matter of right, in the immense Territories yet to claim admission into the Union, beyond the Mississippi, that they may tolerate Slavery.

"6. *Resolved*, (with the concurrence of Council,) That the Governor of this State be requested to transmit a copy of the foregoing resolutions to each of the Senators and Representatives of this State in the Congress of the United States."

PENNSYLVANIA.

HOUSE OF REPRESENTATIVES,
December 11th, 1819.

A motion was made by Mr. Duane and Mr. Thackara, and read as follows:

"The Senate and House of Representatives of the Commonwealth of Pennsylvania, while they cherish the right of the individual States to express their opinion upon all public measures proposed in the Congress of the Union, are aware that its usefulness must in a great degree depend upon the discretion with which it is exercised; they believe that the right ought not to be resorted to upon trivial subjects or unimportant occasions; but they are also persuaded that there are moments when the neglect to exercise it would be a dereliction of public duty.

"Such an occasion, as in their judgment demands the frank expression of the sentiments of Pennsylvania, is now presented. A measure was ardently supported in the last Congress of the United States, and will probably be as earnestly urged during the existing session of that body, which has a palpable tendency to impair the political relations of the several States; which is calculated to mar the social happiness of the present and future generations; which, if adopted, would impede the march of humanity and Freedom through the world; and would transfer from a misguided ancestry an odious stain and fix it indelibly upon the present race—a measure, in brief, which proposes to spread the crimes and cruelties of Slavery from the banks of the Mississippi to the shores of the Pacific. When a measure of this character is seriously advocated in the republican Congress of America, in the nineteenth century, the several States are invoked by the duty which they owe to the Deity, by the veneration which they entertain for the memory of the founders of the Republic, and by a tender regard for posterity, to protest against its adoption, to refuse to covenant with crime, and to limit the range of an evil that already hangs in awful boding over so large a portion of the Union.

"Nor can such a protest be entered by any State with greater propriety than by Pennsylvania. This commonwealth has as sacredly respected the rights of other States as it has been careful of its own; it has been the invariable aim of the people of Pennsylvania to extend to the universe, by their example, the unadulterated blessings of civil and religious freedom; and it is their pride that they have been at all times the practical advocates of those improvements and charities among men which are so well calculated to enable them to answer the purposes of their Creator; and above all, they may boast that they were foremost in removing the pollution of Slavery from among them.

"If, indeed, the measure, against which Pennsylvania considers it her duty to raise her voice, were calculated to abridge any of the rights guaranteed to the several States; if, odious as Slavery is, it was proposed to hasten its extinction by means injurious to the States upon which it was unhappily entailed, Pennsylvania would be among the first to insist upon a sacred observance of the constitutional compact. But it cannot be pretended that the rights of any of the States are at all to be affected by refusing to extend the mischiefs of human bondage over the boundless regions of the West, a territory which formed no part of the Union at the adoption of the Constitution; which has been but lately purchased from a European Power by the people of the Union at large; which may or may not be admitted as a State into the Union at the discretion of Congress; which must establish a republican form of Government, and no other; and whose climate affords none of the pretexts urged for resorting to the labor of natives of the torrid zone; such a territory has no right, inherent or acquired, such as those States possessed which established the existing Constitution. When that Constitution was framed in September, 1787, the concession that three-fifths of the slaves in the States then existing should be represented in Congress, could not have been intended to embrace regions at that time held by a foreign power. On the contrary, so anxious were the Congress of that day to confine human bondage within its ancient home, that on the 13th of July, 1787, that body unanimously declared that Slavery or involuntary servitude should not exist in the extensive territories bounded by the Ohio, the Mississippi, Canada and the Lakes; and in the ninth article of the Constitution itself, the power of Congress to prohibit the emigration of servile persons after 1808, is expressly recognized; nor is there to be found in the statute-book a single instance of the admission of a Territory to the rank of a State in which Congress have not adhered to the right, vested in them by the Constitution, to stipulate with the Territory upon the conditions of the boon.

"The Senate and House of Representatives of Pennsylvania, therefore, cannot but deprecate any departure from the humane and enlightened policy pursued not only by the illustrious Congress which framed the Constitution, but by their successors without exception. They are persuaded that, to open the fertile regions of the West to a servile race, would tend to increase their numbers beyond all past example, would open a new and steady market for the lawless venders of human flesh, and would render all schemes for obliterating this most foul blot upon the American character useless and unavailing.

"Under these convictions, and in the full persuasion that upon this topic there is but one opinion in Pennsylvania—

"*Resolved by the Senate and House of Representatives of the Commonwealth of Pennsylvania*, That the Senators of this State in the Congress of the United States be, and they are hereby instructed, and that the Representatives of this State in the Congress of the United States be, and they are hereby requested, to vote against the admission of any Territory as a State into the Union, unless said Territory shall stipulate and agree that 'the further introduction of Slavery or involuntary servitude, except for the punishment of crimes whereof the party shall have been duly convicted, shall be prohibited; and that all children born within the said Territory, after its admission into the Union as a State, shall be free, but may be held to service until the age of twenty-five years.'

"*Resolved*, That the Governor be, and he is hereby requested to cause a copy of the foregoing preamble and resolution to be transmitted to such of the Senators and Representatives of this State in the Congress of the United States.

"Laid on the table."

"THURSDAY, December 16, 1819.

"Agreeably to the order of the day, the House resumed the consideration of the resolutions postponed on the 14th inst., relative to preventing the introduction of Slavery into States hereafter to be admitted into the Union. And on the question, 'Will the House agree to the resolution?' the Yeas and Nays were required by Mr. Randall and Mr. Souder, and stood—Yeas, 74—(54 Democrats, 20 Federalists); Nays, *none*. Among the Yeas were David R. Porter, late Governor, Josiah Randall of Philadelphia, now a Whig supporter of Buchanan, William Wilkins, late minister to Russia, now in the State Senate, Dr. Daniel Sturgeon, late U. S. Senator, etc., etc. William Duane, editor of *The Aurora*, then the Democratic Organ, also voted for the resolutions, as he had prominently advocated the principle they asserted.

"The Senate unanimously concurred, and the Resolves were signed by Gov. William Findlay."

DELAWARE.

In Senate of the United States, early in 1820, Mr. Van Dyke communicated the following Resolutions of the Legislature of the State of Delaware, which were read:

"*Resolved*, by the Senate and House of Representatives of the State of Delaware, in General Assembly met: That it is, in the opinion of this General Assembly, the constitutional right of the United States, in Congress assembled, to enact and establish, as one of the conditions for the admission of a new State into the Union, a provision which shall effectually prevent the further introduction of Slavery into such State; and that a due regard to the true interests of such State, as well as of the other States, require that the same should be done.

"*Resolved*, That a copy of the above and foregoing resolution be transmitted, by the Speaker of the Senate, to each of the Senators and Representatives from this State in the Congress of the United States."

KENTUCKY.

In Senate, January 24th, 1820, Mr. Logan communicated the following preamble and Resolutions of the Legislature of the State of Kentucky, which were read:

"*Whereas*, The Constitution of the United States provides for the admission of new States into the Union, and it is just and proper that all such States should be established upon the footing of original States, with a view to the preservation of State Sovereignty, the prosperity of such new State, and the good of their citizens; *and whereas*, successful attempts have been heretofore made, and are now making, to prevent the People of the Territory of Missouri from being admitted into the Union as a State, unless trammeled by rules and regulations which do not exist in the original States, particularly in relation to the toleration of Slavery.

"*Whereas*, also, if Congress can thus trammel or control the powers of a Territory in the formation of a State government, that body may, on the same principle, reduce its powers to little more than those possessed by the people of the District of Columbia; and whilst professing to make it a Sovereign State, may bind it in perpetual vassalage, and reduce it to the condition of a province; such State must necessarily become the dependent of Congress, asking such powers, and not the independent State, demanding rights. *And whereas*, it is necessary, in preserving the State Sovereignties in their present rights, that no new State should be subjected to this restriction, any more than an old one, and that there can be no reason or justice why it should not be entitled to the same privileges, when it is bound to bear all the burdens and taxes laid upon it by Congress.

"In passing the following Resolution, the General Assembly refrains from expressing any opinion either in favor or against the principles of Slavery; but to support and maintain State rights, which it conceives necessary to be supported and maintained, to preserve the liberties of the free people of these United States, it avows its solemn conviction, that the States already confederated under one common Constitution, have not a right to deprive new States of equal privileges with themselves. Therefore,

"*Resolved*, by the General Assembly of the Commonwealth of Kentucky, That the Senators in Congress from this State be instructed, and the Representatives be requested, to use their efforts to procure the passage of a law to admit the people of Missouri into the Union, as a State, whether those people will sanction Slavery by their Constitution, or not.

"*Resolved*, That the Executive of this Commonwealth be requested to transmit this Resolution to the Senators and Representatives of this State in Congress, that it may be laid before that body for its consideration."

The bill authorizing Missouri to form a constitution, etc., came up in the House as a special order, Jan. 24th. Mr. Taylor of N. Y. moved that it be postponed for one week: Lost: Yeas 87; Nays 88. Whereupon the House adjourned. It was considered in committee the next day, as also on the 28th and 30th, and thence debated daily until the 19th of February, when a bill came down from the Senate "to admit the State of *Maine* into the Union," but with a rider authorizing the people of Missouri to form a State Constitution, etc., without restriction on the subject of Slavery.

The House, very early in the session, passed a bill providing for the admission of Maine as a State. This bill came to the Senate, and was sent to its Judiciary Committee aforesaid, which amended it by adding a provision for Missouri as above. After several days' debate in Senate, Mr. Roberts of Pa. moved to recommit, so as to strike out all but the admission of Maine; which was defeated (Jan. 14th, 1820)—Yeas 18; Nays 25. Hereupon Mr. Thomas of Ill. (who voted with the majority, as uniformly against any restriction on Missouri) gave notice that he should

"ask leave to bring a bill to prohibit the introduction of Slavery into *the Territories of the United States North and West of the* contemplated *State of Missouri*."

—which he accordingly did on the 19th; when it was read and ordered to a third reading.

[NOTE.—Great confusion and misconception exists in the public mind with regard to "the Missouri Restriction," two totally different propositions being called by that name. The *original* Restriction, which Mr. Clay vehemently opposed, and Mr. Jefferson in a letter characterized as a "fire-bell in the night," contemplated the limitation of Slavery in its exclusion from the *State of Missouri*. This was ultimately defeated, as we shall see. The *second* proposed Restriction was that of Mr. Thomas, just cited, which proposed the exclusion of Slavery, not from the State of Missouri, but *from the Territories of the United States North and West of that State*. This proposition did not emanate from the original Missouri Restrictionists, but from their adversaries, and was but reluctantly and partially accepted by the former.]

The Maine admission bill, with the proposed amendments, was discussed through several days, until, Feb. 16th, the question was taken on the Judiciary Committee's amendments (authorizing Missouri to form a State Constitution, and saying nothing of Slavery), which were adopted by the following vote:

YEAS—Against the Restriction on Missouri:

Messrs. Barbour of Va.	Logan of Ky.
Brown of La.	Macon, of N. C.
Eaton of Tenn.	Pinkney of Md.
Edwards of Ill.	Pleasants of Va.
Elliott of Ga.	Smith of S. C.
Gaillard of S. C.	Stokes of N. C.
Johnson of Ky.	*Taylor* of Ind.
Johnson of La.	*Thomas* of Ill.
King (Wm. R.), Ala.	Walker of Ala.
Leake of Miss.	Walker of Ga.
Lloyd of Md.	Williams of Miss.
Williams of Tenn.—23.	

[20 from Slave States; 3 (in *italics*) from Free States.]

NAYS—For Restriction:

Messrs. Burrill of R. I.	Noble of Ind.
Dana of Ct.	Otis of Mass.
Dickinson of N. J.	Palmer of Vt.
Horsey of Del.	Parrott of N. H.
Hunter of R. I.	Roberts of Pa.
King (Rufus) of N. Y.	Ruggles of Ohio,
Lanman of Conn.	Sanford of N. Y.
Lowrie of Pa.	Tichenor of Vt.
Mellen of Mass.	Trimble of Ohio,
Morrill of N. H.	*Van Dyke* of Del.
Wilson of N. J.—21	

[19 from Free States, 2 (in *italics*) from Delaware.]

Mr. Thomas of Ill. then proposed his amendment, as follows:

"*And be it further enacted,* That the sixth article of compact of the Ordinance of Congress, passed July 13th, 1787, for the government of the Territory of the United States, northwest of the river Ohio, shall, to all intents and purposes, be, and hereby is, deemed and held applicable to, and shall have full force and effect in and over, all that tract of country ceded by France to the United States under the name of Louisiana which lies north of thirty-six degrees and thirty minutes, north latitude, excepting only such part thereof as is included within the limits contemplated by this act."

On the following day Mr. Thomas withdrew the foregoing and substituted the following:

"*And be it further enacted,* That in all that Territory ceded by France to the United States under the name of Louisiana which lies north of thirty-six degrees thirty minutes, north latitude, excepting only such part thereof as is included within the limits of the State contemplated by this act, Slavery and involuntary servitude, otherwise than in the punishment of crime whereof the party shall have been duly convicted, shall be and is hereby forever prohibited. *Provided always,* that any person escaping into the same, from where labor or service is lawfully claimed in any State or Territory of the United States, such fugitive may be lawfully reclaimed and conveyed to the person claiming his or her labor or service as aforesaid."

Mr. Trimble of Ohio moved a substitute for this, somewhat altering the boundaries of the region shielded from Slavery, which was rejected: Yeas 20 (Northern); Nays 24 (Southern, with Noble, Edwards, and Taylor, as aforesaid).

The question then recurred on Mr. Thomas's amendment, which was adopted as follows:

YEAS—For excluding Slavery from all the Territory North and West of Missouri:

Messrs. Brown of La.	Mellen of Mass.
Burrill of R. I.	Morrill of N. H.
Dana of Conn.	Otis of Mass.
Dickerson of N. J.	Palmer of Vt.
Eaton of Tenn.	Parrott of N. H.
Edwards of Ill.	Pinkney of Md.
Horsey of Del.	Roberts of Pa.
Hunter of R. I.	Ruggles of Ohio,
Johnson of Ky.	Sanford of N. Y.
Johnson of La.	Stokes of N. C.
King (Wm. R.) of Ala.	Thomas of Ill.
King (Rufus) of N. Y.	Tichenor of Vt.
Lanman of Conn.	Trimble of Ohio,
Leake of Miss.	Van Dyke of Del.
Lowrie of Pa.	Walker of Ala.
Lloyd of Md.	Williams of Ten.
Logan of Ky.	Wilson of N.J.—34

NAYS—Against such Restriction:

Messrs. Barbour of Va.	Smith (Wm.) of S. C.
Elliott of Ga.	Taylor of Ind.
Gaillard of S. C.	Walker of Ga.
Macon of N. C.	Williams of Miss.—10.
Noble of Ind.	
Pleasants of Va.	

[It will here be seen that the Restriction ultimately adopted, that excluding Slavery from all territory then owned by the United States North and West of the Southwest border of the State of Missouri, was proposed by an early and steadfast opponent of the Restriction originally proposed, relative to Slavery in the contemplated State of Missouri, and was sustained by the votes of fourteen Senators from Slave States, including the Senators from Delaware, Maryland, Kentucky, Tennessee, Alabama, and Louisiana, with one vote each from North Carolina and Mississippi.

The current assumption that this Restriction was proposed by Rufus King of New York, and mainly sustained by the antagonists of Slavery Extension, is wholly mistaken. The truth, doubtless, is, that it was suggested by the more moderate opponents of the proposed Restriction on Missouri—and supported also by Senators from Slave States—as a means of overcoming the resistance of the House to Slavery in Missouri. It was, in effect, an offer from the milder opponents of Slavery Restriction to the more moderate and flexible advocates of that Restriction—"Let us have Slavery in Missouri, and we will unite with you in excluding it from all the uninhabited territories North and West of that State." It was in substance an agreement between the North and the South to that effect, though the more determined champions, whether of Slavery Extension or Slavery Restriction, did not unite in it.]

The bill, thus amended, was ordered to be engrossed for a third reading by the following vote:

YEAS—For the Missouri Bill:

Messrs. Barbour of Va.	Lloyd of Md.
Brown of La.	Logan of Ky.
Eaton of Tenn.	Parrott of N. H.
Edwards of Ill.	Pinkney of Md.
Elliott of Ga.	Pleasants of Va.
Gaillard of S. C.	Stokes of N. C.
Horsey of Del.	Thomas of Ill.
Hunter of R. I.	Van Dyke, Del.
Johnson of Ky.	Walker of Ala.
Johnson of La.	Walker of Ga.
King of Ala.	Williams of Miss.
Leake of Miss.	Williams, Tenn.—24.

NAYS—Against the Bill:

Messrs. Burrill of R. I.	Otis of Mass.
Dana of Conn.	Palmer of Vt.
Dickerson of N. J.	Roberts of Pa.
King of N. Y.	Ruggles of Ohio,
Lanman of Conn.	Sanford of N. Y.
Lowrie of Pa.	Smith of S. C.
Macon of N. C.	Taylor of Ind.
Mellen of Mass.	Tichenor of Vt.
Morrill of N. H.	Trimble of Ohio,
Noble of Ind.	Wilson of N. J. —20.

The bill was thus passed (Feb. 18th) without further division, and sent to the House for concurrence. In the House, Mr. Thomas's amendment (as above) was at first rejected by both parties, and defeated by the strong vote of 159 to 18. The Yeas (to adopt) were,

Messrs	Baldwin of Pa.	Meech of Vt.
	Bayly of Md.	Mercer of Va.
	Bloomfield of N. J.	Quarles of Ky.
	Cocke of Tenn.	Ringgold of Md.
	Crafts of Vt.	Shaw of Mass.
	Culpepper of N. C.	Sloan of Ohio.
	Kinsey of N. J.	Smith of N. J.
	Lathrop of Mass.	Smith of Md.
	Little of Md.	Tarr of Pa.—18.

Prior to this vote, the House disagreed to the log-rolling of Maine and Missouri, into one bill by the strong vote of 93 to 72. [We do not give the Yeas and Nays on this decision; but the majority was composed of the representatives of the Free States with only four exceptions; and Mr. Louis McLane of Delaware, who was constrained by instructions from his legislature. His colleague, Mr. Willard Hall, did not vote.]

The members from Free States who voted with the South to keep Maine and Missouri united in one bill were,

Messrs.	H. Baldwin of Pa.	Henry Meigs of N. Y.
	Bloomfield of N. J.	Henry Shaw of Mass.

The House also disagreed to the remaining amendments of the Senate (striking out the restriction on Slavery in Missouri) by the strong vote of 102 Yeas to 68 Nays.

[Nearly or quite every Representative of a Free State voted in the majority of this division with the following from Slave States:

Louis McLane, Del.	Nelson, Md.
Alney McLean, Ky.	Trimble, Ky.]

So the House rejected all the Senate's amendments, and returned the bill with a corresponding message.

The Senate took up the bill on the 24th, and debated it till the 28th, when, on a direct vote, it was decided *not* to recede from the attachment of Missouri to the Maine bill: Yeas 21; (19 from Free States and 2 from Delaware;) Nays 23; (20 from Slave States, with Messrs. Taylor of Ind., Edwards and Thomas of Ill.)

The Senate also voted not to recede from its amendment prohibiting Slavery west of Missouri, and north of 36° 30′, north latitude. (For receding, 9 from Slave States, with Messrs. Noble and Taylor of Ind.: against it 33—(22 from Slave States, 11 from Free States.) The remaining amendments of the Senate were then insisted on without division, and the House notified accordingly.

The bill was now returned to the House, which, on motion of Mr. John W. Taylor of N. Y., voted to insist on its disagreement to all but sec. 9 of the Senate's amendments, by Yeas 97 to Nays 76: [all but a purely sectional vote: Hugh Nelson of Va. voting with the North; Baldwin of Pa., Bloomfield of N. J., and Shaw of Mass., voting with the South.]

Sec. 9, (the Senate's exclusion of Slavery from the Territory north and west of Missouri) was also rejected—Yeas 160; Nays 14, (much as before.) The Senate thereupon (March 2nd) passed the House's Missouri bill, striking out the restriction of Slavery by Yeas 27 to Nays 15, and adding without a division the exclusion of Slavery from the Territory west and north of said State. Mr. Trimble again moved the exclusion of Slavery from Arkansas also, but was again voted down; Yeas 12; Nays 30.

The Senate now asked a conference, which the House granted without a division. The Committee of Conference was composed of Messrs. Thomas of Ill., Pinkney of Md., and Barbour of Va. (all anti-restrictionists), on the part of the Senate, and Messrs. Holmes of Mass., Taylor of N. Y., Lowndes of S. C., Parker of Mass., and Kinsey of N. J., on the part of the House. [Such constitution of the Committee of Conference was in effect a surrender of the Restriction on the part of the House.] John Holmes of Mass., from this Committee, in due time (March 2nd), reported that,

1. The Senate should give up the combination of Missouri in the same bill with Maine.

2. The House should abandon the attempt to restrict Slavery in Missouri.

3. Both Houses should agree to pass the Senate's separate Missouri bill, with Mr. Thomas's restriction or compromising proviso, excluding Slavery from all Territory north and west of Missouri.

The report having been read,

The first and most important question was put, viz.:

"Will the House concur with the Senate in so much of the said amendments as proposes to strike from the fourth section of the [Missouri] bill the provision prohibiting Slavery or involuntary servitude, in the contemplated State, otherwise than in the punishment of crimes?"

On which question the Yeas and Nays were demanded, and were as follow:

YEAS—For giving up Restriction on Missouri:

MASSACHUSETTS—Mark Langdon Hill, John Holmes, Jonathan Mason, Henry Shaw—4.

RHODE ISLAND.—Samuel Eddy—1.

CONNECTICUT.—Samuel A. Foot, James Stephens—2.

NEW-YORK.—Henry Meigs, Henry R. Storrs—2.

NEW-JERSEY.—Joseph Bloomfield, Charles Kinsey, Bernard Smith—3.

PENNSYLVANIA.—Henry Baldwin, David Fullerton—2.

Total from Free States 14.

DELAWARE.—Louis McLane—1.

MARYLAND.—Stephenson Archer, Thomas Bayly, Thomas Culbreth, Joseph Kent, Peter Little, Raphael Neale, Samuel Ringgold, Samuel Smith, Henry R. Warfield—9.

VIRGINIA.—Mark Alexander, William S. Archer, Philip P. Barbour, William A. Burwell,

John Floyd, Robert S. Garnett, James Johnson, James Jones, William McCoy, Charles F. Mercer, Hugh Nelson, Thomas Nelson, Severn E. Parker, Jas Pindall, John Randolph, Ballard Smith, Alexander Smyth, George F. Strother, Thomas Van Swearingen, George Tucker, John Tyler, Jared Williams—22.

NORTH CAROLINA.—Hutchins G. Burton, John Culpepper, William Davidson, Weldon N. Edwards, Charles Fisher, Thomas H. Hall, Charles Hooks, Thomas Settle, Jesse Slocumb, James S. Smith, Felix Walker, Lewis Williams—12.

SOUTH CAROLINA.—Josiah Brevard, Elias Earle, James Ervin, William Lowndes, James McCreary, James Overstreet, Charles Pinckney, Eldred Simkins, Sterling Tucker—9.

GEORGIA.—Joel A. Abbott, Thomas W. Cobb, Joel Crawford, John A. Cuthbert, Robert R. Reid, William Terrell—6.

ALABAMA.—John Crowell—1.

MISSISSIPPI.—John Rankin—1.

LOUISIANA.—Thomas Butler—1.

KENTUCKY.—Richard C. Anderson, jr., William Brown; Benjamin Hardin, Alney McLean, Thomas Metcalf, Tunstall Quarles, Geo. Robertson, David Trimble—8.

TENNESSEE.—Robert Allen, Henry H. Bryan, Newton Cannon, John Cocke, Francis Jones, John Rhea—5.

Total Yeas from Slave States 76; in all 90.

NAYS—Against giving up the Restriction on Slavery in Missouri:

NEW-HAMPSHIRE.—Joseph Buffum, jr., Josiah Butler, Clifton Clagett, Arthur Livermore, William Plumer, jr., Nathaniel Upham—6.

MASSACHUSETTS (including Maine).—Benjamin Adams, Samuel C. Allen, Joshua Cushman, Edward Dowse, Walter Folger, jr., Timothy Fuller, Jonas Kendall, Martin Kinsley, Samuel Lathrop, Enoch Lincoln, Marcus Morton, Jeremiah Nelson, James Parker, Zabdiel Sampson, Nathaniel Silsbee, Ezekiel Whitman—16.

RHODE ISLAND.—Nathaniel Hazard—1.

CONNECTICUT.—Jonathan O. Moseley, Elisha Phelps, John Russ, Gideon Tomlinson—4.

VERMONT.—Samuel C. Crafts, Rollin C. Mallary, Ezra Meech, Charles Rich, Mark Richards, William Strong—6.

NEW-YORK.—Nathaniel Allen, Caleb Baker, Robert Clark, Jacob H. De Witt, John D. Dickinson, John Fay, William D. Ford, Ezra C. Gross, James Guyon, jr., Aaron Hackley, jr., George Hall, Joseph S. Lyman, Robert Monell, Nathaniel Pitcher, Jonathan Richmond, Randall S. Street, James Strong, John W. Taylor, Albert H. Tracy, Solomon Van Rensselaer, Peter H. Wendover, Silas Wood—22.

NEW-JERSEY.—Ephraim Bateman, John Linn, Henry Southard—3.

PENNSYLVANIA.—Andrew Boden, William Darlington, George Dennison, Samuel Edwards, Thomas Forrest, Samuel Gross, Joseph Hemphill, Jacob Hibschman, Joseph Heister, Jacob Hostetter, William P. Maclay, David Marchand, Robert Moore, Samuel Moore, John Murray, Thomas Patterson, Robert Philson, Thomas J. Rogers, John Sergeant, Christian Tarr, James M. Wallace—21.

OHIO.—Philemon Beecher, Henry Brush, John W. Campbell, Samuel Herrick, Thomas R. Ross, John Sloane—6.

INDIANA.—William Hendricks—1.

ILLINOIS.—Daniel P. Cook—1.

Total Nays 87—all from Free States.

[The members apparently absent on this important division, were Henry W. Edwards of Conn., Walter Case and Honorius Peck of N. Y. and John Condit of N. J., from the Free States; with Lemuel Sawyer of N. C., and David Walker of Ky., from the Slave States. Mr. Clay of Ky., being Speaker, did not vote.]

This defeat broke the back of the Northern resistance to receiving Missouri as a Slave State.

Mr. Taylor, of N. Y., now moved an amendment, intended to include Arkansas Territory under the proposed Inhibition of Slavery West of Missouri; but this motion was cut off by the Previous Question (which then cut off amendments more rigorously, according to the rules of the House, than it now does), and the House proceeded to concur with the Senate in inserting the exclusion of Slavery from the Territory West and North of Missouri, instead of that just stricken out by 134 Yeas to 42 Nays, (the Nays being from the South). So the bill was *passed* in the form indicated above; and the bill admitting Maine as a State, (relieved, by a conference, from the Missouri rider,) passed both Houses without a division, on the following day.

Such was the virtual termination of the struggle for the restriction of Slavery in Missouri, which was beaten by the plan of proffering instead an exclusion of Slavery from all the then Federal Territory West and North of that State. It is unquestionable that, without this compromise or equivalent, the Northern votes, which passed the bill, could not have been obtained for it.

VIII.

THE THIRD MISSOURI STRUGGLE.

THOUGH the acceptance of Missouri as a State, with a Slave Constitution, was forever settled by the votes just recorded, a new excitement sprang up on her presenting herself to Congress (Nov. 16, 1820), with a State Constitution, framed on the 19th of July, containing the following resolutions:

"The General Assembly shall have no power to pass laws, First, for the emancipation of slaves without the consent of their owners, or without paying them, before such emancipation, a full equivalent for such Slaves so emancipated; and, Second, to prevent *bona fide* emigrants to this State, or actual settlers therein, from bringing from any of the United States, or from any of their Territories, such persons as may there be deemed to be Slaves, so long as any persons of the same description are allowed to be held as Slaves by the laws of this State.

* * * "It shall be their duty, as soon as may be, to pass such laws as may be necessary,

"First, to prevent free negroes and mulattoes from coming to, and settling in, this State, under any pretext whatever."

The North, still smarting under a sense of its defeat on the question of excluding Slavery from Missouri, regarded this as needlessly defiant, insulting, and inhuman, and the last quoted as palpably in violation of that clause of the Federal Constitution which gives to the citizens of each State (which blacks are, in several Free States,) the rights of citizens in every State. A determined resistance to any such exclusion was manifested, and a portion of the Northern Members evinced a disposition to renew the struggle against the further introduction of Slaves into Missouri. At the first effort to carry her admission, the House voted it down—Yeas, 79; Nays, 93. A second attempt to admit her, on condition she would expunge the obnoxious clause (last quoted) of her Constitution, was voted down still more decisively—Yeas, 6; Nays, 146.

The House now rested, until a joint resolve, admitting her with but a vague and ineffective qualification, came down from the Senate, where it was passed by a vote of 26 to 18—six Senators from Free States in the affirmative. Mr. Clay, who had resigned in the recess, and been succeeded, as Speaker, by John W. Taylor, of New York, now appeared as the leader of the Missouri admissionists, and proposed terms of compromise, which were twice voted down by the Northern Members, aided by John Randolph and three others from the South, who would have Missouri admitted without condition or qualification. At last, Mr. Clay proposed a Joint Committee on this subject, to be chosen by ballot—which the House agreed to by 101 to 55; and Mr. Clay became its Chairman. By this Committee it was agreed, that a solemn pledge should be required of the Legislature of Missouri, that the Constitution of that State should not be construed to authorize the passage of any Act, and that no Act should be passed, "by which any of the citizens of either of the States should be excluded from the enjoyment of the privileges and immunities to which they are entitled under the Constitution of the United States." The Joint Resolution, amended by the addition of this proviso, passed the House by 86 Yeas to 82 Nays; the Senate concurred (Feb. 27th, 1821,) by 26 Yeas to 15 Nays—(all Northern but Macon, of N. C.) Missouri complied with the condition, and became an accepted member of the Union. Thus closed the last stage of the fierce Missouri Controversy, which for a time seemed to threaten—as so many other controversies have harmlessly threatened—the existence of the Union.

IX.

EXTENSION OF MISSOURI.

The State of Missouri, as originally organized, was bounded on the West by a line already specified, which excluded a triangle West of said line, and between it and the Missouri, which was found, in time, to be exceedingly fertile and desirable. It was free soil by the terms of the Missouri compact, and was also covered by Indian reservations, not to be removed without a concurrence of two-thirds of the Senate. Messrs. Benton and Linn, senators from Missouri, undertook the difficult task of engineering through Congress a bill including this triangle (large enough to form seven Counties) within the State of Missouri; which they effected, at the long Session of 1835–6, so quietly as hardly to attract attention. The bill was first sent to the Senate's Committee on the Judiciary, where a favorable report was procured from Mr. John M. Clayton, of Delaware, its Chairman; and then it was floated through both Houses without encountering the perils of a division. The requisite Indian treaties were likewise carried through the Senate; so Missouri became possessed of a large and desirable accession of territory, which has since become one of her most populous and wealthy sections, devoted to the growing of hemp, tobacco, etc., and cultivated by Slaves. This is the most pro-Slavery section of the State, in which was originated, and has been principally sustained, that series of inroads into Kansas, corruptions of her ballot-boxes, and outrages upon her people, which have earned for their authors the appellation of *Border Ruffians*.

X.

THE ANNEXATION OF TEXAS.

The name of *Texas* was originally applied to a Spanish possession or province, lying between the Mississippi and the Rio Grande del Norte, but not extending to either of these great rivers. It was an appendage of the Viceroyalty of Mexico, but had very few civilized inhabitants down to the time of the separation of Mexico from Spain. On two or three occasions, bands of French adventurers had landed on its coast, or entered it from the adjoining French colony of Louisiana; but they had uniformly been treated as intruders, and either destroyed or made prisoners by the Spanish military authorities. No line had ever been drawn between the two colonies; but the traditional line between them, south of the Red River, ran somewhat within the limits of the present State of Louisiana.

The etymology of *Natchitoches*, a city of Louisiana on the Red River, several miles within the present boundary of that State, attests its claims to a Spanish origin.

When Louisiana was transferred by France to the United States, without specification of boundaries, collisions of claims on this frontier was apprehended. General Wilkinson, commanding the United States troops, moved gradually to the west; the Spanish commandant in Texas likewise drew toward the frontiers, until they stood opposite each other across what was then tacitly settled as the boundary between the two countries. This was never afterward disregarded.

In 1819, Spain and the United States seemed on the verge of war. General Jackson had twice invaded Florida, on the assumption of complicity on the part of her rulers and people—first with our British, then with our savage enemies—and had finally overrun, and, in effect, annexed it to the Union. Spain, on the other hand, had preyed upon our commerce during the long wars in Europe, and honestly owed our merchants large sums for unjustifiable seizures and spoliations. A negotiation for the settlement of these differences was carried on at Washington, between John Quincy Adams, Mr. Monroe's Secretary of State, and Don Onis, the Spanish embassador, in the course of which Mr. Adams set up a claim, on the part of this country, to Texas as a natural geographical appendage not of Mexico, but of Louisiana. This claim, however, he eventually waived and relinquished, in consideration of a cession of Florida by Spain to this country—our government agreeing, on its part, to pay the claims of our merchants for spoliations. Texas remained, therefore, what it always had been—a department or province of Mexico, with a formal quit-claim thereto on the part of the United States.

The natural advantages of this region naturally attracted the attention of American adventurers, and a small colony of Yankees was settled thereon, about 1819–20, by Moses Austin of Connecticut. Other settlements followed. Originally, grants of land in Texas were prayed for, and obtained of the Mexican government, on the assumption that the petitioners were Roman Catholics, persecuted in the United States, because of their religion, and anxious to find a refuge in some Catholic country. Thus all the early emigrants to Texas went professedly as Catholics, no other religion being tolerated.

Slavery was abolished by Mexico soon after the consummation of her independence, when very few slaves were, or ever had been, in Texas. But, about 1834, some years after this event, a quiet, but very general, and, evidently concerted, emigration, mainly from Tennessee and other southwestern States, began to concentrate itself in Texas. The emigrants carried rifles; many of them were accompanied by slaves; and it was well understood that they did not intend to become Mexicans, much less to relinquish their slaves. When Gen. Sam. Houston left Arkansas for Texas, in 1834–5, the Little Rock *Journal*, which announced his exodus and destination, significantly added: "*We shall, doubtless, hear of his raising his flag there shortly.*" That was a foregone conclusion.

Of course, the new settlers in Texas did not lack pretexts or provocations for such a step. Mexico was then much as she is now, misgoverned, turbulent, anarchical, and despotic. The overthrow of her Federal Constitution by Santa Anna was one reason assigned for the rebellion against her authority which broke out in Texas. In 1835, her independence was declared; in 1836, at the decisive battle of San Jacinto, it was, by the rout and capture of the Mexican dictator, secured. This triumph was won by emigrants from this country almost exclusively; scarcely half a dozen of the old Mexican inhabitants participating in the revolution. Santa Anna, while a prisoner, under restraint and apprehension, agreed to a peace on the basis of the independence of Texas—a covenant which he had no power, and probably no desire, to give effect to when restored to liberty. The Texans, pursuing their advantage, twice or thrice penetrated other Mexican provinces—Tamaulipas, Coahuila, etc., and waved their Lone-Star flag in defiance, on the banks of the Rio Grande del Norte; which position, however, they were always compelled soon to abandon—once with severe loss. Their government, nevertheless, in reiterating their declaration of independence, claimed the Rio Grande as their western boundary, from its source to its mouth, including a large share of Tamaulipas, Coahuila, Durango, and by far the more important and populous portion of New Mexico. And it was with this claim, expressly set forth in the treaty, that President Tyler and his responsible advisers negotiated the first official project of annexation, which was submitted to the Senate, during the session of 1843–44, and rejected by a very decisive vote: only fifteen (mainly Southern) senators voting to confirm it. Col. Benton, and others, urged this aggressive claim of boundary, as affording abundant reason for the rejection of this treaty; but it is not known that the Slavery aspect of the case attracted especial attention in the Senate. The measure, however, had already been publicly eulogized by Gen. James Hamilton, of S. C., as calculated to "give a Gibraltar to the South," and had, on that ground, secured a very general and ardent popularity throughout the southwest. And, more than a year previously, several northern members of Congress had united in the following:

TO THE PEOPLE OF THE FREE STATES OF THE UNION.

We, the undersigned, in closing our duties to our constituents and our country as members of the 27th Congress, feel bound to call your attention, very briefly, to the project, long entertained by a portion of the people of these United States, still pertinaciously adhered to, and intended soon to be consummated: THE ANNEXATION OF TEXAS TO THIS UNION. In the press of business incident to the last days of a session of Congress, we have not time, did we deem it necessary, to enter upon a detailed statement of the reasons which force upon our minds the conviction, that this project is *by no means abandoned:* that a large portion of the country, interested in the continuance of Domestic Slavery and the Slave Trade in these United States, have solemnly and unalterably determined: *that it shall be speedily carried into execution;* and that, by this admission of new Slave Territory and

Slave States, *the undue ascendancy of the Slave-holding power in the Government shall be secured and riveted beyond all redemption ! !*

That it was with these views and intentions that settlements were effected in the Province, by citizens of the United States, difficulties fomented with the Mexican Government, a revolt brought about, and an Independent Government declared, *cannot now admit of a doubt* ; and that, hitherto, all attempts of Mexico to reduce her revolted province to obedience, have proved unsuccessful is to be attributed to the unlawful aid and assistance of designing and interested individuals in the United States, and the direct and indirect co-operation of our own Government, *with similar views*, is not the less certain and demonstrable.

The open and repeated enlistment of troops in several States of this Union, in aid of the Texan Revolution, the intrusion of an American Army, by order of the President, far into the Territory of the Mexican Government, at a moment critical for the fate of the insurgents, under pretense of preventing Mexican soldiers from fomenting Indian disturbances, but in reality in aid of, and acting in singular concert and coincidence with, the army of the Revolutionists, the entire neglect of our Government to adopt any efficient measures to prevent the most unwarrantable aggressions of bodies of our own citizens, enlisted, organized and officered within our own borders, and marched in arms and battle array upon the territory, and against the inhabitants of a friendly government, in aid of freebooters and insurgents, and the premature recognition of the Independence of Texas, by a snap vote, at the heel of a session of Congress, and that, too, at the very session when President Jackson had, by special Message, insisted that "the measure would be contrary to the policy invariably observed by the United States in all similar cases;" would be marked with great injustice to Mexico, and peculiarly liable to the darkest suspicions, *inasmuch as the Texans were almost all emigrants from the United States*, AND SOUGHT THE RECOGNITION OF THEIR INDEPENDENCE WITH THE AVOWED PURPOSE OF OBTAINING THEIR ANNEXATION TO THE U. STATES. These occurrences are too well known and too fresh in the memory of all, to need more than a passing notice. These have become matters of history. For further evidence upon all these and other important points, we refer to the memorable speech of John Quincy Adams, delivered in the House of Representatives during the morning hour in June and July, 1838, and to his address to his constituents, delivered at Braintree, 17th September, 1842.

The open avowal of the Texans themselves—the frequent and anxious negotiations of our own Government—the resolutions of various States of the Union—the numerous declarations of members of Congress—the tone of the Southern press—as well as the direct application of the Texan Government, *make it impossible for any man to doubt*, that ANNEXATION, and the formation of several new Slaveholding States, were *originally* the policy and design of the Slaveholding States and the Executive of the Nation.

The same references will show, very conclusively, that the *particular objects* of this new acquisition of Slave Territory, were THE PERPETUATION OF SLAVERY AND THE CONTINUED ASCENDANCY OF THE SLAVE POWER.

The following extracts from a Report on that subject, adopted by the Legislature of Mississippi, from a mass of similar evidence which might be be adduced, will show *with what views* the annexation was *then* urged.

"But we hasten to suggest the importance of the annexation of Texas to this Republic upon grounds somewhat local in their complexion, but of an import infinitely grave and interesting to the people who inhabit the Southern portion of this Confederacy, where it is known that a species of domestic Slavery is tolerated and protected by law, whose existence is prohibited by the legal regulations of other States of this Confederacy; which system of Slavery is held by all, who are familiarly acquainted with its practical effects, *to be of highly beneficial influence to the country within whose limits it is permitted to exist.*

"The Committee feel authorized to say that this system is cherished by our constituents as *the very palladium of their prosperity and happiness*, and whatever ignorant fanatics may elsewhere conjecture, the Committee are fully assured, upon the most diligent observation and reflection on the subject, that *the South does not possess within her limits a blessing with which the affections of her people are so closely entwined and so completely enfibred*, and whose value is more highly appreciated, than that which we are now considering.

* * * * * *

"It may not be improper here to remark, that during the last session of Congress, when a Senator from Mississippi proposed the acknowledgment of Texian independence, it was found, with a few exceptions, *the members of that body were ready to take ground upon it, as upon the subject of Slavery itself.*

"With all these facts before us, we do not hesitate in believing that these feelings influenced the New England Senators, but one voting in favor of the measure; and, indeed, Mr. Webster has been bold enough, in a public speech recently delivered in New York, to many thousand citizens, to declare that the reason that influenced his opposition was his abhorrence to Slavery in the South, and that it might, in the event of its recognition, become a slaveholding State. He also spoke of the efforts making in favor of Abolition; and that being predicated upon, and aided by the powerful influence of religious feeling, it would become irresistible and overwhelming.

"This language, coming from so distinguished an individual as Mr. Webster, so familiar with the feelings of the North, and entertaining so high a respect for public sentiment in New England, speaks so plainly the voice of the North as not to be misunderstood.

"We sincerely hope there is enough good sense and genuine love of country among our fellow-countrymen of the Northern States, *to secure us final justice on this subject* ; yet we cannot consider it safe or expedient for the people of the South to entirely disregard the efforts of the fanatics, and the opinions of such men as Webster, and others who countenance such dangerous doctrines.

"*The Northern States have no interests of their own* which require any *special* safeguards for their defense, save only their domestic manufactures ; and God knows they have already received protection from Government on a most liberal scale; under which encouragement they have improved and flourished beyond example. *The South has very peculiar interests to preserve:* interests already violently assailed and boldly threatened.

"*Your Committee are fully persuaded that this protection to her best interests will be afforded by the annexation of Texas; an equipoise of influence in the halls of Congress will be secured, which will furnish us a permanent guarantee of protection.*"

The speech of Mr. Adams, exposing the whole system of duplicity and perfidy toward Mexico, had marked the conduct of our Government; and the emphatic expressions of opposition which began to come up from all parties in the Free States, however, for a time, nearly silenced the clamors of the South for annexation, and the people of the North have been lulled into the belief, that the project is nearly, if not wholly abandoned, and that, at least, there is now no serious danger of its consummation.

Believing this to be a *false and dangerous security* ; that the project has never been abandoned a moment, by its originators and abettors, but that it has been deferred for a more favorable moment for its accomplishment, we refer to a few evidences of more recent development upon which this opinion is founded.

The last Election of President of the Republic of Texas, is understood to have turned, *mainly*, upon the question of *annexation* or *no annexation*, and the candidate favorable to that measure was successful by an overwhelming majority.

The sovereign States of Alabama, Tennessee, and Mississippi, have *recently* adopted Resolutions, some, if not all of them, *unanimously*, in favor of annexation, and forwarded them to Congress.

The Hon. HENRY A. WISE, a member of Congress from the District in which our present Chief Magistrate resided when elected Vice-President, and who is understood to be more intimately acquainted with the views and designs of the present administration than any other member of Congress, most distinctly avowed his desire for, and expectation of annexation, at the last session of Congress. Among other things, he said, in a speech delivered January 26, 1842:

"True, if Iowa be added on the one side, Florida will be added on the other. But there the equation must stop. Let one more Northern State be admitted, and the equilibrium is gone—gone forever. The *balance of interests* is gone—the *safeguard* of American property--of the American Constitution—of the American Union, vanished into thin air. *This must be the inevitable result, unless by a treaty with Mexico*, THE SOUTH CAN ADD MORE WEIGHT TO HER END OF THE LEVER! *Let the South stop at the Sabine*, (the eastern boundary of Texas,) while the North may spread unchecked beyond the Rocky Mountains, AND THE SOUTHERN SCALE MUST KICK THE BEAM!"

Finding difficulties, perhaps, in the way of a cession by Treaty, in another speech delivered in April, 1842, on a motion made by Mr. Linn, of N. Y., to strike out the salary of the Minister to Mexico, on the ground that the design of the EXECUTIVE, in making the appointment, was to accomplish the annexation of Texas, Mr. Wise said, "he earnestly hoped and trusted that the President was as desirous (of annexation) as he was represented to be. We may well suppose the President to be in favor of it, as every wise statesman must be who is not governed by fanaticism, or local sectional prejudices."

He said of Texas, that

"While she was as a State, weak and almost powerless in resisting invasion, she was herself irresistible as an invading and a conquering power. She had but a sparse population, and neither men nor money of her own, to raise and equip an army for her own defense, but let her once raise the flag of foreign conquest—let her once proclaim a crusade against the rich States to the south of her, and in a moment volunteers would flock to her standard in crowds, *from all the States in the great valley of the Mississippi*—men of enterprise and valor, before whom no Mexican troops could stand for an hour. They would leave their own towns, arm themselves, and travel on their own cost, and would come up in thousands, to plant the lone star of the Texan banner on the Mexican capitol. They would drive Santa Anna to the South, and the boundless wealth of captured towns, and rifled churches, and a lazy, vicious, and luxurious priesthood, would soon enable Texas to pay her soldiery, and redeem her State debt, and push her victorious arms to the very shores of the Pacific. And would not all this extend the bounds of Slavery? Yes, the result would be, that before another quarter of a century, the extension of Slavery would not stop short of the Western Ocean. *We had but two alternatives before us; either to receive Texas into our fraternity of States, and thus make her our own, or to leave her to conquer Mexico, and become our most dangerous and formidable rival.*

"To talk of restraining the people of the great Valley from emigrating to join her armies, was all in vain; and it was equally vain to calculate on their defeat by any Mexican forces, aided by England or not. *They had gone once already; it was they that conquered Santa Anna at San Jacinto; and three-fourths of them*, after winning that glorious field, had peaceably returned to their homes. But once set before them the conquest of the rich Mexican provinces, and you might as well attempt to stop the wind. This Government might send its troops to the frontier, to turn them back, and they would run over them like a herd of buffalo."

"Nothing could keep these booted loafers from rushing on, till they kicked the Spanish priests out of the temples they profaned."

Mr. W. proceeded to insist that a majority of the people of the United States were in favor of the annexation; at all events, he would risk it with the Democracy of the North.

"Sir," said Mr. W., "it is not only the duty of the Government to demand the liquidation of our claims, and the liberation of our citizens, but to go further, and demand the non-invasion of Texas. Shall we sit still while the standard of insurrection is raised on our borders, and let a *horde of slaves, and Indians, and Mexicans roll up to the boundary line of Arkansas and Louisiana?* No. It is our duty at once to say to Mexico, '*If you strike Texas, you strike us*;' and if England, standing by, should dare to intermeddle, and ask, '*Do you take part with Texas?*' his prompt answer should be, '*Yes, and against you.*'

"*Such, he would let gentlemen know, was the spirit of the whole people of the great valley of the West.*"

Several other members of Congress, in the same debate, expressed similar views and desires, and they are still more frequently expressed in conversation.

The Hon. THO'S W. GILMER, a member of Congress from Virginia, and formerly a Governor of that State, numbered as one of the "Guard," and of course understood to be in the counsels of the Cabinet, in a letter bearing date the 10th day of January last, originally designed as a private and confidential letter to a friend, gives it as his deliberate opinion, after much examination and reflection, that TEXAS WILL BE ANNEXED TO THE UNION; and he enters into a spacious argument, and presents a variety of reasons in favor of the measure. He says, among other things:

WASHINGTON, Jan. 10th, 1843.

"DEAR SIR—You ask if I have expressed the opinion, that Texas would be annexed to the United States. I answer, yes; and this opinion has not been adopted without reflection, or without a careful observation of causes, which I believe are rapidly bringing about this result. I do not know how far these causes have made the same impression on others; but I am persuaded that the time is not distant when they will be felt in all their force. The *excitement* which you apprehend, may arise; but it will be *temporary*, and in the end, *salutary.*"

He dodges the Constitutional objections as follows:

"I am, as you know, a strict constructionist of the powers of our federal Government; and I do not admit the force of mere precedent to establish authority under written constitutions. The power conferred by the Constitution over our foreign relations, and the repeated acquisitions of territory under it, seem to me to leave this question open as one of expediency."

"But you anticipate objections with regard to the subject of Slavery. This is indeed a subject of *extreme delicacy*, but *it is one on which the annexation of Texas will have the most salutary influence.* Some have thought that the proposition would endanger our Union. I am of a different opinion. I believe it will bring about a better understanding of our relative rights and obligations."

In conclusion, he says:

"Having acquired Louisiana and Florida, we have an interest and a frontier on the Gulf of Mexico, and along our interior to the Pacific, which will not permit us to close our eyes, or fold our arms, with indifference to the events which a few years may disclose in that quarter. We have already had one question of boundary with Texas; other questions must soon arise, under our revenue laws, and on other points of necessary intercourse, which it will be difficult to adjust. *The institutions of Texas, and her relations with other governments, are yet in that condition which inclines her people (who are our countrymen,) to unite their destinies with ours.* THIS MUST BE DONE SOON, OR NOT AT ALL. There are numerous tribes of Indians along both frontiers, which can easily become the cause or the instrument of border wars. Our own population is pressing onward to the Pacific. No power can restrain it. The pioneer from our Atlantic seaboard will soon kindle his fires, and erect his cabin, beyond the Rocky Mountains, and on the Gulf of California. If Mahomed comes not to the mountain, the mountain will go to Mahomed. Every year adds new difficulties to our progress, as natural and as inevitable as the current of the Mississippi. These difficulties will soon, 'like mountains interposed,'—

"'Make enemies of nations,
Which now, like kindred drops,
Might mingle into one.'

"Truly yours,
"THOMAS W. GILMER."

The impoverished condition of Texas, her inability to raise and sustain troops to defend herself against invasion for any length of time, and her want of character and credit abroad, are urged as reasons for IMMEDIATE ANNEXATION, and the opinion has been frequently expressed, by those who feel a deep interest in this subject, that it would take place AT A VERY EARLY DAY IN THE NEXT SESSION OF CONGRESS!

At the present session, the Resolutions of the State of Alabama, in favor of annexation, and sundry petitions and remonstrances against it, were referred to the Committee on Foreign Relations. A majority of the Committee, consisting of members from the slaveholding States, refused to consider and report upon the subject, and directed Mr. Adams, their Chairman, to report a resolution, asking to be discharged from the further consideration of the subject, which he did on the 28th day of February. At the same time, Mr. Adams asked, as an individual member of the Committee, for leave to present the following resolutions:

"*Resolved*, That by the Constitution of the United States, no power is delegated to their Congress, or to any department or departments of their Government, to affix to this Union any foreign State, or the people thereof.

"*Resolved*, That any attempt of the Government of the United States, by an act of Congress, or by treaty, to annex to this Union the Republic of Texas, or the people thereof, would be a violation of the Constitution of the United States, null and void, and to which the Free States of this Union, and their people, ought not to submit."

Objections being made, the resolutions were not received; the Southern members showing a disinclination to have the subject agitated in the House *at present*. Might it not be considered as savoring too much of a violation of private confidence, we could refer to various declarations of persons high in office in the national government, avowing a fixed determination to bring Texas into the Union, declaring that they had assurances of the aid of the Free States to accomplish the object, and insisting that they prefer a dissolution of the Union to the rejection of Texas, expressing, however, at the same time, their confidence, that if the *annexation* could be effected, the people of the Free States would submit to it, and the institutions of the Slave States would be secured and perpetuated. Contenting ourselves, however, with the above brief glance at some of the most prominent evidence in relation to the subject, we submit to you whether the project of annexation seems to be abandoned, and whether there be not *the most imminent danger* of its speedy accomplishment, unless *the entire mass of the people in the Free States become aroused to a conviction of this danger, and speak out, and act in reference to it, in a manner and with a voice not to be misunderstood, either by the people of the Slave States, or their own public servants and Representatives.*

Although perfectly aware that many important and controlling objections to annexation exist aside from the question of Slavery, we have in this address confined ourselves principally to that, because of its paramount importance, and because *the advocates of annexation distinctly place it upon that ground*—most of the specious arguments and reasons in favor of annexation, with which its advocates attempt *to gild the pill for Northern palates*, are just about as sincere and substantial as were those of Mr. WISE in the speech above referred to, in which he labored a long time to convince Northern philanthropists that they would best promote the objects they had in view, by favoring annexation, that they might have Slavery in Texas within the power and control of our own government, that *they might abolish it or mitigate its evils*, he himself being an advocate of perpetual Slavery, and among the very foremost to trample upon the right of petition itself!!

None can be so blind *now*, as not to know that the real design and object of the South is, to "ADD NEW WEIGHT TO HER END OF THE LEVER." It was upon that ground that Mr. Webster placed his opposition, in his speech on that subject in New-York, in March, 1837. In that speech, after stating that he saw insurmountable objections to the annexation of Texas, that the purchase of Louisiana and Florida furnished no precedent for it, that the cases were not parallel, and that no such policy or necessity as led to that, required the annexation of Texas, he said:

"Gentlemen, we all see, that by whomsoever possessed, Texas is likely to be a slaveholding country; and I frankly avow my entire unwillingness to do anything which shall extend the Slavery of the African race on this continent, or add other slaveholding States to the Union. When I say that I regard Slavery in itself a great moral, social, and political evil, I only use language which has been adopted by distinguished men, themselves citizens of slaveholding States. I shall do nothing, therefore, to favor or encourage its further extension."

And again, he said:

"In my opinion, the people of the United States will not consent to bring a new, vastly extensive, and slaveholding country, large enough for half a dozen or a dozen States, into the Union. IN MY OPINION THEY OUGHT NOT TO CONSENT TO IT. Indeed, I am altogether at a loss to conceive what possible benefit any part of this country can expect to derive from such annexation. All benefit, to any part, is at least doubtful and uncertain, the objections obvious, plain, and strong. On the general question of Slavery, a great portion of the community is already strongly excited. The subject has not only attracted attention as a question of politics, but it has struck a far deeper-toned cord—it has arrested the religious feeling of the country; it has taken a strong hold on the consciences of men. He is a rash man, indeed, and little conversant with human nature, and especially has he a very erroneous estimate of the character of the people of this country, who supposes that a feeling of this kind is to be trifled with, or despised. It will assuredly cause itself to be respected."

In conclusion, he said:

"I see, therefore, no political necessity for the annexation of Texas to the Union; no advantages to be derived from it; and objections to it of a strong, and, in my judgment, decisive character.

"I believe it to be for the interest and happiness of the whole Union, to remain as it is, without diminution and without addition."

We hold that there is not only "no political necessity" for it, "no advantages to be derived from it," but that there is no constitutional power delegated to any department of the national government to authorize it; that no act of Congress, or treaty, for annexation, can impose the least obligation upon the several States of this Union to submit to such an unwarrantable act, or to receive into their family and fraternity such *misbegotten and illegitimate progeny.*

We hesitate not to say, that *annexation*, effected by any act or proceeding of the Federal Government, or any of its departments, WOULD BE IDENTICAL WITH DISSOLUTION. It would be a violation of our national compact, its objects, designs, and the great elementary principles which entered into its formation, of a character so deep and fundamental—and would be an attempt to eternize an institution and a power of a nature so unjust in themselves, so injurious to the interests and abhorrent to the feelings of the people of the Free States, as, in our opinion, not only inevitably to result in a dissolution of the Union, but fully to justify it; and we not only assert that the people of the Free States "ought not to submit to it," but we say, with confidence, THEY WOULD NOT SUBMIT TO IT. We know their present temper and spirit on this subject too well to believe for a moment that they would become *particeps criminis* in any such subtle contrivance for the *irremediable perpetuation* OF AN INSTITUTION, which the wisest and best men who formed our Federal Constitution, as well from the Slave as the Free States, *regarded as an evil and a curse*, soon to become extinct under the operation of laws to be passed, prohibiting the Slave Trade, and the progressive influence of the principles of the Revolution.

To prevent the success of this nefarious project —to preserve from such gross violation the Constitution of our country, adopted expressly "*to secure the blessings of liberty*," and not the perpetuation of Slavery—and to prevent the speedy and violent dissolution of the Union—we invite you to unite, without distinction of party, in an immediate expression of your views on this subject, in such manner as you may deem best calculated to answer the end proposed.

JOHN QUINCY ADAMS,
SETH M. GATES,
WILLIAM SLADE,
WILLIAM B. CALHOUN,
JOSHUA R. GIDDINGS,
SHERLOCK J. ANDREWS,
NATHANIEL B. BORDEN,
THO'S C. CHITTENDEN,
JOHN MATTOCKS,
CHRISTOPHER MORGAN,
JOSHUA M. HOWARD,
VICTORY BIRDSEYE,
HILAND HALL.

WASHINGTON, March 3rd, 1843.

[NOTE.—The above Address was drawn up by Hon. Seth M. Gates of New York, at the suggestion of John Quincy Adams, and sent to Members of Congress at their residences, after the close of the session, for their signatures. Many more than the above approved heartily of its positions and objects, and would have signed it, but for its premature publication, through mistake. Mr. Winthrop of Mass. was one of these, with Gov. Briggs, of course: Mr. Fillmore declined signing it.]

The letters of Messrs. Clay and Van Buren, taking ground against annexation, without the consent of Mexico, as an act of bad faith and aggression, which would necessarily result in war, which appeared in the spring of 1844, make slight allusions, if any, to the Slavery aspect of the case. In a later letter, Mr. Clay declared that he did not oppose annexation on account of Slavery, which he regarded as a temporary institution, which, therefore, ought not to stand in the way of a permanent acquisition. And, though Mr. Clay's last letter on the subject, prior to the election of 1844, reiterated and emphasized all his objections to annexation under the existing circumstances, he did not include the existence of Slavery.

The defeat of Mr. Van Buren, at the Baltimore Nominating Convention—Mr. Polk being selected in his stead, by a body which had been supposed pledged to renominate the ex-President—excited considerable feeling, especially among the Democrats of New York. A number of their leaders united in a letter, termed the "Secret Circular," advising their brethren, while they supported Polk and Dallas, to be careful to vote for candidates for Congress who would set their faces as a flint against annexation. Here is the circular:

"SIR—You will, doubtless, agree with us, that the late Baltimore Convention placed the Democratic Party, at the North, in a position of great difficulty. We are constantly reminded that it rejected Mr. Van Buren, and nominated Mr. Polk, for reasons connected with the immediate annexation of Texas—reasons which had no relation to the principles of the party. Nor was that all. The Convention went beyond the authority delegated to its members, and adopted a resolution on the subject of Texas (a subject not before the country when they were elected, upon which, therefore, they were not instructed), which seeks to interpolate into the party creed a new doctrine, hitherto unknown among us, at war with some of our established principles, and abhorrent to the opinions and feelings of a great majority of Northern freemen. In this position, what was the party at the North to do? Was it to reject the nominations, and abandon the contest? or should it support the nominations, rejecting the untenable doctrine interpolated at the Convention, and taking care that their support should be accompanied by such an expression of their opinion as to prevent its being misinterpreted? The latter alternative has been preferred, and we think wisely; for we conceive that a proper expression of their opinion will save their votes from misconstruction, and that proper efforts will secure the nomination of such Members of Congress as will reject the unwarrantable scheme now pressed upon the country.

"With these views, assuming that you feel on this subject as we do, we have been desired to address you, and invite the coöperation of yourself and other friends throughout the State:

"1st.—In the publication of a joint letter, declaring your purpose to support the nomination, rejecting the resolutions respecting Texas.

"2nd.—In promoting and supporting at the next elections the nomination for Congress of such persons as concur in these opinions.

"If your views in this matter coincide with ours, please write to some one of us, and a draught of the proposed letter will be forwarded for examination.

"Very respectfully,
"GEO. P. BARKER,
WILLIAM C. BRYANT,
J. W. EDMONDS,
DAVID DUDLEY FIELD,
THEODORE SEDGWICK,
THOMAS W. TUCKER,
ISAAC TOWNSEND."

Silas Wright, then a Senator of the United States, and who, as such, had opposed the Tyler Treaty of Annexation, was now run for Governor, as the only man who could carry the State of New York for Polk and Dallas. In a democratic speech at Skaneateles, N. Y., Mr. Wright had recently declared that he could never consent to Annexation on any terms which would give Slavery an advantage over Freedom. This sentiment was reiterated and amplified in a a great Convention of the Democracy, which met at Herkimer, in the autumn of this year.

The contest proceeded with great earnestness throughout the Free States, the supporters of Polk and of Birney (the Abolition candidate for President), fully agreeing in the assertion that Mr. Clay's position was equally favorable to Annexation with Mr. Polk's. Mr. Birney, in a letter published on the eve of the Election, declared that he regarded Mr. Clay's election as *more* favorable to Annexation than Mr. Polk's, because, while equally inclined to fortify and extend Slavery, he possessed more ability to influence Congress in its favor. He says:

"I have no reasons for opposing Mr. Clay on personal grounds. On the contrary, the intercourse we have had has been of the most friendly character. I oppose his election, because he disbelieves the great political truths of the Declaration of Independence, the foundation of all just government, and because he repudiates the paramount objects of the Union, the perpetuation of liberty to all. On the same ground, I oppose the election of Mr. Polk. But I more deprecate the election of Mr. Clay—because, possessing abilities superior to Mr. Polk's, he would proportionately weaken the influence of those truths on the minds of our countrymen.

"Respectfully, &c.,

"JAMES G. BIRNEY."

Before this time, but as yet withheld from, and unknown to, the public, Mr. Calhoun, now President Tyler's Secretary of State, and an early and powerful advocate of Annexation, had addressed to Hon. Wm. R. King, our Embassador at Paris, the following official dispatch:

Mr. Calhoun to Mr. King.

"DEPARTMENT OF STATE,
Washington, August 12, 1844.

"SIR—I have laid your dispatch, No. 1, before the President, who instructs me to make known to you that he has read it with much pleasure, especially the portion which relates to your cordial reception by the King, and his assurance of friendly feelings toward the United States. The President, in particular, highly appreciates the declaration of the King, that, in no event, would any steps be taken by his government in the slightest degree hostile, or which would give to the United States just cause of complaint. It was the more gratifying from the fact, that our previous information was calculated to make the impression that the government of France was prepared to unite with Great Britain in a joint protest against the annexation of Texas, and a joint effort to induce her Government to withdraw the proposition to annex, on condition that Mexico should be made to acknowledge her independence. He is happy to infer from your dispatch that the information, so far as it relates to France, is, in all probability, without foundation. You did not go further than you ought, in assuring the King that the object of Annexation would be pursued with unabated vigor, and in giving your opinion that a decided majority of the American people were in its favor, and that it would certainly be annexed at no distant day. I feel confident that your anticipation will be fully realized at no distant period.

"Every day will tend to weaken that combination of political causes which led to the opposition of the measure, and to strengthen the conviction that it was not only expedient, but just and necessary.

"You were right in making the distinction between the interests of France and England in reference to Texas—or rather, I should say, the apparent interests of the two countries. France cannot possibly have any other than commercial interests in desiring to see her preserve her separate independence, while it is certain that England looks beyond, to political interests, to which she apparently attaches much importance. But, in our opinion, the interest of both against the measure is more apparent than real; and that neither France, England, nor even Mexico herself, has any in opposition to it, when the subject is fairly viewed and considered in its whole extent, and in all its bearings. Thus viewed and considered, and assuming that peace, the extension of commerce, and security, are objects of primary policy with them, it may, as it seems to me, be readily shown that the policy on the part of those powers which would acquiesce in a measure so strongly desired by both the United States and Texas, for their mutual welfare and safety, as the annexation of the latter to the former, would be far more promotive of these great objects than that which would attempt to resist it.

"It is impossible to cast a look at the map of the United States and Texas, and to note the long, artificial and inconvenient line which divides them, and to take into consideration the extraordinary increase of population and growth of the former, and the source from which the latter must derive its inhabitants, institutions, and laws, without coming to the conclusion that it is their destiny to be united, and of course, that Annexation is merely a question of time and mode. Thus regarded, the question to be decided would seem to be, whether it would not be better to permit it to be done now, with the mutual consent of both parties, and the acquiescence of these powers, than to attempt to resist and defeat it.

"If the former course be adopted, the certain fruits would be the preservation of peace, great extension of commerce by the rapid settlement and improvement of Texas, and increased security, especially to Mexico. The last, in reference to Mexico, may be doubted; but I hold it not less clear than the other two.

"It would be a great mistake to suppose that this Government has any hostile feelings toward Mexico, or any disposition to aggrandize itself at her expense. The fact is the very reverse.

"It wishes her well, and desires to see her settled down in peace and security; and is prepared, in the event of the Annexation of Texas, if not forced into conflict with her, to propose to settle with her the question of boundary, and all others growing out of the Annexation, on the most liberal terms. Nature herself has clearly marked the boundary between her and Texas by natural limits, too strong to be mistaken. There are few countries whose limits are so distinctly marked; and it would be our desire, if Texas should be united to us, to see them firmly established, as the most certain means of establishing permanent peace between the two countries, and strengthening and cementing their friendship. Such would be the certain consequence of permitting the Annexation to take place now, with the acquiescence of Mexico; but very different would be the case if it should be attempted to resist and defeat it, whether the attempt should be successful for the present or not. Any attempt of the kind would, not improbably, lead to a conflict between us and Mexico, and involve consequences, in reference to her and the general peace, long to be deplored on both sides, and difficult to be repaired. But, should that not be the case, and the interference of another power defeat the Annexation for the present, without the interruption of peace, it would but postpone the conflict, and render it more fierce and bloody whenever it might occur.

"Its defeat would be attributed to enmity and ambition on the part of that power by whose interference it was occasioned, and excite deep jealousy and resentment on the part of our people, who would be ready to seize the first favorable opportunity to effect by force what was prevented from being done peaceably by mutual consent. It is not difficult to see how greatly such a conflict, come when it might, would endanger the general peace, and how much Mexico might be the loser by it.

"In the mean time, the condition of Texas would be rendered uncertain, her settlement and prosperity in consequence retarded, and her commerce crippled; while the general peace would be rendered much more insecure. It could not but greatly affect us. If the Annexation of Texas should be permitted to take place peaceably now, (as it would, without the interference of other powers,) the energies of our people would, for a long time to come, be directed to the peaceable pursuits of redeeming and bringing within the pale of cultivation, improvement, and civilization, that large portion of the continent lying between Mexico on one side and the British possessions on the other, which is now, with little exception, a wilderness, with a sparse population, consisting, for the most part, of wandering Indian tribes.

"It is our destiny to occupy that vast region; to intersect it with roads and canals; to fill it with cities, towns, villages, and farms; to extend over it our religion, customs, constitution, and laws, and to present it as a peaceful and splendid addition to the domains of commerce and civilization. It is our policy to increase by growing and spreading out into unoccupied regions, assimilating all we incorporate: in a word, to increase by accretion, and not through conquest, by the addition of masses held together by the adhesion of force.

"No system can be more unsuited to the latter process, or better adapted to the former, than our admirable federal system. If it should not be resisted in its course, it will probably fulfill its destiny without disturbing our neighbors, or putting in jeopardy the general peace; but if it be opposed by foreign interference, a new direction would be given to our energy, much less favorable to harmony with our neighbors, and to the general peace of the world.

"The change would be undesirable to us, and much less in accordance with what I have assumed to be primary objects of policy on the part of France, England, and Mexico.

"But, to descend to particulars: it is certain that while England, like France, desires the independence of Texas, with the view to commercial connections, it is not less so that, one of the leading motives of England for desiring it, is the hope that, through her diplomacy and influence, Negro Slavery may be abolished there, and ultimately, by consequence, in the United States and throughout the whole of this continent. That its ultimate abolition throughout the entire continent is an object ardently desired by her, we have decisive proofs in the declaration of the Earl of Aberdeen, delivered to this Department, and of which you will find a copy among the documents transmitted to Congress with the Texan treaty. That she desires its abolition in Texas, and has used her influence and diplomacy to effect it there, the same document, with the correspondence of this Department with Mr. Packenham, also to be found among the documents, furnishes proof not less conclusive. That one of the objects of abolishing it there is to facilitate its abolition in the United States, and throughout the continent, is manifest from the declaration of the Abolition party and societies both in this country and in England. In fact, there is good reason to believe that the scheme of abolishing it in Texas, with a view to its abolition in the United States, and over the continent, originated with the prominent members of the party in the United States; and was first broached by them in the (so called) World's Convention, held in London in the year 1840, and through its agency brought to the notice of the British Government.

"Now, I hold, not only that France can have no interest in the consummation of this grand scheme, which England hopes to accomplish through Texas, if she can defeat the Annexation, but that her interests, and those of all the Continental powers of Europe are directly and deeply opposed to it.

"It is too late in the day to contend that humanity or philanthropy is the great object of the policy of England in attempting to abolish African Slavery on this Continent. I do not question but humanity may have had a considerable influence in abolishing Slavery in her West India possessions, aided, indeed, by the fallacious calculation that the labor of the Negroes would be at least as profitable, if not more so, in consequence of the measure. She acted on the principle that tropical products can be produced cheaper by free African labor and East India labor, than by slave labor. She knew full well the value of such products to her commerce, navigation, navy, manufacturers, revenue, and power. She was not ignorant that the support and maintenance of her political preponderance depended on her tropical possessions, and had no intention of diminishing their productiveness, nor any anticipation that such would be the effect, when the scheme of abolishing Slavery in her colonial possessions was adopted. On the contrary, she calculated to combine philanthropy with profit and power, as is not unusual with fanaticism. Experience has convinced her of the fallacy of her calculations. She has failed in all her objects. The labor of her Negroes has proved far less productive, without affording the consolation of having improved their condition.

"The experiment has turned out to be a costly one. She expended nearly one hundred millions of dollars in indemnifying the owners of the emancipated Slaves. It is estimated that the increased price paid since, by the people of Great Britain, for sugar and other tropical productions, in consequence of the measure, is equal to half that sum; and that twice that amount has been expended in the suppression of the Slave-trade; making together two hundred and fifty millions of dollars as the cost of the experiment. Instead of realizing her hope, the result has been a sad disappointment. Her tropical products have fallen off to a vast amount. Instead of supplying her own wants, and those of nearly all Europe with them, as formerly, she has now, in some of the most important articles, scarcely enough to supply her own. What is worse, her own colonies are actually consuming sugar produced by Slave-labor, brought direct to England, or refined in bond, and exported and sold in her colonies as cheap, or cheaper, than can be produced there; while the Slave-trade, instead of diminishing, has been in fact carried on to a greater extent than ever. So disastrous has been the result, that her fixed capital invested in tropical possessions, estimated at the value of nearly five hundred millions of dollars, is said to stand on the brink of ruin.

"But this is not the worst; while this costly

scheme has had such ruinous effects on the tropical productions of Great Britain, it has given a powerful stimulus, followed by a corresponding increase of products, to those countries which had had the good sense to shun her example. There has been vested, it has been estimated by them, in the production of tropical products, since 1808, in fixed capital, nearly $4,000,000,000, wholly dependent on Slave-labor. In the same period, the value of their products has been estimated to have risen from about $72,000,000, annually, to nearly $220,000,000; while the whole of the fixed capital of Great Britain, vested in cultivating tropical products, both in the East and West Indies, is estimated at only about $830,000,000, and the value of the products annually at about $50,000,000. To present a still more striking view of three articles of tropical products (sugar, coffee, and cotton), the British possessions, including the East and West Indies, and Mauritius, produced in 1842, of sugar, only 3,993,771 pounds; while Cuba, Brazil, and the United States, excluding other countries having tropical possessions, produced 9,600,000 pounds; of coffee, the British possessions produced only 27,393,003 pounds, while Cuba and Brazil produced 201,590,125 pounds; and of cotton, the British possessions, including shipments to China, only 137,443,446 pounds, while the United States alone produced 790,479,275 pounds.

"The above facts and estimate have all been drawn from a British periodical of high standing and authority,* and are believed to be entitled to credit.

"The vast increase of the capital and production on the part of those nations, who have continued their former policy toward the negro race, compared with that of Great Britain, indicates a corresponding relative increase of the means of commerce, navigation, manufactures, wealth, and power. It is no longer a question of doubt, that the great source of wealth, prosperity, and power of more civilized nations of the temperate zone (especially Europe, where the arts have made the greatest advance), depends, in a great degree, on the exchange of their products with those of the tropical regions. So great has been the advance made in the arts, both chemical and mechanical, within the few last generations, that all the old civilized nations can, with but a small part of their labor and capital, supply their respective wants; which tends to limit, within narrow bounds, the amount of the commerce between them, and forces them all to seek for markets in the tropical regions, and the more newly-settled portions of the globe. Those who can best succeed in commanding those markets, have the least prospect of outstripping the others in the career of commerce, navigation, manufactures, wealth, and power.

This is seen and felt by British statesmen, and has opened their eyes to the errors which they have committed. The question now with them is, how shall it be counteracted? What has been done cannot be undone. The question is, by what means can Great Britain regain and keep a superiority in tropical cultivation, commerce, and influence? Or, shall that be abandoned, and other nations be suffered to acquire the supremacy, even to the extent of supplying British markets, to the destruction of the capital already vested in their production? These are the questions which now profoundly occupy the attention of her statesmen, and have the greatest influence over her councils.

"In order to regain her superiority, she not only seeks to revive and increase her own capacity to produce tropical productions, but to diminish and destroy the capacity of those who have so far outstripped her in consequence of her error. In pursuit of the former, she has cast her eyes to her East India possessions—to Central and Eastern Africa—with the view of establishing colonies there, and even to restore, substantially, the Slave-trade itself, under the specious name of transporting her free laborers from Africa to her West India possessions, in order, if possible, to compete successfully with those who have refused to follow her suicidal policy. But these all afford but uncertain and distant hopes of recovering her lost superiority. Her main reliance is on the other alternative—to cripple or destroy the productions of her successful rivals. There is but one way by which it can be done, and that is by abolishing African Slavery throughout this continent; and that she openly avows to be the constant object of her policy and exertions. It matters not how, or from what motive, it may be done—whether it be by diplomacy, influence, or force; by secret or open means; and whether the motive be humane or selfish, without regard to manner, means, or motive. The thing itself, should it be accomplished, would put down all rivalry, and give her the undisputed supremacy in supplying her own wants, and those of the rest of the world; and thereby more than fully retrieve what she lost by her errors. It would give her the monopoly of tropical productions, which I shall next proceed to show.

"What would be the consequence if this object of her unceasing solicitude and exertions should be effected by the abolition of Negro Slavery throughout this continent, some idea may be formed from the immense diminution of productions, as has been shown, which has followed abolition in her West India possessions. But, as great as that has been, it is nothing compared with what would be the effect, if she should succeed in abolishing Slavery in the United States, Cuba, Brazil, and throughout this continent. The experiment in her own colonies was made under the most favorable circumstances. It was brought about gradually and peaceably by the steady and firm operation of the parent country, armed with complete power to prevent or crush at once all insurrectionary movements on the part of the negroes, and able and disposed to maintain to the full, the political and social ascendancy of the former Masters over their former Slaves. It is not at all wonderful that the change of the relations of Master and Slave took place, under such circumstances, without violence and bloodshed, and that order and peace should have been since preserved. Very different would be the result of abolition, should it be effected by her influence and exertions in the possessions of other countries on this continent—and especially in the United States, Cuba, and Brazil, the great cultivators of the principal tropical products of America. To form a correct conception of what would be the result with them, we must look, not to Jamaica, but to St. Domingo, for example. The change would be followed by unforgiving hate between the two races, and end in a bloody and deadly struggle between them for the superiority. One or the other would have to be subjugated, extirpated, or expelled; and desolation would overspread their territories, as in St. Domingo, from which it would take centuries to recover. The end would be, that the superiority in cultivating the great tropical staples would be transferred from them to the British tropical possessions.

"They are of vast extent, and those beyond the Cape of Good Hope, possessed of an unlimited amount of labor, standing ready, by the aid of British capital, to supply the deficit which would be occasioned by destroying the tropical productions of the United States, Cuba, Brazil, and other countries cultivated by Slave-labor on this continent, as soon as the increased prices, in consequence, would yield a profit. It is the

* Blackwood's Magazine for June, 1841.

successful competition of that labor which keeps the prices of the great tropical staples so low as to prevent their cultivation with profit in the possessions of Great Britain, by what she is pleased to call free-labor.

"If she can destroy its competition, she would have a monopoly of these productions. She has all the means of furnishing an unlimited supply—vast and fertile possessions in both Indies, boundless command of capital and labor, and ample power to suppress disturbances and preserve order throughout her wide domain.

"It is unquestionable that she regards the abolition of Slavery in Texas as a most important step toward this great object of policy, so much the aim of her solicitude and exertions; and the defeat of the Annexation of Texas to our Union as indispensable to the abolition of Slavery there. She is too sagacious not to see what a fatal blow it would give to Slavery in the United States, and how certainly its abolition with us will abolish it over the whole continent, and thereby give her a monopoly in the productions of the great tropical staples, and the command of the commerce, navigation, and manufactures of the world, with an established naval ascendancy and political preponderance. To this continent, the blow would be calamitous beyond description. It would destroy, in a great measure, the cultivation and productions of the great tropical staples, amounting annually in value to nearly $300,000,000, the fund which stimulates and upholds almost every other branch of its industry, commerce, navigation, and manufactures. The whole, by their joint influence, are rapidly spreading population, wealth, improvement and civilization over the whole continent, and vivifying, by their overflow, the industry of Europe, thereby increasing its population, wealth, and advancement in the arts, in power, and in civilization.

"Such must be the result, should Great Britain succeed in accomplishing the constant object of her desire and exertions—the abolition of Negro Slavery over this continent—and towards the effecting of which she regards the defeat of the Annexation of Texas to our Union so important.

"Can it be possible that governments so enlightened and sagacious as those of France and the other great continental powers, can be so blinded by the plea of philanthropy as not to see what must inevitably follow, be her motive what it may, should she succeed in her object? It is little short of mockery to talk of philanthropy, with the example before us of the effects of abolishing Negro Slavery in her own colonies, in St. Domingo, and in the Northern States of our Union, where statistical facts, not to be shaken, prove that the free Negro, after the experience of sixty years, is in a far worse condition than in the other States, where he has been left in his former condition. No: the effect of what is called abolition, where the number is few, is not to raise the inferior race to the condition of freemen, but to deprive the Negro of the guardian care of his owner, subject to all the depression and oppression belonging to his inferior condition. But, on the other hand, where the number is great, and bears a large proportion to the whole population, it would be still worse. It would be to substitute for the existing relation a deadly strife between the two races, to end in the subjection, expulsion, or extirpation of one or the other; and such would be the case over the greater part of this continent where Negro Slavery exists. It would not end there; but would, in all probability, extend, by its example, the war of races over all South America, including Mexico, and extending to the Indian as well as the African race, and make the whole one scene of blood and devastation.

"Dismissing, then, the stale and unfounded plea of philanthropy, can it be that France and the other great continental powers—seeing what must be the result of the policy, for the accomplishment of which England is constantly exerting herself, and that the defeat of the Annexation of Texas is so important towards its consummation—are prepared to back or countenance her in her efforts to produce either? What possible motives can they have to favor her cherished policy? Is it not better for them that they should be supplied with tropical products in exchange for their labor from the United States, Brazil, Cuba, and this continent generally, than to be dependent on one great monopolizing power for their supply? Is it not better that they should receive them at the low prices which competition, cheaper means of production, and nearness of market, would furnish them by the former, than to give the high prices which monopoly, dear labor, and great distance from market, would impose? Is it not better that their labor should be exchanged with a new continent, rapidly increasing in population and capacity for consuming, and which would furnish, in the course of a few generations, a market nearer to them, and almost of unlimited extent, for the products of their industry and arts, than with old and distant regions, whose population has long since reached its growth?

"The above contains those enlarged views of policy which, it seems to me, an enlightened European statesman ought to take, in making up his opinion on the subject of the Annexation of Texas, and the grounds, as it may be inferred, on which England vainly opposes it. They certainly involve considerations of the deepest importance, and demanding the greatest attention. Viewed in connection with them, the question of Annexation becomes one of the first magnitude, not only to Texas and the United States, but to this continent and Europe. They are presented, that you may use them on all suitable occasions where you think they may be with effect, in your correspondence, where it can be done with propriety or otherwise. The President relies with confidence on your sagacity, prudence, and zeal. Your mission is one of the first magnitude at all times, but especially now; and he feels assured that nothing will be left undone on your part to do justice to the country and the Government in reference to this measure.

"I have said nothing as to our right of treaty with Texas, without consulting Mexico. You so fully understand the grounds on which we rest our right, and are so familiar with all the facts necessary to maintain them, that it was thought unnecessary to add anything in reference to it.

"I am, Sir, very respectfully,
"Your obedient Servant,
"J. C. CALHOUN."

"WILLIAM R. KING, Esq., &c., &c."

The election of James K. Polk as President, and George M. Dallas as Vice-President, (Nov. 1844) having virtually settled, affirmatively, the question of annexing Texas, the XXVIIIth Congress commenced its second session at Washington on the 2nd of December, 1844—Mr. John Tyler being still acting President up to the end of the Congress, March 4th following.

Dec. 19. Mr. John B. Weller, (then member from Ohio, now Senator from California) by leave, introduced a joint resolution, No. 51, providing for the annexation of Texas to the United States, which he moved to the Committee of the Whole.

Mr. E. S. Hamlin of Ohio moved a reference of said resolve to a committee of one from each State, with instructions to report to the House,

"1st. Whether Congress has any constitutional power to annex a *foreign*, independent nation to this Government; and if so, by what article and section of the Constitution it is conferred; whether it is among the powers expressly granted, or among those which are *implied*; whether it is necessary to carry into effect any expressly-granted power; and if so, which one.

"2d. Whether annexation of Texas would not extend and perpetuate Slavery in the Slave States, and also, the internal slave-trade; and whether the United States Government has any constitutional power over Slavery *in the States*, either to perpetuate it there, *or to do it away*.

"3d. Whether the United States, having acknowledged the independence of Texas, Mexico is thereby deprived of her right to reconquer that province.

"4th. That they report whether Texas is owing any debts or not; and, if she is, what is the amount, and to whom payable; and whether, if she should be annexed to the United States, the United States Government would be bound to pay them all.

"5th. That they report what treaties are in existence between Texas and foreign governments; and, if she should be annexed to the United States, whether the United States Government would be bound, by the law of nations, to fulfill those treaties."

The question on commitment was insisted upon, and first taken—Yeas, 109 (Democrats); Nays, 61 (Whigs); whereupon it was held that Mr. Hamlin's amendment was defeated, and the original proposition alone committed.

Jan. 10*th*, 1845. Mr. John P. Hale, N. H., (then a Democratic Representative, now a Republican Senator) proposed the following as an amendment to any act or resolve contemplating the annexation of Texas to this Union:

"*Provided*, That immediately after the question of boundary between the United States of America and Mexico shall have been definitively settled by the two governments, and before any State formed out of the territory of Texas shall be admitted into the Union, the said territory of Texas shall be divided as follows, to wit: beginning at a point on the Gulf of Mexico, midway between the Northern and Southern boundaries thereof on the coast; and thence by a line running in a northwesterly direction to the extreme boundary thereof, so as to divide the same as nearly as possible into two equal parts, and in that portion of said territory lying south and west of the line to be run as aforesaid, there shall be neither Slavery nor involuntary servitude, otherwise than in the punishment of crimes, whereof the party shall have been duly convicted.

"*And provided further*, That this provision shall be considered as a compact between the people of the United States and the people of the said territory, and forever remain unalterable, unless by the consent of three-fourths of the States of the Union."

Mr. Hale asked a suspension of the rules, to enable him to offer it now, and have it printed and committed. Refused—Yeas, 92, (not two-thirds;) Nays, 81.

Yeas—All the Whigs and most of the Democrats from the Free States, with Messrs. Duncan L. Clinch and Alex. H. Stephens of Georgia, and Geo. W. Summers of Va.

Nays—All the members from Slave States, except the above, with the following from Free States:

MAINE.—Sheppard Cary—1.

NEW-HAMPSHIRE.—Edmund Burke, Moses Norris, jr—2.

NEW-YORK.—James G. Clinton, Selah B. Strong—2.

PENNSYLVANIA.—James Black, Richard Brodhead, Henry D. Foster, Joseph R. Ingersoll, Michael H. Jenks—5.

OHIO.—Joseph J. McDowell—1.

INDIANA.—William J. Brown, John W. Davis, John Pettit—3.

ILLINOIS.—Orlando B. Ficklin, Joseph P. Hoge, Robert Smith—3.

Total Democrats from Free States, 17.

Dec. 12*th*.—Mr. C. J. Ingersoll of Pa., from the Committee on Foreign Affairs, reported a Joint. Resolution for annexing Texas to the Union, which was committed and discussed in Committee of the Whole from time to time, through the next month.

Jan. 7*th*.—Mr. J. P. Hale presented resolves of the Legislature of New Hampshire, thoroughly in favor of Annexation, and silent on the subject of Slavery, except as follows:

"*Resolved*, That we agree with Mr. Clay, that the re-annexation of Texas will add more Free than Slave States to the Union; and that it would be unwise to refuse a permanent acquisition, which will exist as long as the globe remains, on account of a temporary institution."

Jan. 13*th*.—Mr. Cave Johnson of Tenn. moved that all further debate on this subject be closed at 2 P. M. on Thursday next. Carried—Yeas, 126; Nays, 57; (nearly all the Nays from Slave States).

Jan. 25*th*.—The debate, after an extension of time, was at length brought to a close, and the Joint Resolution taken out of Committee, and reported to the House in the following form; (that portion relating to Slavery, having been added in Committee, on motion of Mr. Milton Brown (Whig) of Tennessee:

"*Resolved, by the Senate and House of Representatives in Congress assembled*, That Congress doth consent that the Territory properly included within, and rightfully belonging to, the Republic of Texas, may be erected into a new State, to be called the State of Texas, with a republican form of government, to be adopted by the people of said republic, by deputies in convention assembled, with the consent of the existing government, in order that the same may be admitted as one of the States of this Union.

"2. *And be it further resolved*, That the foregoing consent of Congress is given upon the following conditions, and with the following guarantees, to wit:

"First. Said State to be formed, subject to the adjustment by this Government of all questions of boundary that may arise with other governments; and the Constitution thereof, with the proper evidence of its adoption by the people of said Republic of Texas, shall be transmitted to the President of the United States, to be laid before Congress for its final action, on or before the 1st day of January, 1846.

"Second. Said State, when admitted into the Union, after ceding to the United States all public edifices, fortifications, barracks, ports, and harbors, navy and navy-yards, docks, magazines, arms, armaments, and all other property and means pertaining to the public defense, belonging to the said Republic of Texas, shall retain all the public funds, debts, taxes, and dues of every kind which may belong to, or be due or owing said republic; and shall also retain all the vacant and unappropriated lands lying within its limits, to be applied to the payment of the debts and liabilities of said Republic of Texas; and the residue of said lands, after discharging said debts and liabilities, to be disposed of as said State may direct; but in no event are said debts and liabilities to become a charge upon the United States.

"Third. New States of convenient size, not exceeding four in number, in addition to said State of Texas, and having sufficient population, may hereafter, by the consent of said State, be formed out of the Territory thereof, which shall be entitled to admission under the provisions of the Federal Constitution. And such States as may be formed out of that portion of said Territory, lying south of thirty-six degrees thirty minutes north latitude, commonly known as the Missouri Compromise line, shall be admitted into the Union, with or without Slavery, as the people of each State asking admission may desire; and in such State or States as shall be formed out of said Territory, north of said Missouri Compromise line, Slavery or involuntary servitude (except for crime) shall be prohibited."

Mr. Cave Johnson of Tenn. moved the previous question, which the House seconded —Yeas 113; Nays 106—and then the amendment aforesaid was agreed to—Yeas 118; Nays 101.

Yeas, 114 Democrats, and Messrs. Milton Brown of Tenn., James Dellet of Ala., and Duncan L. Clinch and Alex. H. Stephens of Ga. (4), Southern Whigs.

Nays, all the Whigs present from Free States, with all from Slave States, but the four just named; with the following Democrats from Free States:

MAINE.—Robert P. Dunlap, Hannibal Hamlin —2.

VERMONT.—Paul Dillingham, jr.—1.

NEW-HAMPSHIRE.—John P. Hale—1.

CONNECTICUT.—George S. Catlin—1.

NEW-YORK.—Joseph H. Anderson, Charles S. Benton, Jeremiah E. Carey, Amasa Dana, Richard D. Davis, Byram Green, Preston King, Smith M. Purdy, George Rathbun, Orville Robinson, David L. Seymour, Lemuel Stetson—12.

OHIO.—Jacob Brinckerhoff, William C. McCauslen, Joseph Morris, Henry St. John—4.

MICHIGAN.—James B. Hunt, Robert McClelland—2.

Total Democrats from Free States, 23.
" Whigs from Free and Slave States, 78.

The House then ordered the whole proposition to a third reading forthwith—Yeas 120; Nays 97—and passed it by Yeas 120; Nays 98.

Yeas, all the Democrats from Slave States, and all the Democrats from Free States, except as below; with Messrs. Duncan L. Clinch, Milton Brown, James Dellet, Willoughby Newton, of Va. (who therefrom turned Democrat), and Alex. H. Stephens of Ga. (now Democrat), from Slave States.

Nays, all the Whigs from Free States; all those from Slave States except as above; with the following Democrats from Free States, viz.:

MAINE.—Hannibal Hamlin—1.

NEW-HAMPSHIRE.—John P. Hale, John R. Reding—2.

VERMONT.—Paul Dillingham, jr.—1.

CONNECTICUT.—George S. Catlin—1.

NEW-YORK.—Joseph H. Anderson, Charles S. Benton, Levi D. Carpenter, Jeremiah E. Carey, Amasa Dana, Richard D. Davis, Byram Green, Preston King, Smith M. Purdy, George Rathbun, Lemuel Stetson, Horace Wheaton, David L. Seymour—14.

OHIO.—Henry St. John—1.

MICHIGAN.—James B. Hunt, Robert McClelland—2.

Total Democrats from Free States 23.

So the resolve passed the House, and was sent to the Senate for concurrence.

In Senate, several attempts to originate action in favor of Annexation were made at this session, but nothing came of them.

Feb. 24th. The joint resolution aforesaid from the House was taken up for consideration by 30 Yeas to 11 Nays (all Northern Whigs). On the 27th, Mr. Walker of Wis. moved to add an alternative proposition, contemplating negotiation as the means of effecting the meditated end.

Mr. Foster (Whig) of Tenn. proposed the following:

"*And provided further*, That in fixing the terms and conditions of such admission, it shall be expressly stipulated and declared, that the State of Texas, and such other States as may be formed out of that portion of the present Territory of Texas lying south of thirty-six deg. thirty min. north latitude, commonly known as the Missouri Compromise line, shall be admitted into the Union with or without Slavery, as the people of each State, so hereafter asking admission, may desire: *And provided furthermore*, That it shall be also stipulated and declared, that the public debt of Texas shall in no event become a charge upon the government of the United States."

The question was first taken on the first (Slavery) proviso of the foregoing, which was defeated, by Yeas and Nays, as follows:

YEAS—For the Slavery Proviso:

Messrs.	Archer, Va.	Jarnagin, Tenn.
	Barrow, La.	Johnson, La.
	Bayard, Del.	Mangum, N. C.
	Berrien, Ga.	Merrick, Md.
	Clayton, Del.	Morehead, Ky.
	Crittenden, Ky.	Pearce, Md.
	Foster, Tenn.	Phelps, Vt.
	Hannegan, Ind.	Rives, Va.
	Huger, S. C.	*Sevier*, Ark.—18.

All Whigs but three (in *Italics*).

NAYS—Against the Slavery Proviso:

Messrs. Allen, Ohio. Ashley, Ark. Atchison, Mo. Atherton, N. H. Bagby, Ala. Bates, Mass. Benton, Mo. Breese, Ind. Buchanan, Pa. Choate, Mass. Colquitt, Ga. Dayton, N. J. Dickinson, N. Y. Dix, N. Y. Evans, Me. Fairfield, Me. Francis, R. I. Haywood, N. C. Henderson, Miss. Huntington, Conn. Lewis, Ala. McDuffie, S. C. Miller, N. Y. Niles, Conn. Porter, La. Semple, Ill. Sturgeon, Pa. Tappan, Ohio. Upham, Vt. Walker, Wis. White, Ind. Woodbridge, Mich. Woodbury, N. H.—34.

The other branch of the amendment was voted down. Yeas, 20 (Whigs); Nays, 31 (25 Democrats and 6 Whigs).

Various amendments were proposed and voted down. Among them, Mr. Foster, of Tenn., moved an express stipulation that Slavery should be tolerated in all States formed out of the Territory of Texas, south of the Missouri line of 36° 30′. Rejected—Yeas, 16 (Southern Whigs, and Sevier of Arkansas); Nays, 33.

Mr. Miller, of N. J., moved to strike out all after the enacting clause, and insert:

"That the President of the United States be, and he hereby is, authorized and advised to open negotiations with Mexico and Texas, for the adjustment of boundaries, and the annexation of the latter to the United States, on the following basis, to wit:

"I. The boundary of the annexed territory to be in the desert prairie west of the Nueces, and along the highlands and mountain heights which divide the waters of the Mississippi from the waters of the Rio del Norte, and to latitude forty-two degrees north.

"II. The people of Texas, by a legislative act, or by any authentic act which shows the will of the majority, to express their assent to said annexation.

"III. A State to be called 'the State of Texas,' with boundaries fixed by herself, and an extent not exceeding the largest State of the Union, be admitted into the Union, by virtue of this act, on an equal footing with the original States.

"IV. The remainder of the annexed territory, to be held and disposed of by the United States as one of their Territories, to be called 'the Southwest Territory.'

"V. The existence of Slavery to be forever prohibited in the northern and northwestern part of said Territory, west of the 100th degree of latitude west from Greenwich, so as to divide, as equally as may be, the whole of the annexed country between slaveholding and non-slaveholding States.

"VI. The assent of Mexico to be obtained by treaty to such annexation and boundary, or to be dispensed with when the Congress of the United States may deem such assent to be unnecessary.

"VII. Other details of the annexation to be adjusted by treaty, so far as the same may come within the scope of the treaty-making power."

Rejected by the following vote:

YEAS—For Mr. Miller's Substitute:

Messrs. Archer of Va. Berrien of Ga. Choate of Mass. Crittenden of Ky. Dayton of N. J. Evans of Me. Francis of R. I. Miller of N. J. Phelps of Vt. Upham of Vt. Woodbridge of Mich.—11 (all Whigs).

NAYS—Against Mr. Miller's Substitute:

Messrs. Allen, Ohio. Ashley, Ark. Atchison, Mo. Atherton, N. H. Bagby, Ala. Barrow, La. Benton, Mo. Breese, Ind. Buchanan, Pa. Clayton, Del. Colquitt, Ga. Dickinson, N. Y. Dix, N. Y. Fairfield, Me. Foster, Tenn. Hannegan, Ind. Haywood, N. C. Henderson, Miss. Huger, S. C. Jarnagin, Tenn. Johnson, La. Lewis, Ala. McDuffie, S. C. Merrick, Md. Niles, Conn. Pearce, Md. Rives, Va. Semple, Ill. Sevier, Ark. Sturgeon. Pa. Tappan, Ohio. Walker, Wis. Woodbury, N. H.—33.

The Walker amendment aforesaid was carried, by Yeas 27, to Nays 25, as follows:

YEAS—For Walker's Amendment:

Messrs. Allen, Ashley, Atchison, Atherton, Bagby, Benton, Breese, Buchanan, Colquitt, Dickinson, Dix, Fairfield, Hannegan. Haywood, Henderson, Huger, Johnson, Lewis, McDuffie, Merrick, Niles, Semple, Sevier, Sturgeon, Tappan, Walker, Woodbury—27.

NAYS—Against Walker's Amendment:

Messrs. Archer, Barrow, Bates, Bayard, Berrien, Choate, Clayton, Crittenden, Dayton, Evans, Foster, Francis, Huntington, Jarnagin, Mangum, Miller, Morehead, Pearce, Phelps, Porter, Rives, Simmons, Upham, White, Woodbridge—25.

The resolution as thus amended was adopted (Feb. 27,) by Yeas and Nays as follows:

YEAS—For the Proposition as amended:

Messrs. Allen, Ashley, Atchison, Atherton, Bagby, Benton, Breese, Buchanan, Colquitt, Dickinson, Dix, Fairfield, Hannegan, Haywood, *Henderson*, Huger, *Johnson*, Lewis, McDuffie, *Merrick*. Niles, Semple, Sevier, Sturgeon, Tappan, Walker, Woodbury—26.

[Yeas—All Democrats but three in *italics*, of whom Messrs. Henderson and Merrick have since been Democrats.]

NAYS—Against the proposed Annexation:

Messrs. Archer,	Huntington,
Barrow,	Jarnagin,
Bates,	Mangum,
Bayard,	Miller,
Berrien,	Morehead,
Choate,	Pearce,
Clayton,	Phelps,
Crittenden,	Porter,
Dayton,	Rives,
Evans,	Simmons,
Foster,	Upham,
Francis,	White,

Woodbridge—25—[all Whigs].

The joint resolve being thus returned to the House as amended by the Senate, a vote was almost immediately taken on concurring, and the amendment of the Senate was assented to—Yeas, 134; Nays, 77. [A strict party vote, except that Mr. Dellet of Alabama, (Whig) voted in the majority]. So the Annexation of Texas was decreed, and in the following terms:

JOINT RESOLUTION FOR ANNEXING TEXAS TO THE UNITED STATES.

"*Resolved, by the Senate and House of Representatives of the United States in Congress assembled*, That Congress doth consent that the territory properly included within, and rightfully belonging to, the Republic of Texas, may be erected into a new State, to be called *the State of Texas*, with a Republican form of government, to be adopted by the people of said Republic, by deputies in convention assembled, with the consent of the existing government, in order that the same may be admitted as one of the States of this Union.

"SEC. 2. *And be it further resolved*, That the foregoing consent of Congress is given upon the following conditions, and with the following guaranties, to wit:

"*First.* Said State to be formed, subject to the adjustment by this Government of all questions of boundary that may arise with other Governments; and the constitution thereof, with the proper evidence of its adoption by the people of said Republic of Texas, shall be transmitted to the President of the United States, to be laid before Congress for its final action, on or before the first day of January, one thousand eight hundred and forty-six.

"*Second.* Said State, when admitted into the Union, after ceding to the United States all public edifices, fortifications, barracks, ports, and harbors, navy and navy-yards, docks, magazines, arms, armaments, and all other property and means pertaining to the public defense, belonging to the said Republic of Texas, shall retain all the public funds, debts, taxes, and dues of every kind which may belong to, or be due or owing said Republic; and shall also retain all the vacant or unappropriated lands lying within its limits, to be applied to the payment of the debts and liabilities of said Republic of Texas; and the residue of said lands, after discharging said debts and liabilities, to become a charge upon the United States.

"*Third.* New States of convenient size, not exceeding four in number, in addition to the said State of Texas, and having sufficient population, may hereafter, by the consent of said State, be formed out of the territory thereof, which shall be entitled to admission under the provision of the Federal Constitution; and such States as may be formed out of that portion of said territory lying South of thirty-six degrees thirty minutes north latitude, commonly known as the Missouri Compromise line, shall be admitted into the Union with or without Slavery, as the people of each State asking admission may desire. And in such State or States as shall be formed out of said territory north of said Missouri Compromise line, Slavery or involuntary servitude (except for crime) shall be prohibited.

[WALKER'S AMENDMENT—ADDED.]

"*And be it further resolved*, That if the President of the United States shall, in his judgment and discretion, deem it most advisable, instead of proceeding to submit the foregoing resolution to the republic of Texas, as an overture on the part of the United States, for admission, to negotiate with that Republic; then,

"*Be it resolved*, That a State to be formed out of the present Republic of Texas, with suitable extent and boundaries, and with two representatives in Congress, until the next apportionment of representation, shall be admitted into the Union by virtue of this act, on an equal footing with the existing States, as soon as the terms and conditions of such admission, and the cession of the remaining Texan territory to the United States, shall be agreed upon by the Governments of Texas and the United States.

"*And be it further enacted*, That the sum of one hundred thousand dollars be, and the same is hereby, appropriated to defray the expenses of missions and negotiations, to agree upon the terms of said admission and cession, either by treaty to be submitted to the Senate, or by articles to be submitted to the two Houses of Congress, as the President may direct.

"Approved, *March* 2, 1845."

XI.

THE WILMOT PROVISO.

TEXAS having been annexed during the summer of 1845, in pursuance of the foregoing joint resolution of the two Houses of Congress, a portion of the United States Army, under Gen. Taylor, was, early in the Spring of 1846, moved down to the east bank of the Rio Grande del Norte, claimed by Texas as her Western boundary, but not so regarded by Mexico. A hostile collision ensued, resulting in war between the United States and Mexico.

It was early thereafter deemed advisable that a considerable sum should be placed by Congress at the President's disposal, to negotiate an advantageous Treaty of Peace and Limits with the Mexican government. A Message to this effect was submitted by President Polk to Congress, August 8th, 1846, and a bill in accordance with its suggestions laid before the House, which proceeded to consider the subject in Committee of the Whole. The bill appropriating $30,000 for immediate use in negotiations with Mexico, and placing $2,000,000 more at the disposal of the President, to be employed in making peace, Mr. David Wilmot, of Pa., after consultation with other Northern Democrats, offered the following Proviso, in addition to the first section of the bill:

"*Provided*, That as an express and fundamental condition to the acquisition of any territory from the Republic of Mexico by the United States, by virtue of any treaty which may be negotiated between them, and to the use by the Executive of the moneys herein appropriated, neither Slavery nor involuntary servitude shall ever exist in any part of said territory, except for crime, whereof the party shall first be duly convicted."

This proviso was carried in Committee, by the strong vote of eighty-three to sixty-four—only three Members (Democrats) from the Free States, it was said, opposing it. [No record is made of individual votes in Committee of the Whole.] The bill was then reported to the House, and Mr. Rathbun of N. Y. moved the previous question on its engrossment.

Mr. Tibbatts of Ky. moved that it do lie on the table. Defeated—Yeas 79; [Stephen A. Douglas, John A. McClernand, John Pettit, and Robert C. Schenck, voting with the South to lay on the table]; Nays 93; [Henry Grider and William P. Thomasson of Ky. (Whigs) voting with the North against it].

The bill was then engrossed for its third reading by Yeas 85, Nays 80; and thus passed without further division. A motion to reconsider was laid on the table—Yeas 71; Nays 83. So the bill was passed and sent to the Senate, where Mr. Dixon H. Lewis of Ala. moved that the Proviso above cited be stricken out; on which debate arose, and Mr. John Davis of Mass. was speaking when, at noon of August 10th, the time fixed for adjournment having arrived, both Houses adjourned without day.

[Note.—We do not give the Yeas and Nays on the divisions just above, the House having been quite thin when they were taken, and some Northern Members voting with the South from hostility to the whole project of buying either peace or territory. Generally, however, the vote ran much as former divisions would lead one to expect. Mr. Stephen A. Douglas, and some other friends of the original bill, voted against it at every stage after the Proviso was added.]

The XXXth Congress assembled Dec. 6, 1847.

Feb. 28*th*, 1848, Mr. Putnam of N. York moved the following:

"*Whereas*, In the settlement of the difficulties pending between this country and Mexico, territory may be acquired in which Slavery does not now exist:

"*And whereas*, Congress, in the organization of a territorial government, at an early period of our political history, established a principle worthy of imitation in all future time, forbidding the existence of Slavery in free territory; Therefore,

"*Resolved*, That in any territory, that may be acquired from Mexico, over which shall be established territorial governments, Slavery, or involuntary servitude, except as a punishment for crime, whereof the party shall have been duly convicted, shall be forever prohibited; and that in any act or resolution establishing such governments, a fundamental provision ought to be inserted to that effect."

Mr. R. Brodhead of Penn. moved that this resolution lie on the table. Carried; Yeas, 105; Nays, 93.

[Yeas—all the members from Slave States, but John W. Houston (Whig), of Delaware, with the following from Free States (all Democrats but Levin):

Maine.—Asa W. H. Clapp, Franklin Clark, Jas. S. Wiley, Hezekiah Williams—4.

New-York.—Ausburn Birdsall, David S. Jackson, Frederick W. Lord, William B. Maclay—4.

Pennsylvania.—Richard Brodhead, Charles Brown, *Lewis C. Levin*, Job Mann—4.

Ohio.—William Kennon, jr., John K. Miller, Thomas Richey, William Sawyer—4.

Indiana.—Charles W. Cathcart, Thomas J. Henley, John Petitt, John L. Robinson, William W. Wick—5.

Illinios.—Orlando B. Ficklin, John A. McClernand, William A. Richardson, Robert Smith, Thomas J. Turner—5.

Nays—all the Whigs and a large majority of the Democrats from Free States, with John W. Houston aforesaid.

This vote terminated all direct action in favor of the Wilmot proviso for that Session.

July 18*th*.—In Senate, Mr. Clayton of Del., from the Select Committee to which was referred, on the 12th inst., the bill providing a territorial government for Oregon, reported a bill to establish Territorial governments for Oregon, New Mexico, and California, which was read. [It proposed to submit all questions as to the rightful existence or extent of Slavery in the Territories to the decision of the Supreme Court of the United States.]

July 24*th*.—Second reading. Mr. Baldwin of Conn. moved to strike out so much of said bill as relates to California and New Mexico. Rejected; Yeas, 17 (Northern Free Soil men of both parties); Nays, 37.

The bill was discussed through several succeeding days. On the 26th, Mr. Clarke of R. I. moved to add to the 6th section:

"*Provided, however*, That no law, regulation, or act of the provisional government of said Territory permitting Slavery or involuntary servitude therein shall be valid, until the same shall be approved by Congress."

Rejected; Yeas, 10 [Col. Benton, and 18 Northern Freesoilers of both parties]; Nays, 33.

Mr. Reverdy Johnson of Md. moved to amend the bill by inserting—

"Except only, that in all cases of title to Slaves, the said writs of error or appeals shall be allowed and decided by the said Supreme Court without regard to the value of the matter, property, or title in controversy; and except, also, that a writ of error or appeal shall also be allowed to the Supreme Court of the United States from the decision of the said Supreme Court created by this act, or of any judge thereof, or of the district Courts created by this act, or of any judge upon any writ of habeas corpus involving the question of personal freedom."

Carried: Yeas, 31 (all sorts); Nays, 19

(all Southern, but Bright, Dickinson, and Hannegan).

Mr. Baldwin of Conn. moved an additional section, as follows:

"SEC. 37. *And be it further enacted*, That it shall be the duty of the attorneys for said Territories, respectively, on the complaint of any person held in involuntary servitude therein, to make application in his behalf in due form of law, to the court next thereafter to be holden in said Territory, for a writ of habeas corpus, to be directed to the person so holding such applicant in service as aforesaid, and to pursue all needful measures in his behalf; and if the decision of such court shall be adverse to the application, or if, on the return of the writ, relief shall be denied to the applicant, on the ground that he is a slave held in servitude in said Territory, said attorney shall cause an appeal to be taken therefrom, and the record of all the proceedings in the case to be transmitted to the Supreme Court of the United States as speedily as may be, and to give notice thereof to the Attorney General of the United States, who shall prosecute the same before said Court, who shall proceed to hear and determine the same at the first term thereof."

Yeas, 15 (all Northern, except Benton); Nays, 31.

Mr. Davis of Mass. moved to strike out section 12, and insert as follows:

"Sec. 12. *And be it further enacted*, That so much of the sixth section of the ordinance of the 13th July, 1787, as is contained in the following words; viz: 'There shall be neither Slavery nor involuntary servitude in the said Territory, otherwise than in the punishment of crimes, whereof the party shall have been duly convicted,' shall be and remain in force in the Territory of Oregon."

This was defeated; Yeas, 21; Nays, 33, as follows:

YEAS—For the Slavery Prohibition:

Messrs. Allen, Ohio, Atherton, N. H., Baldwin, Conn., Benton, Mo., Bradbury, Mo., Clarke, R. I., Corwin, Ohio, Davis, Mass., Dayton, N. J., Dix, N. Y., Dodge, Wisc., Felch, Mich., Fitzgerald, Mich., Greene, R. I., Hale, N. H., Hamlin, Me., Miller, N. J., Niles, Conn., Spruance, Del., Upham, Vt., Walker, Wis.—21.

NAYS—Against the Slavery Prohibition:

Messrs. Atchison, Mo., Badger, N. C., Bell, Tenn., Berrien, Ga., Borland, Ark., Breese, Ill., Bright, Ind., Butler, S. C., Calhoun, S. C., Clayton, Del., Davis, Miss., Dickinson, N. Y., Douglas, Ill., Downs, La., Foote, Miss., Hannegan, Ind., Houston, Texas, Hunter, Va., Johnson, Md., Johnson, La., Johnson, Ga., King, Ala., Lewis, Ala., Mangum, N. C., Mason, Va., Metcalf, Ky., Rusk, Texas, Sebastian, Ark., Sturgeon, Pa., Turney, Tenn., Underwood, Ky., Westcott, Fla., Yulee—33.

The bill was then engrossed for a third reading; Yeas, 33; Nays, 22; as follows:

YEAS—For Clayton's Compromise:

Messrs. Atchison, Atherton, Benton, Berrien, Borland, Breese, Bright, Butler, Calhoun, Clayton, Davis, Miss., Dickinson, Douglas, Downs, Foote, Hannegan, Houston, Hunter, Johnson, Md., Johnson, La., Johnson, Ga., King, Lewis, Mangum, Mason, Phelps, Rusk, Sebastian, Spruance, Sturgeon, Turney, Westcott, Yulee—33.

NAYS—Against Clayton's bill:

Messrs. Allen, Badger, Baldwin, Bell, Bradbury, Clarke, Corwin, Davis, Mass., Dayton, Dix, Dodge, Felch, Fitzgerald, Greene, Hale, Hamlin, Metcalf, Miller, Niles, Underwood, Upham, Walker—22.

So the bill was engrossed, and immediately passed without a division.

July 28th.—This bill reached the House, and was taken up and read twice.

Mr. Linn Boyd of Ky. moved it to a Committee of the Whole on the State of the Union.

Mr. C. B. Smith of Ind. moved and obtained a call of the House, when all but eighteen Members responded.

Mr. A. H. Stephens of Ga. moved that the bill *do lie on the table.* Yeas and Nays ordered, and the motion prevailed: Yeas, 112; Nays, 97.

Yeas all the Free State Whigs, with the following Whigs from Slave States:

VIRGINIA.—John S. Pendleton—1.

NORTH CAROLINA.—Nathaniel Boydon, Richard S. Donnell—2.

GEORGIA.—Alex. H. Stephens—1.

KENTUCKY.—Green Adams, Aylett Buckner, John B. Thompson—3.

TENNESSEE.—John H. Crozier—1.

Total, eight Whigs from Slave States. Democrats from Free States:

MAINE.—Asa W. H. Clapp, David Hammons, Ephraim K. Smart, James S. Wiley—4.

NEW-HAMPSHIRE.—Charles H. Peaslee—1.

VERMONT.—Lucius B. Peck—1.

RHODE ISLAND.—Benjamin B. Thurston—1.

NEW YORK.—William Collins, Timothy Jenkins, Sidney Lawrence, Frederick W. Lord, William B. Maclay, Henry Nicoll, George A. Starkweather—7.

PENNSYLVANIA.—Wm. Strong, James Thompson, David Wilmot—3.

OHIO.—James J. Faran, George Fries, Samuel Lahm, Jonathan D. Morris—4.

INDIANA.—Thomas J. Henley—1.

ILLINOIS.—Robert Smith, John Wentworth—2.

MICHIGAN. — Kinsley S. Bingham, Robert McClelland, Charles E. Stuart—3.

WISCONSIN.—Mason C. Darling, William Pitt Lynde—2.

IOWA.—William Thompson.—1.

Total Democrats from Free States—30.

Total Whigs from Free States—74.

Nays, 21 Democrats from Free States, with 76 Democrats and Whigs from Slave States.

Mr. Pollock of Pa. moved that this vote be reconsidered, and that the motion to reconsider do lie on the table; which prevailed —Yeas, 113; Nays, 96. (Vote same as before, except that Mr. Franklin Clark of Maine changed from the minority to the majority.)

So Mr. Clayton's project of Compromise was defeated.

GEN. CASS'S NICHOLSON LETTER.

Immediately after the adjournment of Congress, in 1847, Gen. Cass was currently reported to have expressed his favorable opinion of the Wilmot Proviso, and his regret that Mr. Davis's untimely remarks in the Senate had deprived him (Cass) of an opportunity of recording his vote in its favor. This remark he was said to have made in a railroad car, on his homeward journey from Washington. If such a position were taken by him, however, it was not long maintained; as the following letter from his pen appeared during the winter of 1847–8, and proved a prelude to the nomination of the writer for President, by the Democratic National Convention which assembled at Baltimore in the spring of 1848. It may be regarded as the first logical and well-considered enunciation of the doctrine of "Squatter Sovereignty."

Gen. Cass to A. O. P. Nicholson.

WASHINGTON, Dec. 24, 1847.

DEAR SIR,—I have received your letter, and shall answer it as frankly as it is written.

You ask me whether I am in favor of the acquisition of Mexican territory, and what are my sentiments with regard to the Wilmot Proviso.

I have so often and so explicitly stated my views of the first question, in the Senate, that it seems almost unnecessary to repeat them here. As you request it, however, I shall briefly give them.

I think, then, that no peace should be granted to Mexico, till a reasonable indemnity is obtained for the injuries which she has done us. The territorial extent of this indemnity is, in the first instance, a subject of Executive consideration. There the Constitution has placed it, and there I am willing to leave it: not only because I have full confidence in its judicious exercise, but because, in the ever-varying circumstances of a war, it would be indiscreet, by a public declaration, to commit the country to any line of indemnity, which might otherwise be enlarged, as the obstinate injustice of the enemy prolongs the contest, with its loss of blood and treasure.

It appears to me, that the kind of metaphysical magnanimity which would reject all indemnity at the close of a bloody and expensive war, brought on by a direct attack upon our troops by the enemy, and preceded by a succession of unjust acts for a series of years, is as unworthy of the age in which we live, as it is revolting to the common sense and practice of mankind. It would conduce but little to our future security, or, indeed, to our present reputation, to declare that we repudiate all expectation of compensation from the Mexican Government, and are fighting, not for any practical result, but for some vague, perhaps philanthropic object, which escapes my penetration, and must be defined by those who assume this new principle of national intercommunication. All wars are to be deprecated, as well by the statesman as by the philanthropist. They are great evils; but there are greater evils than these, and submission to injustice is among them. The nation which should refuse to defend its rights and its honor, when assailed, would soon have neither to defend; and, when driven to war, it is not by professions of disinterestedness and declarations of magnanimity that its rational objects can be best obtained, or other nations taught a lesson of forbearance—the strongest security for permanent peace. We are at war with Mexico, and its vigorous prosecution is the surest means of its speedy termination, and ample indemnity the surest guaranty against the recurrence of such injustice as provoked it.

The Wilmot Proviso has been before the country some time. It has been repeatedly discussed in Congress, and by the public Press. I am strongly impressed with the opinion, that a great change has been going on in the public mind upon this subject, in my own as well as others; and that doubts are resolving themselves into convictions, that the principle it involves should be kept out of the National Legislature, and left to the people of the confederacy in their respective local governments.

The whole subject is a comprehensive one, and fruitful of important consequences. It would be ill-timed to discuss it here. I shall not assume that responsible task, but shall confine myself to such general views as are necessary to the fair exhibition of my opinions.

We may well regret the existence of Slavery in the Southern States, and wish they had been saved from its introduction. But there it is, not by the act of the present generation; and we must deal with it as a great practical question, involving the most momentous consequences. We have neither the right nor the power to touch it where it exists; and if we had both, their exercise, by any means heretofore suggested, might lead to results which no wise man would willingly encounter, and which no good man could contemplate without anxiety.

The theory of our Government presupposes that its various members have reserved to themselves the regulation of all subjects relating to what may be termed their internal police. They are sovereign within their boundaries, except in those cases where they have surrendered to the General Government a portion of their rights, in order to give effect to the objects of the Union, whether these concern foreign nations or the several States themselves. Local institutions, if I may so speak, whether they have reference to Slavery or to any other relations, domestic or public, are left to local authority, either original or derivative. Congress has no right to say that there shall be Slavery in New-York, or that there shall be no Slavery in Georgia; nor is there any other human power, but the people of those States, respectively, which can change the relations existing therein; and they can say, if they will, We will have Slavery in the former, and we will abolish it in the latter.

In various respects, the Territories differ from the States. Some of their rights are inchoate, and they do not possess the peculiar attributes of sovereignty. Their relation to the General Government is very imperfectly defined by the Constitution; and it will be found, upon examination, that in that instrument the only grant of power concerning them is conveyed in the phrase, "Congress shall have the power to dispose of and make all needful rules and regulations, respecting the territory and other property belonging to the United States." Certainly this phraseology is very loose, if it were designed to include in the grant the whole power of legislation over persons, as well as things. The expression, the "territory and other property," fairly construed, relates to the public lands, as such; to arsenals, dockyards, forts, ships, and all the various kinds of property which the United States may and must possess.

But surely the simple authority *to dispose of and regulate* these does not extend to the unlimited power of legislation; to the passage of all *laws*, in the most general acceptation of the word; which, by-the-by, is carefully excluded from the sentence. And, indeed, if this were so, it would render unnecessary another provision of the Constitution, which grants to Congress the power to legislate, with the consent of the States, respectively, over all places purchased for the "erection of forts, magazines, arsenals, dockyards," etc. These being the "*property*" of the United States, if the power to make "needful rules and regulations concerning" them includes the general power of legislation, then the grant of authority to regulate "the territory and other property of the United States" is unlimited, wherever subjects are found for its operation, and its exercise needed no auxiliary provision. If, on the other hand, it does not include such power of legislation over the "other property" of the United States, then it does not include it over their "*territory*;" for the same terms which grant the one, grant the other. "*Territory*" is here classed with property, and treated as such; and the object was evidently to enable the General Government, as a property-holder—which, from necessity, it must be—to manage, preserve and "*dispose of*" such property as it might possess, and which authority is essential almost to its being. But the lives and persons of our citizens, with the vast variety of objects connected with them, cannot be controlled by an authority which is merely called into existence for the purpose of making *rules and regulations for the disposition and management of property*.

Such, it appears to me, would be the construction put upon this provision of the Constitution, were this question now first presented for consideration, and not controlled by imperious circumstances. The original ordinance of the Congress of the Confederation, passed in 1787, and which was the only act upon this subject in force at the adoption of the Constitution, provided a complete frame of government for the country north of the Ohio, while in a territorial condition, and for its eventual admission in separate States into the Union. And the persuasion that this ordinance contained within itself all the necessary means of execution, probably prevented any direct reference to the subject in the Constitution, further than vesting in Congress the right to admit the States formed under it into the Union. However, circumstances arose, which required legislation, as well over the territory north of the Ohio as over other territory, both within and without the original Union, ceded to the general Government, and, at various times, a more enlarged power has been exercised over the *Territories*—meaning thereby the different Territorial Governments—than is conveyed by the limited grant referred to. How far an existing necessity may have operated in producing this legislation, and thus extending, by rather a violent implication, powers not directly given, I know not. But certain it is that the principle of interference should not be carried beyond the necessary implication, which produces it. It should be limited to the creation of proper governments for new countries, acquired or settled, and to the necessary provision for their eventual admission into the Union; leaving, in the mean time, to the people inhabiting them, to regulate their internal concerns in their own way. They are just as capable of doing so as the people of the States; and they can do so, at any rate as soon as their political independence is recognized by admission into the Union. During this temporary condition, it is hardly expedient to call into exercise a doubtful and invidious authority, which questions the intelligence of a respectable portion of our citizens, and whose limitation, whatever it may be, will be rapidly approaching its termination—an authority which would give to Congress despotic power, uncontrolled by the Constitution, over most important sections of our common country. For, if the relation of master and servant may be regulated or annihilated by its legislation, so may the regulation of husband and wife, of parent and child, and of any other condition which our institutions and the habits of our society recognize. What would be thought if Congress should undertake to prescribe the terms of marriage in New-York, or to regulate the authority of parents over their children in Pennsylvania? And yet it would be as vain to seek one justifying the interference of the national legislature in the cases referred to in the original States of the Union. I speak here of the inherent power of Congress, and do not touch the question of such contracts as may be formed with new States when admitted into the confederacy.

Of all the questions that can agitate us, those which are merely sectional in their character are the most dangerous, and the most to be deprecated. The warning voice of him who from his character and services and virtue had the best right to warn us, proclaimed to his countrymen, in his Farewell Address—that monument of wisdom for him, as I hope it will be of safety for them—how much we had to apprehend from measures peculiarly affecting geographical sections of our country. The grave circumstances in which we are now placed make these words words of safety; for I am satisfied, from all I have seen and heard here, that a successful attempt to engraft the principles of the Wilmot Proviso upon the legislation of this Government, and to apply them to new territory, should new territory be acquired, would seriously affect our tranquillity. I do not suffer myself to foresee or to foretell the consequences that would ensue; for I trust and believe there is good sense and good feeling enough in the country to avoid them, by avoiding all occasions which might lead to them.

Briefly, then, I am opposed to the exercise of any jurisdiction by Congress over this matter; and I am in favor of leaving to the people of any territory, which may be hereafter acquired, the right to regulate it for themselves, under the general principles of the Constitution. Because—

1. I do not see in the Constitution any grant of the requisite power to Congress; and I am not disposed to extend a doubtful precedent beyond its necessity—the establishment of territorial governments when needed—leaving to the inhabitants all the rights compatible with the relations they bear to the confederation.

2. Because I believe this measure, if adopted, would weaken, if not impair, the union of the States; and would sow the seeds of future discord, which would grow up and ripen into an abundant harvest of calamity.

3. Because I believe a general conviction that such a proposition would succeed, would lead to an immediate withholding of the supplies, and

thus to a dishonorable termination of the war. I think no dispassionate observer at the seat of Government can doubt this result.

4. If, however, in this I am under a misapprehension, I am under none in the practical operation of this restriction, if adopted by Congress, upon a treaty of peace, making any acquisition of Mexican territory. Such a treaty would be rejected as certainly as presented to the Senate. More than one-third of that body would vote against it, viewing such a principle as an exclusion of the citizens of the slaveholding States from a participation in the benefits acquired by the treasure and exertions of all, and which should be common to all. I am repeating—neither advancing nor defending these views. That branch of the subject does not lie in my way, and I shall not turn aside to seek it.

In this aspect of the matter, the people of the United States must choose between this restriction and the extension of their territorial limits. They cannot have both; and which they will surrender must depend upon their representatives first, and then, if these fail them, upon themselves.

5. But after all, it seems to be generally conceded that this restriction, if carried into effect, could not operate upon any State to be formed from newly-acquired territory. The well-known attributes of sovereignty, recognized by us as belonging to the State Governments, would sweep before them any such barrier, and would leave the people to express and exert their will at pleasure. Is the object, then, of temporary exclusion for so short a period as the duration of the Territorial Governments, worth the price at which it it would be purchased?—worth the discord it would engender, the trial to which it would expose our Union, and the evils that would be the certain consequence, let the trial result as it might? As to the course, which has been intimated, rather than proposed, of engrafting such a restriction upon any treaty of acquisition, I persuade myself it would find but little favor in any portion of this country. Such an arrangement would render Mexico a party, having a right to interfere in our internal institutions in questions left by the Constitution to the State Governments, and would inflict a serious blow upon our fundamental principles. Few, indeed, I trust, there are among us who would thus grant to a foreign power the right to inquire into the constitution and conduct of the sovereign States of this Union; and if there are any, I am not among them, nor never shall be. To the people of this country, under God, now and hereafter, are its destinies committed; and we want no foreign power to interrogate us, treaty in hand, and to say, Why have you done this, or why have you left that undone? Our own dignity and the principles of national independence unite to repel such a proposition.

But there is another important consideration, which ought not to be lost sight of, in the investigation of this subject. The question that presents itself is not a question of the increase, but of the diffusion of Slavery. Whether its sphere be stationary or progressive, its amount will be the same. The rejection of this restriction will not add one to the class of servitude, nor will its adoption give freedom to a single being who is now placed therein. The same numbers will be spread over greater territory; and, so far as compression, with less abundance of the necessaries of life, is an evil, so far will that evil be mitigated by transporting slaves to a new country, and giving them a larger space to occupy.

I say this in the event of the extension of Slavery over any new acquisition. But can it go there? This may well be doubted. All the descriptions which reach us of the condition of the Californias and of New-Mexico, to the acquisition of which our efforts seem at present directed, unite in representing those countries as agricultural regions, similar in their products to our Middle States, and generally unfit for the production of the great staples which can alone render Slave labor valuable. If we are not grossly deceived—and it is difficult to conceive how we can be—the inhabitants of those regions, whether they depend upon their plows or their herds, cannot be slaveholders. Involuntary labor, requiring the investment of large capital, can only be profitable when employed in the production of a few favored articles confined by nature to special districts, and paying larger returns than the usual agricultural products spread over more considerable portions of the earth.

In the able letter of Mr. Buchanan upon this subject, not long since given to the public, he presents similar considerations with great force. "Neither," says the distinguished writer, "the soil, the climate, nor the productions of California south of 36° 30′, nor indeed of any portion of it, North or South, is adapted to Slave labor; and beside every facility would be there afforded for the slave to escape from his master. Such property would be entirely insecure in any part of California. It is morally impossible, therefore, that a majority of the emigrants to that portion of the territory south of 36° 30′, which will be chiefly composed of our citizens, will ever re-establish Slavery within its limits.

"In regard to New-Mexico, east of the Rio Grande, the question has already been settled by the admission of Texas into the Union.

"Should we acquire territory beyond the Rio Grande and east of the Rocky Mountains, it is still more impossible that a majority of the people would consent to *re-establish* Slavery. They are themselves a colored population, and among them the negro does not belong socially to a degraded race."

With this last remark, Mr. Walker fully coincides in his letter written in 1844, upon the annexation of Texas, and which everywhere produced so favorable an impression upon the public mind, as to have conduced very materially to the accomplishment of that great measure. "Beyond the Del Norte," says Mr. Walker, "Slavery will not pass; not only because it is forbidden by law, but because the colored race there preponderates in the ratio of ten to one over the whites; and holding, as they do, the government and most of the offices in their possession, they will not permit the enslavement of any portion of the colored race, which makes and executes the laws of the country."

The question, it will be therefore seen on examination, does not regard the exclusion of Slavery from a region where it now exists, but a prohibition against its introduction where it does not exist, and where, from the feelings of the inhabitants and the laws of nature, "it is morally impossible," as Mr. Buchanan says, that it can ever re-establish itself.

It augurs well for the permanence of our confederation, that during more than half a century, which has elapsed since the establishment of this Government, many serious questions, and some of the highest importance, have agitated the public mind, and more than once threatened the gravest consequences; but that they have all in succession passed away, leaving our institutions unscathed, and our country advancing in numbers, power, and wealth, and in all the other elements of national prosperity, with a rapidity unknown in ancient or in modern days. In times of political excitement, when difficult and delicate questions present themselves for solution, there is one ark of safety for us; and that is, an honest appeal to the fundamental principles of our Union, and a stern determination to abide their dictates.

This course of proceeding has carried us in safety through many a trouble, and I trust will carry us safely through many more, should many more be destined to assail us. The Wilmot Proviso seeks to take from its legitimate tribunal a question of domestic policy, having no relation to the Union, as such, and to transfer it to another, created by the people for a special purpose, and foreign to the subject matter involved in this issue. By going back to our true principles, we go back to the road of peace and safety. Leave to the people, who will be affected by this question, to adjust it upon their own responsibility, and in their own manner, and we shall render another tribute to the original principles of our Government, and furnish another guaranty for its permanence and prosperity. I am, dear sir, respectfully, your obedient servant, LEWIS CASS.

A. O. P. NICHOLSON, Esq., Nashville, Tenn.

The next session of the same Congress opened under very different auspices. The Mexican War had been terminated, so that none could longer be deterred from voting for Slavery Exclusion by a fear that the prosecution of hostilities would thereby be embarrassed. General Taylor had been elected President, receiving the votes of Delaware, Maryland, North Carolina, Georgia, Kentucky, Tennessee, Louisiana, and Florida—a moiety of the Slave States—over Gen. Cass, now the avowed opponent of Slavery Restriction. Many of the Northern Democrats considered themselves absolved by this vote from all extra-constitutional obligations to the South, and voted accordingly.

Dec. 13.—Mr. J. M. Root of Ohio, offered the following:

"*Resolved*, That the Committee on Territories be instructed to report to this House, with as little delay as practicable, a bill or bills providing a territorial government for each of the Territories of New Mexico and California, and excluding Slavery therefrom."

A call of the House was had, and the previous question ordered.

Mr. W. P. Hall of Mo. moved that the same do lie on the table. Lost: Yeas, 80; Nays, 106.

The resolve then passed: Yeas, 108; Nays, 80, viz.:

Yeas—All the Whigs from Free States, and all the Democrats, but those noted as Nays below, including the following, who had voted against the same principle at the former session:

MAINE.—Asa W. H. Clapp, James S. Wiley—2.
NEW YORK.—Frederick W. Lord—1.
OHIO.—Thomas Richey—1.
INDIANA.—Charles W Cathcart, Thomas J. Henley, John L. Robinson, William W. Wick—4.
ILLINOIS.—Robert Smith—1.

Messrs. Clark and H. Williams of Maine, Birdsall and Maclay of New-York, Brodhead and Mann of Pa., Pettit of Ind., Ficklin and McClelland of Ill., who voted with the South at the former session—now failed to vote.

Mr. Jackson of N.Y., who then voted with the South, had been succeeded by Mr. H. Greeley, who voted with the North.

Nays—All the Members voting from the Slave States, with the following from the Free States:

NEW-YORK.—Henry C. Murphy—1.
PENNSYLVANIA—Charles Brown, Charles J. Ingersoll—2.
OHIO—William Kennon, jun., John K. Miller William Sawyer—3.
ILLINOIS.—William A. Richardson—1.
IOWA.—Shepherd Leffler—1.

Total Nays from Free States—8.

Mr. Robinson of Ind. moved a reconsideration of this vote, which motion (Dec. 18), on motion of Mr. Wentworth of Ill., was laid on the table: Yeas, 105; Nays, 83.

[Messrs. Clapp, Clark, and Wiley of Me., voted to lay on the table, as did Messrs. Lord of N. Y., Job Mann of Pa., Richey of Ohio, Henley and Wick of Indiana, R. Smith of Ill. Messrs. C. Brown and Levin of Pa. did not now vote. The rest, very much as before, except that a few more voted.]

Dec. 20th.—Mr. C. B. Smith accordingly reported a bill, establishing the Territorial Government of Upper California, which was read twice and committed.

Jan. 3rd.—He reported a similar bill for the organization of New Mexico, which took the same direction.

Jan. 15th.—Mr. Julius Rockwell of Mass. moved that these bills be made the special order for the 23d instant. Negatived: Yeas, 114 (not two-thirds); Nays, 71 (nearly a sectional vote).

Feb. 26–7th.—The bill was taken out of committee, and engrossed for a third reading.

Mr. Meade of Va. moved that it do lie on the table. Negatived: Yeas, 86; Nays, 127.

It was then passed by the following similar vote:

Yeas—All the Whigs from the Free States, with Aylett Buckner (Whig) of Ky., and all the Democrats also, except

PENSYLVANIA.—Samuel A. Bridges—1.
OHIO.—William Kennon, jun., John K. Miller, William Sawyer—3.
Total—4.

Nays—All the Members from Slave States, except Mr. Buckner aforesaid, with the addition of those from Free States just mentioned.

This bill was read twice in the Senate, (Feb. 28th), and referred to the Committee on Territories.

March 3d.—Said Committee was discharged from its further consideration, and Mr. Douglas moved that it be taken up in Senate, which was negatived. Yeas, 25; Nays, 28 (all but a sectional vote). That was the end of the bill; the Senate having already determined to affix its essential provisions to the Civil and Diplomatic Appropriation bill, and thus avoid and defeat the Slavery Exclusion contained in the House bill, and force the House to agree to organize the Territories, *without* such provision, or leave the Government without appropriations. How this succeeded, we shall see.

The Civil and Diplomatic Appropriation bill having passed the House in the usual form, came up to the Senate, where it was debated several days.

Feb. 21*st.*—Mr. Walker of Wisc. moved an amendment, extending all the laws of the United States, so far as applicable, to the Territories acquired from Mexico.

Mr. Bell of Tenn. moved to add further sections organizing the State of California, to be admitted into the Union on the 1st of October next. This was rejected: Yeas 4 (Bell, Dodge of Iowa, Douglas, Davis); Nays 39.

Feb. 26*th.*—Mr. Dayton of N. J. moved that the President be vested with power to provide a suitable temporary government for the Territories. Rejected; Yeas 8; Nays 47.

The question recurred on Mr. Walker's amendment, modified so as to read as follows:

"Sec. 5. *And be it further enacted*, That the Constitution of the United States, in so far as the provisions of the same be applicable to the condition of a Territory of the United States, and all and singular the several acts of Congress respecting the registering, recording, enrolling, or licensing ships, or vessels, and the entry and clearance thereof, and the foreign and coasting trade and fisheries, and all the acts respecting the imposing and collecting the duties on imports, and all the acts respecting trade and intercourse with the Indian tribes, and all the acts respecting the public lands, or the survey or sale thereof, and all and singular the other acts of Congress of a public and general character, and the provisions whereof are suitable and proper to be applied to the territory West of the Rio del Norte, acquired from Mexico by the treaty of the second day of February, 1848, be, and the same are hereby, extended over, and given full force and efficiency in all said territory; and the President of the United States is hereby authorized to prescribe and establish all proper and needful rules and regulations (in conformity with the Constitution of the United States) for the enforcement of the provisions of the Constitution hereinbefore referred to, of said laws in said territory, and for the preservation of order and tranquillity, and the establishment of justice therein, and from time to time to modify or change the said rules and regulations in such manner as may seem to him discreet and proper; and to establish, temporarily, such divisions, districts, ports, offices, and all arrangements proper for the execution of said laws, and appoint and commission such officers as may be necessary to administer such laws in said territory, for such term or terms as he may prescribe, whose authority shall continue until otherwise provided by Congress; said officers to receive such compensation as the President may prescribe, not exceeding double the compensation heretofore paid to similar officers of the United States or its territories, for like services; and to enable the same to be done, the sum of two hundred thousand dollars be appropriated, out of any money in the treasury not otherwise appropriated."

YEAS—For Mr. Walker's proposition:

Messrs. Atchison, Bell, Berrien, Borland, Butler, Houston, Hunter, Johnson of La. Johnson of Ga. King, Davis of Miss. Dickinson, Dodge, Iowa, Douglas, Downs, Fitzgerald, Fitzpatrick, Foote, Miss. Hannegan, Mangum, Mason, Rusk, Sebastian, Sturgeon, Turner, Underwood, Walker, Westcott, Yulee—29.

NAYS—Against Mr. Walker's proposition:

Messrs. Allen, Atherton, Badger, Baldwin, Bradbury, Bright, Cameron, Clarke, Corwin, Davis of Mass. Dayton, Dix, Dodge, Wisc. Felch, Greene, Hale, Hamlin, Johnson, Md. Jones, Miller, Niles, Pearce, Phelps, Spruance, Upham, Wales, Webster—27.

The bill being returned to the House, thus amended, this amendment was (March 2d) voted down—Yeas 101; Nays 115—as follows:

Yeas, all the members from the Slave States, with the following from the Free States, viz.:

MAINE—Hezekiah Williams—1.

NEW YORK—Ausburn Birdsall—1.

PENNSYLVANIA—Samuel A. Bridges, Richard Brodhead, Charles Brown, Charles J. Ingersoll, *Lewis C. Levin*—5.

OHIO—William Kennon, jr., William Sawyer—2.

ILLINOIS—Orlando B. Ficklin, John A. McClernand, William A. Richardson—3.

IOWA—Shepherd Leffler—1.

Total, thirteen from Free States; eighty-eight from Slave States. (Only two from Slave States absent or silent.)

Nays, all the Whigs from Free States, and all the Democrats from Free States, except those named above.

So the House refused to concur in this amendment, and the bill was returned to the Senate accordingly.

The Senate resolved to insist on its amendment, and ask a conference, which was granted, but resulted in nothing. Messrs. Atherton of N. H., Dickinson of N. Y., and Berrien of Ga., were managers on the part of the Senate, and insisted on its amendment, organizing the Territories without restriction as to Slavery. Messrs. Vinton of Ohio, Nicoll of N. Y., and Morehead of Ky., were appointed on the part of the House. These, after a long sitting, reported their inability to agree, and were discharged.

The bill being now returned to the House, Mr. McClernand of Ill. moved that the House do *recede* from its disagreement; Carried: Yeas 111; Nays 106.

Mr. Morehead of Ky. moved to amend so as to provide that nothing in this section shall affect the question, as to the boundary of Texas. Carried: Yeas 187; Nays 19.

Mr. R. W. Thompson of Ind. moved that the House concur with the Senate, with an amendment, which was a substitute, extending the laws of the United States over said Territories, but leaving them unorganized, as follows:

"That the President of the United States be, and he hereby is, authorized to hold possession of and occupy the Territories ceded by Mexico to the United States, by the treaty of the 2nd of Feb., eighteen hundred and forty-eight, and that he be, and hereby is, authorized for that purpose, and in order to maintain the authority of the United States, and preserve peace and order in said Territory, to employ such parts of the army and navy of the United States as he may deem necessary, and that the Constitution of the United States, so far as the same is applicable, be extended over said Territories.

"Sec. 2nd. *And be it further enacted*, That, until the fourth day of July, eighteen hundred and fifty, unless Congress shall sooner provide for the government of said Territories, *the existing laws thereof shall be retained and observed*, and that the civil and judicial authority heretofore exercised in said Territories shall be vested in, and exercised by, such person or persons as the President of the United States shall appoint and direct, to the end that the inhabitants of said Territories may be protected in the full and free enjoyment of their liberty, property, and religion: *provided, nevertheless*, that martial law shall not be proclaimed or declared in said Territories, or either of them, nor any military court established or instituted, except ordinary courts-martial for the trial of persons belonging to the army and navy of the United States; and the imprisonment of any citizen of said Territories for debt is hereby forbidden.

"Sec. 3. *And be it further enacted*, That, to enable the President to carry into execution the provisions of this act, the sum of two hundred thousand dollars is hereby appropriated out of any money in the Treasury not otherwise appropriated."

The question being reached on amending the Senate's proposition as proposed by Mr. Thompson, it was carried: Yeas 111; Nays 105.

[All the Southern Members in the negative, with Levin and a few of the Northern Democrats; the residue with all the Northern Whigs in the affirmative.]

The House now proceeded to agree to the Senate's amendment, *as amended;* Yeas 110; Nays 103, [the same as before; the friends of the Senate's proposition voting against it, as amended, and *vice versa*, on the understanding that Mr. Thompson's amendment would exclude Slavery.]

The bill as thus amended being returned to the Senate, it refused to agree to the House's amendment, and receded from its own proposition; so the bill was passed and the session closed, with no provision for the government of the newly-acquired Territories.

XII.

OREGON.

Aug. 6, 1846.—Mr. Douglas, from the Committee on Territories, reported to the House a bill organizing the Territory of Oregon.

Said bill was discussed in Committee of the Whole, and the following amendment agreed to:

"And neither Slavery, nor involuntary servitude shall ever exist in said Territory, except for crime whereof the party shall have been duly convicted."

On coming out of Committee, this amendment was agreed to—Yeas 108; Nays 44. [The Nays are all Southern, but Charles J. Ingersoll, Orlando B. Ficklin, and possibly one or two others; and all Democrats, but some half a dozen from the South, of whom Robert Toombs has since turned Democrat.] Stephen A. Douglas did not vote. The bill passed the House without further opposition, was read twice in the Senate, and referred; and Mr. Westcott of Florida made a report thereon from the Committee on Territories; but the Session closed without further action on the bill.

This Congress reassembled, Dec. 7th, 1846. On the 23d, Mr. Douglas again reported his bill to provide a territorial government for Oregon, which was read twice and committed: Jan. 11th, 1847, was discussed in Committee, as also on the 12th and 14th, when it was resolved to close the debate. On the 15th, it was taken out of Committee, when Gen. Burt of S. C. moved the following addition (already moved, debated, and voted down in Committee) to the clause forbidding Slavery in said Territory:

"Inasmuch as the whole of said Territory lies north of thirty-six degrees thirty minutes north latitude, known as the line of the Missouri Compromise."

The purpose of this is clear enough. It was intended to recognize the Missouri line, not as limited to the territories possessed by the United States at the time said line was established, but as extending to all that had since been, or hereafter should be, acquired, so as to legalize Slavery in any territory henceforth to be acquired by us south of 36° 30′.

Mr. Burt's amendment was negatived—Yeas 82; Nays 114.

The vote was very nearly sectional; but the following Members from Free States voted in the minority:

PENNSYLVANIA.—Charles J. Ingersoll—1.
ILLINOIS—Stephen A. Douglas, Robt. Smith—2.
IOWA.—S. C. Hastings—1.

In all, 5.

No Member from a Slave State voted in

the majority. The bill then passed—Yeas 134; Nays 35 (all Southern).

Jan. 15th.—The bill reached the Senate, and was sent to the Judiciary Committee, consisting of

Messrs. Ashley, Ark. Berrien, Ga.
Breese, Ill. Dayton, N. J.
Westcott, Fla.

Jan. 25.—Mr. Ashley reported the Oregon bill with amendments, which were ordered to be printed.

29th.—Said bill, on motion of Mr. Westcott, was recommitted to the Judiciary Committee.

Feb. 10*th.*—Mr. Ashley again reported it with amendments.

March 3*d.*—It was taken up as in Committee of the Whole, when Mr. Evans of Me. moved that it be laid on the table. Defeated—Yeas 19, (all Whigs but Calhoun of S. C., and Yulee of Florida); Nays 26; (24 Dem., with Corwin of Ohio, and Johnson of La.).

Mr. Westcott of Fla. immediately moved that the bill do lie on the table, which prevailed—Yeas 26; Nays 18, (a mixed vote, evidently governed by various motives); but the negatives were all Democrats, but Corwin and Johnson aforesaid. This being the last day of the session, it was evident that the bill, if opposed, as it was certain to be, could not get through, and it was, doubtless, in behalf of other pressing business that many Senators voted to lay this aside. It was, of course, dead for the session.

Dec. 6*th*, 1847.—The XXXth Congress assembled; Robert C. Winthrop (Whig) of Mass. was chosen Speaker of the House. President Polk, in his Annual Message, regretted that Oregon had not already been organized, and urged the necessity of action on the subject.

Feb. 9*th.*—Mr. Caleb B. Smith of Indiana reported to the House a bill to establish the territorial government of Oregon; which, by a vote of two-thirds, was made a special order for March 14th. It was postponed, however, to the 28th; when it was taken up and discussed, as on one or two subsequent days. *May* 29th, it was again made a special order next after the Appropriation bills. The President that day sent a special message, urging action on this subject. *July* 25th, it was taken up in earnest; Mr. Wentworth of Illinois moving that debate on it in Committee cease at two o'clock this day.

Mr. Geo. S. Houston of Ala. endeavored to put this motion on the table. Defeated—Yeas 85; Nays 89, (nearly, but not fully, a sectional division). Mr. Geo. W. Jones of Tenn. moved a reconsideration, which was carried—Yeas 100; Nays 88; and the resolution laid on the table—Yeas 96; Nays 90.

The bill continued to be discussed, and finally (Aug. 1st) was got out of Committee; when Mr. C. B. Smith moved the Previous Question thereon, which was ordered.

August 2*d.*—The House came to a vote on an amendment made in Committee, whereby the following provision of the original bill was stricken out:

"That the inhabitants of said Territory shall be entitled to enjoy, all and singular, the rights, privileges, and advantages granted and secured to the people of the Territory of the United States northwest of the river Ohio, by the articles of compact contained in the ordinance for the government of said Territory, passed the 13th day of July, seventeen hundred and eighty-seven; and shall be subject to all the conditions, and restrictions, and prohibitions in said articles of compact imposed upon the people of said territory and—"

The House refused to agree to this amendment—Yeas 88; Nays 114.

The Members from the Free States who voted with the South to strike out, were—

NEW-YORK—Ausburn Birdsall—1.

OHIO—William Kennon, jr., John K. Miller—2.

ILLINOIS—Orlando B. Ficklin, John A. McClernand, William A. Richardson—3.

INDIANA—John L. Robinson, William W. Wick—2.

Mr. John W. Houston of Delaware voted in the majority.

The bill was then passed: Yeas 128; Nays 71.

[This vote was almost completely sectional. Mr. Houston of Delaware voting in the majority as before: otherwise, Members from Free States in the affirmative; those from Slave States in the negative.]

Aug. 3*rd.*—This bill reached the Senate, when Mr. Badger of N. C. moved its indefinite postponement: negatived, 47 to 1, (Yulee). It was then sent to the Committee on Territories.

The Senate had had under consideration, from time to time through the Session, a bill of its own, reported by Mr. Douglas, which was finally referred to a Select Committee—Mr. Clayton of Delaware, Chairman—and by said committee reported some days before the reception of the House bill. It was then dropped.

Aug. 5*th.*—Mr. Douglas reported the House Bill, with amendments, which were printed.

Aug. 10*th.*—After some days' debate, the Senate proceeded to vote. Mr. Foote of Miss. moved that the bill do lie on the table. Defeated: Yeas 15 (Southern); Nays 36.

On the question of agreeing to this amendment:

"Inasmuch as the said Territory is north of thirty-six deg. thirty min., usually known as the [line of the] Missouri Compromise."

It was rejected: Yeas 2 (Bright and Douglas); Nays 52.

Mr. Douglas moved to amend the bill, by inserting after the word "enacted":

"That the line of thirty-six degrees and thirty minutes of north latitude, known as the Missouri Compromise line, as defined in the eighth section of an act entitled, 'An Act to authorize the people of the Missouri Territory to form a Constitutional and State Government, and for the admission of such State into the Union, on an equal footing with the original States, and to prohibit Slavery in certain Territories, approved March 6th, 1820,' be, and the same is hereby, declared to extend to the Pacific Ocean; and the said eighth section, together with the compromise therein effected, is hereby revived, and declared to be in full force and binding, for the future organization of the Territories of the United States in the same sense, and with the same understanding with which it was originally adopted; and—"

Which was carried—Yeas 33; Nays 21—as follows:

YEAS—For recognizing the Missouri line as rightfully extending to the Pacific:

Messrs. Atchison, Badger, Bell, Benton, Berrien, Borland, Bright, Butler, Calhoun, Cameron, Davis of Miss., Dickinson, Douglas, Downs, Fitzgerald, Foote of Miss., Hannegan, Houston, Hunter, Johnson of Md., Johnson of La., Johnson of Ga., King, Lewis, Mangum, Mason, Metcalf, Pearce, Sebastian, Spruance, Sturgeon, Turney, Underwood—33.

NAYS—Against recognizing said line:

Messrs. Allen, Atherton, Baldwin, Bradbury, Breese, Clarke, Corwin, Davis of Mass., Dayton, Dix, Dodge, Felch, Greene, Hale, Hamlin, Miller, Niles, Phelps, Upham, Walker, Webster—21.

The bill was then engrossed for a third reading: Yeas 33; Nays 22 (nearly same as the above—Westcott of Florida, added to the Nays—and thus passed).

Aug. 11th.—The bill, thus amended, having been returned to the House, the amendment of Mr. Douglas, just recited, was rejected: Yeas 82; Nays 121.

Yeas from Free States:

New York—Ausburn Birdsall—1.

Pennsylvania—Charles Brown, Charles J. Ingersoll.—2.

Total—3.

Otherwise, from Slave States, all Yeas; from Free States, all Nays.

Aug. 12th.—The Senate, after voting down various propositions to lay on the table, etc., finally decided to *recede* from its amendments to the Oregon bill, and pass it as it came from the House: Yeas 29; Nays 25, as follows:

YEAS—For Receding:

Messrs. Allen, Baldwin, Benton, Bradbury, Breese, Bright, Cameron, Clarke, Corwin, Davis of Mass., Dayton, Dickinson, Dix, Dodge, Douglas, Felch, Fitzgerald, Greene, Hale, Hamlin, Hannegan, Houston, Miller, Niles, Phelps, Spruance, Upham, Walker, Webster—29.

NAYS—Against Receding:

Messrs. Atchison, Badger, Bell, Berrien, Borland, Butler, Calhoun, Davis of Miss., Downs, Foote, Hunter, Johnson of Md., Johnson of La., Johnson of Ga., Lewis, Mangum, Mason, Metcalf, Pearce, Rusk, Sebastian, Turney, Underwood, Westcott, Yulee—25.

(All from Slave States.)

So the bill became a law, and Oregon a Territory, under the original Jefferson or Dane Proviso against Slavery.

XIII.

THE COMPROMISE OF 1850.

The XXXIst Congress commenced its first Session at Washington, Dec. 3d, 1849; but the House was unable to organize—no person receiving a majority of all the votes for Speaker—until the 22nd, when, the Plurality rule having been adopted by a vote of 113 to 106, Mr. Howell Cobb of Ga. was elected, having 102 votes to 100 for Robert C. Winthrop of Mass., and 20 scattering. It was thereupon resolved—Yeas 149; Nays 35—"That Howell Cobb be declared duly elected Speaker;" and on the 24th President Zachary Taylor transmitted to both Houses his first Annual Message, in the course of which he says:

"No civil government having been provided by Congress for California, the people of that Territory, impelled by the necessities of their political condition, recently met in Convention, for the purpose of forming a Constitution and State Government; which, the latest advices give me reason to suppose, has been accomplished; and it is believed they will shortly apply for the admission of California into the Union, as a Sovereign State. Should such be the case, and should their constitution be conformable to the requisitions of the Constitution of the United States, I recommend their application to the favorable consideration of Congress.

"The people of New-Mexico will also, it is believed, at no very distant period, present themselves for admission into the Union. Preparatory to the admission of California and New-Mexico, the people of each will have instituted for themselves a republican form of government, laying its foundation in such principles, and organizing its power in such form, as to them shall seem most likely to effect their safety and happiness.

"By awaiting their action, all causes of uneasiness may be avoided, and confidence and kind feeling preserved. With a view of maintaining the harmony and tranquillity so dear to all, we should abstain from the introduction of those exciting topics of a sectional character which have hitherto produced painful apprehensions in the public mind; and I repeat the solemn warning of the first and most illustrious of my predecessors, against furnishing any ground for characterizing parties by geographical discriminations."

Jan. 4th.—Gen. Sam. Houston of Texas submitted to the Senate the following proposition:

"*Whereas*, The Congress of the United States, possessing only a delegated authority, have no power over the subject of Negro Slavery within the limits of the United States, either to prohibit or interfere with it, in the States, Territories, or District, where, by municipal law, it now exists, or to establish it in any State or Territory where it does not exist; but, as an assurance and guarantee to promote harmony, quiet apprehension, and remove sectional prejudice, which by possibility might impair or weaken love and devotion to the Union in any part of the country, it is hereby

"*Resolved*, That, as the people in Territories have the same inherent rights of self-government as the people in the States, if, in the exercise of such inherent rights, the people in the newly-acquired Territories, by the Annexation of Texas and the acquisition of California and New-Mexico, south of the parallel of 36 degrees and 30 minutes of north latitude, extending to the Pacific Ocean, shall establish Negro Slavery in the formation of their state governments, it shall be deemed no objection to their admission as a State or States into the Union, in accordance with the Constitution of the United States."

Jan. 21st.—Gen. Taylor, in answer to a resolution of inquiry, sent a message to the House, stating that he had urged the formation of State Governments in California and New-Mexico. He adds:

"In advising an early application by the people of these Territories for admission as States, I was actuated principally by an earnest desire to afford to the wisdom and patriotism of Congress the opportunity of avoiding occasions of bitter and angry discussions among the people of the United States.

"Under the Constitution, every State has the right to establish, and, from time to time, alter its municipal laws and domestic institutions, independently of every other State and of the General Government, subject only to the prohibitions and guarantees expressly set forth in the Constitution of the United States. The subjects thus left exclusively to the respective States, were not designed or expected to become topics of National agitation. Still as, under the Constitution, Congress has power to make all needful rules and regulations respecting the Territories of the United States, every new acquisition of territory has led to discussions on the question whether the system of involuntary servitude, which prevails in many of the States, should or should not be prohibited in that Territory. The periods of excitement from this cause, which have heretofore occurred, have been safely passed; but, during the interval, of whatever length, which may elapse before the admission of the Territories ceded by Mexico, as States, it appears probable that similar excitement will prevail to an undue extent.

"Under these circumstances, I thought, and still think, that it was my duty to endeavor to put it in the power of Congress, by the admission of California and New-Mexico as States, to remove all occasion for the unnecessary agitation of the public mind.

"It is understood that the people of the Western part of California have formed the plan of a State Constitution, and will soon submit the same to the judgment of Congress, and apply for admission as a State. This course on their part, though in accordance with, was not adopted exclusively in consequence of, any expression of my wishes, inasmuch as measures tending to this end had been promoted by officers sent there by my predecessor, and were already in active progress of execution, before any communication from me reached California. If the proposed constitution shall, when submitted to Congress, be found to be in compliance with the requisitions of the Constitution of the United States, I earnestly recommend that it may receive the sanction of Congress."

He adds—

"Should Congress, when California shall present herself for incorporation into the Union, annex a condition to her admission as a State affecting her domestic institutions contrary to the wishes of her people, and even compel her temporarily to comply with it, yet the State could change her constitution at any time after admission, when to her it should seem expedient. Any attempt to deny to the people of the State the right of self-government, in a matter which peculiarly affects themselves, will infallibly be regarded by them as an invasion of their rights; and, upon the principles laid down in our own Declaration of Independence, they will certainly be sustained by the great mass of the American people. To assert that they are a conquered people, and must, as a State, submit to the will of their conquerors, in this regard, will meet with no cordial response among American freemen. Great numbers of them are native citizens of the United States, and not inferior to the rest of our countrymen in intelligence and patriotism; and no language of menace to restrain them in the exercise of an undoubted right, substantially guarantied to them by the treaty of cession itself, shall ever be uttered by me, or encouraged and sustained by persons acting under my authority. It is to be expected that, in the residue of the territory ceded to us by Mexico, the people residing there will, at the time of their incorporation into the Union as a State, settle all questions of domestic policy to suit themselves."

Feb. 13, 1850.—Gen. Taylor communicated to Congress the Constitution (free) of the State of California.

Jan. 29th, 1850.—Mr. Henry Clay of Ky. submitted to the Senate the following propositions, which were made a special order and printed:

"1. *Resolved*, That California, with suitable boundaries, ought, upon her application, to be admitted as one of the States of this Union, without the imposition by Congress of any restriction in respect to the exclusion or introduction of Slavery within those boundaries.

"2. *Resolved*, That as Slavery does not exist by law, and is not likely to be introduced into any of the territory acquired by the United States from the Republic of Mexico, it is inexpedient for Congress to provide by law either for its introduction into, or exclusion from, any part of the said territory; and that appropriate territorial governments ought to be established by Congress in all the said territory, not assigned as within the boundaries of the proposed State of California, without the adoption of any restriction or condition on the subject of Slavery.

"3. *Resolved*, That the western boundary of the State of Texas ought to be fixed on the Rio del Norte, commencing one marine league from its mouth, and running up that river to the southern line of New-Mexico; thence with that line eastwardly, and so continuing in the same direction to the line as established between the United States and Spain, excluding any portion of New-Mexico, whether lying on the east or west of that river.

"4. *Resolved*, That it be proposed to the State of Texas, that the United States will provide for the payment of all that portion of the legitimate and *bona fide* public debt of that State contracted prior to its annexation to the United States, and for which the duties on foreign imports were pledged by the said State to its creditors, not exceeding the sum of —— dollars, in consideration of the said duties so pledged having been no longer applicable to that object after the said annexation, but having thenceforward become payable to the United States; and upon the condition, also, that the said State of Texas shall, by some solemn and authentic act of her legislature, or of a convention, relinquish to the United States any claim which she has to any part of New-Mexico.

"5. *Resolved*, That it is inexpedient to abolish Slavery in the District of Columbia whilst that institution continues to exist in the State of Maryland, without the consent of that State, without the consent of the people of the District, and without just compensation to the owners of Slaves within the District.

"6. *But Resolved*, that it *is* expedient to prohibit, within the District, the slave trade in slaves brought into it from States or places beyond the limits of the District, either to be sold therein as merchandise, or to be transported to other markets without the District of Columbia.

"7. *Resolved*, That more effectual provision ought to be made by law, according to the requirement of the Constitution, for the restitution and delivery of persons bound to service or labor in any State, who may escape into any other State or Territory in the Union. And,

"8. *Resolved*, That Congress has no power to prohibit or obstruct the trade in slaves between the Slaveholding States, but that the admission or exclusion of Slaves brought from one into another of them, depends exclusively upon their own particular laws."

Feb. 28th.—Mr. John Bell of Tenn. submitted to the Senate the following propositions:

"*Whereas*, Considerations of the highest interest to the whole country demand that the existing and increasing dissensions between the North and the South, on the subject of Slavery, should be speedily arrested, and that the questions in controversy be adjusted upon some basis which shall tend to give present quiet, repress sectional animosities, remove, as far as possible, the causes of future discord, and secure the uninterrupted enjoyment of those benefits and advantages which the Union was intended to confer in equal measure upon all its members;

"*And, whereas*, It is manifest, under present circumstances, that no adjustment can be effected of the points of difference unhappily existing between the Northern and Southern sections of the Union, connected with the subject of Slavery, which shall secure to either section all that is contended for, and that mutual concessions upon questions of mere policy, not involving the violation of any constitutional right or principle, must be the basis of every project affording any assurance of a favorable acceptance;

"*And, whereas*, The joint resolution for annexing Texas to the United States, approved March 1, 1845, contains the following condition and guarantee—that is to say: 'New States of convenient size, not exceeding four in number, in addition to said State of Texas, and having sufficient population, may hereafter, by the consent of said State, be formed out of the territory thereof, which shall be entitled to admission under the provisions of the Federal Constitution; and such States as may be formed out of that portion of said territory lying south of thirty-six degrees thirty minutes north latitude, commonly known as the Missouri Compromise line, shall be admitted into the Union with or without Slavery, as the people of each State asking admission may desire; and in such State or States as shall be formed out of said territory north of said Missouri Compromise line, Slavery, or involuntary servitude (except for crime), shall be prohibited:' Therefore,

"1. *Resolved*, That the obligation to comply with the condition and guarantee above recited in good faith be distinctly recognized; and that, in part compliance with the same, as soon as the people of Texas shall, by an act of their legislature, signify their assent by restricting the limits thereof, within the territory lying east of the Trinity and south of the Red River, and when the people of the residue of the territory claimed by Texas adopt a constitution, republican in form, they be admitted into the Union upon an equal footing in all respects with the original States.

"2. *Resolved*, That if Texas shall agree to cede, the United States will accept, a cession of all the unappropriated domain in all the territory claimed by Texas, lying west of the Colorado and extending north to the forty-second parallel of north latitude, together with the jurisdiction and sovereignty of all the territory claimed by Texas, north of the thirty-fourth parallel of north latitude, and to pay therefor a sum not exceeding —— millions of dollars, to be applied in the first place to the extinguishment of any portion of the existing public debt of Texas, for the discharge of which the United States are under any obligation, implied or otherwise, and the remainder as Texas shall require.

"3. *Resolved*, That when the population of that portion of the territory claimed by Texas, lying south of the thirty-fourth parallel of north latitude and west of the Colorado, shall be equal to the ratio of representation in Congress, under the last preceding apportionment, according to the provisions of the Constitution, and the people of such territory shall, with the assent of the new State contemplated in the preceding resolution, have adopted a State Constitution, republican in form, they be admitted into the Union as a State, upon an equal footing with the original States.

"4. *Resolved*, That all the territory now claimed by Texas, lying north of the thirty-fourth parallel of north latitude, and which may be ceded to the United States by Texas, be incorporated with the Territory of New-Mexico, except such part thereof as lies east of the Rio Grande and south of the thirty-fourth degree of north latitude, and that the Territory so composed form a State, to be admitted into the Union when the inhabitants thereof shall adopt a State Constitution, republican in form, with the consent of Congress; but, in the mean time, and until Congress shall give such consent, provision be made for the government of the inhabitants of said Territory suitable to their condition, but without any restriction as to Slavery.

"5. *Resolved*, That all the territory ceded to the United States, by the Treaty of Guadaloupe Hidalgo, lying west of said Territory of New-Mexico, and east of the contemplated new State of California, for the present, constitute one Territory, and for which some form of government suitable to the condition of the inhabitants be provided, without any restriction as to Slavery.

"6. *Resolved*, That the constitution recently formed by the people of the western portion of California, and presented to Congress by the President on the 13th day of February, 1850, be accepted, and that they be admitted into the Union as a State, upon an equal footing in all respects with the original States.

"7. *Resolved*, That, in future, the formation of State Constitutions, by the inhabitants of the territories of the United States, be regulated by law; and that no such constitution be hereafter formed or adopted by the inhabitants of any Territory belonging to the United States, without the consent and authority of Congress.

"8. *Resolved*, That the inhabitants of any Territory of the United States, when they shall be authorized by Congress to form a State Constitution, shall have the sole and exclusive power to regulate and adjust all questions of internal State policy, of whatever nature they may be, controlled only by the restrictions expressly imposed by the Constitution of the United States.

"9. *Resolved*, That the Committee on Territories be instructed to report a bill in conformity with the spirit and principles of the foregoing resolutions."

A debate of unusual duration, earnestness, and ability ensued, mainly on Mr. Clay's Resolutions. They were regarded by uncompromising champions, whether of Northern or of Southern views, but especially of the latter, as conceding substantially the matter in dispute to the other side. Thus,

Jan. 29th.—Mr. Clay having read and briefly commented on his propositions, *seriatim*, he desired that they should be held over without debate, to give time for consideration, and made a special order for Monday or Tuesday following. But this was not assented to.

Mr. Rusk rose at once to protest against that portion of them which called in question the right of Texas to so much of New-Mexico as lies east of the Rio del Norte.

Mr. Foote of Miss. spoke against them generally, saying:

"If I understand the resolutions properly, they are objectionable, as it seems to me,

"1. Because they only assert that it is not *expedient* that Congress should abolish Slavery in the District of Columbia; thus allowing the implication to arise that Congress has power to legislate on the subject of Slavery in the District, which may hereafter be exercised, if it should become expedient to do so; whereas, I hold that Congress has, under the Constitution, no such power at all, and that any attempt thus to legislate would be a gross fraud upon all the States of the Union.

"2. The Resolutions of the honorable Senator assert that Slavery does not now exist by law in the territories recently acquired from Mexico; whereas, I am of opinion that the treaty with the Mexican republic carried the Constitution, *with all its guaranties*, to all the territory obtained by treaty, and secured the privilege to every Southern slaveholder to enter any part of it, attended by his slave-property, and to enjoy the same therein, free from all molestation or hindrance whatsoever.

"3. Whether Slavery is or is not likely to be introduced into these territories, or into any of them, is a proposition too uncertain, in my judgment, to be at present positively affirmed; and I am unwilling to make a solemn legislative declaration on the point. *Let the future provide the appropriate solution of this interesting question.*

"4. Considering, as I have several times heretofore formally declared, the title of Texas to all the territory embraced in her boundaries, as laid down in her law of 1836, full, complete, and undeniable, I am unwilling to say anything, by resolution or otherwise, which may in the least degree draw that title into question, as I think is done in one of the resolutions of the honorable Senator from Kentucky.

"5. I am, upon constitutional and other grounds, wholly opposed to the principle of *assuming State debts*, which I understand to be embodied in one of the resolutions of the honorable Senator from Kentucky. If Texan soil is to be bought, (and with certain appropriate *safeguards*, I am decidedly in favor of it,) let us pay to the sovereign State of Texas the value thereof in money, to be used by her as she pleases. It will be, as I think, more delicate and respectful to let her provide for the management of this matter, which is strictly *domestic* in its character, in such manner as she may choose—presuming that she will act wisely, justly, and honorably toward all to whom she may be indebted.

"6. As to the abolition of the *slave-trade* in the District of Columbia, I see no particular objection to it, provided it is done in a delicate and judicious manner, and is not a concession to the menaces and demands of factionists and fanatics. If other questions can be adjusted, this one will, perhaps, occasion but little difficulty.

"7. The resolutions which provide for the restoration of fugitives from labor or service, and for the establishment of territorial governments, free from all restriction on the subject of Slavery, have my hearty approval. The last resolution—which asserts that Congress has no power to prohibit the trade in Slaves from State to State—I equally approve.

"8. If all other questions connected with the subject of Slavery can be satisfactorily adjusted, I can see no objection to admitting all California, above the line of 36 deg. 30 min., into the Union; *provided another new Slave State can be laid off within the present limits of Texas*, so as to keep the present *equiponderance* between the Slave and Free States of the Union; and provided further, all this is done by way of *compromise*, and in order to save the Union, (as dear to me as to any man living.")

Mr. Mason of Va., after expressing his deep anxiety to "go with him who went furthest, but within the limits of strict duty, in adjusting these unhappy differences," added:

"Sir, so far as I have read these resolutions, there is but one proposition to which I can give a hearty assent, and that is the resolution which proposes to organize Territorial governments at once in these Territories, without a declaration one way or the other as to their domestic institutions. But there is another which I deeply regret to see introduced into this Senate, by a Senator from a slaveholding State; it is that which assumes that Slavery does not now exist by law in those countries. I understand one of these propositions to declare that, by law, Slavery is now abolished in New-Mexico and California. That was the very proposition advanced by the non-slaveholding

States at the last session; combated and disproved, as I thought, by gentlemen from the slaveholding States, and which the Compromise bill was framed to test. So far, I regarded the question of law as disposed of, and it was very clearly and satisfactorily shown to be against the spirit of the resolution of the Senator from Kentucky. If the contrary is true, I presume the Senator from Kentucky would declare that if a law is now valid in the Territories abolishing Slavery, that it could not be introduced there, even if a law was passed creating the institution, or repealing the statutes already existing; a doctrine never assented to, so far as I know, until now, by any Senator representing one of the slaveholding States. Sir, I hold the very opposite, and with such confidence, that at the last session I was willing and did vote for a bill to test this question in the Supreme Court. Yet this resolution assumes the other doctrine to be true, and our assent is challenged to it as a proposition of law.

"I do not mean to detain the Senate by any discussion; but I deemed it to be my duty to enter a decided protest, on the part of Virginia, against such doctrines. They concede the whole question at once, that our people shall not go into the new Territories and take their property with them; a doctrine to which I never will assent, and for which, sir, no law can be found. There are other portions of the resolutions, for which, if they could be separated, I should be very willing to vote. That respecting fugitive slaves, and that respecting the organization of governments in these Territories, I should be willing to vote for; and I am happy to declare the gratification I experience at finding the Senator from Kentucky differing so much, on this subject, from the Executive message recently laid before the Senate. I beg not to be understood as having spoken in any spirit of unkindness towards the Senator from Kentucky, for whom I entertain the warmest and most profound respect; but I cannot but express also my regret that he has felt it to be his duty, standing as he does before this people, and representing the people he does, to introduce into this body resolutions of this kind."

Mr. Jefferson Davis of Miss. (since and now Secretary of War) objected specially to so much of Mr. Clay's propositions as relates to the boundary of Texas, to the Slave-trade in the Federal district, and to Mr. Clay's avowal in his speech that he did not believe Slavery ever would or could be established in any part of the territories acquired from Mexico. He continued:

"But, sir, we are called upon to receive this as a measure of compromise! As a measure in which we of the minority are to receive nothing. A measure of compromise! I look upon it as but a modest mode of taking that, the claim to which has been more boldly asserted by others; and, that I may be understood upon this question, and that my position may go forth to the country in the same columns that convey the sentiments of the Senator from Kentucky, I here assert, that never will I take less than the Missouri Compromise line extended to the Pacific ocean, with the specific recognition of the right to hold slaves in the territory below that line; and that, before such territories are admitted into the Union as States, slaves may be taken there from any of the United States at the option of the owners. I can never consent to give additional power to a majority to commit further aggressions upon the minority in this Union; and will never consent to any proposition which will have such a tendency, without a full guaranty or counteracting measure is connected with it."

Mr. Clay in reply said:

"I am extremely sorry to hear the Senator from Mississippi say that he requires, first, the extension of the Missouri Compromise line to the Pacific; and also that he is not satisfied with that, but requires, if I understood him correctly, a positive provision for the admission of Slavery south of that line. And now, sir, coming from a Slave State, as I do, I owe it to myself, I owe it to truth, I owe it to the subject, to state that no earthly power could induce me to vote for a specific measure for the introduction of Slavery where it had not before existed, either south or north of that line. Coming as I do from a Slave State, it is my solemn, deliberate, and well-matured determination that no power—no earthly power—shall compel me to vote for the positive introduction of Slavery either south or north of that line. Sir, while you reproach, and justly, too, our British ancestors for the introduction of this institution upon the continent of America, I am, for one, unwilling that the posterity of the present inhabitants of California and of New-Mexico shall reproach us for doing just what we reproach Great Britain for doing to us. If the citizens of those Territories choose to establish Slavery, I am for admitting them with such provisions in their constitutions; but then, it will be their own work, and not ours, and their posterity will have to reproach them, and not us, for forming constitutions allowing the institution of Slavery to exist among them. These are my views, sir, and I choose to express them; and I care not how extensively and universally they are known. The honorable Senator from Virginia has expressed his opinion that Slavery exists in these Territories, and I have no doubt that opinion is sincerely and honestly entertained by him; and I would say with equal sincerity and honesty, that I believe that Slavery nowhere exists within any portion of the Territory acquired by us from Mexico. He holds a directly contrary opinion to mine, as he has a perfect right to do; and we will not quarrel about that difference of opinion."

Mr. William R. King of Ala. was inclined to look with favor on Mr. Clay's propositions, and assented to some of them; but he objected to the mode in which California had formed what is called a State Constitution. He preferred the good old way of first organizing Territories, and so training up their people "for the exercise and enjoyment of our institutions." Besides, he thought "there was not that kind of population there that justified the formation of a State Government." On the question of Slavery in the new Territories, he said:

"With regard to the opinions of honorable Senators, respecting the operation of the laws of Mexico in our newly-acquired territories, there may be, and no doubt is, an honest difference of opinion with regard to that matter. Some believe that the municipal institutions of Mexico overrule the provisions of our Constitution, and prevent us from carrying our slaves there. That is a matter which I do not propose to discuss; it has been discussed at length in the debate upon the Compromise bill, putting it on the ground of a judicial decision. Sir, I know not—nor is it a matter of much importance with me—whether that which the honorable Senator states to be a fact, and which, as has been remarked by the Senator from Mississippi, can only be conjectural, be in reality so or not—that Slavery never can go there. This is what is stated, however. Well, be it so. If slave labor be not profitable there, it will not go there; or, if it go, who will be benefited? Not the South. They will never compel it to go there. We are misunderstood—grossly, I may say—by honorable Senators, though not intentionally; but we are contending for a principle, and a great principle—a principle lying at the very foundation of our constitutional rights—involving, as has been remarked, our property; in one word, involving our safety, our honor, all that is dear to us, as American freemen. Well, sir, for that principle we will be compelled to contend to the utmost, and to resist aggression at every hazard and at every sacrifice. That is the position in which we are placed. We ask no act of Congress—as has been properly intimated by the Senator from Mississippi—to carry Slavery anywhere. Sir, I believe we have as much constitutional power to prohibit Slavery from going into the territories of the United States, as we have to pass an act carrying Slavery there. We have no right to do either the one or the other. I would as soon vote for the Wilmot Proviso as I would vote for any law which required that Slavery should go into any of the Territories."

Mr. Downs of Louisiana said:

"I must confess that, in the whole course of my life, my astonishment has never been greater than it was when I saw this [Mr. Clay's] proposition brought forward as a compromise; and I rise now, sir, not for the purpose of discussing it at all, but to protest most solemnly against it. I consider this compromise as no compromise at all. What, sir, does it grant to the South? I can see nothing at all. The first resolution offered by the honorable Senator proposes to admit the State of California with a provision prohibiting Slavery in territory which embraces all our possessions on the Pacific. It is true, there may be a new regulation of the boundary hereafter; but, if there were to be such a regulation, why was it not embraced in this resolution? As no boundary is mentioned, we have a right to presume that the boundary established by the Constitution of California was to be received as the established boundary. What concession, then, is it from the North, that we admit a State thus prohibiting Slavery, embracing the whole of our possessions on the Pacific coast, according to these resolutions? As to the resolution relating to New-Mexico and Deseret, if it had simply contained the provision that a constitutional government shall be established there, without any mention of Slavery whatever, it would have been well enough. But, inasmuch as it is affirmed that Slavery does not now exist in these Territories, does it not absolutely preclude its admission there? and the resolutions might just as well affirm that Slavery should be prohibited in these Territories. The Senator from Alabama, if I understood him aright, maintains that the proposition is of the same import as the Wilmot Proviso; and, in view of these facts, I would ask, is there anything conceded to us of the South?"

Mr. Butler of South Carolina said:

"Perhaps our Northern brethren ought to understand that all the Compromises that have been made, have been by concessions—acknowledged concessions—on the part of the South. When other compromises are proposed, that require new concessions on their part, whilst none are exacted on the other, the issue, at least, should be presented for their consideration before they come to the decision of their great question. If I understand it, the Senator from Kentucky's whole proposition of compromise is nothing more than this: That California is already disposed of having formed a State Constitution, and tha. Territorial Governments shall be organized for Deseret and New-Mexico, under which, by the operation of laws already existing, a slaveholding population could not carry with them, or own slaves there. What is there in the nature of a compromise here, coupled, as it is, with the proposition that, by the existing laws in the Territories, it is almost certain that slaveholders cannot, and have no right to, go there with their property? What is there in the nature of a compromise here? I am willing, however, to run the risks, and am ready to give to the Territories the governments they require. I shall always think that, under a constitution giving equal rights to all parties, the slaveholding people, as such, can go to these Territories, and retain their property there. But, if we adopt this proposition of the Senator from Kentucky, it is clearly on the basis that Slavery shall not go there.

"I do not understand the Senator from Mississippi (Mr. Davis) to maintain the proposition, that the South asked or desired a law declaring that Slavery should go there, or that it maintained the policy even that it was the duty of Congress to pass such a law. We have only asked, and it is the only compromise to which we will submit, that Congress shall withhold the hand of violence from the Territories. The only way in which this question can be settled is, for gentlemen from the North to withdraw all their opposition to the Territorial Governments, and not insist on their Slavery Prohibition. The Union is then safe enough. Why, then, insist on a compromise, when those already made are sufficient for the peace of the North and South, if faithfully observed? These propositions are in the name of a compromise, when none is necessary."

The debate having engrossed the attention of the Senate for nearly two months—

March 25th.—Mr. Douglas, from the Committee on Territories, reported the following bills:

Senate, 169.—A bill for the admission of California into the Union.

Senate, 170.—A bill to establish the Territorial Governments of Utah and New-Mexico, and for other purposes.

These bills were read, and passed to a second reading.

April 11th.—Mr. Douglas moved that Mr. Bell's resolves do lie on the table. Lost: Yeas 26; Nays 28.

April 15th.—The discussion of Mr. Clay's resolutions still proceeding, Colonel Benton moved that the previous orders be postponed, and that the Senate now proceed to consider the bill (S. 169) for the admission of the State of California.

Mr. Clay moved that this proposition do lie on the table. Carried: Yeas 27 (for a Compromise); Nays 24 (for a settlement without compromise).

The Senate now took up Mr. Bell's resolves aforesaid, when Mr. Benton moved that they lie on the table. Lost: Yeas 24; Nays 28.

Mr. Benton next moved that they be so amended as not to connect or mix up the admission of California with any other question. Lost: Yeas 23; Nays 28.

Various modifications of the generic idea were severally voted down, generally by large majorities.

On motion of Mr. Foote of Miss., it was now

"*Ordered*, That the resolution submitted by Mr. Bell on the 28th February, together with the resolutions submitted on the 29th of January by Mr. Clay, be referred to a Select Committee of thirteen; *Provided*, that the Senate does not deem it necessary, and therefore declines, to express in advance any opinion, or to give any instruction, either general or specific, for the guidance of the said Committee."

April 19*th*.—The Senate proceeded to elect by ballot such Select Committee, which was composed as follows:

Mr. Henry Clay of Ky. *Chairman.*

Messrs. Dickinson of N. Y.	Cooper of Pa.
Phelps of Vt.	Downs of La.
Bell of Tenn.	King of Ala.
Cass of Mich.	Mangum of N. C.
Webster of Mass.	Mason of Va.
Berrien of Ga.	Bright of Ind.

May 8*th*.—Mr. Clay, from said Committee, reported as follows:

REPORT.

The Senate's Committee of thirteen, to whom were referred various resolutions relating to California, to other portions of the territory recently acquired by the United States from the Republic of Mexico, and to other subjects connected with the institution of Slavery, have, according to order, had these resolutions and subjects under consideration, and beg leave to submit the following Report:

The Committee entered on the discharge of their duties with a deep sense of their great importance, and with earnest and anxious solicitude to arrive at such conclusions as might be satisfactory to the Senate and to the country. Most of the matters referred have not only been subjected to extensive and serious public discussion throughout the country, but to a debate in the Senate itself, singular for its elaborateness and its duration; so that a full exposition of all those motives and views which, on several subjects confided to the Committee, have determined the conclusions at which they have arrived, seems quite unnecessary. They will, therefore, restrict themselves to a few general observations, and to some reflections which grow out of those subjects.

Out of our recent territorial acquisitions, and in connection with the institution of Slavery, questions most grave sprung, which, greatly dividing and agitating the people of the United States, have threatened to disturb the harmony, if not to endanger the safety, of the Union. The Committee believe it to be highly desirable and necessary speedily to adjust all those questions, in a spirit of concord, and in a manner to produce, if practicable, general satisfaction. They think it would be unwise to leave any of them open and unsettled, to fester in the public mind, and to prolong, if not aggravate, the existing agitation. It has been their object, therefore, in this Report, to make such proposals and recommendations as would accomplish a general adjustment of all these questions.

Among the subjects referred to the Committee which command their first attention, are the resolutions offered to the Senate by the Senator from Tennessee, Mr. Bell. By a provision in the resolution of Congress annexing Texas to the United States, it is declared that "new States of convenient size, not exceeding four in number, by the consent of said State, be formed out of the territory thereof, which shall be *entitled to admission*, under the provisions of the Federal Constitution; and such States as may be formed out of that portion of said territory lying South of 36° 30′ North latitude, commonly known as the Missouri Compromise line, *shall be* admitted into the Union with or without Slavery, as the people of each State asking admission may desire."

The Committee are unanimously of opinion, that whenever one or more States, formed out of the territory of Texas, not exceeding four, having sufficient population, with the consent of Texas, may apply to be admitted into the Union, they are entitled to such admission, beyond all doubt, upon the clear, unambiguous, and absolute terms of the solemn compact contained in the Resolution of Annexation adopted by Congress, and assented to by Texas. But, whilst the Committee conceive that the right of admission into the Union of any new State, carved out of the Territory of Texas, not exceeding the number specified, and under the conditions stated, cannot be justly controverted, the Committee do not think that the formation of any new States should now originate with Congress. The initiative, in conformity with the usage which has hitherto prevailed, should be taken by a portion of the people of Texas themselves, desirous of constituting a new State, with the consent of Texas. And in the formation of such new States, it will be, for the people composing it to decide for themselves whether they will admit, or whether they will exclude, Slavery. And however they may decide that purely municipal question, Congress is bound to acquiesce, and to fulfill in good faith the stipulations of the compact with Texas. The Committee are aware that it has been contended that the resolution of Congress annexing Texas was unconstitutional. At a former epoch of our country's history, there were those (and Mr. Jefferson, under whose auspices the treaty of Louisiana was concluded, was among them,) who believed that the States formed out of Louisiana could not be received into the Union without an amendment of the constitution. But the States of Louisiana, Missouri, Arkansas, and Iowa have been all, nevertheless, admitted. And who would now think of opposing Minnesota, Oregon, or new States formed out of the ancient province of Louisiana, upon the ground of an alleged original defect of constitutional power? In grave national transactions, while yet in their earlier or incipient stages, differences may well exist; but when once they have been decided by a constitutional majority, and are consummated, or in a process of consummation, there can be no other safe and prudent alternative than to respect the decision already rendered, and to acquiesce in it. Entertaining these views, a majority of the Committee do not think it necessary or proper to recommend, at this time, or prospectively, any new State or States to be formed out of the territory of Texas. Should any such State be hereafter formed, and present itself for admission into the Union, whether with or without the establishment of Slavery, it cannot be doubted that Congress will admit it, under the influence of similar considerations, in regard to new States formed of or out of New-Mexico and Utah, with or without the institution of Slavery, according to the constitutions and judgment of the people who compose them, as to what may be best to promote their happiness.

In considering the question of the admission of California as a State into the Union, a majority of the Committee conceive that any irregularity, by which that State was organized without the previous authority of an act of Congress, ought to be overlooked, in consideration of the omission by Congress to establish any territorial government for the people of California, and the consequent necessity which they were under to create a government for themselves, best adapted to their own wants. There are various instances, prior to the case of California, of the admission of new States into the Union without any previous authorization by Congress. The sole condition required by the Constitution of the United States, in respect to the admission of a new State, is, that its constitution shall be republican in form. California presents such a constitution; and there is no doubt of her having a greater population than that which, according to the practice of the government, has been heretofore deemed sufficient to receive a new State into the Union.

In regard to the proposed boundaries of California, the Committee would have been glad if there existed more full and accurate geographical knowledge of the territory which these boundaries include. There is reason to believe that, large as they are, they embrace no very disproportionate quantity of land adapted to cultivation. And it is known that they contain extensive ranges of mountains, deserts of sand, and much unproductive soil. It might have been, perhaps, better to have assigned to California a more limited front on the Pacific; but even if there had been reserved, on the shore of that ocean, a portion of the boundary which it presents, for any other State or States, it is not very certain that an accessible interior of sufficient extent could have been given to them to render an approach to the ocean, through their own limits, of very great importance.

A majority of the Committee think that there are many and urgent concurring considerations in favor of admitting California, with the proposed boundaries, and of securing to her at this time the benefits of a State government. If, hereafter, upon an increase of her population, a more thorough exploration of her territory, and an ascertainment of the relations which may arise between the people occupying its various parts, it should be found conducive to their convenience and happiness to form a new State out of California, we have every reason to believe, from past experience, that the question of its admission will be fairly considered and justly decided.

A majority of the Committee, therefore, recommend to the Senate the passage of the bill reported by the Committee on Territories, for the admission of California as a State into the Union. To prevent misconception, the Committee also recommend that the amendment reported by the same Committee to the bill be adopted, so as to leave incontestable the right of the United States to the public domain and other public property of California.

Whilst a majority of the Committee believe it to be necessary and proper, under actual circumstances, to admit California, they think it quite as necessary and proper to establish governments for the residue of the territory derived from Mexico, and to bring it within the pale of the federal authority. The remoteness of that territory from the seat of the general government; the dispersed state of its population; the variety of races—pure and mixed—of which it consists; the ignorance of some of the races of our laws, language, and habits; their exposure to inroads and wars of savage tribes; and the solemn stipulations of the treaty by which we acquired dominion over them—impose upon the United States the imperative obligation of extending to them protection, and of providing for them government and laws suited to their condition. Congress will fail in the performance of a high duty, if it do not give, or attempt to give to them, the benefit of such protection, government, and laws. They are not now, and for a long time to come may not be, prepared for State government. The territorial form, for the present, is best suited to their condition. A bill has been reported by the Committee on Territories, dividing all the territory acquired from Mexico, not comprehended within the limits of California, into two territories, under the names of New-Mexico and Utah, and proposing for each a territorial government.

The Committee recommend to the Senate the establishment of those territorial governments; and, in order more certainly to secure that desirable object, they also recommend that the bill for their establishment be incorporated in the bill for the admission of California, and that, united together, they both be passed.

The combination of the two measures in the same bill is objected to on various grounds. It is said that they are incongruous, and have no necessary connection with each other. A majority of the Committee think otherwise. The object of both measures is the establishment of a government suited to the conditions, respectively, of the proposed new State and of the new Territories. Prior to their transfer to the United States, they both formed a part of Mexico, where they stood in equal relations to the government of that republic. They were both ceded to the United States by the same treaty. And, in the same article of that treaty, the United States engaged to protect and govern both. Common in their origin, common in their alienation from one foreign government to another, common in their wants of good government, and conterminous in some of their boundaries, and alike in many particulars of physical condition, they have nearly everything in common in the relation in which they stand to the rest of this Union. There is, then, a general fitness and propriety in extending the parental care of government to both in common. If California, by a sudden and extraordinary augmentation of population, has advanced so rapidly as to mature for herself a State Government, that furnishes no reason why the less fortunate Territories of New-Mexico and Utah should be abandoned and left ungoverned by the United States, or should be disconnected with California, which, although she has organized for herself a State Government, must, legally and constitutionally, be regarded as a Territory until she is actually admitted as a State into the Union.

It is further objected that, by combining the two measures in the same bill, members who may be willing to vote for one, and unwilling to vote for the other, would be placed in an embarrassing condition. They would be constrained, it is urged, to take or reject both. On the other hand, there are other members who would be willing to vote for both united, but would feel themselves constrained to vote against the California bill if it stood alone. Each party finds in the bill which it favors something which commends it to acceptance, and in the other something which it disapproves. The true ground, therefore, of the objection to the union of the measures is not any want of affinity between them, but because of the favor or disfavor with which they are respectively regarded. In this conflict of opinion, it seems to a majority of the Committee that a spirit of mutual concession enjoins that the two measures should be connected together—the effect of which will be, that neither opinion will exclusively triumph, and that both may find, in such an amicable arrangement, enough of good to reconcile them to the acceptance of the combined measure. And such a course of legisla tion is not at all unusual. Few laws have ever passed in which there were not parts to which exception was taken. It is inexpedient, if not impracticable, to separate these parts, and embody them in distinct bills, so as to accommodate the diversity of opinion which may exist. The Constitution of the United States contained in it a great variety of provisions, to some of which serious objection was made in the convention which formed it, by different members of that body; and, when it was submitted to the ratification of the States, some of them objected to some parts, and others to other parts, of the same instrument. Had these various parts and provisions been separately acted on in the convention, or separately submitted to the people of the United States, it is by no means certain that the Constitution itself would ever have been adopted or ratified. Those who did not like particular provisions found compensation in other parts of it. And in all cases of constitution and laws, when either is presented as a whole, the question to be decided is, whether the good which it contains is not of greater amount, and capable of neutralizing anything objectionable in it. And, as nothing human is perfect, for the sake of that harmony so desirable in such a confederacy as this, we must be reconciled to secure as much as we can of what we wish, and be consoled by the reflection that what we do not exactly like is a friendly concession, and agreeable to those who, being united with us in a common destiny, it is desirable, should always live with us in peace and concord.

A majority of the Committee have, therefore, been led to the recommendation to the Senate that the two measures be united. The bill for establishing the two Territories, it will be observed, omits the Wilmot proviso on the one hand, and, on the other, makes no provision for the introduction of Slavery into any part of the new Territories.

That proviso has been the fruitful source of distraction and agitation. If it were adopted and applied to any Territory, it would cease to have any obligatory force as soon as such Territory were admitted as a State into the Union. There was never any occasion for it to accomplish the professed object with which it was originally offered. This has been clearly demonstrated by the current of events. California, of all the recent territorial acquisitions from Mexico, was that in which, if anywhere within them, the introduction of Slavery was most likely to take place; and the constitution of California, by the unanimous vote of her convention, has expressly interdicted it. There is the highest degree of probability that Utah and New-Mexico will, when they come to be admitted as States, follow the example. The proviso is, as to all those regions in common, a mere abstraction. Why should it be any longer insisted on? Totally destitute as it is of any practical import, it has, nevertheless, had the pernicious effect to excite serious, if not alarming, consequences. It is high time that the wounds which it has inflicted should be healed up and closed. And, to avoid, in all future time, the agitations which must be produced by the conflict of opinion on the Slavery question, existing as this institution does in some of the States, and prohibited as it is in others, the true principle which ought to regulate the action of Congress in forming Territorial Governments for each newly-acquired domain, is to refrain from all legislation on the subject in the Territory acquired, so long as it retains the Territorial form of Government—leaving it to the people of such Territory, when they have attained to the condition which entitles them to admission as a State, to decide for themselves the question of the allowance or prohibition of domestic Slavery. The Committee believe that they express the anxious desire of an immense majority of the people of the United States, when they declare that it is high time that good feeling, harmony, and fraternal sentiment should be again revived, and that the Government should be able once more to proceed in its great operations to promote the happiness and prosperity of the country, undisturbed by this distracting cause.

As for California—far from seeing her sensibility affected by her being associated with other kindred measures—she ought to rejoice and be highly gratified that, in entering into the Union, she may have contributed to the tranquillity and happiness of the great family of States, of which, it is to be hoped, she may one day be a distinguished member.

The Committee beg leave next to report on the subject of the Northern and Western boundary of Texas. On that question a great diversity of opinion has prevailed. According to one view of it, the western limit of Texas was the Nueces; according to another, it extended to the Rio Grande, and stretched from its mouth to its source. A majority of the Committee having come to the conclusion of recommending an amicable adjustment of the boundary with Texas, abstain from expressing any opinion as to the true and legitimate western and northern boundary of that State. The terms proposed for such an adjustment are contained in the bill herewith reported, and they are, with inconsiderable variation, the same as that reported by the Committee on Territories.

According to these terms, it is proposed to Texas that her boundary be recognized to the Rio Grande, and up that river to the point commonly called El Paso, and thence running up that river twenty miles, measured thereon by a straight line, and thence eastwardly to a point where the hundredth degree of west longitude crosses Red River; being the southwest angle in the line designated between the United States and Mexico, and the same angle in the line of the territory set apart for the Indians by the United States.

If this boundary be assented to by Texas, she will be quieted to that extent in her title. And some may suppose that, in consideration of this concession by the United States, she might, without any other equivalent, relinquish any claim she has beyond the proposed boundary; that is, any claim to any part of New-Mexico. But, under the influence of sentiments of justice and great liberality, the bill proposes to Texas, for her relinquishment of any such claim, a large pecuniary equivalent. As a consideration for it, and considering that a portion of the debt of Texas was created on a pledge to her creditors of the duties on foreign imports, transferred by the resolution of Annexation to the United States, and now received and receivable in her treasury, a majority of the Committee recommend the payment of the sum of —— millions of dollars to Texas, to be applied in the first instance to the extinction of that portion of her debt for the reimbursement of which the duties on foreign imports were pledged as aforesaid, and the residue in such manner as she may direct. The sum is to be paid by the United States, in a stock, to be created, bearing five per cent. interest annually, payable half-yearly, at the treasury of the United States, and the principal reimbursable at the end of fourteen years.

According to an estimate which has been made, there are included in the territory to which it is proposed that Texas shall relinquish her claim, embracing that part of New-Mexico lying east of the Rio Grande, a little less than 124,933 square miles, and about 79,957,120 acres of land. From the proceeds of the sale of this land, the United States may ultimately be reimbursed a portion, if not the whole, of the amount of what is thus proposed to be advanced to Texas.

It cannot be anticipated that Texas will decline to accede to these liberal propositions; but if she should, it is to be distinctly understood that the title of the United States to any territory acquired from Mexico east of the Rio Grande will remain unimpaired, and in the same condition as if the proposals of adjustment now offered had never been made.

A majority of the Committee recommend to the Senate that the section containing these proposals to Texas shall be incorporated into the bill embracing the admission of California as a State, and the establishment of territorial governments for Utah and New-Mexico. The definition and establishment of the boundary between New-Mexico and Texas have an intimate and necessary connection with the establishment of a territorial government for New-Mexico. To form a territorial government for New-Mexico, without prescribing the limits of the Territory, would leave the work imperfect and incomplete, and might expose New-Mexico to serious controversy, if not dangerous collisions, with the State of Texas. And most, if not all, the considerations which unite in favor of combining the bill for the admission of California as a State and the Territorial bills, apply to the boundary question of Texas. By the union of the three measures, every question of difficulty and division which has arisen out of the territorial acquisitions from Mexico, will, it is hoped, be adjusted, or placed in a train of satisfactory adjustment. The Committee, availing themselves of the arduous and valuable labors of the Committee on Territories, report a bill, herewith annexed, (marked A,) embracing those three measures, the passage of which, uniting them together, they recommend to the Senate.

The Committee will now proceed to the consideration of, and to report upon, the subject of persons owing service or labor in one State escaping into another. The text of the Constitution is quite clear: "No person held to labor or service in one State, *under the laws thereof*, escaping into another, shall, in consequence of any law or regulation therein, be discharged from such service or labor, but *shall be delivered up* on the claim of the party to whom such service or labor is due." Nothing can be more explicit than this language —nothing more manifest than the right to demand, and the obligation to deliver up to the claimant, any such fugitive. And the Constitution addresses itself alike to the States composing the Union and to the General Government. If, indeed, there were any difference in the duty to enforce this portion of the Constitution between the States and the Federal Government, it is more clear that it is that of the former than of the latter. But it is the duty of both. It is well known and incontestable that citizens of slaveholding States encounter the greatest difficulty in obtaining the benefit of this provision of the Constitution.

The attempt to recapture a fugitive is almost always a subject of great irritation and excitement, and often leads to most unpleasant, if not perilous, collisions. An owner of a slave, it is quite notorious, cannot pursue his property, for the purpose of its recovery, in some of the States, without imminent personal hazard. This is a deplorable state of things, which ought to be remedied. The law of 1793 has been found wholly ineffectual, and requires more stringent enactments. There is especially a deficiency in the number of public functionaries authorized to afford aid in the seizure and arrest of fugitives. Various States have declined to afford aid and coöperation in the surrender of fugitives from labor, as the Committee believe, from a misconception of their duty, arising under the Constitution of the United States. It is true that a decision of the Supreme Court of the United States has given countenance to them in withholding their assistance. But the Committee cannot but believe that the intention of the Supreme Court has been misunderstood. They cannot but think that that Court merely meant that laws of the several States, which created obstacles in the way of the recovery of fugitives, were not authorized by the Constitution, and not that the State laws affording facilities in the recovery of fugitives were forbidden by that instrument. The non-slaveholding States, whatever sympathies any of their citizens may feel for persons who escape from other States, cannot discharge themselves from an obligation to enforce the Constitution of the United States. All parts of the instrument being dependent upon, and connected with, each other, ought to be fairly and justly enforced. If some States may seek to exonerate themselves from one portion of the Constitution, other States may endeavor to evade the performance of the other portions of it; and thus the instrument, in some of the most important provisions, might become inoperative and invalid.

But, whatever may be the conduct of individual States, the duty of the General Government is perfectly clear. That duty is, to amend the existing law, and provide an effectual remedy for the recovery of fugitives from service or labor. In devising such a remedy, Congress ought, whilst, on the one hand, securing to the owner the fair restoration of his property, effectually to guard, on the other, against any abuses in the application of that remedy.

In all cases of arrest, within a State, of persons charged with offenses; in all cases of the pursuit of fugitives from justice from one State to another State; in all cases of extradition, provided for by treaties between foreign powers—the proceeding uniformly is summary. It has never been thought necessary to apply, in cases of that kind, the forms and ceremonies of a final trial. And, when that trial does take place, it is in the State or country from which the party has fled, and not in that in which he has found refuge. By the express language of the Constitution, whether the fugitive is held to service or labor, or not, is to be determined *by the laws of the State from which he fled*; and, consequently, it is most proper that the tribunals of that State should expound and administer its own laws. If there have been any instances of abuse, in the erroneous arrest of fugitives from service or labor, the Committee have not obtained knowledge of them. They believe that none have occurred, and that such are not likely to occur. But, in order to guard against the possibility of their occurrence, the committee have prepared, and herewith report, a section, (marked B,) to be offered to the fugitive bill now before the Senate. According to this section, the owner of a fugitive from service or labor is, when practicable, to carry with him to the State in which the person is found a record from a competent tribunal, adjudicating the fact of elopement and slavery, with a general description of the fugitive. This record, properly attested and certified under the official seal of the court, being taken to the State where the person owing service or labor is found, is to be held competent and sufficient evidence of the facts which had been adjudicated, and will leave nothing more to be done than to identify the fugitive.

Numerous petitions have been presented praying for a trial by jury, in the case of arrest of fugitives from service or labor in the non-slaveholding States. It has been already shown that this would be entirely contrary to practice and uniform usage in all similar cases. Under the name of a popular and cherished institution—an institution, however, never applied in cases of preliminary proceeding, and only in cases of final trial—there would be a complete mockery of justice, so far as the owner of the fugitive is concerned. If the trial by jury be admitted, it would draw after it its usual consequences; of continuance from time to time, to bring evidence from distant places; of second or new trials, in cases where the jury is hung, or the verdict is set aside; and of revisals of the verdict and conduct of the juries by competent tribunals. During the progress of all these dilatory and expensive proceedings, what security is there as to the custody and forthcoming of the fugitive upon their termination? And if, finally, the claimant should be successful, contrary to what happens in ordinary litigation between free persons, he would have to bear all the burdens and expenses of the litigation, without indemnity, and would learn, by sad experience, that he had by far better abandon his right in the first instance, than to establish it at such unremunerated cost and heavy sacrifice.

But, whilst the Committee conceive that a trial by jury in a State where a fugitive from service or labor is recaptured, would be a virtual denial of justice to the claimant of such fugitive, and would be tantamount to a positive refusal to execute the provision of the Constitution, the same objections do not apply to such a trial in the State from which he fled. In the slaveholding States. full justice is administered, with entire fairness and impartiality, in cases of all actions for freedom. The person claiming his freedom is allowed to sue in *forma pauperis;* counsel is assigned him; time is allowed him to collect his witnesses and to attend the sessions of the court; and his claimant is placed under bond and security, or is divested of the possession during the progress of the trial, to insure the enjoyment of these privileges; and, if there be any leaning on the part of courts and juries, it is always to the side of the claimant for freedom.

In deference to the feelings and prejudices which prevail in non-slaveholding States, the Committee propose such a trial in the State from which the fugitive fled, in all cases where he declares to the officer giving the certificate for his return that he has a right to his freedom. Accordingly, the Committee have prepared, and report herewith, (marked C), two sections which they recommend should be incorporated in the fugitive bill, pending in the Senate. According to these sections, the claimant is placed under bond, and required to return the fugitive to that county in the State from which he fled, and there to take him before a competent tribunal, and allow him to assert and establish his freedom, if he can, affording to him for that purpose all needful facilities.

The Committee indulge the hope that if the Fugitive bill, with the proposed amendments, shall be passed by Congress, it will be effectual to secure the recovery of all fugitives from service or labor, and it will remove all causes of complaint which have hitherto been experienced on that irritating subject. But, if in its practical operation it shall be found insufficient, and if no adequate remedy can be devised for the restoration to their owners of fugitive slaves, those owners shall have a just title to indemnity out of the Treasury of the United States.

It remains to report upon the resolutions in relation to Slavery and the Slave-Trade in the District of Columbia. Without discussing the power of Congress to abolish Slavery within the District, in regard to which a diversity of opinion exists, the Committee are of opinion that it ought not to be abolished. It could not be done without indispensable conditions which are not likely to be agreed to. It could not be done without exciting great apprehension and alarm in the Slave States. If the power were exercised within this District, they would apprehend that, under some pretext or another, it might hereafter be attempted to be exercised within the slaveholding States. It is true that, at present, all such power within those States is almost unanimously disavowed and disclaimed in the Free States. But, experience in public affairs has too often shown that where there is a desire to do a particular thing, the power to accomplish it, sooner or later, will be found or assumed.

Nor does the number of Slaves within the District make the abolition of Slavery an object of any such consequence as appears to be attached to it in some parts of the Union. Since the retrocession of Alexandria county to Virginia on the south side of the Potomac, the District now consists only of Washington county on the north side of that river; and the returns of the decennary enumeration of the people of the United States show a rapidly progressing decrease in the number of slaves in Washington county. According to the census of 1830, the number was 4,505; and in 1840, it was reduced to 3,320; showing a reduction in ten years of nearly one-third. If it should continue in the same ratio, the number, according to the census now about to be taken, will be only a little upward of two thousand.

But a majority of the Committee think differently in regard to the Slave-Trade within the District. By that trade is meant the introduction of slaves from adjacent States into the District, for sale, or to be placed in dépôt for the purpose of subsequent sale or transportation to other and distant markets. That trade, a majority of the Committee are of opinion, ought to be abolished. Complaints have always existed against it, no less on the part of members of Congress from the South than on the part of members from the North. It is a trade sometimes exhibiting revolting spectacles, and one in which the people of the District have no interest, but, on the contrary, are believed to be desirous that it should be discontinued. Most, if not all, of the slaveholding States have, either in their constitutions or by penal enactments, prohibited a trade in slaves as merchandise within their respective jurisdictions. Congress, standing in regard to this District, on this subject, in a relation similar to that of the State Legislatures, to the people of the States, may safely follow the example of the States. The Committee have prepared, and herewith report, a bill for the abolition of that trade (marked D), the passage of which they recommend to the Senate. This bill has been framed after the model of what the law of Maryland was when the General Government was removed to Washington.

The views and recommendations contained in this report may be recapitulated in a few words:

1. The admission of any new State or States formed out of Texas to be postponed until they shall hereafter present themselves to be received into the Union, when it will be the duty of Congress fairly and faithfully to execute the compact with Texas, by admitting such new State or States;

2. The admission forthwith of California into the Union, with the boundaries which she has proposed;

3. The establishment of territorial governments, without the Wilmot Proviso, for New-Mexico and Utah, embracing all the territory recently acquired by the United States from Mexico, not contained in the boundaries of California;

4. The combination of these two last-mentioned measures in the same bill;

5. The establishment of the western and north-

ern boundaries of Texas, and the exclusion from her jurisdiction of all New-Mexico, with the grant to Texas of a pecuniary equivalent; and the section for that purpose to be incorporated in the bill admitting California and establishing territorial governments for Utah and New-Mexico;

6. More effectual enactments of law to secure the prompt delivery of persons bound to service or labor in one State, under the laws thereof, who escape into another State; and,

7. Abstaining from abolishing Slavery; but, under a heavy penalty, prohibiting the slave-trade in the District of Columbia.

If such of these several measures as require legislation should be carried out by suitable acts of Congress, all controversies to which our late territorial acquisitions have given rise, and all existing questions connected with the institution of Slavery, whether resulting from those acquisitions, or from its existence in the States and the District of Columbia, will be amicably settled and adjusted, in a manner, it is confidently believed, to give general satisfaction to an overwhelming majority of the people of the United States. Congress will have fulfilled its whole duty in regard to the vast country which, having been ceded by Mexico to the United States, has fallen under their dominion. It will have extended to it protection, provided for its several parts the inestimable blessing of free and regular government, adapted to their various wants, and placed the whole under the banner and the flag of the United States. Meeting courageously its clear and entire duty, Congress will escape the unmerited reproach of having, from considerations of doubtful policy, abandoned to an undeserved fate territories of boundless extent, with a sparse, incongruous, and alien, if not unfriendly population, speaking different languages, and accustomed to different laws, whilst that population is making irresistible appeals to the new sovereignty to which they have been transferred for protection, for government, for law, and for order.

The Committee have endeavored to present to the Senate a comprehensive plan of adjustment, which, removing all causes of existing excitement and agitation, leaves none open to divide the country and disturb the general harmony. The nation has been greatly convulsed, not by measures of general policy, but by questions of a sectional character, and, therefore, more dangerous, and more to be deprecated. It wants repose. It loves and cherishes the Union. And it is most cheering and gratifying to witness the outbursts of deep and abiding attachment to it, which have been exhibited in all parts of it, amidst all the trials through which we have passed, and are passing. A people so patriotic as those of the United States, will rejoice in an accommodation of all troubles and difficulties by which the safety of that Union might have been brought into the least danger. And, under the blessing of that Providence who, amidst all vicissitudes, has never ceased to extend to them His protecting care, His smiles, His blessings, they will continue to advance in population, power, and prosperity, and work out triumphantly the glorious problem of man's capacity for self-government.

The Senate proceeded to debate from day to day the provisions of the principal bill thus reported, commonly termed "the Omnibus."

June 28th.—Mr. Soulé of Louisiana moved that all south of 36° 30′ be cut off from California, and formed into a territory entitled South California, and that said territory "shall, when ready, able, and willing to become a State, and deserving to be such, be admitted with or without Slavery, as the people thereof shall desire, and make known through their Constitution."

This was rejected: Yeas 19 (all Southern); Nays 36.

July 10th.—The discussion was interrupted by the death of President Taylor. Millard Fillmore succeeded to the Presidency, and William R. King of Alabama was chosen President of the Senate, *pro tempore.*

July 15th.—The bill was reported to the Senate and amended so as to substitute "that Congress shall make no law establishing or prohibiting" Slavery in the new territories, instead of "in respect to" it. Yeas 27; Nays 25.

Mr. Seward moved to add at the end of the 37th section:

"But neither Slavery nor involuntary servitude shall be allowed in either of the Territories of New-Mexico or Utah, except on legal conviction for crime."

Which was negatived; Yeas and Nays not taken.

July 17th.—The Senate resumed the consideration of the "Omnibus bill."

Mr. Benton moved a change in the proposed boundary between Texas and New-Mexico. Rejected: Yeas 18; Nays 36.

Mr. Foote moved that the 34th parallel of north latitude be the northern boundary of Texas throughout. Lost: Yeas 20; Nays 34.

July 19th.—Mr. King moved that the parallel of 35° 30′ be the southern boundary of the State of California. Rejected: Yeas 20; Nays 37.

Mr. Davis of Mississippi moved 36° 30′. Rejected: Yeas 23; Nays 32.

July 23d.—Mr. Turney of Tenn. moved that the people of California be enabled to form a new State Constitution. Lost: Yeas 19; Nays 33.

Mr. Jeff. Davis of Mississippi moved to add:

"And that all laws and usages existing in said Territory, at the date of its acquisition by the United States, which deny or obstruct the right of any citizen of the United States to remove to, and reside in, said Territory, with any species of property legally held in any of the States of this Union, be, and are hereby declared to be, null and void."

This was rejected: Yeas 22; Nays 33.

YEAS—For Davis's amendment:

Messrs.	Atchison, Mo.	King, Ala.
	Barnwell, S. C.	Mangum, N. C.
	Bell, Tenn.	Mason, Va.
	Berrien, Ga.	Morton, Fla.
	Butler, S. C.	Pratt, Md.
	Clemens, Ala.	Rusk, Texas,
	Davis, Miss.	Sebastian, Ark.
	Dawson, Ga.	Soulé, La.
	Downs, La.	Turney, Tenn.
	Houston, Texas,	Underwood, Ky.
	Hunter, Va.	Yulee, Fla.—22.

NAYS—Against Davis's amendment:

Messrs. Badger, N. C., Baldwin, Conn., Benton, Mo., Bradbury, Me., Bright, Ind., Cass, Mich., Chase, Ohio., Clarke, R. I., Clay, Ky., Cooper, Pa., Davis, Mass., Dayton, N. J, Dickinson, N. Y., Dodge, Wisc., Dodge, Iowa, Felch, Mich., Foote, Miss., Greene, R. I., Hale, N. H., Hamlin, Me., Jones, Iowa, Miller, N. J., Norris, N. H., Pearce, Md., Seward, N. Y., Shields, Ill., Smith, Conn., Spruance, Del., Sturgeon, Pa., Upham, Vt., Wales, Del., Walker, Wisc., Whitcomb, Ind.—33.

July 24th.—Mr. Rusk moved that the Rio Grande del Norte be the western boundary of Texas throughout, as defined in her statute of limits. Rejected: Yeas 18 (all Southern); Nays 34 (Douglas not voting).

July 25th.—Mr. Hale moved that the true boundary of Texas be ascertained and conformed to, without prejudice on account of anything contained in this bill. Rejected: Yeas 23; Nays 30.

Mr. Benton moved an amendment intended to exclude from Texas every portion of New-Mexico. Rejected: Yeas 16; Nays 38.

July 26th.—Mr. Seward moved that New-Mexico be admitted as a State into the Union. Rejected: Yeas 1 (Seward); Nays 42.

July 29th.—Mr. Dayton of N. J. moved that the true northern boundary of Texas be ascertained and settled by an amicable suit before the Supreme Court. Rejected: Yeas 18; Nays 34.

Mr. Mason of Virginia moved that the proposed commissioners to settle the boundary of Texas be authorized, in case the true legal boundary be found impracticable, to agree on and fix a convenient compromise boundary. Lost, by a tie: Yeas 29; Nays 29.

Mr. Turney moved that no pecuniary consideration be given for any change from the rightful boundary of Texas. Rejected: Yeas 20; Nays 31.

July 30th.—Mr. Walker of Miss. moved that this bill do lie on the table. Lost: Yeas 25; Nays 32.

Mr. Dawson of Ga. now moved the following additional section:

"*And be it further enacted*, That, until such time as the boundary line between the State of Texas and the territory of the United States be agreed to by the Legislature of the State of Texas and the government of the United States, the Territorial government authorized by this act shall not go into operation east of the Rio Grande, nor shall any State be established for New-Mexico, embracing any territory east of the Rio Grande."

This prevailed by the following vote—30 to 28—and gave the death-blow to the "Omnibus Bill."

YEAS—For Dawson's amendment:

Messrs. Atchison, Badger, Barnwell, Bell, Berrien, Butler, Clay, Clemens, Cooper, Davis, Miss., Dawson, Dickinson, Dodge, Iowa, Downs, Foote, Houston, Hunter, Jones, King, Mangum, Mason, Morton, Phelps, Pratt, Rusk, Sebastian, Soule, Sturgeon, Turney, Yulee—30.

NAYS—Against Dawson's amendment:

Messrs. Baldwin, Benton, Bradbury, Bright, Chase, Clarke, Davis, Mass., Dayton, Dodge of Wisc., Douglas, Ewing, Felch, Greene, Hale, Hamlin, Miller, Norris, Pearce, Seward, Shields, Smith, Spruance, Underwood, Upham, Wales, Walker, Whitcomb, Winthrop—28.

Mr. Bradbury's amendment, thus amended, prevailed by a similar vote: Yeas 30; Nays 28.

[It provided for the appointment of commissioners to determine, in connection with commissioners to be chosen by Texas, the Northern boundary of that State.]

July 31st.—Mr. Norris of N. H. moved to strike from the bill the words, "nor establishing nor prohibiting African Slavery" (which words deny to the Territorial Legislatures the power to establish or prohibit Slavery). Carried: Yeas 32; Nays 20. (Nays all Southern, but Ewing of Ohio and Whitcomb of Ind.—Cass, Clay, Dayton, Dickinson, Douglas, Seward, etc., in the affirmative.)

Mr. Pearce of Md. now moved to strike from the bill so much thereof as provides a Territorial Government for New-Mexico, and for settling the boundary between her and Texas. Carried: Yeas 33 (including all the opponents of a compromise, whether from the North or the South, and all those averse to paying Texas ten millions of dollars for relinquishing her pretensions to absorb New-Mexico, with some who would not vote in this conjunction for the portions of "the Omnibus" severally disapproved of;) Nays 22:

YEAS—For breaking up "the Omnibus":

Messrs. Baldwin, Barnwell, Benton, Berrien, Butler, Chase, Clarke, Davis, Mass., Davis, Miss., Hunter, Mason, Miller, Morton, Pearce, Phelps, Seward, Shields, Smith,

Dayton,	Soule,
Dodge, Wisc.	Turney,
Douglas,	Underwood,
Ewing,	Upham,
Greene,	Wales,
Hale,	Walker,
Hamlin,	Winthrop,
Yulee—33.	

NAYS—Against breaking up "the Omnibus":

Messrs. Atchison,	Houston,
Badger,	Jones,
Bright,	King,
Cass,	Mangum,
Clay,	Norris,
Clemens,	Pratt,
Dawson,	Rusk,
Dickinson,	Sebastian,
Dodge of Iowa,	Spruance,
Downs,	Sturgeon,
Foote,	Whitcomb—22.

Mr. Pearce moved a substitute for the sections so stricken out.

Mr. Hale moved that the bill be postponed indefinitely. Negatived: Yeas 27; Nays 32.

Mr. Douglas moved an amendment to Mr. Pearce's substitute, providing that the Territorial Government thereby provided for New-Mexico shall not go into operation until the boundary of Texas be adjusted. Lost: Yeas 24; Nays 33.

Mr. Turney of Tenn. moved that the bill be indefinitely postponed. Lost: Yeas 29; Nays 30.

Mr. Underwood of Ky. moved to strike out so much of Mr. Pearce's substitute as postponed the organization of a Territorial Government in New-Mexico to the 4th of March ensuing. Lost: Yeas 25; Nays 32.

Mr. Yulee moved to strike out so much of said substitute as provided for the appointment of commissioners to settle the boundary between Texas and New-Mexico, and with it the section just struck at by Mr. Underwood. Carried: Yeas 29; Nays 28.

Mr. Chase now moved that the bill be postponed indefinitely: Lost; Yeas 28; Nays 29.

The Senate now refused to adopt Mr. Pearce's substitute as amended: Yeas 25; Nays 28.

Mr. Davis of Miss. moved a new boundary line for Utah, which was rejected: Yeas 22; Nays 34.

Mr. Walker moved to strike out all that remained of the bill except so much as provides for the admission of California: Lost; Yeas 22; Nays 33.

Mr. Phelps of Vt. moved the indefinite postponement of the bill: Lost: Yeas 28; Nays 30.

Mr. Atchison of Mo. moved to strike out so much of the bill as relates to California: Lost by a tie; Yeas 29; Nays 29.

Mr. Winthrop of Mass. moved a reconsideration of this vote: Carried; Yeas 33; Nays 26.

Mr. Clemens of Alabama moved that the bill be postponed to the next session: Lost; Yeas 25; Nays 30.

Mr. Atchison's reconsidered motion, to strike California out of the bill, now prevailed: Yeas 34; Nays 25.

The bill being now reduced so as to provide merely for the organization of the Tertory of Utah, Mr. Douglas proposed to amend so as to make its southern boundary the parallel of 36° 30′ instead of 38° north latitude: Lost; Yeas 26; (all Southern but Dickinson of N. Y. and Douglas of Ill.) Nays 27; (all Northern but Spruance and Wales of Delaware—Mr. Clay not present).

After some further attempts to amend, adjourn, etc., the bill, providing only for the organization of the Territory of Utah, was passed to its third reading: Yeas 32; Nays 18. [Nays all Northern but Bell of Tennessee.]

Aug. 1st.—Said bill passed its third reading without a division.

Mr. Douglas now called up the original bill providing for the admission of California, which was again made a special order.

Aug. 2nd.—Mr. Foote of Miss. again moved "that the line of 36° 30′ be the southern boundary of said State: Lost; Yeas 23 (all Southern); Nays 33.

Aug. 6th.—Mr. Turney moved "that the line of 36° 30′, commonly known as the Missouri Compromise line, be, and the same hereby is, extended to the Pacific ocean." He proposed to admit California with one representative, on her assent, by convention, to this boundary; rejected: Yeas 24 (all Southern); Nays, 32 (including Benton, Underwood, Walker, Spruance, and Wales, from Slave States; the rest Northern).

Various motions to adjourn, postpone, etc., were now made and voted down; finally, the Senate was, by the withdrawal of Southern Members, left without a quorum, and adjourned.

Aug. 7th.—The game of moving to postpone, adjourn, etc., consumed all this day also.

Meantime (August 5th), Mr. Pearce of Md. had introduced a bill to settle the Northern and Western boundaries of Texas, (a part of the old overturned "Omnibus,") which was also sent to the Committee of the Whole.

Aug. 6th.—President Fillmore sent a Message announcing that Gov. Bell of Texas had notified the Government of his determination to extend the authority and jurisdiction of Texas over all New-Mexico east of the Rio Grande. The President considers himself bound to resist this pretension —if necessary, by force—does not believe anything would be effected by commissioners to adjust the boundary, as the facts in the case are already generally understood, but intimates that—

"The Government of the United States would be justified, in my opinion, in allowing an indemnity to Texas, not unreasonable or extravagant, but fair, liberal, and awarded in a just spirit of accommodation."

He urges Congress not to adjourn without settling this boundary question, and says:

"I think no event would be hailed with more gratification by the people of the United States than the amicable adjustment of questions of difficulty which have now for a long time agitated the country, and occupied, to the exclusion of other subjects, the time and attention of Congress."

The Texas boundary bill being now put ahead of the bill admitting California, Mr. Dayton moved (Aug. 8th), that Texas be required to cede her public lands to the United States in consideration of the payment to her of $10,000,000 herein given her for the relinquishment of her claim to New-Mexico. After the United States shall have been repaid the $10,000,000 out of the proceeds of these lands, the residue to revert to Texas: Rejected; Yeas 17 (all Northern); Nays 32.

Aug. 9th.—Mr. Underwood moved that the Northern boundary of Texas run due east from a point on the Rio Grande, twenty miles above El Paso, to the Red River of Louisiana: Rejected; Yeas 24; (all Northern, but Wales, Spruance, and Underwood;) Nays 25.

Mr. Mason of Va. moved the giving up to Texas of all New-Mexico east of the Rio Grande: Lost: Yeas 14; Nays 37.

Mr. Sebastian moved that the (New-Mexican) Territory, surrendered by Texas in pursuance of the provisions of this bill, shall be admitted in due time as a State, with or without Slavery, as its people may determine: Rejected: Yeas 19; (all Southern but Dodge of Iowa;) Nays 29—(including Badger of N. C., Cass and Dickinson—Clay absent—Douglas, who voted just before and just after, did not vote on this.)

The bill was now engrossed: Yeas 27; Nays 24; and finally passed: Yeas 30; Nays 20.

Aug. 10th.—The California bill was now taken up. Mr. Yulee of Fla. moved a substitute, remanding California to a territorial condition, and limiting her southern boundary: Rejected; Yeas 12 (all Southern); Nays 35.

Mr. Foote moved a like project, cutting off so much of California as lies south of 36 deg. 30 min., and erecting it into the territory of Colorado: Rejected; Yeas 13 (ultra Southern); Nays 29.

Aug. 12th.—Still another proposition to limit California southwardly, by the line of 36 deg. 30 min., was made by Mr. Turney, and rejected: Yeas 20 (all Southern); Nays 30. After defeating Southern motions to adjourn, postpone, and lay on the table, the bill was engrossed for a third reading: Yeas 33; (all the Senators from Free States, with Bell, Benton, Houston, Spruance, Wales and Underwood;) Nays 19; (all from Slave States. Mr. Clay still absent—endeavoring to restore his failing health.)

Aug. 13th.—The California bill passed its third reading: Yeas 34; Nays 18; (all Southern.)

Aug. 14th.—The Senate now took up the bill organizing the Territories of New-Mexico and Utah, (as it was originally reported, prior to its inclusion in Mr. Clay's "Omnibus.")

Mr. Chase of Ohio moved to amend the bill by inserting:

"Nor shall there be in said Territory either Slavery or involuntary servitude, otherwise than in the punishment of crimes whereof the party shall have been duly convicted to have been personally guilty."

Which was rejected: Yeas 20; Nays 25.

YEAS—For Prohibiting Slavery:

Messrs. Baldwin, Bradbury, Bright, Chase, Cooper, Davis, of Mass. Dodge, of Wisc. Felch, Greene, Hale, Hamlin, Miller, Norris, Phelps, Shields, Smith, Upham, Walker, Whitcomb, Winthrop—20.

NAYS—Against Prohibiting Slavery:

Messrs. Atchison, Badger, Bell, Benton, Berrien, Cass, Davis of Miss. Dawson, Dodge of Iowa, Downs, Foote, Houston, Hunter, Jones, King, Mangum, Mason, Morton, Pratt, Rusk, Sebastian, Soule, Sturgeon, Underwood, Yates—25.

The bill was then reported complete, and passed to be engrossed.

Aug. 15th.—Said bill had its third reading, and was finally passed: Yeas 27; Nays 10.

[The Senate proceeded to take up, consider, mature, and pass the Fugitive Slave bill, and the bill excluding the Slave-Trade from the District of Columbia; but the history of these is but remotely connected with our theme.] We return to the House.

Aug. 19th—The several bills which we have been watching on their tedious and dubious course through the Senate, having reached the House, Mr. William J. Brown of Ind. moved that they be taken off the Speaker's table, and made the special order for to-morrow: Defeated; Yeas 87; Nays 98.

Mr. Ashmun of Mass. made a similar motion, which was likewise beaten: Yeas 94; Nays 94.

Aug. 28*th*.—The California bill was taken up, read twice, and committed.

The Texas bill coming up, Mr. Inge of Ala. objected to it, and a vote was taken on its rejection: Yeas 34; Nays 168; so it was not rejected.

Mr. Boyd of Ky. moved to amend it so as to create and define thereby the territories of New-Mexico and Utah, to be slave-holding or not as their people shall determine when they shall come to form State governments. [In other words, to append the bill organizing the territory of New-Mexico to the Texas bill.]

Mr. Meade of Va. raised the question of order; but the Speaker ruled the amendment in order, and his ruling was sustained by the House: Yeas 122; Nays 84.

Aug. 29*th*.—The Texas bill was taken up. Mr. Clingman of N. C. moved to amend so as to limit California by the line of 36 deg. 30 min., and establish the Territory of Colorado.

The Speaker ruled this amendment in order, and the House sustained him—122 to 67.

Mr. McClernand of Ill. moved the bill to the Committee of the Whole, to which Mr. Root of Ohio moved to add instructions, to exclude Slavery from all the Territory acquired from Mexico, east of California (which had already taken care of itself).

Sept. 2*nd*.—This bill was, by a two-third vote, made a special order henceforth.

Sept. 3*rd*.—Mr. McClernand withdrew his motion, (and Mr. Root's fell with it).

Sept. 4*th*.—Mr. R. M. McLane called the Previous Question, which was seconded, and the main question ordered.—Yeas 133; Nays 68.

The bill was then committed; Yeas 101; Nays 99.

Mr. Walden of N. Y. moved a reconsideration.

Mr. Root moved that this do lie on the table: Yeas 103; Nays 103. The Speaker voted Nay; so the motion was not laid on the table.

The motion to reconsider prevailed: Yeas 104; Nays 101. The House then refused to commit: Yeas 101; Nays 103.

Mr. Clingman's amendment, creating the Territory of Colorado out of Southern California and Utah, was now defeated: Yeas 69; Nays 130.

Mr. Boyd's amendment was then beaten: Yeas 98; Nays 106.

Mr. Boyd moved a reconsideration, which prevailed: Yeas 131; Nays 75.

Mr. Wentworth of Ill. moved to commit the bill, with instructions to provide for the exclusion of Slavery from all the territory ceded by Mexico: Lost: Yeas 80; Nays 119.

Mr. Tombs of Ga. having moved, as an amendment to Mr. Boyd's, that the Constitution of the United States and such statutes thereof as may not be locally inapplicable, and the common law as it existed on the 4th of July, 1776, should be the exclusive laws of said territory, until altered by the proper authority, it was voted down: Yeas 65; Nays 132.

Mr. Boyd's amendment prevailed: Yeas 107; Nays 99.

The question was now taken on the engrossment of the bill, and it was defeated: Yeas 99; Nays 107.

Mr. Howard of Texas moved a reconsideration.

The Speaker decided it out of order, the bill having already been once reconsidered.

Mr. Howard appealed, and the House overruled the Speaker's decision: Yeas (to sustain) 82; Nays 124.

The vote rejecting the bill was reconsidered: Yeas 122; Nays 84.

Mr. Howard again moved the Previous Question, which was seconded, and the Main Question ordered: Yeas 115; Nays 97; and the bill was ordered to a third reading: Yeas 108; Nays 98. It was then passed (as amended on motion of Mr. Boyd): Yeas 108; Nays 97.

Sept. 7*th*.—The California bill now came up. Mr. Boyd moved his amendment already moved to the Texas bill. Mr. Vinton of Ohio declared it out of order. The Speaker again ruled it in order. Mr. Vinton appealed, and the House overruled the Speaker: Yeas (to sustain) 87; Nays 115.

Mr. Jacob Thompson of Miss. moved to cut off from California all below 36° 30′: Rejected: Yeas 76; Nays 131.

The bill was now ordered to a third reading: Yeas 151; Nays 57, and then passed: Yeas 150; Nays 56 (all Southern).

The Senate bill organizing the Territory of Utah (without restriction as to Slavery) was then taken up, and rushed through the same day: Yeas 97; Nays 85. [The Nays were mainly Northern Free Soil men; but some Southern men, for a different reason, voted with them.]

Sept. 9*th*.—The House having returned the Texas Boundary bill, with an amendment (Linn Boyd's), including the bill organizing the Territory of New-Mexico therein, the Senate proceeded to consider and agree to the same: Yeas 31; Nays 10, namely:

Messrs. Baldwin, Conn.	Ewing, Ohio,
Benton, Mo.	Hamlin, Me.
Chase, Ohio,	Seward, N. Y.
Davis, Mass.	Upham, Vt.
Dodge, Wisc.	Winthrop, Mass.

So all the bills originally included in Mr. Clay's "Omnibus" were passed—two of them in the same bill—after the Senate had once voted to sever them.

These acts are substantially as follows:

ADMISSION OF CALIFORNIA.

An Act for the admission of the State of California into the Union.

Whereas, the people of California have presented a Constitution and asked admission into the Union, which constitution was submitted to Congress by the President of the United States, by message, dated February 13th, 1850, which, on due examination, is found to be republican in its form of government—

Be it enacted by the Senate and House of Representatives of the United States of America in Congress assembled, That the State of California shall be one, and is hereby declared to be one, of the United States of America, and admitted into the Union on an equal footing with the original States, in all respects whatever.

SEC. 2. *And be it further enacted*, That until the Representatives in Congress shall be apportioned according to an actual enumeration of the inhabitants of the United States, the State of California shall be entitled to two representatives in Congress.

SEC. 3. *And be it further enacted*, That the said State of California is admitted into the Union upon the express condition that the people of said State, through their legislature or otherwise, shall never interfere with the primary disposal of the public lands within its limits, and shall pass no law, and do no act, whereby the title of the United States to, and right to dispose of, the same, shall be impaired or questioned; and they shall never lay any tax or assessment of any description whatsoever on the public domain of the United States; and in no case shall non-resident proprietors, who are citizens of the United States, be taxed higher than residents; and that all the navigable waters within the said State shall be common highways, and for ever free, as well to the inhabitants of said State as to the citizens of the United States, without any tax, duty, or impost therefor: *Provided*, that nothing herein contained shall be construed as recognizing or rejecting the propositions tendered by the people of California as articles of compact in the ordinance adopted by the Convention which formed the constitution of that State.

Approved, Sept. 9, 1850.

THE TEXAS BOUNDARY.

An Act proposing to the State of Texas the establishment of her Northern and Western Boundaries, the relinquishment by the said State of all territory claimed by her exterior to said boundaries, and of all her claims upon the United States, and to establish a Territorial Government for New-Mexico.

Be it enacted by the Senate and House of Representatives of the United States of America in Congress assembled, that the following propositions shall be, and the same hereby are, offered to the State of Texas; which, when agreed to by the said State, in an act passed by the General Assembly, shall be binding and obligatory upon the United States, and upon the said State of Texas: *Provided*, That said agreement by the said General Assembly shall be given on or before the first day of December, eighteen hundred and fifty.

First.—The State of Texas will agree that her boundary on the North shall commence at the point at which the meridian of one hundred degrees west from Greenwich is intersected by the parallel of thirty-six degrees, and thirty minutes north latitude, and shall run from said point due west to the meridian of one hundred and three degrees west from Greenwich; hence her boundary shall run due south to the thirty-second degree of north latitude; thence on the said parallel of thirty-two degrees of north latitude to the Rio Bravo del Norte; and thence with the channel of said river to the Gulf of Mexico.

Second.—The State of Texas cedes to the United States all her claims to territories exterior to the limits and boundaries, which she agrees to establish by the first article of this agreement.

Third.—The State of Texas relinquishes all claim upon the United States for liability for the debts of Texas, and for compensation or indemnity for the surrender to the United States of her ships, forts, arsenals, custom-houses, custom-house revenue, arms and munitions of war, and public buildings, with their sites, which became the property of the United States at the time of the Annexation.

Fourth.—The United States, in consideration of said establishment of boundaries, cession of claims to territory, and relinquishment of claims, will pay to the State of Texas the sum of ten millions of dollars, in a stock bearing five per cent. interest, and redeemable at the end of fourteen years, the interest payable half-yearly at the Treasury of the United States.

Fifth.—Immediately after the President of the United States shall have been furnished with an authentic copy of the act of the general assembly of Texas, accepting these propositions, he shall cause the stock to be issued in favor of the State of Texas, as provided for in the fourth article of this agreement.

Provided also, That no more than five millions of said stock shall be issued until the creditors of the State, holding bonds and other certificates of stock of Texas, for which duties on imports were specially pledged, shall first file, at the treasury of the United States, releases of all claims against the United States for or on account of said bonds or certificates, in such form as shall be prescribed by the Secretary of the Treasury, and approved by the President of the United States.

ORGANIZATION OF NEW-MEXICO.

The second section of this act enacts, that all that portion of the territory of the United States, bounded as follows, to wit: beginning at a point on the Colorado river where the boundary line of the republic of Mexico crosses the same; thence eastwardly with the said boundary line to the Rio Grande; thence following the main channel of said river to the parallel of the thirty-second degree of north latitude; thence eastwardly with said degree to its intersection with the one hundred and third degree of longitude west from Greenwich; thence north with said degree of longitude to the parallel of the thirty-eighth degree of north latitude; thence west with said parallel to the summit of the Sierra Madre; thence south with the crest of said mountains to the thirty-seventh parallel of north latitude; thence west with the said parallel to its intersection with the boundary line of the State of California; thence with the said boundary line to the place of beginning, be, and the same is hereby, erected into a temporary government by the name of the Territory of New-Mexico; *Provided*, That nothing in this act contained shall be construed to inhibit the Government of the United States from dividing said Territory into two or more territories, in such manner and at such times as Congress shall deem convenient and proper, or from attaching any portion thereof to any other Territory or State; *Provided further*, That when admitted as a State, the said Territory, or any portion of the same, shall be received into the Union, with or without Slavery, as their Constitution may prescribe at the time of their admission.

The eighteenth section enacts, that the pro

visions of this act be suspended until the boundary between the United States and the State of Texas shall be adjusted, and when such adjustment shall have been effected, the President of the United States shall issue his proclamation declaring this act to be in full force and operation, and shall proceed to appoint the officers herein provided to be appointed for the said Territory.

Approved Sept. 9, 1850.

ORGANIZATION OF UTAH.

An Act to establish a Territorial Government for Utah.

Be it enacted by the Senate and House of Representatives of the United States of America in Congress assembled, That all that part of the Territory of the United States included within the following limits, to wit: bounded on the west by the State of California, on the north by the Territory of Oregon, on the east by the summit of the Rocky Mountains, and on the south by the thirty-seventh parallel of north latitude, be, and the same is hereby, created into a temporary government, by the name of the Territory of Utah; and, when admitted as a State, the said Territory, or any portion of the same, shall be received into the Union, with or without Slavery, as their constitution may prescribe at the time of their admission: *Provided*, That nothing in this act contained shall be construed to prohibit the government of the United States from dividing said Territory into two or more territories, in such manner and at such time as Congress shall deem convenient and proper, or from attaching any portion of said Territory to any other State or Territory of the United States.

[The act proceeds to provide for the appointment of a territorial governor, secretary, marshal, judges, etc., etc., and for the election of a council of thirteen, and a house of representatives of twenty-six members; also for a delegate in Congress. All recognized citizens to be voters.]

The governor shall receive an annual salary of fifteen hundred dollars as governor, and one thousand dollars as superintendent of Indian affairs. The chief justice and associate justices shall each receive an annual salary of eighteen hundred dollars. The secretary shall receive an annual salary of eighteen hundred dollars. The said salaries shall be paid quarter-yearly, at the Treasury of the United States. The members of the legislative assembly shall be entitled to receive each three dollars per day during their attendance at the sessions thereof, and three dollars each for every twenty miles' travel in going to and returning from said sessions, estimated according to the nearest usually traveled route.

Sec. 6. *And be it further enacted*, That the legislative power of said Territory shall extend to all rightful subjects of legislation, consistent with the Constitution of the United States and the provisions of this act; but no law shall be passed interfering with the primary disposal of the soil; no tax shall be imposed upon the property of the United States; nor shall the lands or other property of non-residents be taxed higher than the lands or other property of residents. All the laws passed by the legislative assembly and Governor shall be submitted to the Congress of the United States, and, if disapproved, shall be null and of no effect.

Sec. 17. *And be it further enacted*, That the Constitution and laws of the United States are hereby extended over, and declared to be in force in, said Territory of Utah, so far as the same, or any provision thereof, may be applicable.

Approved Sept. 9, 1850.

[We have omitted several matter-of-course provisions.]

XIV.

THE KANSAS-NEBRASKA STRUGGLE.

Out of the Louisiana Territory, since the admission first of Louisiana and then of Missouri as Slave States, there had been formed the Territories of Arkansas, Iowa, and Minnesota; the first without, and the two others with, Congressional inhibition of Slavery. Arkansas, in due course, became a Slave, and Iowa a Free, State; Minnesota was and is following surely in the track of Iowa. The destiny of one tier of States, fronting upon, and westward of, the Mississippi, was thus settled. What should be the fate of the next tier?

The region lying immediately westward of Missouri, with much territory north, as well as a more clearly defined district south of it, was long since dedicated to the uses of the Aborigines—not merely those who had originally inhabited it, but the tribes from time to time removed from the States eastward of the Mississippi. Very little, if any, of it was legally open to settlement by Whites; and, with the exception of the few and small military and trading posts thinly scattered over its surface, it is probable that scarcely two hundred white families were located in the spacious wilderness bounded by Missouri, Iowa, and Minnesota on the east, the British possessions on the north, the crest of the Rocky Mountains on the west, and the settled portion of New-Mexico and the line of 36° 30′ on the south, at the time when Mr. Douglas first, at the session of 1852-3, submitted a bill organizing the Territory of Nebraska, by which title the region above bounded had come to be vaguely indicated.

This region was indisputably included within the scope of the exclusion of Slavery from all Federal territory north of 36° 30′, to which the South had assented by the terms of the Missouri compact, in order thereby to secure the admission of Missouri as a Slave State. Nor was it once intimated, during the long, earnest, and searching debate in the Senate on the Compromise measures of 1850, that the adoption of those measures, whether together or separately, would involve or imply a repeal of the Missouri Restriction. We have seen in our last chapter how Mr. Clay's original suggestion of a compromise, which was substantially that ultimately adopted, was received by the Southern Senators who spoke on its introduction, with hardly a qualification, as a virtual surrender of all that the South had ever claimed with respect to the new territories. And, from the beginning to the close of the long and able discussion which followed, neither friend nor foe of the Compromises, nor of any of them, hinted that one effect of their adoption would be the lifting of the Missouri restriction from the territory now covered by it. When the Compromises of 1850 were accepted in 1852 by the National Conventions of the two great parties, as a settlement of the distracting controversy therein contemplated, no hint was added that the Nebraska region was opened thereby to Slavery.

Several petitions for the organization of a Territory westward of Missouri and Iowa were presented at the session of 1851-2, but no decisive action taken thereon until the next session, when,

Dec. 13th.—Mr. W. P. Hall of Mo., pursuant to notice, submitted to the House a bill to organize the Territory of Platte, which was read twice, and sent to the Committee on Territories. From that Committee,

Feb. 2d, 1853.—Mr. W. A. Richardson of Ill. reported a bill to organize the Territory of Nebraska, which was read twice and committed.

Feb. 9th.—The bill was ordered to be taken out of Committee, on motion of W. P. Hall.

Feb. 10th.—The bill was reported from the Committee of the Whole to the House, with a recommendation that it do *not* pass.

Mr. Richardson moved the previous question, which prevailed.

Mr. Letcher of Va. moved that the bill do lie on the table: Lost; Yeas 49 (mainly Southern); Nays 107.

The bill was then engrossed, read a third time, and passed; Yeas 98; Nays 43, (as before).

Feb. 11th.—The bill reached the Senate and was referred to the Committee on Territories.

Feb. 17th.—Mr. Douglas reported it without amendment.

March 2nd.—(Last day but one of the session), Mr. Douglas moved that the bill be taken up: Lost: Yeas 20; (all Northern but Atchison and Geyer of Mo.); Nays 25; (21 Southern, 4 Northern).

March 3rd.—Mr. Douglas again moved that the bill be taken up.

Mr. Borland of Ark. moved that it do lie on the table: Carried: Yeas 23; (all Southern but 4;) Nays 17; (all Northern but Atchison and Geyer). So the bill was put to sleep for the session.

On the motion to take up—Mr. Rusk of Texas objecting—Mr. Atchison said:

"I must ask the indulgence of the Senate to say one word in relation to this matter. Perhaps there is not a State in the Union more deeply interested in this question than the State of Missouri. If not the largest, I will say the best, portion of that Territory, perhaps the only portion of it that in half a century will become a State, lies immediately west of the State of Missouri. It is only a question of time, whether we will organize the territory at this session of Congress, or whether we will do it at the next session; and, for my own part, I acknowledge now that, as the Senator from Illinois well knows, when I came to this city, at the beginning of the last session, I was perhaps as much opposed to the proposition, as the Senator from Texas now is. The Senator from Iowa knows it; and *it was for reasons which I will not now mention or suggest.* But, sir, I have from reflection and investigation in my own mind, and from the opinions of others—my constituents, whose opinions I am bound to respect—come to the conclusion that now is the time for the organization of this Territory. It is the most propitious time. The treaties with the various Indian tribes, the titles to whose possessions must be extinguished, can better be made now than at any future time; for, as the question is agitated, and as it is understood, white men, speculators, will interpose, and interfere, and the longer it is postponed the more we will have to fear from them, and the more difficult it will be to extinguish the Indian title in that country, and the harder the terms to be imposed. Therefore, Mr. President, for this reason, without going into detail, I am willing now that the question shall be taken, whether we will proceed to the consideration of the bill or not."

The meaning is here diplomatically veiled, yet is perfectly plain. Gen. Atchison had been averse to organizing this Territory until he could procure a relaxation of the Missouri Restriction as to Slavery; but, seeing no present hope of this, he was willing to waive the point, and assent to an organization under a bill silent with respect to Slavery, and of course leaving the Missouri Restriction unimpaired.

Gen. Pierce was inaugurated President on the 4th March, 1853; and, in his Inaugural Address, referred to the discussions concerning Slavery and the Compromises of 1850 in the following terms:

"I believe that involuntary servitude, as it exists in different States of this confederacy, is recognized by the Constitution. I believe that it stands like any other admitted right, and that the States where it exists are entitled to efficient remedies to enforce the constitutional provisions. I hold that the laws of 1850, commonly called the "Compromise Measures," are strictly constitutional, and to be unhesitatingly carried into effect. I believe that the constituted authorities of this Republic are bound to regard the rights of the South in this respect, as they would view any other legal and constitutional right, and that the laws to enforce them should be respected and obeyed, not with a reluctance encouraged by abstract opinions as to their propriety in a different state of society, but cheerfully, and according to the decisions of the tribunal to which their exposition belongs. Such have been, and are, my convictions, and upon them shall I act. I fervently hope that the question is at rest, and that no sectional, or ambitious, or fanatical excitement may again threaten the durability of our institutions, or obscure the light of our prosperity."

The XXXIIId Congress assembled at Washington, Dec. 5th, 1853, with a large Administration majority in either House. Linn Boyd of Ky. was chosen Speaker of the House. The President's Annual Message contained the following allusion to the subject of Slavery:

"It is no part of my purpose to give prominence to any subject which may properly be regarded as set at rest by the deliberate judgment of the people. But, while the present is bright with promise, and the future full of demand and inducements for the exercise of active intelligence, the past can never be without useful lessons of admonition and instruction. If its dangers serve not as beacons, they will evidently fail to fulfill the object of a wise design. When the grave shall have closed over all, who are now endeavoring to meet the obligations of duty, the year 1850 will be recurred to as a period filled with anxious apprehension. A successful war had just terminated. Peace brought with it a vast augmentation of territory. Disturbing questions arose, bearing upon the domestic institutions of one portion of the confederacy, and involving the constitutional rights of the States. But, notwithstanding differences of opinion and sentiment which then existed in relation to details and specific provisions, the acquiescence of distinguished citizens, whose devotion to the Union can never be doubted, has given renewed vigor to our institutions, and restored a sense of repose and security to the public mind throughout the confederacy. That this repose is to suffer no shock during my official term, if I have power to avert it, those who placed me here may be assured."

Dec. 15th.—Mr. A. C. Dodge of Iowa submitted to the Senate a bill (No. 22) "To organize the Territory of Nebraska," which was read twice, and referred to the Committee on Territories.

Jan. 4th.—Mr. Douglas, from said Committee, reported said bill with amendments, which were printed. The following is the accompanying Report:

The Committee on Territories, to whom was referred a bill for an act to establish the Territory of Nebraska, have given the same that serious and deliberate consideration which its great importance demands, and beg leave to report it back to the Senate with various amendments, in the form of a substitute for the bill:

The principal amendments which your committee deem it their duty to commend to the favorable action of the Senate, in a special report, are those in which the principles established by the Compromise Measures of 1850, so far as they are applicable to territorial organizations, are proposed to be affirmed and carried into practical operation within the limits of the new Territory.

The wisdom of those measures is attested, not less by their salutary and beneficial effects, in allaying sectional agitation and restoring peace and harmony to an irritated and distracted people, than by the cordial and almost universal approbation with which they have been received and sanctioned by the whole country. In the judgment of your Committee, those measures were intended to have a far more comprehensive and enduring effect than the mere adjustment of difficulties arising out of the recent acquisition of Mexican territory. They were designed to establish certain great principles, which would not only furnish adequate remedies for existing evils, but, in all time to come, avoid the perils of similar agitation, by withdrawing the question of Slavery from the Halls of Congress and the political arena, and committing it to the arbitration of those who were immediately interested in, and alone responsible for, its consequences. With a view of conforming their action to what they regard as the settled policy of the Government, sanctioned by the approving voice of the American People, your Committee have deemed it their duty to incorporate and perpetuate, in their territorial bill, the principles and spirit of those measures. If any other consideration were necessary to render the propriety of this course imperative upon the Committee, they may be found in the fact that the Nebraska country occupies the same relative position to the Slavery question, as did New-Mexico and Utah, when those Territories were organized.

It was a disputed point, whether Slavery was prohibited by law in the country acquired from Mexico. On the one hand, it was contended, as a legal proposition, that Slavery, having been prohibited by the enactments of Mexico, according to the laws of nations, we received the country with all its local laws and domestic institutions attached to the soil, so far as they did not conflict with the Constitution of the United States; and that a law either protecting or prohibiting Slavery, was not repugnant to that instrument, as was evidenced by the fact that one-half of the States of the Union tolerated, while the other half prohibited, the institution of Slavery. On the other hand, it was insisted that, by virtue of the Constitution of the United States, every citizen had a right to remove to any Territory of the Union, and carry his property with him under the protection of law, whether that property consisted of persons or things. The difficulties arising from this diversity of opinion, were greatly aggravated by the fact that there were many persons on both sides of the legal controversy, who were unwilling to abide the decision of the courts on the legal matters in dispute; thus, among those who claimed that the Mexican laws were still in force, and, consequently, that Slavery was already prohibited in those Territories by valid enactment, there were many who insisted upon Congress making the matter certain, by enacting another prohibition. In like manner, some of those who argued that Mexican law had ceased to have any binding force, and that the Constitution tolerated and protected Slave property in those territories, were unwilling to trust the decision of the courts upon the point, and insisted that Congress should, by direct enactment, remove all legal obstacles to the introduction of Slaves into those Territories.

Such being the character of the controversy in respect to the territory acquired from Mexico, a similar question has arisen in regard to the right to hold slaves in the Territory of Nebraska, when the Indian laws shall be withdrawn, and the country thrown open to emigration and settlement. By the 8th section of "an act to authorize the people of Missouri Territory to form a Constitution and State Government, and for the admission of such State into the Union on an equal footing with the original States, and to prohibit Slavery in certain Territories," approved March 6th, 1820, it was provided; "That in all that territory ceded by France to the United States under the name of Louisiana, which lies north of 36 degrees 30 minutes north latitude, not included within the limits of the State contemplated by this act, Slavery and involuntary servitude, otherwise than in the punishment of crimes whereof the parties shall have been duly convicted, shall be, and are hereby, prohibited: *Provided always*, That any person escaping into the same, from whom labor or service is lawfully claimed in any State or Territory of the United States, such fugitive may be lawfully reclaimed, and conveyed to the persons claiming his or her labor or service, as aforesaid."

Under this section, as in the case of the Mexican law in New-Mexico and Utah, it is a disputed point whether Slavery is prohibited in the Nebraska country by *valid* enactment. The decision of this question involves the constitutional power of Congress to pass laws prescribing and regulating the domestic institutions of the various Territories of the Union. In the opinion of those eminent statesmen who hold that Congress is invested with no rightful authority to legislate upon the subject of Slavery in the Territories, the 8th section of the act preparatory to the admission of Missouri is null and void; while the prevailing sentiment in large portions of the Union sustains the doctrine that the Constitution of the United States secures to every citizen an inalienable right to move into any of the Territories with his property, of whatever kind and description, and to hold and enjoy the same under the sanction of law. Your Committee do not feel themselves called upon to enter upon the discussion of these controverted questions. They involve the same grave issues which produced the agitation, the sectional strife, and the fearful struggle of 1850. As Congress deemed it wise and prudent to refrain from deciding the matters in controversy then, either by affirming or repealing the Mexican laws, or by an act declaratory of the true intent of the Constitution, and the extent of the protection afforded by it to Slave property in the Territories, so your Committee are not prepared to recommend a departure from the course pursued on that memorable occasion, either by affirming or repealing the 8th section of the Missouri act, or by any act declaratory of the meaning of the Constitution in respect to the legal points in dispute.

Your Committee deem it fortunate for the peace of the country, and the security of the Union, that the controversy then resulted in the adoption of the Compromise Measures, which the two great political parties, with singular unanimity, have affirmed as a cardinal article of their faith, and proclaimed to the world as a final settlement of the controversy and an end of the agitation. A due respect, therefore, for the avowed opinions of Senators, as well as a proper sense of patriotic duty, enjoins upon your Committee the propriety and necessity of a strict adherence to the principles, and even a literal adoption of the enactments of that adjustment, in all their territorial bills, so far as the same are not locally inapplicable. Those enactments embrace, among other things, less material to the matters under consideration, the following provisions:

When admitted as a State, the said Territory, or any portion of the same, shall be received into the Union, with or without Slavery, as their constitution may prescribe at the time of their admission;

That the legislative power and authority of said Territory shall be vested in the Governor and a Legislative Assembly;

That the legislative power of said Territory shall extend to all rightful subjects of legislation, consistent with the Constitution of the United States, and the provisions of this act; but no law shall be passed interfering with the primary disposal of the soil; no tax shall be imposed upon the property of the United States; nor shall the lands or other property of non-residents be taxed higher than the lands or other property of residents.

Writs of error and appeals from the final decisions of said Supreme Court shall be allowed, and may be taken to the Supreme Court of the United States in the same manner and under the same regulations as from the Circuit Courts of the United States, where the value of the property or amount in controversy, to be ascertained by the oath or affirmation of either party, or other competent witness, shall exceed one thousand dollars; except only that, in all cases involving title to slaves, the said writs of error or appeals shall be allowed and decided by the said Supreme Court, without regard to the value of the matter, property, or title in controversy; and except, also, that a writ of error or appeal shall also be allowed to the Supreme Court of the United States from the decisions of the said Supreme Court by this act, or of any judge thereof, or of the district courts created by this act, or of any judge thereof, upon any writ of *habeas corpus* involving the question of personal freedom; and each of the said district courts shall have and exercise the same jurisdiction, in all cases arising under the Constitution and laws of the United States, as is vested in the circuit and district courts of the United States; and the said supreme and district courts of the said territory, and the respective judges thereof, shall and may grant writs of *habeas corpus*, in all cases in which the same are granted by the judges of the United States in the District of Columbia.

To which may be added the following proposition affirmed by the act of 1850, known as the fugitive slave law:

That the provisions of the "act respecting fugitives from justice, and persons escaping from the service of their masters," approved February 12, 1793, and the provisions of the act to amend and supplementary to the aforesaid act, approved September 18, 1850, shall extend to, and be in force in, all the organized Territories, as well as in the various States of the Union.

From these provisions, it is apparent that the Compromise Measures of 1850 affirm, and rest upon, the following propositions:

First.—That all questions pertaining to Slavery in the Territories, and the new States to be formed therefrom, are to be left to the decision of the people residing therein, by their appropriate representatives, to be chosen by them for that purpose.

Second.—That "all cases involving title to slaves," and "questions of personal freedom," are to be referred to the adjudication of the local tribunals, with the right of appeal to the Supreme Court of the United States.

Third.—That the provisions of the Constitution of the United States, in respect to fugitives from service, is to be carried into faithful execution in all "the original Territories," the same as in the States.

The substitute for the bill which your Committee have prepared, and which is commended to the favorable action of the Senate, proposes to carry these propositions and principles into practical operation, in the precise language of the Compromise Measures of 1850.

Jan. 24th.—The bill thus reported was considered in Committee of the Whole and postponed to Monday next, when it was made the order of the day.

The bill was further considered Jan. 31st, Feb. 3rd, Feb. 5th, and Feb. 6th, when an amendment reported by Mr. Douglas, declaring the Missouri Restriction on Slavery "inoperative and void," being under consideration, Mr. Chase of Ohio moved to strike out the assertion that said Restriction

"was superseded by the principles of the legislation of 1850, commonly called the Compromise Measures."

This motion was defeated by Yeas 13; Nays 30, as follows:

YEAS—To strike out:

Messrs. Allen, *Ohio,*	Hamlin, *Me.*
Cass, *Mich.*	Seward, *N. Y.*
Chase, *Ohio,*	Smith, *Conn.*
Everett, *Mass.*	Stuart, *Mich.*
Fish, *N. Y.*	Sumner, *Mass.*
Foot, *Vt.*	Wade, *Ohio,*
Walker, *Wisc.*—13.	

NAYS—Against striking out:

Messrs. Adams, *Miss.*	Fitzpatrick, *Ala.*
Atchison, *Mo.*	Geyer, *Mo.*
Badger, *N. C.*	Hunter, *Va.*
Bayard, *Del.*	Jones, (J. C.) *Tenn.*
Bell, *Tenn.*	Mallory, *Fla.*
Benjamin, *La.*	Mason, *Va.*
Bright, *Ind.*	Norris, *N. H.*
Brodhead, *Pa.*	Pettit, *Ind.*
Butler, *S. C.*	Sebastian, *Ark.*
Clay, (C. C.) *Ala.*	Shields, *Ill.*
Dawson, *Ga.*	Slidell, *La.*
Dixon, *Ky.*	Thompson, *Ky.*
Dodge, *Iowa,*	Toucey, *Conn.*
Douglas, *Ill.*	Weller, *Cal.*
Evans, *S. C.*	Williams, *N. H.*—30.

Feb. 15th.—The bill having been discussed daily until now, Mr. Douglas moved to strike out of his amendment the words above quoted (which the Senate had refused to strike out on Mr. Chase's motion,) and insert instead the following:

"Which, being inconsistent with the principle of non-intervention by Congress with Slavery in the States and Territories, as recognized by the legislation of 1850, (commonly called the Compromise Measures,) is hereby declared inoperative and void; it being the true intent and meaning of this act not to legislate Slavery into any Territory or State, nor to exclude it therefrom, but to leave the people thereof perfectly free to form and regulate their domestic institutions in their own way, subject only to the Constitution of the United States"—

which prevailed—Yeas 35; Nays 10—as follows:

YEAS—For Douglas's new Amendment:

Messrs. Adams,	Gwin,
Atchison,	Hunter,
Bayard,	Johnson,
Bell,	Jones of Iowa,
Benjamin,	Jones of Tenn.
Brodhead,	Mason,
Brown,	Morton,
Butler,	Norris,
Cass,	Pearce,
Clayton,	Pettit,
Dawson,	Pratt,
Dixon,	Sebastian
Dodge of Iowa,	Slidell,
Douglas,	Stuart,
Evans,	Thompson of Ky.
Fitzpatrick,	Toombs,
Geyer,	Weller,
Williams—35.	

NAYS—Against said Amendment:

Messrs. Allen,	Foot,
Chase,	Houston,
Dodge of Wisc.	Seward,
Everett,	Sumner,
Fish,	Wade—10.

[NOTE.—Prior to this move of Mr. Douglas, Mr. Dixon (Whig) of Ky. had moved to insert a clause directly and plainly *repealing* the Missouri Restriction. Mr. Dixon thought if that was the object, (and he was in favor of it), it should be approached in a direct and manly way. He was assailed for this in *The Union* newspaper next morning; but his suggestion was substantially adopted by Douglas, after a brief hesitation. Mr. Dixon's proposition, having been made in Committee, does not appear in the Journal of the Senate, or it would here be given in terms.]

The bill was further discussed daily until March 2nd, when the vote was taken on Mr. Chase's amendment, to add to Sec. 14 the following words:

"*Under which the people of the Territory, through their appropriate representatives, may, if they see fit, prohibit the existence of Slavery therein*"—

which was rejected: Yeas 10; Nays 36, as follows:

YEAS—For Mr. Chase's Amendment:

Messrs. Chase,	Hamlin,
Dodge of Wisc.	Seward,
Fessenden,	Smith,
Fish,	Sumner,
Foot,	Wade—10.

NAYS—Against Chase's Amendment:

Messrs. Adams,	Hunter,
Atchison,	Johnson,
Badger,	Jones of Iowa,
Bell,	Jones of Tenn.
Benjamin,	Mason,
Brodhead,	Morton,
Brown,	Norris,
Butler,	Pettit,
Clay, (C. C.)	Pratt,
Clayton,	Rusk,
Dawson,	Sebastian,
Dixon,	Shields,
Dodge of Iowa,	Slidell,
Douglas,	Stuart,
Evans,	Toucey,
Fitzpatrick,	Walker,
Gwin,	Weller,
Houston,	Williams—36.

Mr. Badger of N. C. moved to add to the aforesaid section:

"*Provided, That nothing herein contained shall be construed to revive or put in force any law or regulation which may have existed prior to the act of 6th of March, 1820, either protecting establishing, prohibiting, or abolishing Slavery.*"

Carried; Yeas 35; Nays 6, as follows:

YEAS—For Badger's Amendment:

Messrs. Atchison,	Houston,
Badger,	Hunter,
Bell,	Jones of Iowa,
Benjamin,	Jones of Tenn.
Brodhead,	Mason,
Butler,	Morton,
Clay,	Norris,
Dawson,	Pettit,
Dixon,	Pratt,
Dodge of Iowa,	Seward,
Douglas,	Shields
Evans,	Slidell,
Fish,	Smith,
Fitzpatrick,	Stuart,

Foot,	Toucey,
Gwin,	Walker,
Hamlin,	Weller,
Williams—35.	

NAYS—Against said Amendment:

Messrs. Adams,	Johnson,
Brown,	Rusk,
Dodge of Wisc.	Sebastian—6.

Mr. Clayton now moved to strike out so much of said Douglas amendment as permits emigrants from Europe, who shall have declared their intention to become citizens, to vote: Carried; Yeas 23; Nays 21—as follows:

YEAS—For Clayton's Amendment:

Messrs. Adams,	Dixon,
Atchison,	Evans,
Badger,	Fitzpatrick,
Bell,	Houston,
Benjamin,	Hunter,
Brodhead,	Johnson,
Brown,	Jones of Tenn.
Butler,	Mason,
Clay,	Morton,
Clayton,	Pratt,
Dawson,	Sebastian,
Slidell—23.	

NAYS—Against Clayton's Amendment:

Messrs. Chase,	Norris,
Dodge of Wisc.	Pettit,
Dodge of Iowa,	Seward,
Douglas,	Shields,
Fessenden,	Smith,
Fish,	Stuart,
Foot,	Sumner,
Gwin,	Toucey,
Hamlin,	Wade,
Jones of Iowa,	Walker,
Williams—21.	

Mr. Chase moved to amend, by providing for the appointment of three Commissioners residing in the Territory to organize the Territory, divide it into election districts, notify an election on the first Monday in September then ensuing, etc., at which election the people should choose their own Governor, as well as a Territorial Legislature—the Governor to serve for two years, and the Legislature to meet not later than May, 1855.

This extension of the principle of "Squatter Sovereignty" was defeated—Yeas 10; Nays 30—as follows:

YEAS—To enable the People of the Territory to choose their own Governor, etc.

Messrs. Chase,	Seward,
Fessenden,	Shields,
Foot,	Smith,
Hamlin,	Sumner,
Norris,	Wade—10.

NAYS—Against said proposition:

Messrs. Atchison,	Gwin,
Badger,	Houston,
Bell,	Hunter,
Benjamin,	Johnson,
Brodhead,	Jones of Iowa,
Brown,	Jones of Tenn.
Butler,	Mason,
Clay,	Morton,
Dawson,	Pettit,
Dixon,	Pratt,
Dodge of Wisc.	Rusk,
Dodge of Iowa,	Sebastian,
Douglas,	Slidell,
Evans,	Stuart,
Fitzpatrick,	Williams—30.

Mr. Chase then moved to amend the Boundary section of Mr. Douglas's amendment, so as to have but one Territory named Nebraska, instead of two, entitled respectively, Nebraska and Kansas; which was defeated—Yeas 8; Nays 34—as follows:

YEAS—For having but one Territory.

Messrs. Chase,	Seward,
Fessenden,	Smith,
Foot,	Sumner,
Hamlin,	Wade—8.

NAYS—For severing Nebraska from Kansas:

Messrs. Adams,	Houston,
Atchison,	Hunter,
Badger,	Johnson,
Bell,	Jones of Iowa,
Benjamin,	Jones of Tenn.
Brodhead,	Mason,
Brown,	Morton,
Butler,	Norris,
Clay,	Pettit,
Dawson,	Pratt,
Dixon,	Rusk,
Dodge of Wisc.	Sebastian,
Dodge of Iowa,	Shields,
Douglas,	Slidell,
Evans,	Stuart,
Fitzpatrick,	Walker,
Gwin,	Williams—34.

Mr. Douglas's amendment was then agreed to, and the bill reported from the Committee of the Whole to the Senate.

A motion to strike out the amendment, allowing emigrant aliens who have declared their intention to become citizens to vote, was agreed to—Yeas 22; Nays 20—as follows:

YEAS—To strike out said provision:

Messrs. Adams,	Evans,
Atchison,	Fitzpatrick,
Badger,	Houston,
Bell,	Hunter,
Benjamin,	Johnson,
Brodhead,	Jones of Tenn.
Brown,	Mason,
Butler,	Morton,
Clay,	Pratt,
Dawson,	Sebastian,
Dixon,	Slidell—22.

NAYS—Against striking out:

Messrs. Chase,	Norris,
Dodge of Wisc.	Pettit,
Dodge of Iowa,	Seward,
Douglas,	Shields,
Fessenden,	Smith,
Fish,	Stuart,
Foot,	Sumner,
Hamlin,	Wade,
James,	Walker,
Jones of Iowa,	Williams—20.

The question on the engrossment of the bill was now reached, and it was carried—Yeas 29; Nays 12—as follows:

YEAS—To engross the bill for its third reading:

Messrs.	Adams,	Gwin,
	Atchison,	Hunter,
	Badger,	Johnson,
	Benjamin,	Jones of Iowa,
	Brodhead,	Jones of Tenn.
	Brown,	Mason,
	Butler,	Morton,
	Clay,	Norris,
	Dawson,	Pettit,
	Dixon,	Pratt,
	Dodge of Iowa,	Sebastian,
	Douglas,	Shields,
	Evans,	Slidell,
	Fitzpatrick,	Stuart,
	Williams—29.	

NAYS—Against the engrossment:

Messrs.	Chase,	James,
	Dodge of Wisc.	Seward,
	Fessenden,	Smith,
	Fish,	Sumner,
	Foot,	Wade,
	Hamlin,	Walker—12.

March 3rd.—The rule assigning Fridays for the consideration of private bills, having been suspended, on motion of Mr. Badger, the Senate proceeded to put the Nebraska-Kansas bill on its final passage, when a long and earnest debate ensued. At a late hour of the night, Mr. Seward of N. Y. addressed the Senate, in opposition to the bill, as follows:

Mr. President:—I rise with no purpose of further resisting or even delaying the passage of this bill. Let its advocates have only a little patience, and they will soon reach the object for which they have struggled so earnestly and so long. The sun has set for the last time upon the guaranteed and certain liberties of all the unsettled and unorganized portions of the American continent that lie within the jurisdiction of the United States. To-morrow's sun will rise in dim eclipse over them. How long that obscuration shall last, is known only to the Power that directs and controls all human events. For myself, I know only this—that now no human power will prevent its coming on, and that its passing off will be hastened and secured by others than those now here, and perhaps by only those belonging to future generations.

Sir, it would be almost factious to offer further resistance to this measure here. Indeed, successful resistance was never expected to be made in this Hall. The Senate-floor is an old battle-ground, on which have been fought many contests, and always, at least since 1820, with fortune adverse to the cause of equal and universal freedom. We were only a few here who engaged in that cause in the beginning of this contest. All that we could hope to do—all that we did hope to do—was to organize and to prepare the issue for the House of Representatives, to which the country would look for its decision as authoritative, and to awaken the country that it might be ready for the appeal which would be made, whatever the decision of Congress might be. We are no stronger now. Only fourteen at the first, it will be fortunate if, among the ills and accidents which surround us, we shall maintain that number to the end.

We are on the eve of the consummation of a great national transaction—a transaction which will close a cycle in the history of our country—and it is impossible not to desire to pause a moment and survey the scene around us, and the prospect before us. However obscure we may individually be, our connection with this great transaction will perpetuate our names for the praise or for the censure of future ages, and perhaps in regions far remote. If, then, we had no other motive for our actions but that of an honest desire for a just fame, we could not be indifferent to that scene and that prospect. But individual interests and ambition sink into insignificance in view of the interests of our country and of mankind. These interests awaken, at least in me, an intense solicitude.

It was said by some in the beginning, and it has been said by others later in this debate, that it was doubtful whether it would be the cause of Slavery or the cause of Freedom that would gain advantages from the passage of this bill. I do not find it necessary to be censorious, nor even unjust to others, in order that my own course may be approved. I am sure that the honorable Senator from Illinois [Mr. Douglas] did not mean that the Slave States should gain an advantage over the Free States; for he disclaimed it when he introduced the bill. I believe in all candor, that the honorable Senator from Georgia [Mr. Toombs], who comes out at the close of the battle as one of the chiefest leaders of the victorious party, is sincere in declaring his own opinion that the Slave States will gain no unjust advantage over the Free States, because he disclaims it as a triumph in their behalf. Notwithstanding all this, however, what has occurred here and in the country, during this contest, has compelled a conviction that Slavery will gain something, and Freedom will endure a severe, though I hope not an irretrievable, loss. The slaveholding States are passive, quiet, content, and satisfied with the prospective boon, and the Free States are excited and alarmed with fearful forebodings and apprehensions. The impatience for the speedy passage of the bill, manifested by its friends, betrays a knowledge that this is the condition of public sentiment in the Free States. They thought in the beginning that it was necessary to guard the measure by inserting the Clayton amendment, which would exclude unnaturalized foreign inhabitants of the Territories from the right of suffrage. And now they seem willing, with almost perfect unanimity, to relinquish that safeguard, rather than to delay the adoption of the principal measure for at most a year, perhaps for only a week or a day. Suppose that the Senate should adhere to that condition, which so lately was thought so wise and so important—what then? The bill could only go back to the House of Representatives, which must either yield or insist! In the one case or in the other, a decision in favor of the bill would be secured; for even if the House should disagree, the Senate would have time to recede. But the majority will hazard nothing, even on a prospect so certain as this. They will recede at once, without a moment's further struggle, from the condition, and thus secure the passage of this bill now, to-night. Why such haste? Even if the question were to go to the country before a final decision here, what would there be wrong in that? There is no man living who will say that the country anticipated, or that *he* anticipated, the agitation of this measure in Congress, when this Congress was elected, or even when it assembled in December last.

Under such circumstances, and in the midst of agitation, and excitement, and debates, it is only fair to say, that certainly the country has not decided in favor of the bill. The refusal, then, to let the question go to the country is a conclusive proof that the Slave States, as represented here, expect from the passage of this bill what the Free States insist that they will lose by it—an advantage, a material advantage, and not a mere ab straction. There are men in the Slave States, as in the Free States, who insist always too pertinaciously upon mere abstractions. But that is not the policy of the Slave States to-day. They are in earnest in seeking for, and securing, an object, and an important one. I believe they are going to have it. I do not know how long the advantage gained will last, nor how great or comprehensive it will be. Every Senator who agrees with me in opinion must feel as I do—that under such circumstances he can forego nothing that can be done decently, with due respect to difference of opinion, and consistently with the constitutional and settled rules of legislation, to place the true merits of the question before the country. Questions sometimes occur which seem to have two right sides. Such were the questions that divided the English nation between Pitt and Fox—such the contest between the assailant and the defender of Quebec. The judgment of the world was suspended by its sympathies, and seemed ready to descend in favor of him who should be most gallant in conduct. And so, when both fell with equal chivalry on the same field, the survivors united in raising a common monument to the glorious but rival memories of Wolfe and Montcalm. But this contest involves a moral question. The Slave States so present it. They maintain that African Slavery is not erroneous, not unjust, not inconsistent with the advancing cause of human nature. Since they so regard it, I do not expect to see statesmen representing those States indifferent about a vindication of this system by the Congress of the United States. On the other hand, we of the Free States regard Slavery as erroneous, unjust, oppressive, and therefore absolutely inconsistent with the principles of the American Constitution and Government. Who will expect us to be indifferent to the decisions of the American people and of mankind on such an issue?

Again: there is suspended on the issue of this contest the political equilibrium between the Free and the Slave States. It is no ephemeral question, no idle question, whether Slavery shall go on increasing its influence over the central power here, or whether Freedom shall gain the ascendancy. I do not expect to see statesmen of the Slave States indifferent on so momentous a question, and as little can it be expected that those of the Free States will betray their own great cause. And now it remains for me to declare, in view of the decision of this controversy so near at hand, that I have seen nothing and heard nothing during its progress to change the opinions which at the earliest proper period I deliberately expressed. Certainly, I have not seen the evidence then promised, that the Free States would acquiesce in the measure. As certainly, too, I may say that I have not seen the fulfillment of the promise that the history of the last thirty years would be revised, corrected, and amended, and that it would then appear that the country, during all that period, had been resting in prosperity, and contentment, and peace, not upon a valid, constitutional, and irrevocable compromise between the Slave States and the Free States, but upon an unconstitutional and false, and even infamous, act of Congressional usurpation.

On the contrary, I am now, if possible, more than ever satisfied that, after all this debate, the history of the country will go down to posterity just as it stood before, carrying to them the everlasting facts, that until 1820 the Congress of the United States legislated to prevent the introduction of Slavery into new Territories whenever that object was practicable; and that in that year they so far modified that policy, under alarming apprehensions of civil convulsion, by a constitutional enactment in the character of a compact, as to admit Missouri a new Slave State, but upon the express condition, stipulated in favor of the Free States, that Slavery should be forever prohibited in all the residue of the existing and unorganized Territories of the United States lying north of the parallel of 36 deg. 30 min. north latitude. Certainly, I find nothing to win my favor toward the bill in the proposition of the Senator from Maryland [Mr. Pearce] to restore the Clayton amendment, which was struck out in the House of Representatives. So far from voting for that proposition, I shall vote against it now, as I did when it was under consideration here before, in accordance with the opinion adopted as early as any political opinions I ever had, and cherished as long, that the right of suffrage is not a mere conventional right, but an inherent natural right, of which no government can rightly deprive any adult man who is subject to its authority, and obligated to its support.

I hold, moreover, sir, that inasmuch as every man is, by force of circumstances beyond his own control, a subject of government somewhere, he is, by the very constitution of human society, entitled to share equally in the conferring of political power on those who wield it, if he is not disqualified by crime; that in a despotic government he ought to be allowed arms, in a free government the ballot or the open vote, as a means of self-protection against unendurable oppression. I am not likely, therefore, to restore to this bill an amendment which would deprive it of an important feature imposed upon it by the House of Representatives, and that one, perhaps, the only feature that harmonizes with my own convictions of justice. It is true that the House of Representatives stipulates such suffrage for white men as a condition for opening it to the possible proscription and slavery of the African. I shall separate them. I shall vote for the former and against the latter, glad to get universal suffrage of white men, if only that can be gained now, and working right on, full of hope and confidence, for the prevention or the abrogation of Slavery in the Territories hereafter.

Sir, I am surprised at the pertinacity with which the honorable Senator from Delaware, mine ancient and honorable friend, [Mr. Clayton,] perseveres in opposing the granting of the right of suffrage to the unnaturalized foreigner in the Territories. Congress cannot deny him that right. Here is the third article of that convention by which Louisiana, including Kansas and Nebraska, was ceded to the United States:

"The inhabitants of the ceded territory shall be incorporated in the Union of the United States, and admitted as soon as possible, according to the principles of the Federal Constitution, to the enjoyment of the rights, privileges, and immunities of citizens of the United States; and in the mean time they shall be maintained and protected in the free enjoyment of their liberty, property, and the religion they profess."

The inhabitants of Kansas and Nebraska are citizens already, and by force of this treaty must continue to be, and as such to enjoy the right of suffrage, whatever laws you may make to the contrary. My opinions are well known, to wit: That Slavery is not only an evil, but a local one, injurious and ultimately pernicious to society, wherever it exists, and in conflict with the constitutional principles of society in this country. I am not willing to extend nor to permit the extension of that local evil into regions now free within our empire. I know that there are some who differ from me, and who regard the Constitution of the United States as an instrument which sanctions Slavery as well as Freedom. But if I could admit a proposition so incongruous with the letter and spirit of the Federal Constitution, and the known sentiments of its illustrious founders, and so should conclude that Slavery was national, I must still cherish the opinion that it is an evil; and because it is a national one, I am the more firmly held and bound to prevent an increase of it, tending, as I think it manifestly does, to the weakening and ultimate overthrow of the Constitution itself, and therefore to the injury of all mankind. I know there have been States which have endured long, and achieved much, which tolerated Slavery; but that was not the Slavery of caste, like African Slavery. Such Slavery tends to demoralize equally the subject-ed race and the superior one. It has been the absence of such Slavery from Europe that has given her nations their superiority over other countries in that hemisphere. Slavery, wherever it exists, begets fear, and fear is the parent of weakness. What is the secret of that eternal, sleepless anxiety in the legislative halls, and even at the firesides of the Slave States, always asking new stipulations, new compromises and abrogation of compromises, new assumptions of power and abnegations of power, but fear? It is the apprehension, that, even if safe now, they will not always or long be secure against some invasion or some aggression from the Free States. What is the secret of the humiliating part which proud old Spain is acting at this day, trembling between alarms of American intrusion into Cuba on one side, and British dictation on the other, but the fact that she has cherished Slavery so long and still cherishes it, in the last of her American colonial possessions? Thus far Kansas and Nebraska are safe, under the laws of 1820, against the introduction of this element of national debility and decline. The bill before us, as we are assured, contains a great principle, a glorious principle; and yet that principle, when fully ascertained, proves to be nothing less than the subversion of that security, not only within the Territories of Kansas and Nebraska, but within all the other present and future Territories of the United States. Thus it is quite clear that it is not a principle alone that is involved, but that those who crowd this measure with so much zeal and earnestness must expect that either Freedom or Slavery shall gain something by it in those regions. The case, then, stands thus in Kansas and Nebraska: Freedom may lose, but certainly can gain nothing; while Slavery may gain, but as certainly can lose nothing.

So far as I am concerned, the time for looking on the dark side has passed. I feel quite sure that Slavery at most can get nothing more than Kansas; while Nebraska—the wider northern region—will, under existing circumstances, escape, for the reason that its soil and climate are uncongenial with the staples of slave culture—rice, sugar, cotton, and tobacco. Moreover, since the public attention has been so well and so effectually directed toward the subject, I cherish a hope that Slavery may be prevented even from gaining a foothold in Kansas. Congress only gives consent, but it does not and cannot introduce Slavery there. Slavery will be embarrassed by its own overgrasping spirit. No one, I am sure, anticipates the possible re-establishment of the African Slave-trade. The tide of emigration to Kansas is therefore to be supplied there solely by the domestic fountain of slave production. But Slavery has also other regions besides Kansas to be filled from that fountain. There are all of New-Mexico and all of Utah already within the United States; and then there is Cuba that consumes slave labor and life as fast as any one of the slaveholding States can supply it; and besides these regions, there remains all of Mexico down to the Isthmus. The stream of slave labor flowing from so small a fountain, and broken into several divergent channels, will not cover so great a field; and it is reasonably to be hoped that the part of it nearest to the North Pole will be the last to be inundated. But African slave emigration is to compete with free emigration of white men, and the source of this latter tide is as ample as the civilization of the two entire continents. The honorable Senator from Delaware mentioned, as if it were a startling fact, that twenty thousand European immigrants arrived in New-York in one month. Sir, he has stated the fact with too much moderation. On my return to the capital a day or two ago, I met twelve thousand of these emigrants who had arrived in New-York on one morning, and who had thronged the churches on the following Sabbath, to return thanks for deliverance from the perils of the sea, and for their arrival in the land, not of Slavery but of Liberty. I also thank God for their escape, and for their coming. They are now on their way westward, and the news of the passage of this bill, preceding them, will speed many of them towards Kansas and Nebraska. Such arrivals are not extraordinary—they occur almost every week; and the immigration from Germany, from Great Britain, and from Norway, and from Sweden, during the European war, will rise to six or seven hundred thousand souls in a year. And with this tide is to be mingled one rapidly swelling from Asia and from the islands of the South Seas. All the immigrants under this bill, as the House of Representatives overruling you have ordered, will be good, loyal, Liberty-loving, Slavery-fearing citizens. Come on, then, gentlemen of the Slave States. Since there is no escaping your challenge, I accept it in behalf of the cause of Freedom. We will engage in competition for the virgin soil of Kansas, and God give the victory to the side which is stronger in numbers as it is in right.

There are, however, earnest advocates of this bill, who do not expect, and who, I suppose, do not desire, that Slavery shall gain possession of Nebraska. What do they expect to gain? The honorable Senator from Indiana [Mr. Pettit] says that by thus obliterating the Missouri Compromise restriction, they will gain a *tabula rasa*, on which the inhabitants of Kansas and Nebraska may write whatever they will. This is the great principle of the bill, as he understands it. Well, what gain is there in that? You obliterate a Constitution of Freedom. If they write a new Constitution of Freedom, can the new be better than the old? If they write a Constitution of Slavery, will it not be a worse one? I ask the honorable Senator that. But the honorable Senator says that the people of Nebraska will have the privilege of establishing institutions for themselves. They have now the privilege of establishing free institutions. Is it a privilege, then, to establish Slavery? If so, what a mockery are all our Constitutions, which prevent the inhabitants from capriciously subverting free institutions and establishing institutions of Slavery! Sir, it is a sophism, a subtlety, to talk of conferring upon a country, already secure in the blessings of Freedom, the power of self-destruction.

What mankind everywhere want, is not the removal of the Constitutions of Freedom which they have, that they may make at their pleasure Constitutions of Slavery or of Freedom, but the privilege of retaining Constitutions of Freedom when they already have them, and the removal of Constitutions of Slavery when they have them, that they may establish Constitutions of Freedom in their place. We hold on tenaciously to all existing Constitutions of Freedom. Who denounces any man for diligently adhering to such Constitutions? Who would dare to denounce any one for disloyalty to our existing Constitutions, if they were Constitutions of Despotism and Slavery? But it is supposed by some that this principle is less important in regard to Kansas and Nebraska than as a general one—a general principle applicable to all other present and future Territories of the United States. Do honorable Senators then indeed suppose they are establishing a principle at all? If so, I think they egregiously err, whether the principle is either good or bad, right or wrong. They are not establishing it, and cannot establish it in this way. You subvert one law capriciously, by making another law in its place. That is all. Will your law have any more weight, authority, solemnity, or binding force on future Congresses, than the first had? You abrogate the law of your predecessors—others will have equal power and equal liberty to abrogate yours. You allow no barriers around the old law, to protect it from abrogation. You erect none around your new law, to stay the hand of future innovators.

On what ground do you expect the new law to stand? If you are candid, you will confess that you rest your assumption on the ground that the Free States will never agitate repeal, but always *acquiesce*. It may be that you are right. I am not going to predict the course of the Free States. I claim no authority to speak for them, and still less to say what they will do. But I may venture to say, that if they shall not repeal this law, it will not be because they are not strong enough to do it. They have power in the House of Representatives greater than that of the Slave States, and, when they choose to exercise it, a power greater even here in the Senate. The Free States are not dull scholars, even in practical political strategy. When you shall have taught them that a compromise law establishing Freedom can be abrogated, and the Union nevertheless stand, you will have let them into another secret, namely: that a law permitting or establishing Slavery can be repealed, and the Union nevertheless remain firm. If you inquire why they do not stand by their rights and their interests more firmly, I will tell you to the best of my ability. It is because they are conscious of their strength, and, therefore, unsuspecting, and slow to apprehend danger. The reason why you prevail in so many contests, is because you are in perpetual fear.

There cannot be a convocation of Abolitionists, however impracticable, in Faneuil Hall or the Tabernacle, though it consists of men and women who have separated themselves from all effective political parties, and who have renounced all political agencies, even though they resolve that they will vote for nobody, not even for themselves, to carry out their purposes, and though they practice on that resolution, but you take alarm, and your agitation renders necessary such compromises as those of 1820 and of 1850. We are young in the arts of politics; you are old. We are strong; you are weak. We are, therefore, over-confident, careless, and indifferent; you are vigilant and active. These are traits that redound to your praise. They are mentioned not in your disparagement. I say only, that there may be an extent of intervention, of aggression on your side, which may induce the North, at some time, either in this or in some future generation, to adopt your tactics and follow your example. Remember now, that by unanimous consent, this new law will be a repealable statute, exposed to all the chances of the Missouri Compromise. It stands an infinitely worse chance of endurance than that compromise did.

The Missouri Compromise was a transaction which wise, learned, patriotic statesmen agreed to surround and fortify with the principles of a compact for mutual considerations, passed and executed, and therefore, although not irrepealable in fact, yet irrepealable in honor and conscience, and down at least until this very session of the Congress of the United States, it has had the force and authority not merely of an act of Congress, but of a covenant between the Free States and the Slave States, scarcely less sacred than the Constitution itself. Now then, who are your contracting parties in the law establishing Governments in Kansas and Nebraska, and abrogating the Missouri Compromise? What are the equivalents in this law? What has the North given, and what has the South got back, that makes this a contract? Who pretends that it is anything more than an ordinary act of ordinary legislation? If, then, a law which has all the forms and solemnities recognized by common consent as a compact, and is covered with traditions, cannot stand amid this shuffling of the balance between the Free States and the Slave States, tell me what chances this new law that you are passing will have?

You are, moreover, setting a precedent which abrogates all compromises. Four years ago, you obtained the consent of a portion of the Free States—enough to render the effort at immediate repeal or resistance alike impossible—to what we regard as an unconstitutional act for the surrender of fugitive slaves. That was declared, by the common consent of the persons acting in the name of the two parties, the Slave States and the Free States in Congress, an irrepealable law—not even to be questioned, although it violated the Constitution. In establishing this new principle, you expose that law also to the chances of repeal. You not only so expose the fugitive slave law, but there is no solemnity about the articles for the annexation of Texas to the United States, which does not hang about the Missouri Compromise; and when you have shown that the Missouri Compromise can be repealed, then the articles for the annexation of Texas are subject to the will and pleasure and the caprice of a temporary majority in Congress. Do you, then, expect that the Free States are to observe compacts, and you to be at liberty to break them; that they are to submit to laws and leave them on the statute-book, however unconstitutional and however grievous, and that you are to rest under no such obligation? I think it is not a reasonable expectation. Say, then, who from the North will be bound to admit Kansas, when Kansas shall come in here, if she shall come as a Slave State?

The honorable Senator from Georgia, [Mr. Toombs,] and I know he is as sincere as he is ardent, says if he shall be here when Kansas comes as a Free State, he will vote for her admission. I doubt not that he would; but he will not be here, for the very reason, if there be no other, that he would vote that way. When Oregon or Minnesota shall come here for admission—within one year, or two years, or three years from this time—we shall then see what your new principle is worth in its obligation upon the slaveholding States. No; you establish no principle, you only abrogate a principle which was established for your own security as well as ours; and while you think you are abnegating and resigning all power and all authority on this subject into the hands of the people of the Territories, you are only getting over a difficulty in settling this question in the organization of two new Territories, by postponing it till they come here to be admitted as States, slave or free.

Sir, in saying that your new principle will not be established by this bill, I reason from obvious, clear, well settled principles of human nature. Slavery and Freedom are antagonistical elements in this country. The founders of the Constitution framed it with a knowledge of that antagonism, and suffered it to continue, that it might work out its own ends. There is a commercial antagonism, an irreconcilable one, between the systems of free labor and slave labor. They have been at war with each other ever since the Government was established, and that war is to continue forever. The contest, when it ripens between these two antagonistic elements, is to be settled somewhere; it is to be settled in the seat of central power, in the Federal Legislature. The Constitution makes it the duty of the central Government to determine questions, as often as they shall arise, in favor of one or the other party, and refers the decision of them to the majority of the votes in the two Houses of Congress. It will come back here, then, in spite of all the efforts to escape from it.

This antagonism must end either in a separation of the antagonistic parties—the Slaveholding States and the Free States—or, secondly, in the complete establishment of the influence of the Slave power over the Free—or else, on the other hand, in the establishment of the superior influence of Freedom over the interests of Slavery. It will not be terminated by a voluntary secession of either party. Commercial interests bind the Slave States and the Free States together in links of gold that are riveted with iron, and they cannot be broken by passion or by ambition. Either party will submit to the ascendancy of the other, rather than yield the commercial advantages of this Union. Political ties bind the Union together—a common necessity, and not merely a common necessity, but the common interests of empire—of such empire as the world has never before seen. The control of the national power is the control of the great Western Continent; and the control of this continent is to be, in a very few years, the controlling influence in the world. Who is there, North, that hates Slavery so much, or who, South, that hates emancipation so intensely, that he can attempt, with any hope of success, to break a Union thus forged and welded together? I have always heard, with equal pity and disgust, threats of disunion in the Free States, and similar threats in the Slaveholding States. I know that men may rave in the heat of passion, and under great political excitement; but I know that when it comes to a question whether this Union shall stand, either with Freedom or with Slavery, the masses will uphold it, and it will stand until some inherent vice in its Constitution, not yet disclosed, shall cause its dissolution. Now, entertaining these opinions, there are for me only two alternatives, viz.: either to let Slavery gain unlimited sway, or so to exert what little power and influence I may have, as to secure, if I can, the ultimate predominance of Freedom.

In doing this, I do no more than those who believe the Slave Power is rightest, wisest, and best, are doing, and will continue to do, with my free consent, to establish its complete supremacy. If they shall succeed, I still shall be, as I have been, a loyal citizen. If we succeed, I know they will be loyal also, because it will be safest, wisest, and best for them to be so. The question is one, not of a day, or of a year, but of many years, and, for aught I know, many generations. Like all other great political questions, it will be attended sometimes by excitement, sometimes by passion, and sometimes, perhaps, even by faction; but it is sure to be settled in a constitutional way, without any violent shock to society, or to any of its great interests. It is, moreover, sure to be settled rightly; because it will be settled under the benign influences of Republicanism and Christianity, according to the principles of truth and justice, as ascertained by human reason. In pursuing such a course, it seems to me obviously as wise as it is necessary to save all existing laws and Constitutions which are conservative of Freedom, and to permit, as far as possible, the establishment of no new ones in favor of Slavery; and thus to turn away the thoughts of the States which tolerate Slavery, from political efforts to perpetuate what in its nature cannot be perpetual, to the more wise and benign policy of emancipation.

This, in my humble judgment, is the simple, easy path of duty for the American Statesman. I will not contemplate that other alternative—the greater ascendancy of the Slave Power. I believe that if it shall ever come, the voice of Freedom will cease to be heard in these Halls, whatever may be the evils and dangers which Slavery shall produce. I say this without disrespect for Representatives of Slave States, and I say it because the rights of petition and of debate on that are effectually suppressed—necessarily suppressed—in all the Slave States, and because they are not always held in reverence, even now, in the two Houses of Congress. When freedom of speech on a subject of such vital interest shall have ceased to exist in Congress, then I shall expect to see Slavery not only luxuriating in all new Territories, but stealthily creeping even into the Free States themselves. Believing this, and believing, also, that complete responsibility of the Government to the people is essential to public and private safety, and that decline and ruin are sure to follow, always, in the train of Slavery, I am sure that this will be no longer a land of Freedom and constitutional liberty when Slavery shall have thus become paramount. *Auferre trucidare falsis nominibus imperium atque, ubi solitudinem faciunt, pacem appellant.*

Sir, I have always said that I should not despond, even if this fearful measure should be effected; nor do I now despond. Although, reasoning from my present convictions, I should not have voted for the compromise of 1820, I have labored, in the very spirit of those who established it, to save the landmark of Freedom which it assigned. I have not spoken irreverently even of the compromise of 1850, which, as all men know, I opposed earnestly and with diligence. Nevertheless, I have always preferred the compromises of the Constitution, and have wanted no others. I feared all others. This was a leading principle of the great statesman of the South, [Mr. Calhoun]. Said he:

"I see my way in the Constitution; I cannot in a compromise. A compromise is but an act of Congress. It may be overruled at any time. It gives us no security. But the Constitution is stable. It is a rock on which we can stand, and on which we can meet our friends from the non-slaveholding States. It is a firm and stable ground, on which we can better stand in opposition to fanaticism than on the shifting sands of compromise. Let us be done with compromises. Let us go back and stand upon the Constitution."

I stood upon this ground in 1850, defending Freedom upon it as Mr. Calhoun did in defending Slavery. I was overruled then, and I have waited since without proposing to abrogate any compromises.

It has been no proposition of mine to abrogate them now; but the proposition has come from another quarter—from an adverse one. It is about to prevail. The shifting sands of compromise are passing from under my feet, and they are now, without agency of my own, taking hold again on the rock of the Constitution. It shall be no fault of mine if they do not remain firm. This seems to me auspicious of better days and wiser legislation. Through all the darkness and gloom of the present hour, bright stars are breaking, that inspire me with hope, and excite me to perseverance. They show that the day of compromises has past forever, and that henceforward all great questions between Freedom and Slavery legitimately coming here—and none other can come—shall be decided, as they ought to be, upon their merits, by a fair exercise of legislative power, and not by bargains of equivocal prudence, if not of doubtful morality.

The House of Representatives has, and it always will have, an increasing majority of members from the Free States. On this occasion, that House has not been altogether faithless to the interests of the Free States; for although it has taken away the charter of Freedom from Kansas and Nebraska, it has, at the same time, told this proud body, in language which compels acquiescence, that in submitting the question of its restoration, it would submit it not merely to interested citizens, but to the alien inhabitants of the Territories also. So the great interests of humanity are, after all, thanks to the House of Representatives, and thanks to God, submitted to the voice of human nature.

Sir, I see one more sign of hope. The great support of Slavery in the South has been its alliance with the Democratic party of the North. By means of that alliance, it obtained paramount influence in this Government about the year 1800, which from that time to this, with but few and slight interruptions, it has maintained. While Democracy in the North has thus been supporting Slavery in the South, the people of the North have been learning more profoundly the principles of republicanism and of free government. It is an extraordinary circumstance, which you, sir, the present occupant of the chair, [Mr. Stuart], I am sure will not gainsay, that at this moment, when there seems to be a more complete divergence of the Federal Government, in favor of Slavery, than ever before, the sentiment of Universal Liberty is stronger in all Free States than it ever was before. With that principle, the present Democratic party must now come into a closer contest. Their prestige of Democracy is fast waning, by reason of the hard service which their alliance with their slaveholding brethren has imposed upon them. That party perseveres, as indeed it must, by reason of its very constitution, in that service, and thus comes into closer conflict with elements of true Democracy, and for that reason is destined to lose, and is fast losing, the power which it has held so firmly and long. That power will not be restored until the principle established here now shall be reversed, and a Constitution shall be given, not only to Kansas and Nebraska, but also to every other national Territory, which will be not a *tabula rasa*, but a Constitution securing equal, universal, and perpetual Freedom.

Mr. Douglas closed the debate, reiterating and enforcing the views set forth in his Report already given; and at last the vote was taken, and the bill passed: Yeas 37; Nays 14; as follows:

YEAS—For the Kansas-Nebraska bill:

Messrs. Adams, Atchison, Badger, Bayard, Benjamin, Brodhead, Brown, Butler, Cass, Clay, Dawson, Dixon, Dodge of Iowa, Douglas, Evans, Hunter, Johnson, Jones of Iowa, Jones of Tenn. Mason, Morton, Norris, Pettit, Pratt, Rusk, Sebastian, Shields, Slidell, Stuart, Thompson of Ky. Fitzpatrick, Geyer, Gwin, Thomson of N. J. Toucey, Weller, Williams—37.

NAYS—Against the said bill;

Messrs. Bell, Chase, Dodge of Wisc. Fessenden, Fish, Foot, Hamlin, Houston, James, Seward, Smith, Sumner, Wade, Walker—14.

So the bill was passed, and its title declared to be "An Act to organize the Territories of Nebraska and Kansas," and the Senate adjourned over to the Tuesday following.

In the House, a bill to organize the Territory of Nebraska had been noticed on the first day of the session, by Mr. John G. Miller of Mo., who introduced it December 22nd.

Jan. 24th.—Mr. Giddings gave notice of a bill to organize said Territory.

Jan. 30th.—Mr. Pringle of N. Y. endeavored to have the bill passed at the last session (leaving the Missouri Restriction intact), reported by the Committee on Territories; but debate arose, and his resolution lay over.

Jan. 31st.—Mr. Richardson of Ill., chairman of the Committee on Territories, reported a bill "To organize the Territories of Nebraska and Kansas," which was read twice and committed.

Mr. Richardson's bill was substantially Mr. Douglas's last bill, and was accompanied by no report. Mr. English of Ind. submitted the views of a minority of said Committee on Territories, proposing, without argument, the two following amendments:

1. Amend the section defining the boundary of Kansas, so as to make "the summit of the Rocky Mountains" the western boundary of said Territory.

2. Strike out of the 14th and 34th sections of said bill all after the words "United States," and insert in each instance (the one relating to Kansas, and the other to Nebraska) as follows:

Provided, That nothing in this act shall be so construed as to prevent the people of said Territory, through the properly-constituted legislative authority, from passing such laws, in relation to the institution of Slavery, as they may deem best adapted to their locality, and most conducive to their happiness and welfare; and so much of any existing act of Congress as may conflict with the above right of the people to regulate their domestic institutions in their own way, be, and the same is hereby, repealed."

This appears to have been an attempt to give practical effect to the doctrine of Squatter Sovereignty; but it was not successful.

May 8th.—On motion of Mr. Richardson, the House—Yeas 109; Nays 88—resolved itself into a Committee of the Whole, and took up the bill (House No. 236) to organize the Territories of Nebraska and Kansas, and discussed it—Mr. Olds of Ohio in the chair.

On coming out of Committee, Mr George W. Jones of Tenn. moved that the rules be suspended so as to enable him to move the printing of Senate bill (No. 22, passed the Senate as aforesaid) and the amendment now pending to the House bill. No quorum voted—adjourned.

May 9th.—This motion prevailed. After debate in Committee on the Kansas-Nebraska bill, the Committee found itself without a quorum, and thereupon rose and reported the fact to the House—only 106 Members were found to be present. After several fruitless attempts to adjourn, a call was ordered and a quorum obtained, at 9 P. M. At 10, an adjournment prevailed.

May 10th.—Debate in Committee continued.

May 11th.—Mr. Richardson moved that all debate in Committee close to-morrow at noon.

Mr. English moved a call of the House: Refused; Yeas 88; Nays 97.

Mr. Mace moved that Mr. Richardson's motion be laid on the table: Defeated; Yeas 95; Nays 100.

Mr. Edgerton of Ohio moved a call of the House: Refused; Yeas 45; Nays 80.

[The day was spent in what has come to be called "Filibustering"—that is, the minority moving adjournments, calls of the House, asking to be excused from voting, taking appeals, etc., etc. In the midst of this, Mr. Richardson withdrew his original motion, and moved instead that the debate in Committee be closed in five minutes after the House shall have resumed it.

The hour of noon of the 12th having arrived, Messrs. Dean and Banks raised points of order as to the termination of the legislative day. The Speaker decided that the legislative day could only be terminated by the adjournment of the House, except by constitutional conclusion of the session. Mr. Banks appealed, but at length withdrew his appeal.

Finally, at 11½ o'clock, P. M., of Friday, 12th, after a continuous sitting of thirty-six hours, the House, on motion of Mr. Richardson, adjourned.

May 13th.—The House sat but two hours, and effected nothing.

May 15th.—Mr. Richardson withdrew his demand for the Previous Question on closing the debate, and moved instead that the debate close at noon on Friday the 19th instant. This he finally modified by substituting Saturday the 20th; and in this shape his motion prevailed by a two-thirds majority—Yeas 137; Nays 66—the following opponents of the bill voting for the motion, namely:

MAINE.—Thomas J. D. Fuller, Samuel Mayall—2.

NEW-HAMPSHIRE.—Geo. W. Kittredge, Geo. W. Morrison—2.

MASSACHUSETTS.—Nathaniel P. Banks, jr.—1.

CONNECTICUT.—Origen S. Seymour—1.

NEW-YORK.—Gilbert Dean, Charles Hughes —2.

PENNSYLVANIA.—Michael C. Trout—1.

OHIO.—Alfred P. Edgerton, Harvey H. Johnson, Andrew Ellison, William D. Lindsley, Thomas Richey—5.

INDIANA.—Andrew J. Harlan, Daniel Mace—2.

ILLINOIS.—John Wentworth—1.

MICHIGAN.—David A. Noble, Hestor L. Stevens—2.

WISCONSIN.—John B. Macy—1.

VIRGINIA.—John S. Millson—1.

Total—21.

Mr. Richardson, having thus got in his resolution to close the debate, put on the previous question again, and the House—Yeas, 113; Nays, 59—agreed to close the debate on the 20th.

Debate having been closed, the opponents of the measure expected to defeat or cripple it by moving and taking a vote in Committee on various propositions of amendment, kindred to those moved and rejected in the Senate; some of which it was believed a majority of the House would not choose (or dare) to vote down; and, though the names of those voting on one side or the other in Committee of the Whole are not recorded, yet any proposition moved and rejected there, may be renewed in the House after taking the bill out of committee, and is no longer cut off by the Previous Question; as it formerly was. But, when the hour for closing debate in Committee had arrived, Mr. Alex. H. Stephens moved that *the enacting clause of the bill be stricken out;* which was carried by a rally of the friends of the bill, and of course cut off all amendments. The bill was thus reported to the House with its head off; when, after a long struggle, the House *refused to agree to the report of the Committee of the Whole*—Yeas (for agreeing) 97; Nays 117—bringing the House to a direct vote on the engrossment of the bill.

Mr. Richardson now moved an amendment, which was a substitute for the whole bill, being substantially the Senate's bill, with the clause admitting aliens, who have declared their intention to become citizens, to the right of suffrage. He thereupon called the Previous Question, which the House sustained—Yeas 116; Nays 90—when the House adopted his amendment—Yeas 115; Nays 95—and proceeded to engross the bill—Yeas 112; Nays 99—when he put on the Previous Question again, and passed the bill finally—Yeas 113; Nays 100—as follows:

YEAS—113.

FROM THE FREE STATES.

MAINE—Moses McDonald—1.

NEW-HAMPSHIRE—Harry Hibbard—1.

CONNECTICUT—Colin M. Ingersoll—1.

VERMONT—*None.* MASSACHUSETTS—*None.*

RHODE ISLAND—*None.*

NEW-YORK—Thomas W. Cumming, Francis B. Cutting, Peter Rowe, John J. Taylor, William M. Tweed, Hiram Walbridge, William A. Walker, Mike Walsh, Theo. R. Westbrook—9.

PENNSYLVANIA—Samuel A. Bridges, John L. Dawson, Thomas B. Florence, J. Glancy Jones, William H. Kurtz, John McNair, Asa Packer, John Robbins, Jr., Christian M. Straub, William H. Witte, Hendrick B. Wright—11.

NEW-JERSEY—Samuel Lilly, George Vail—2.

OHIO—David T. Disney, Frederick W. Green, Edson B. Olds, Wilson Shannon—4.

INDIANA—John G. Davis, Cyrus L. Dunham, Norman Eddy, William H. English, Thomas A. Hendricks, James H. Lane, Smith Miller—7.

ILLINOIS—James C. Allen, Willis Allen, Wm. A. Richardson—3.

MICHIGAN—Samuel Clark, David Stuart—2.

IOWA—Bernhart Henn—1.

WISCONSIN—*None.*

CALIFORNIA—Milton S. Latham, J. A. McDougall—2. Total 44.

FROM THE SLAVE STATES.

DELAWARE—George R. Riddle—1.

MARYLAND—William T. Hamilton, Henry May, Jacob Shower, Joshua Vansant—4.

VIRGINIA—Thomas H. Bayly, Thomas S. Bocock, John S. Caskie, Henry A. Edmundson, Charles J. Faulkner, William O. Goode, Zedekiah Kidwell, John Letcher, Paulus Powell, William Smith, John F. Snodgrass—11.

NORTH CAROLINA—William S. Ashe, Burton Craige, Thomas L. Clingman, *John Kerr*, Thos. Ruffin, Henry M. Shaw—6.

SOUTH CAROLINA—William W. Boyce, Preston S. Brooks, James L. Orr—3.

GEORGIA—David J. Bailey, Elijah W. Chastain, Alfred H. Colquitt, Junius Hillyer, *David A. Reese*, Alex. H. Stephens—6.

ALABAMA—*James Abercrombie*, Williamson R. W. Cobb, James F. Dowdell, Sampson W. Harris, George S. Houston, Philip Phillips, William R. Smith—7.

MISSISSIPPI—William S. Barry, William Barksdale, Otho R. Singleton, Daniel B. Wright—4.

LOUISIANA—William Dunbar, Roland Jones, John Perkins, Jr.—3

KENTUCKY—John C. Breckenridge, James S. Chrisman, *Leander M. Cox, Clement S. Hill*, John M. Elliot, *Benj. E. Grey, William Preston*, Richard H. Stanton—8.

TENNESSEE—William M. Churchwell, George W. Jones, *Charles Ready*, Samuel A. Smith, Frederick P. Stanton, *Felix K. Zollicoffer*—6.

MISSOURI—Alfred W. Lamb, *James J. Lindley, John G. Miller, Mordecai Oliver*, John S. Phelps—5.

ARKANSAS—Alfred B. Greenwood, Edwin A. Warren—2.

FLORIDA—Augustus E. Maxwell—1.

TEXAS—Peter H. Bell, Geo. W. Smyth—2.

Total—69.

Total, Free and Slave States—113.

NAYS—100.

FREE STATES.

MAINE—*Samuel P. Benson, E. Wilder Farley*, Thomas J. D. Fuller, Samuel Mayall, *Israel Washburn, Jr.*—5.

NEW-HAMPSHIRE—George W. Kittredge, George W. Morrison—2.

MASSACHUSETTS—Nathaniel P. Banks, Jr., *Samuel L. Crocker*, ALEX. DE WITT, *Edward Dickinson, J. Wiley Edmands, Thomas D. Eliot, John Z. Goodrich, Charles W. Upham, Samuel H. Walley, Tappan Wentworth*—10.

RHODE ISLAND—Thomas Davis, Benjamin B. Thurston—2.

CONNECTICUT—Nathan Belcher, James T. Pratt, Origen S. Seymour—3.

VERMONT—*James Meacham, Alvah Sabin, Andrew Tracy*—3.

NEW-YORK—*Henry Bennett, Davis Carpenter*, Gilbert Dean, Caleb Lyon, Reuben E. Fenton, *Thomas T. Flagler*, George Hastings, *Solomon G. Haven*, Charles Hughes, Daniel T. Jones, *Orsamus B. Matteson, Edwin B. Morgan*, William Murray, Andrew Oliver, Jared V. Peck, Rufus W. Peckham, Bishop Perkins, *Benjamin Pringle, Russell Sage, George A. Simmons*, GERRIT SMITH, John Wheeler—22.

NEW-JERSEY—*Alex. C. M. Pennington*, Charles Skelton, Nathan T. Stratton—3.

PENNSYLVANIA—*Joseph R. Chandler*, Carlton B. Curtis, *John Dick*, Augustus Drum, *William Everhart*, James Gamble, Galusha A. Grow, *Isaac E. Hiester, Thomas M. Howe, John McCulloch, Ner Middleswarth, David Ritchie, Samuel L. Russell*, Michael C. Trout—14.

OHIO—*Edward Ball, Lewis D. Campbell*, Alfred P. Edgerton, Andrew Ellison, JOSHUA R. GIDDINGS, *Aaron Harlan, John Scott Harrison*, H. H. Johnson, William D. Lindsley, M. H. Nichols, Thomas Richey, *William R. Sapp*, Andrew Stuart, *John L. Taylor*, EDWARD WADE—15.

INDIANA—Andrew J. Harlan, Daniel Mace, *Samuel W. Parker*—3.

ILLINOIS—*James Knox, Jesse O. Norton, Elihu B. Washburne*, John Wentworth, *Richard Yates*—5.

MICHIGAN—David A. Noble, Hestor L. Stevens—2.

WISCONSIN—Benjamin C. Eastman, Daniel Wells, Jr.—2.

IOWA—*None.* CALIFORNIA—*None.* Total—91.

SOUTHERN STATES.

VIRGINIA—John S. Millson—1.

NORTH CAROLINA—*Richard C. Puryear, Sion H. Rogers*—2.

TENNESSEE—*Robert M. Bugg, William Cullom, Emerson Etheridge, Nathaniel G. Taylor*—4.

LOUISIANA—*Theodore G. Hunt*—1.

MISSOURI—Thomas H. Benton—1.

OTHER SOUTHERN STATES—*None.* Total—9.

Total, Free and Slave States—100.

ABSENT, OR NOT VOTING—21.

N. ENGLAND STATES—*William Appleton* of Mass.—1.

NEW-YORK—*Geo. W. Chase*, James Maurice—2.

PENNSYLVANIA—*None.* NEW-JERSEY—*None.*

OHIO—George Bliss, *Moses B. Corwin*—2.

ILLINOIS—Wm. H. Bissell—1.

CALIFORNIA—*None.*

INDIANA—Eben M. Chamberlain—1.

MICHIGAN—*None.* IOWA—*John P. Cook*—1.

WISCONSIN—John B. Macy—1.

Total from Free States—9.

MARYLAND—*John R. Franklin, Augustus R Sollers*—2.

VIRGINIA—Fayette McMullen—1.

NORTH CAROLINA—*None.* DELAWARE—*None.*

SOUTH CAROLINA—Wm. Aiken, Lawrence M. Keitt, John McQueen—3.

GEORGIA—Wm. B. W. Dent, James L. Seward—2.

ALABAMA—*None.*

MISSISSIPPI—Wiley P. Harris—1.

KENTUCKY—Linn Boyd, (Speaker,) *Presley Ewing*—2.

MISSOURI—*Samuel Caruthers*—1.

ARKANSAS—*None.* FLORIDA—*None.*

TEXAS—*None.* TENNESSEE—*None.*

LOUISIANA—*None.*

Total from Slave States—12.

Whigs in *Italics.* Abolitionists in SMALL CAPITALS. Democrats in Roman.

May 23d.—The bill being thus sent to the Senate (not as a Senate but as a House bill), was sent at once to the Committee of the Whole, and there briefly considered.

May 24th.—Mr. Pearce of Md. moved to strike out the clause in sec. 5 which extends the right of suffrage to

"those who shall have declared on oath their intention to become such, [citizens] and shall have taken an oath to support the Constitution of the United States, and the provisions of this act."

Negatived—Yeas; Bayard, Bell, Brodhead, Brown, Clayton, Pearce, and Thompson of Ky Nays 41.

The bill was then ordered to be engrossed for a third reading—Yeas 35; Nays 13, as follows:

YEAS—For Engrossing:

Messrs. Atchison, Mo. | Mason, Va.
Badger, N. C. | *Morton*, Fla.
Benjamin, La. | Norris, N. H.
Brodhead, Pa. | *Pearce*, Md.
Brown, Miss. | Pettit, Ind.
Butler, S. C. | *Pratt*, Md.
Cass, Mich. | Rusk, Texas,
Clay, Ala. | Sebastian, Ark.
Dawson, Ga. | Shields, Ill.
Douglas, Ill. | Slidell, La.
Fitzpatrick, Ala. | Stuart, Mich.
Gwin, Cal. | *Thompson*, Ky.
Hunter, Va. | Thomson, N. J.
Johnson, Ark. | Toombs, Ga.
Jones, Iowa, | Toucey, Ct.
Jones, Tenn. | Weller, Cal.
Mallory, Fla. | Williams, N. H.
Wright, N. J.—35.

NAYS—Against Engrossing:

Messrs. Allen, R. I. | GILLETTE, Ct.
Bell, Tenn. | Hamlin, Me.
CHASE, Ohio, | James, R. I.
Clayton, Del. | *Seward*, N. Y.
Fish, N. Y. | SUMNER, Mass.
Foot, Vt. | *Wade*, Ohio,
Walker, Wisc.—13.

Democrats in Roman; Whigs in *Italics*; Free Democrats in SMALL CAPS.

The bill was then passed without further division, and, being approved by the President, became a law. Its provisions are as follows:

An Act to organize the Territories of Nebraska and Kansas.

Be it enacted by the Senate and House of Representatives of the United States of America in Congress assembled: That all that part of the Territory of the United States included within the following limits, except such portions thereof as are hereinafter expressly exempted from the operations of this act, to wit: beginning at a point in the Missouri river where the fortieth parallel of north latitude crosses the same; thence west on said parallel to the east boundary of the Territory of Utah on the summit of the Rocky Mountains; thence on said summit northward to the forty-ninth parallel of north latitude; thence east on said parallel to the western boundary of the Territory of Minnesota; thence southward on said boundary to the Missouri river; thence down the main channel of said river to the place of beginning, be, and the same is hereby created into a temporary government by the name of the Territory of Nebraska; and when admitted as a State or States, the said Territory, or any portion of the same, shall be received into the Union with or without Slavery, as their constitution may prescribe at the time of their admission: *Provided*, That nothing in this act contained shall be construed to inhibit the government of the United States from dividing said Territory into two or more territories, in such manner and at such times as Congress shall deem convenient and proper, or from attaching any portion of said Territory to any other State or Territory of the United States: *Provided* further, That nothing in this act contained shall be construed to impair the rights of person or property now pertaining to the Indians in said Territory, so long as such rights shall remain unextinguished by treaty between the United States and such Indians, or to include any Territory which, by treaty with any Indian tribe, is not, without the consent of said tribe, to be included within the territorial limits or jurisdiction of any State or Territory; but all such Territory shall be excepted out of the boundaries, and constitute no part of the Territory of Nebraska, until said tribe shall signify their assent to the President of the United States to be included within the said Territory of Nebraska, or to affect the authority of the government of the United States to make any regulations respecting such Indians, their lands, property, or other rights, by treaty, law, or otherwise, which it would have been competent to the government to make if this act had never passed.

SEC. 2. That the executive power and authority in and over said Territory of Nebraska shall be vested in a governor, who shall hold his office for four years, and until his successor shall be appointed and qualified, unless sooner removed by the President of the United States. The governor shall reside within said Territory, and shall be commander-in-chief of the militia thereof. He may grant pardons and respites for offenses against the laws of said Territory, and reprieves for offenses against the laws of the United States, until the decision of the President can be made known thereon; he shall commission all officers who shall be appointed to office under the laws of the said Territory, and shall take care that the laws be faithfully executed.

SEC. 3. That there shall be a secretary of said Territory, who shall reside therein, and hold his office for five years, unless sooner removed by the President of the United States; he shall record and preserve all the laws and proceedings of the legislative assembly hereinafter constituted, and all the acts and proceedings of the governor in his executive department; he shall transmit one copy of the laws and journals of the legislative assembly, within thirty days after the end of each session, and one copy of the executive proceedings and official correspondence semi-annually on the first days of January and July in each year, to the President of the United States, and two copies of the laws to the President of the Senate and to the Speaker of the

House of Representatives, to be deposited in the libraries of Congress; and, in case of the death, removal, resignation, or absence of the governor from the Territory, the secretary shall be, and he is hereby authorized and required to execute and perform all the powers and duties of the governor during such vacancy or absence, or until another governor shall be duly appointed and qualified to fill such vacancy.

SEC. 4. That the legislative power and authority of said Territory shall be vested in the governor and a legislative assembly. The legislative assembly shall consist of a council and house of representatives. The council shall consist of thirteen members, having the qualifications of voters as hereinafter prescribed, whose term of service shall continue two years. The house of representatives shall, at its first session, consist of twenty-six members, possessing the same qualifications as prescribed for members of the council, and whose term of service shall continue one year. The number of representatives may be increased by the legislative assembly, from time to time, in proportion to the increase of qualified voters; *Provided*, That the whole number shall never exceed thirty-nine; an apportionment shall be made as nearly equal as practicable, among the several counties or districts, for the election of the council and representatives, giving to each section of the territory representation in the ratio of its qualified voters as nearly as may be. And the members of the council and of the house of representatives shall reside in, and be inhabitants of, the district or county, or counties, for which they may be elected, respectively. Previous to the first election, the governor shall cause a census, or enumeration of the inhabitants and qualified voters of the several counties and districts of the territory, to be taken by such persons and in such mode as the governor shall designate and appoint; and the persons so appointed shall receive a reasonable compensation therefor. And the first election shall be held at such times, and places, and be conducted in such manner, both as to the persons who shall superintend such election, and the returns thereof, as the governor shall appoint and direct; and he shall at the same time declare the number of members of the council and house of representatives to which each of the counties or districts shall be entitled under this act. The persons having the highest number of legal votes in each of said council districts for members of the council, shall be declared by the governor to be duly elected to the council; and the persons having the highest number of legal votes for the house of representatives, shall be declared by the governor to be duly elected members of said house: *Provided*, That in case two or more persons voted for shall have an equal number of votes, and in case a vacancy shall otherwise occur in either branch of the legislative assembly, the governor shall order a new election; and the persons thus elected to the legislative assembly shall meet at such place and on such day as the governor shall appoint; but thereafter, the time, place, and manner of holding and conducting all elections by the people, and the apportioning the representation in the several counties or districts to the council and house of representatives, according to the number of qualified voters, shall be prescribed by law, as well as the day of the commencement of the regular sessions of the legislative assembly: *Provided*, That no session in any one year shall exceed the term of forty days, except the first session, which may continue sixty days.

SEC. 5. That every free white male inhabitant above the age of twenty-one years, who shall be an actual resident of said territory, and shall possess the qualifications hereinafter prescribed, shall be entitled to vote at the first election, and shall be eligible to any office within the said territory; but the qualifications of voters, and of holding office, at all subsequent elections, shall be such as shall be prescribed by the legislative assembly: *Provided*, That the right of suffrage and of holding office shall be exercised only by citizens of the United States and those who shall have declared on oath their intention to become such, and shall have taken an oath to support the Constitution of the United States and the provisions of this act: *And provided further*, That no officer, soldier, seaman, or marine, or other person in the army or navy of the United States, or attached to troops in the service of the United States, shall be allowed to vote or hold office in said territory, by reason of being on service therein.

SEC. 6. That the legislative power of the territory shall extend to all rightful subjects of legislation consistent with the Constitution of the United States and the provisions of this act; but no law shall be passed interfering with the primary disposal of the soil; no tax shall be imposed upon the property of the United States; nor shall the lands or other property of non-residents be taxed higher than the lands or other property of residents. Every bill which shall have passed the council and house of representatives of the said territory, shall, before it become a law, be presented to the governor of the territory; if he approve, he shall sign it; but if not, he shall return it with his objections, to the house in which it originated, who shall enter the objections at large on their journal, and proceed to reconsider it. If, after such reconsideration, two-thirds of that house shall agree to pass the bill, it shall be sent, together with the objections to the other house, by which it shall likewise be reconsidered, and if approved by two-thirds of that house, it shall become a law. But in all such cases the votes of both houses shall be determined by yeas and nays, to be entered on the journal of each house respectively. If any bill shall not be returned by the governor, within three days (Sundays excepted) after it shall have been presented to him, the same shall be a law in like manner as if he had signed it, unless the assembly, by adjournment, prevent its return, in which case it shall not be a law.

SEC. 7. That all township, district, and county officers, not herein otherwise provided for, shall be appointed or elected, as the case may be, in such manner as shall be provided by the governor and legislative assembly of the Territory of Nebraska. The governor shall nominate, and, by and with the advice and consent of the legislative council, appoint all officers not herein otherwise provided for; and in the first instance the governor alone may appoint all said officers, who shall hold their offices until the end of the first session of the legislative assembly; and shall lay off the necessary districts for members of the council and house of representatives, and all other officers.

SEC. 8. That no member of the legislative assembly shall hold, or be appointed to, any office which shall have been created, or the salary or or emoluments of which shall have been increased, while he was a member, during the term for which he was elected, and for one year after the expiration of such term; but this restriction shall not be applicable to members of the first legislative assembly; and no person holding a commission or appointment under the United States, except postmasters, shall be a member of the legislative assembly, or shall hold any office under the government of said territory.

SEC. 9. That the judicial power of said Territory shall be vested in a supreme court, district courts, probate courts, and in justices of the peace. The supreme court shall consist of a chief justice and two associate justices, any two of whom shall constitute a quorum, and who shall hold a term at the seat of government of said Territory annually, and they shall hold their offices during the period of four years, and until their successors shall be appointed and qualified. The said Territory shall be divided into three judicial districts, and a district court shall be held in each of said districts by one of the justices of the supreme court, at such times and places as may be prescribed by law; and the said judges shall, after their appointments, respectively, reside in the district which shall be assigned them. The jurisdiction of the several courts herein provided for, both appellate and original, and that of the probate courts and of justices of the peace, shall be as limited by law: *Provided*, That justices of the peace shall not have jurisdiction of any matter in controversy when the title or boundaries of land may be in dispute, or where the debt or sum claimed shall exceed one hundred dollars; and the said supreme and district courts, respectively, shall possess chancery as well as common law jurisdiction. Each district court, or the judge thereof, shall appoint its clerk, who shall also be the register in chancery, and shall keep his office at the place where the court may be held. Writs of error, bills of exception, and appeals shall be allowed in all cases from the final decision of said district courts to the supreme court, under such regulations as may be prescribed by law; but in no case removed to the supreme court shall trial by jury be allowed in said court. The supreme court, or the justices thereof, shall appoint its own clerk, and every clerk shall hold his office at the pleasure of the court for which he shall have been appointed. Writs of error, and appeals from the final decision of said supreme court, shall be allowed, and may be taken to the supreme court of the United States, in the same manner and under the same regulations as from the circuit courts of the United States, where the value of the property, or the amount in controversy, to be ascertained by the oath or affirmation of either party, or other competent witness, shall exceed one thousand dollars; except only that in all cases involving title to slaves, the said writs of error or appeals shall be allowed and decided by the said supreme court, without regard to the value of the matter, property, or title in controversy; and except also that a writ of error or appeal shall also be allowed to the supreme court of the United States, from the decisions of the said supreme court created by this act, or of any judge thereof, or of the district courts created by this act, or of any judge thereof, upon any writ of habeas corpus, involving the question of personal freedom; *Provided*, That nothing herein contained shall be construed to apply to or affect the provisions of the "act respecting fugitives from justice, and persons escaping from the service of their masters," approved February twelfth, seventeen hundred and ninety-three, and the "act to amend and supplementary to the aforesaid act," approved September eighteenth, eighteen hundred and fifty; and each of the said district courts shall have and exercise the same jurisdiction in all cases arising under the Constitution and laws of the United States, as is vested in the circuit and district courts of the United States; and the said supreme and district courts of the said Territory, and the respective judges thereof, shall and may grant writs of habeas corpus in all cases in which the same are granted by the judges of the United States in the District of Columbia; and the first six days of every term of said courts, or so much thereof as shall be necessary, shall be appropriated to the trial of causes arising under the said Constitution and laws, and writs of error and appeal in all such cases shall be made to the supreme court of said Territory, the same as in other cases. The said clerk shall receive in all such cases the same fees which the clerks of the district courts of Utah Territory now receive for similar services.

SEC. 10. That the provisions of an act entitled "An act respecting fugitives from justice, and persons escaping from the service of their masters," approved February twelve, seventeen hundred and ninety-three, and the provisions of the act entitled "An act to amend, and supplementary to, the aforesaid act," approved September eighteen, eighteen hundred and fifty, be, and the same are hereby, declared to extend to, and be in full force within, the limits of said Territory of Nebraska.

SEC. 11. That there shall be appointed an attorney for said Territory, who shall continue in office for four years, and until his successor shall be appointed and qualified, unless sooner removed by the President, and who shall receive the same fees and salary as the attorney of the United States for the present Territory of Utah. There shall also be a marshal for the Territory appointed, who shall hold his office for four years, and until his successor shall be appointed and qualified, unless sooner removed by the President, and who shall execute all processes issuing from the said courts when exercising their jurisdiction as circuit and district courts of the United States; he shall perform the duties, be subject to the same regulations and penalties, and be entitled to the same fees as the marshal of the district court of the United States for the present Territory of Utah, and shall, in addition, be paid two hundred dollars annually as a compensation for extra services.

SEC. 12. That the governor, secretary, chief justice, and associate justices, attorney and marshal, shall be nominated, and, by and with the advice and consent of the Senate, appointed by the President of the United States. The governor and secretary to be appointed as aforesaid, shall, before they act as such, respectively take an oath or affirmation by the laws now in force therein, or before the chief justice or some associate justice of the Supreme Court of the United States, to support the Constitution of the United States, and faithfully to discharge the duties of their respective offices, which said oaths, when so taken, shall be certified by the person by whom the same shall have been taken; and such certificates shall be received and recorded by the said secretary among the executive proceedings: and the chief justice and associate justices, and all other civil officers in said Territory, before they act as such, shall take a like oath or affirmation before the said governor or secretary, or some judge or justice of the peace of the territory who may be duly commissioned and qualified, which said oath or affirmation shall be certified and transmitted by the person taking the same to the secretary, to be by him recorded as aforesaid; and afterwards the like oath or affirmation shall be taken, certified, and recorded, in such manner and form as may be prescribed by law. The governor shall receive an annual salary of two thousand five hundred dollars. The chief justice and associate justices shall receive an annual salary of two thousand dollars. The secretary shall receive an annnal salary of two thousand dollars. The said salaries shall be paid quarter-yearly, from the dates of the respective appointments, at the Treasury of the United States; but no such payment shall be made until said officers shall have entered upon the duties of their respective appointments. The members of the legislative assembly shall be entitled to receive three dollars each per day during their attendance at the sessions thereof, and three dollars each for every twenty miles' travel in going to, and returning from, the said sessions, estimated according to the nearest usually-traveled route; and an additional allowance of three dollars shall be paid to the presiding officer of each house for each day he shall so preside. And a chief clerk, one assistant clerk, a sergeant-at-arms, and door-keeper may be chosen for each house; and the chief clerk shall receive four dollars per day, and the said other officers three dollars per day, during the session of the legislative assembly; but no other officer shall be paid by the United States: *Provided*, That there shall be but one session of the legislature annually, unless, on an extraordinary occasion, the governor shall think proper to call the legislature together. There shall be appropriated, annually, the usual sum, to be expended by the governor to defray the contingent expenses of the territory, including the salary of a clerk of the executive department; and there shall also be appropriated annually, a sufficient sum, to be expended by the secretary of the Territory, and upon an estimate to be made by the secretary of the Treasury of the United States, to defray the expenses of the legislative assembly, the printing of the laws, and other incidental expenses; and the governor and secretary of the Territory shall, in the disbursement of all moneys intrusted to them, be governed solely by the instructions of the secretary of the Treasury of the United States, and shall, semi-annually, account to the said secretary for the manner in which the aforesaid moneys shall have been expended; and no expenditure shall be made by said legislative assembly for objects not specially authorised by the acts of Congress making the appropriations, nor beyond the sums thus appropriated for such objects.

SEC. 13. That the legislative assembly of the Territory of Nebraska shall hold its first session at such time and place in said Territory as the governor thereof shall appoint and direct; and at said first session, or as soon thereafter as they shall deem expedient, the governor and legislative assembly shall proceed to locate and establish the seat of government for said Territory at such place as they may deem eligible; which place, however, shall thereafter be subject to be changed by the said governor and legislative assembly.

SEC. 14. That a delegate to the House of Representatives of the United States, to serve for the term of two years, who shall be a citizen of the United States, may be elected by the voters qualified to elect members of the legislative assembly, who shall be entitled to the same rights and privileges as are exercised and enjoyed by the delegates from the several other territories of the United States to the said House of Representatives; but the delegate first elected shall hold his seat only during the term of the Congress to which he shall be elected. The first election shall be held at such time and places, and be conducted in such manner, as the governor shall appoint and direct; and at all subsequent elections, the times, places, and manner of holding the elections shall be prescribed by law. The person having the greatest number of votes shall be declared by the governor to be duly elected, and a certificate thereof shall be given accordingly. That the Constitution and all the laws of the United States which are not locally inapplicable, shall have the same force and effect within the said Territory of Nebraska as elsewhere within the United States, except the eighth section of the act preparatory to the admission of Missouri into the Union, approved March sixth, eighteen hundred and twenty, which being inconsistent with the principle of non-intervention by Congress with Slavery in the States and Territories, as recognized by the legislation of eighteen hundred and fifty, commonly called the Compromise Measures, is hereby declared inoperative and void; it being the true intent and meaning of this act not to legislate Slavery into any Territory or State, nor to exclude it therefrom, but to leave the people thereof perfectly free to form and regulate their domestic institutions in their own way, subject only to the Constitution of the United States: *Provided*, That nothing herein contained shall be construed to revive or put in force any law or regulation which may have existed prior to the act of sixth of March, eighteen hundred and twenty, either protecting, establishing, prohibiting or abolishing, Slavery.

SEC. 15. That there shall hereafter be appropriated, as has been customary for the territorial governments, a sufficient amount, to be expended under the direction of the said governor of the Territory of Nebraska, not exceeding the sums heretofore appropriated for similar objects, for the erection of suitable public buildings at the seat of government, and for the purchase of a library to be kept at the seat of government for the use of the governor, legislative assembly, judges of the supreme court, secretary, marshal, and attorney of said territory, and such other persons, and under such regulations as shall be prescribed by law.

SEC. 16. That when the lands in the said territory shall be surveyed under the direction of the government of the United States, preparatory to bringing same into market, sections numbered sixteen and thirty-six, in each township in said territory, shall be, and the same are hereby, reserved for the purpose of being applied to schools in said teritory, and in the States and Territories hereafter to be erected out of the same.

SEC. 17. That, until otherwise provided by law, the governor of said Territory may define the judicial districts of said Territory, and assign the judges who may be appointed for said Territory to the several districts; and also appoint the times and places for holding courts in the several counties or subdivisions in each of said judicial districts by proclamation, to be issued by him; but the legislative assembly, at their first, or any subsequent session, may organize, alter, or modify such judicial districts, and assign the judges, and alter the times and places of holding the courts, as to them shall seem proper and convenient.

SEC. 18. That all officers to be appointed by the President, by and with the advice and consent of the Senate, for the Territory of Nebraska, who, by virtue of the provisions of any law now existing, or which may be enacted during the present Congress, are required to give security for moneys that may be intrusted with them for disbursements, shall give such security, at such time and place, and in such manner as the Secretary of the Treasury may prescribe.

SEC. 19. That all that part of the territory of the United States included within the following limits, except such portions thereof as are hereinafter expressly exempted from the operations of this act, to wit: beginning at a point on the western boundary of the State of Missouri, where the thirty-seventh parallel of north latitude crosses the same; thence west on said parallel to the eastern boundary of New-Mexico; thence north on said boundary to latitude thirty-eight; thence following said boundary westward to the east boundary of the Territory of Utah, on the summit of the Rocky Mountains; thence northward on said summit to the fortieth parallel of latitude; thence east on said parallel to the western boundary of the State of Missouri; thence south with the western boundary of said State to the place of beginning, be, and the same is hereby, created into a temporary government by the name of the Territory of Kansas; and when admitted as a

State or States, the said Territory, or any portion of the same, shall be received into the Union with or without Slavery, as their Constitution may prescribe at the time of their admission: *Provided*, That nothing in this act contained shall be construed to inhibit the Government of the United States from dividing said Territory into two or more territories, in such manner and at such times as Congress shall deem convenient and proper, or from attaching any portion of said Territory to any other State or Territory of the United States: *Provided further*, That nothing in this act contained shall be so construed as to impair the rights of person or property now pertaining to the Indians in said Territory, so long as such rights shall remain unextinguished by treaty between the United States and such Indians, or to include any territory which, by treaty with any Indian tribe, is not, without the consent of said tribe, to be included within the territorial limits or jurisdiction of any State or Territory; but all such territory shall be excepted out of the boundaries, and constitute no part of the Territory of Kansas, until said tribe shall signify their assent to the President of the United States to be included within the said Territory of Kansas, or to affect the authority of the Government of the United States to make any regulation respecting such Indians, their lands, property, or other rights, by treaty, law, or otherwise, which it would have been competent to the Government to make if this act had never passed.

[The next seventeen sections substantially repeat the foregoing, save that their provisions apply to Kansas instead of Nebraska. The final section refers to both Territories, as follows:]

SEC. 37. And be it further enacted, that all treaties, laws, and other engagements made by the Government of the United States with the Indian tribes inhabiting the territories embraced within this act, shall be faithfully and rigidly observed, notwithstanding anything contained in this act; and that the existing agencies and superintendencies of said Indians be continued with the same powers and duties which are now prescribed by law, except that the President of the United States may, at his discretion, change the location of the office of superintendent.

No action of any moment with regard to Slavery in the Territories was taken in either House at the Second (short) Session of this Congress.

KANSAS ORGANIZED.

The struggle respecting Slavery in Kansas which followed the organization of that Territory, under the Provisions of the act just recited, is yet too recent and incomplete to justify an attempt to write its history. All that can be prudently done as yet, is to collect and arrange the most important documents in which its incidents are detailed, and its principles discussed, and this we now proceed to do, without attempting to reconcile the gloomy discrepancies between the statements submitted on the one side and on the other, respectively. Though it will not be possible in this course to avoid repeated statements of the same fact, and an occasional devotion of undue space to a point undeserving of such elaborate treatment, yet, the measurable authenticity of statement, thus secured, and the light cast on the general theme by the conflicting views thus presented, serve to give this the preference over any other mode of narrating so nearly cotemporaneous with their chronicle as these. We proceed, then, with our record, which must henceforth consist mainly of public documents, submitted to the current Congress, connected by the merest thread of narrative.

Dec. 3rd, 1855.—The XXXIVth Congress convened at the Capital, in Washington,—Jesse D. Bright of Ind. holding over as President *pro tempore* of the Senate, in place of Vice-President William R. King of Alabama, deceased. A quorum of either House was found to be present.

But the House found itself unable to organize by the choice of a Speaker, until after an unprecedented struggle of nine weeks' duration. Finally, on Saturday, Feb. 20th, 1856, the plurality-rule was adopted—Yeas 113; Nays 104—and the House proceeded under it to its *one hundred and thirty-third* ballot for speaker, when Nathaniel P. Banks, Jr., (anti-Nebraska) of Massachusets, was chosen, having 103 votes to 100, for William Aiken of South Carolina. Eleven votes scattered on other persons did not count against a choice. It was therefore resolved—Yeas 155; Nays 40—that Mr. Banks was duly elected Speaker,

But, during the pendency of this election, the President had transmitted to both Houses, first (Dec. 31st) his Annual Message, and next (Jan. 24th) a special message with regard to the condition of Kansas, which is as follows:

MESSAGE OF THE PRESIDENT.

WASHINGTON, Jan. 24, 1856.

To the Senate and House of Representatives:

Circumstances have occurred to disturb the course of governmental organization in the Territory of Kansas, and produce there a condition of things which renders it incumbent on me to call your attention to the subject, and urgently recommend the adoption by you of such measures of legislation as the grave exigencies of the case appear to require.

A brief exposition of the circumstances referred to, and of their causes, will be necessary to the full understanding of the recommendations which it is proposed to submit.

The act to organize the Territories of Nebraska and Kansas was a manifestation of the legislative opinion of Congress on two great points of constitutional construction: One that the designation of the boundaries of a new Territory, and provision for its political organization and administration as a Territory, are measures which of right fall within the powers of the General Government; and the other, that the inhabitants of any such Territory, considered as an inchoate State, are entitled, in the exercise of self-government, to determine for themselves what shall be their own domestic institutions, subject only to the Constitution and the laws duly enacted by Congress under it, and to the power of the existing States to decide, according to the provisions and principles of the Constitution, at what time the Territory shall be received as a State into the Union. Such are the great political rights which are solemnly declared and affirmed by that act.

Based upon this theory, the act of Congress defined for each Territory the outlines of republican government, distributing public authority among the lawfully created agents—executive, judicial and legislative—to be appointed either by the General Government or by the Territory. The legislative functions were intrusted to a Council and a House of Representatives, duly elected and empowered to enact all the local laws which they might deem essential to their prosperity, happiness and good government. Acting in the same spirit, Congress also defined the persons who were in the first instance to be considered as the people of each Territory; enacting that every free white male inhabitant of the same above the age of twenty-one years, being an actual resident thereof, and possessing the qualifications hereafter described, should be entitled to vote at the first election, and be eligible to any office within the Territory; but that the qualifications of voters and holding office at all subsequent elections should be such as might be prescribed by the Legislative Assembly: *Provided, however*, That the right of suffrage and of holding office should be exercised only by citizens of the United States, and those who should have declared on oath their intention to become such, and have taken an oath to support the Constitution of the United States and the provisions of the act: *And provided, further*, That no officer, soldier, seaman or marine, or other person in the army or navy of the United States, or attached to troops in their service, should be allowed to vote or hold office in either Territory by reason of being on service therein.

Such of the public officers of the Territories as, by the provisions of the act, were to be appointed by the General Government, including the Governors, were appointed and commissioned in due season—the law having been enacted on the 30th of May, 1854, and the commission of the Governor of the Territory of Nebraska being dated on the 2nd day of August, 1854, and of the Territories of Kansas on the 29th day of June, 1854.

Among the duties imposed by the act on the governors, was that of directing and superintending the political organization of the respective Territories. The Governor of Kansas was required to cause a census or enumeration of the inhabitants and qualified voters of the several counties and districts of the Territory to be taken, by such persons and in such mode as he might designate and appoint; to appoint and direct the time and places of holding the first elections, and the manner of conducting them, both as to the persons to superintend such elections, and the returns thereof; to declare the number of the members of the Council and House of Representatives for each county or district; to declare what persons might appear to be duly elected; and to appoint the time and place of the first meeting of the Legislative Assembly. In substance, the same duties were devolved on the Governor of Nebraska.

While, by this act, the principle of constitution for each of the Territories was one and the same, and the details of organic legislation regarding both were as nearly as could be identical, and while the Territory of Nebraska was tranquilly and successfully organized in the due course of law, and its first Legislative Assembly met on the 16th of January, 1855, the organization of Kansas was long delayed, and has been attended with serious difficulties and embarrassments, partly the consequence of local maladministration, and partly of the unjustifiable interference of the inhabitants of some of the States, foreign by residence, interests, and rights to the Territory.

The Governor of the Territory of Kansas, commissioned, as before stated, on the 29th of June, 1854, did not reach the designated seat of his government until the 7th of the ensuing October, and even then failed to make the first step in its legal organization—that of ordering the census or enumeration of its inhabitants—until so late a day that the election of the members of the Legislative Assembly did not take place until the 30th of March, 1855, nor its meeting until the 2d of July, 1855; so that, for a year after the Territory was constituted by the act of Congress, and the officers to be appointed by the Federal Executive had been commissioned, it was without a complete government, without any legislative authority, without local law, and, of course, without the ordinary guarantees of peace and public order.

In other respects, the Governor, instead of exercising constant vigilance and putting forth all his energies to prevent or counteract the tendencies to illegality which are prone to exist in all imperfectly-organized and newly-associated communities, allowed his attention to be diverted from official obligation by other objects, and himself set an example of the violation of law in the performance of acts which rendered it my duty, in the sequel, to remove him from the office of chief executive magistrate of the Territory.

Before the requisite preparation was accomplished for election of a Territorial Legislature, an election of delegate to Congress had been held in the Territory on the 29th day of November, 1854, and the delegate took his seat in the House of Representatives without challenge. If arrangements had been perfected by the Governor so that the election for members of the Legislative Assembly might be held in the several precincts at the same time as for delegate to Congress, any question appertaining to the qualification of the persons voting as people of the Territory, would have passed necessarily and at once under the supervision of Congress, as the judge of the validity of the return of the delegate, and would have been determined before conflicting passions had become inflamed by time, and before opportunity could have been afforded for systematic interference of the people of individual States.

This interference, in so far as concerns its primary causes and its immediate commencement, was one of the incidents of that pernicious agitation on the subject of the condition of the colored persons held to service in some of the States, which has so long disturbed the repose of our country, and excited individuals, otherwise patriotic and law-abiding, to toil with misdirected zeal in the attempt to propagate their social theories by the perversion and abuse of the powers of Congress.

The persons and parties whom the tenor of the act to organize the Territories of Nebraska and Kansas thwarted in the endeavor to impose, through the agency of Congress, their particular views of social organization on the people of the future new States, now perceiving that the policy of leaving the inhabitants of each State to judge for themselves in this respect was ineradicably rooted in the convictions of the people of the Union, then had recourse, in the pursuit of their general object, to the extraordinary measure of propagandist colonization of the Territory of Kansas, to prevent the free and natural action of its inhabitants in its internal organization and thus to anticipate or to force the determination of that question in this inchoate State.

With such views, associations were organized in some of the States, and their purpose was proclaimed through the press in language extremely irritating and offensive to those of whom the colonists were to become the neighbors. Those designs and acts had the necessary consequence to awaken emotions of intense indignation in States near to the Territory of Kansas, and especially in the adjoining State of Missouri, whose domestic peace was thus the most directly endangered; but they are far from justifying the illegal and reprehensible counter-movements which ensued.

Under these inauspicious circumstances, the primary elections for members of the Legislative Assembly were held in most, if not all, of the precincts, at the time and the places and by the persons designated and appointed by the Governor, according to law.

Angry accusations that illegal votes had been polled, abounded on all sides, and imputations were made both of fraud and violence. But the Governor, in the exercise of the power and the discharge of the duty conferred and imposed by law on him alone, officially received and considered the returns; declared a large majority of the members of the Council and the House of Representatives "duly elected;" withheld certificates from others because of alleged illegality of votes; appointed a new election to supply the place of the persons not certified; and thus, at length, in all the forms of statute, and with his own official authentication, complete legality was given to the first Legislative Assembly of the Territory.

Those decisions of the returning-officers and of the Governor are final, except that by the parliamentary usage of the country applied to the organic law, it may be conceded that each House of the Assembly must have been competent to determine, in the last resort, the qualifications and the election of its members. The subject was, by its nature, one appertaining exclusively to the jurisdiction of the local authorities of the Territory. Whatever irregularities may have occurred in the elections, it seems too late now to raise that question as to which, neither now nor at any previous time, has the least possible legal authority been possessed by the President of the United States. For all present purposes the legislative body, thus constituted and elected, was the legitimate assembly of the Territory.

Accordingly, the Governor, by proclamation, convened the Assembly thus elected to meet at a place called Pawnee City. The two Houses met, and were duly organized in the ordinary parliamentary form; each sent to and received from the Governor the official communications usual on such occasions; an elaborate Message opening the session was communicated by the Governor, and the general business of legislation was entered upon by the Legislative Assembly.

But, after a few days, the Assembly resolved to adjourn to another place in the Territory. A law was accordingly passed, against the consent of the Governor, but in due form otherwise, to remove the seat of government temporarily to the "Shawnee Manual-labor School" (or mission), and thither the Assembly proceeded. After this, receiving a bill for the establishment of a ferry at the town of Kickapoo, the Governor refused to sign it, and, by special message, assigned for reason of refusal, not anything objectionable in the bill itself, nor any pretense of the illegality or incompetency of the Assembly as such, but only the fact that the Assembly had, by its act, transferred the seat of government temporarily from Pawnee City to Shawnee Mission. For the same reason he continued to refuse to sign other bills, until, in the course of a few days, he, by official Message, communicated to the Assembly the fact that he had received notification of the termination of his functions as Governor, and that the duties of the office were legally devolved on the Secretary of the Territory; thus to the last recognizing the body as a duly-elected and constituted Legislative Assembly.

It will be perceived that if any constitutional defect attached to the legislative acts of the Assembly, it is not pretended to consist in irregularity of election or want of qualification of the members, but only in the change of its place of session. However trivial the objection may seem to be, it requires to be considered, because upon it is founded all that superstructure of acts, plainly against law, which now threatens the peace not only of the Territory of Kansas but of the Union.

Such an objection to the proceedings of the Legislative Assembly was of exceptionable origin, for the reason that, by the express terms of the organic law, the seat of government of the Territory was "located temporarily at Fort Leavenworth;" and yet the Governor himself remained there less than two months, and of his own discretion transferred the seat of Government to the Shawnee Mission, where it in fact was at the time the Assembly were called to meet at Pawnee City. If the Governor had any such right to change temporarily the seat of Government, still more had the Legislative Assembly. The objection is of exceptional origin for the further reason that the place indicated by the Governor, without having an exclusive claim of preference in itself, was a proposed town-site only, which he and others were attempting to locate unlawfully upon land within a military reservation, and for participation in which illegal act the commandant of a post, a superior officer of the Army, has been dismissed by sentence of court-martial.

Nor is it easy to see why the Legislative Assembly might not with propriety pass the Territorial act transferring its sittings to the Shawnee Mission. If it could not, that must be on account of some prohibitory or incompatible provision of act of Congress. But no such provision exists. The organic act, as already quoted, says "the seat of Government is hereby located temporarily at Fort Leavenworth;" and it then provides that certain of the public buildings there "may be occupied and used under the direction of the Governor and Legislative Assembly." These expressions might possibly be construed to imply that when, in a previous section of the act, it was enacted that "the first Legislative Assembly shall meet at such place and on such day as the Governor shall appoint," the word "place" means place at Fort Leavenworth, not place anywhere in the Territory. If so, the Governor would have been the first to err in this matter, not only in himself having removed the seat of Government to the Shawnee Mission, but in again removing it to Pawnee City. If there was any departure from the letter of the law, therefore, it was his in both instances.

But, however this may be, it is most unreasonable to suppose that by the terms of the organic act, Congress intended to do impliedly what it has not done expressly—that is, to forbid to the Legislative Assembly the power to choose any place it might see fit as the temporary seat of its deliberations. That is proved by the significant language of one of the subsequent acts of Congress on the subject, that of March 3, 1855, which, in making appropriation for public buildings of the Territory, enacts that the same shall not be expended "until the Legislature of said Territory shall have fixed by law the permanent seat of government." Congress, in these expressions, does not profess to be granting the power to fix the permanent seat of government, but recognizes the power as one already granted. But how? Undoubtedly by the comprehensive provision of the organic act itself, which declares that "the legislative power of the Territory shall extend to all rightful subjects of legislation consistent with the Constitution of the United States and the provisions of this act." If, in view of this act, the Legislative Assembly had the large power to fix the permanent seat of government at any place in its discretion, of course by the same enactment it had the less and the included power to fix it temporarily.

Nevertheless, the allegation that the acts of the Legislative Assembly were illegal by reason of this removal of its place of session, was brought forward to justify the first great movement in disregard of law within the Territory. One of the acts of the Legislative Assembly provided for the election of a Delegate to the present Congress, and a Delegate was elected under that law. But, subsequently to this, a portion of the people of the Territory proceeded, without authority of law, to elect another Delegate.

Following upon this movement was another and more important one of the same general character. Persons confessedly not constituting the body politic, or all the inhabitants, but merely a party of the inhabitants, and without law, have undertaken to summon a convention for the purpose of transforming the Territory into a State, and have framed a constitution, adopted it, and under it elected a Governor and other officers, and a representative to Congress.

In extenuation of these illegal acts, it is alleged that the State of California, Michigan, and others, were self-organized, and as such were admitted into the Union, without a previous enabling act of Congress. It is true that, while in a majority of cases a previous act of Congress has been passed to authorize the Territory to present itself as a State, and that this is deemed the most regular course, yet such an act has not been held to be indispensable, and in some cases the Territory has proceeded without it, and has nevertheless been admitted into the Union as a State. It lies with Congress to authorize beforehand, or to confirm afterward, in its discretion; but in no instance has a State been admitted upon the application of persons acting against authorities duly constituted by act of Congress. In every case it is the people of the Territory, not a party among them, who have the power to form a constitution and ask for admission as a State. No principle of public law, no practice or precedent under the Constitution of the United States, no rule of reason, right, or common sense, confers any such power as that now claimed by a mere party in the Territory. In fact, what has been done is of revolutionary character. It is avowedly so in motive and in aim as respects the local law of the Territory. It will become treasonable insurrection if it reach the length of organized resistance by force to the fundamental or any other federal law, and to the authority of the General Government.

In such an event, the path of duty for the Executive is plain. The Constitution requiring him to take care that the laws of the United States be faithfully executed, if they be opposed in the Territory of Kansas, he may and should place at the disposal of the marshal any public force of the United States which happens to be within the jurisdiction, to be used as a portion of the *posse comitatus*; and, if that do not suffice to maintain order, then he may call forth the militia of one or more States for that object, or employ for the same object any part of the land or naval force of the United States. So also if the obstruction be to the laws of the Territory, and it be duly presented to him as a case of insurrection, he may employ for its suppression the militia of any State, or the land or naval force of the United States. And if the Territory be invaded by the citizens of other States, whether for the purpose of deciding elections or for any other, and the local authorities find themselves unable to repel or withstand it, they will be entitled to, and upon the fact being fully ascertained, they shall most certainly receive, the aid of the General Government.

But it is not the duty of the President of the United States to volunteer interposition by force to preserve the purity of elections either in a State or Territory. To do so would be subversive of public freedom. And whether a law be wise or unwise, just or unjust, is not a question for him to judge. If it be constitutional—that is, if it be the law of the land—it is his duty to cause it to be executed, or to sustain the authorities of any State or Territory in executing it in opposition to all insurrectionary movements.

Our system affords no justification of revolutionary acts; for the constitutional means of relieving the people of unjust administration and laws, by a change of public agents and by repeal, are ample, and more prompt and effective than illegal violence. These constitutional means must be scrupulously guarded—this great prerogative of popular sovereignty sacredly respected.

It is the undoubted right of the peaceable and orderly people of the Territory of Kansas to elect their own legislative body, make their own laws, and regulate their own social institutions, without foreign or domestic molestation. Interference, on the one hand, to procure the abolition or prohibition of slave-labor in the Territory, has produced mischievous interference on the other for its maintenance or introduction. One wrong begets another. Statements entirely unfounded or grossly exaggerated, concerning events within the Territory, are sedulously diffused through remote States to feed the flame of sectional animosity there; and the agitators there exert themselves indefatigably in return to encourage and stimulate strife within the Territory.

The inflammatory agitation, of which the present is but a part, has for twenty years produced nothing save unmitigated evil, North and South. But for it the character of the domestic institutions of the future new State would have been a matter of too little interest to the inhabitants of the contiguous States, personal or collectively, to produce among them any political emotion. Climate, soil, production, hopes of rapid advancement, and the pursuit of happiness on the part of settlers themselves, with good wishes but with no interference from without, would have quietly determined the question which is at this time of such disturbing character.

But we are constrained to turn our attention to the circumstances of embarrassment as they now exist. It is the duty of the people of Kansas to discountenance every act or purpose of resistance to its laws. Above all, the emergency appeals to the citizens of the States and especially of those contiguous to the Territory, neither by intervention of non-residents in elections, nor by unauthorized military force, to attempt to encroach upon or usurp the authority of the inhabitants of the Territory.

No citizen of our country should permit himself to forget that he is a part of its government, and entitled to be heard in the determination of its policy and its measures; and that, therefore, the highest considerations of personal honor and patriotism require him to maintain, by whatever of power or influence he may possess, the integrity of the laws of the Republic.

Entertaining these views, it will be my imperative duty to exert the whole power of the Federal Executive to support public order in the Territory; to vindicate its laws, whether Federal or local, against all attempts of organized resistance; and so to protect its people in the establishment of their own institutions, undisturbed by encroachment from without, and in the full enjoyment of the rights of self-government assured to them by the Constitution and the organic act of Congress.

Although serious and threatening disturbances in the Territory of Kansas, announced to me by the Governor, in December last, were speedily quieted without the effusion of blood, and in a satisfactory manner, there is, I regret to say, reason to apprehend that disorders will continue to occur there, with increasing tendency to violence, until some decisive measures be taken to dispose of the question itself which constitutes the inducement or occasion of internal agitation and of external interference.

This, it seems to me, can best be accomplished by providing that, when the inhabitants of Kansas may desire it, and shall be of sufficient numbers to constitute a State, a convention of delegates, duly elected by the qualified voters, shall assemble to frame a Constitution, and thus to prepare, through regular and lawful means, for its admission into the Union as a State. I respectfully recommend the enactment of a law to that effect.

I recommend, also, that a special appropriation be made to defray any expense which may become requisite in the execution of the laws or the maintenance of public order in the Territory of Kansas. FRANKLIN PIERCE.

March 12*th*.—In Senate, Mr. Douglas of Illinois, from the Committee on Territories, made the following

REPORT:

The Committee on Territories, to whom was referred so much of the annual message of the President of the United States as relates to territorial affairs, together with his special message of the 24th day of January, 1856, in regard to Kansas Territory, and his message of the 18th of February, in compliance with the resolution of the Senate of the 4th of February, 1856, requesting transcripts of certain papers relative to the affairs of the Territory of Kansas, having given the same that serious and mature deliberation which the importance of the subject demands, beg leave to submit the following report:

Your Committee deem this an appropriate occasion to state briefly, but distinctly, the principles upon which new States may be admitted and Territories organized under the authority of the Constitution of the United States.

The Constitution (section 3, article 4) provides that "new States may be admitted by the Congress into this Union."

Section 8, Article 1: "Congress shall have power to make all laws which shall be necessary and proper for carrying into execution the foregoing powers, and all other powers vested by this constitution in the government of the United States, or in any department or office thereof."

10th amendment: "The powers not delegated to the United States by the Constitution, nor prohibited by it to the States, are reserved to the States respectively, or to the people."

A State of the Federal Union is a sovereign power, limited only by the Constitution of the United States.

The limitations which that instrument has imposed are few, specific, and uniform—applicable alike to all the States, old and new. There is no authority for putting a restriction upon the sovereignty of a new State, which the Constitution has not placed on the original States. Indeed, if such a restriction could be imposed on any State, it would instantly cease to be a *State* within the meaning of the Federal Constitution, and, in consequence of the inequality, would assimilate to the condition of a province or dependency. Hence, equality among all the States of the Union is a fundamental principle in our federative system—a principle embodied in the Constitution, as the basis upon which the American Union rests.

African Slavery existed in all the colonies, under the sanction of the British government, prior to the Declaration of Independence. When the Constitution of the United States was adopted, it became the supreme law and bond of union between twelve slaveholding States and one non-slaveholding State. Each State reserved the right to decide the question of Slavery for itself—to continue it as a domestic institution so long as it pleased, and to abolish it when it chose.

In pursuance of this reserved right, six of the original slaveholding States have since abolished and prohibited Slavery within their limits respectively, without consulting Congress or their sister States; while the other six have retained and sustained it as a domestic institution, which, in their opinion, had become so firmly engrafted on their social systems, that the relation between the master and slave could not be dissolved with safety to either. In the mean time, eighteen new States have been admitted into the Union, in obedience to the Federal Constitution, on an equal footing with the original States, including, of course, the right of each to decide the question of Slavery for itself. In deciding this question, it has so happened that nine of these new States have abolished and prohibited Slavery, while the other nine have retained and regulated it. That these new States had at the time of their admission, and still retain, an equal right, under the Federal Constitution, with the original States, to decide all questions of domestic policy for themselves, including that of African Slavery, ought not to be seriously questioned, and certainly cannot be successfully controverted.

They are all subject to the same supreme law, which, by the consent of each, constitutes the only limitation upon their sovereign authority.

Since we find the right to admit new States enumerated among the powers expressly delegated in the Constitution, the question arises, Whence does Congress derive authority to organize temporary governments for the Territories preparatory to their admission into the Union on an equal footing with the original States? Your Committee are not prepared to adopt the reasoning which deduces the power from that other clause of the Constitution, which says:

"Congress shall have power to dispose of and make all needful rules and regulation respecting the territory or other property belonging to the United States."

The language of this clause is much more appropriate when applied to property than to persons. It would seem to have been employed for the purpose of conferring upon Congress the power of disposing of the public lands and *other property belonging to the United States*, and to make all needful rules and regulations for that purpose, rather than to govern the people who might purchase those lands from the United States and become residents thereon. The word "territory" was an appropriate expression to designate that large area of public lands of which the United States had become the owner by virtue of the revolution and the cession by the several States. The additional words, "or other property belonging to the United States," clearly show that the term "territory" was used in its ordinary geographical sense to designate the public domain, and not as descriptive of the whole body of the people, constituting a distinct political community, who have no representation in Congress, and consequently no voice in making the laws upon which all their rights and liberties would depend, if it were conceded that Congress had the general and unlimited power to make all "needful rules and regulations concerning" their internal affairs and domestic concerns. It is under this clause of the constitution, and from this alone, that Congress derives authority to provide for the surveys of the public lands, for securing pre-emption rights to actual settlers, for the establishment of land-offices in the several States and Territories, for exposing the lands to private and public sale, for issuing patents and confirming titles, and, in short, for making all needful rules and regulations for protecting and disposing of the public domain and other property belonging to the United States.

These needful rules and regulations may be embraced, and usually are found, in general laws applicable alike to States and Territories, wherever the United States may be the owner of the lands or other property to be regulated or disposed of. It can make no difference, under this clause of the Constitution, whether the "territory, or other property, belonging to the United States," shall be situated in Ohio or Kansas, in Alabama or Minnesota, in California or Oregon. The power of Congress to make needful rules and regulations is the same in the States and Territories, to the extent that the title is vested in the United States. Inasmuch as the right of legislation in such cases rests exclusively upon the fact of ownership, it is obvious it can extend only to the tracts of land to which the United States possess the title, and must cease in respect to each tract the instant it becomes private property by purchase from the United States. It will scarcely be contended that Congress possesses the power to legislate for the people of those States in which public lands may be located, in respect to their internal affairs and domestic concerns, merely because the United States may be so fortunate as to own a portion of the territory and other property within the limits of those States. Yet it should be borne in mind that this clause of the Constitution confers upon Congress the same power to make needful rules and regulations in the States as it does in the Territories, concerning the territory or other property belonging to the United States.

In view of these considerations, your Committee are not prepared to affirm that Congress derives authority to institute governments for the people of the Territories, from that clause of the Constitution which confers the right to make needful rules and regulations concerning the territory or other property belonging to the United States; much less can we deduce the power from any supposed necessity, arising outside of the Constitution and not provided for in that instrument. The federal government is one of delegated and limited powers, clothed with no rightful authority which does not result directly and necessarily from the Constitution. Necessity, when experience shall have clearly demonstrated its existence, may furnish satisfactory reasons for enlarging the authority of the federal government, by amendments to the Constitution, in the mode prescribed in the instrument; but cannot afford the slightest excuse for the assumption of powers not delegated, and which, by the tenth amendment, are expressly "reserved to the States respectively, or to the people." Hence, before the power can be safely exercised, the right of Congress to organize Territories, by instituting temporary governments, must be traced directly to some provision of the Constitution conferring the authority in express terms, or as a means necessary and proper to carry into effect some one or more of the powers which are specifically delegated. Is not the organization of a Territory eminently necessary and proper as a means of enabling the people thereof to form and mould their local and domestic institutions, and establish a State government under the authority of the Constitution, preparatory to its admission into the Union? If so, the right of Congress to pass the organic act for the temporary government is clearly included in the provision which authorizes the admission of new States. This power, however, being an incident to an express grant, and resulting from it by necessary implication, as an appropriate means for carrying it into effect, must be exercised in harmony with the nature and objects of the grant from which it is deduced. The organic act of the Territory, deriving its validity from the power of Congress to admit new States, must contain no provision or restriction which would destroy or impair the equality of the proposed State with the original States, or impose any limitation upon its sovereignty which the Constitution has not placed on all the States. So far as the organization of a Territory may be necessary and proper as a means of carrying into effect the provision of the Constitution for the admission of new States, and when exercised with reference only to that end, the power of Congress is clear and explicit; but beyond that point the authority cannot extend, for the reason that all "powers not delegated to the United States by the Constitution, nor prohibited by it to the States, are reserved to the States respectively, or to the people." In other words, the organic act of the Territory, conforming to the spirit of the grant from which it receives its validity, must leave the people entirely free to form and regulate their domestic institutions and internal concerns in their own way, subject only to the Constitution of the United States, to the end that when they attain the requisite population, and establish a State government in conformity to the Federal Constitution, they may be admitted into the Union on an equal footing with the original States in all respects whatsoever.

The act of Congress for the organization of the Territories of Kansas and Nebraska, was designed to conform to the spirit and letter of the Federal Constitution, by preserving and maintaining the fundamental principle of equality among all the States of the Union, notwithstanding the restriction contained in the 8th section of the act of March 6, 1820, (preparatory to the admission of Missouri into the Union,) which assumed to deny to the people forever the right to settle the question of Slavery for themselves, provided they should make their homes and organize States north of thirty-six degrees and thirty minutes north latitude. Conforming to the cardinal principles of State equality and self-government, in obedience to the Constitution, the Kansas-Nebraska act declared, in the precise language of the Compromise Measures of 1850, that, "when admitted as a State, the said Territory, or any portion of the same, shall be received into the Union, with or without Slavery, as their constitutions may prescribe at the time of their admission." Again, after declaring the said 8th section of the Missouri act (sometimes called the Missouri Compromise, or Missouri Restriction) inoperative and void as being repugnant to these principles, the purpose of Congress, in passing the act, is declared in these words: "It being the true intent and meaning of this act not to legislate Slavery into any State or Territory, nor to exclude it therefrom, but to leave the people thereof perfectly free to form and regulate their domestic institutions in their own way, subject only to the Constitution of the United States."

The passage of the Kansas-Nebraska act was strenuously resisted by all persons who thought it a less evil to deprive the people of new States and Territories of the right of State equality and self-government under the Constitution, than to allow them to decide the Slavery question for themselves, as every State of the Union had done, and must retain the undeniable right to do, so long as the Constitution of the United States shall be maintained as the supreme law of the land. Finding opposition to the principles of the act unavailing in the halls of Congress and under the forms of the Constitution, combinations were immediately entered into in some portions of the Union to control the political destinies, and form and regulate the domestic institutions, of those Territories and future States, through the machinery of emigrant aid societies. In order to give consistency and efficiency to the movement, and surround it with the color of legal authority, an act of incorporation was procured from the legislature of the State of Massachusetts, in which it was provided, in the first section, that twenty persons therein named, and their "associates, successors, and assigns, are hereby made a corporation, by the name of the Massachusetts Emigrant Aid Company, for the purpose of assisting emigrants to settle in the West; and for this purpose they shall have all the powers and privileges, and be subject to all the duties, restrictions, and liabilities set forth in the 38th and 44th chapters of the revised statutes" of Massachusetts.

The second section limited the capital stock of the company to five millions of dollars, and authorized the whole to be invested in real and personal estate, with the proviso that "the said corporation shall not hold real estate in this commonwealth (Massachusetts) to an amount exceeding twenty thousand dollars."

The third section provided for dividing the capital stock of the corporation into shares of one hundred dollars each, and prescribed the mode, time, and amounts in which assessments might be made on each share.

The fourth and last section was in these words:

"At all meetings of the stockholders, each stockholder shall be entitled to cast one vote for each share held by him; *provided*, that no stockholder shall be entitled to cast more than fifty votes on shares held by himself, nor more than fifty votes by proxy."

Although the act of incorporation does not distinctly declare that the company was formed for the purpose of controlling the domestic institutions of the Territory of Kansas, and forcing it into the Union with a prohibition of Slavery in her constitution, regardless of the rights and wishes of the people as guarantied by the Constitution of the United States, and secured by their organic law, yet the whole history of the movement, the circumstances in which it had its origin, and the professions and avowals of all engaged in it, render it certain and undeniable that such was its object.

To remove all doubt upon this point, your committee will here present a few extracts from a pamphlet published by the company soon after its organization, under the following caption:

"Organization, objects, and plan of operations of the Emigrant Aid Company; also, a description of Kansas, for the information of emigrants.

"*Trustees*—Amos A. Lawrence, Boston; J. M. S. Williams, Cambridge; Ely Thayer, Worcester.

"*Treasurer*, Amos A. Lawrence.

"*Secretary*, Thomas H. Webb, Boston.

"For the purpose of answering numerous communications concerning the plan of operations of the Emigrant Aid Company, and the resources of Kansas Territory, which it is proposed now to settle, the secretary of the company has deemed it expedient to publish the following definite information in regard to this particular: * * * *

"For these purposes it is recommended. 1st. That the trustees contract immediately with some one of the competing lines of travel for the conveyance of 20,000 persons from Massachusetts to that place in the West which the trustees shall select for their first settlement." * * * * *

"It is recommended that the company's agents locate and take up for the company's benefit, the sections of land in which the boarding-houses and mills are located, and no others. And further, whenever the Territory shall be organized as a free State, the trustees shall dispose of all its interests there, replace by the sales the money laid out, declare a dividend to the stockholders, and that they then select a new field, and make similar arrangements for the settlement and organization of another free State of this Union." * * * *

"With the advantages attained by such a system of effort, the territory selected as the scene of operations would, it is believed, be filled up with free inhabitants. * * * * *

"There is reason to suppose several thousand men of New-England origin propose to emigrate under the auspices of some such arrangement, this very summer. Of the whole emigration from Europe, amounting to some 400,000 persons, there can be no difficulty in inducing some thirty or forty thousand to take the same direction." * * *

"Especially will it prove an advantage to Massachusetts, if she create the new State by her foresight, supply the necessities of its inhabitants, and open in the outset communications between their homes and her ports and factories." * * *

"It determines in the right way the institutions of the unsettled Territories, in less time than the discussion of them has required in Congress."

Having thus secured from the State of Massachusetts the color of legal authority to sanction their proceedings, in perversion of the plain provisions of an act of Congress passed in pursuance of the Constitution, the company commenced its operations by receiving subscriptions to its capital stock, and exerting its whole power to harmonize, combine, and direct, in the channel it should mark out, all the elements of opposition to the principles of the Kansas and Nebraska act. The plan adopted was to make it the interest of a large body of men, who sympathized with them in the objects of the corporation, to receive their aid and protection, and, under the auspices of the company, to proceed to Kansas, and acquire whatever residence, and do whatever acts, might be found necessary to enable them to vote at the elections, and through the ballot-box, if possible, to gain control over the legislation of the Territory. This movement is justified by those who originated and control the plan, upon the ground that the persons whom they sent to Kansas were free men, who, under the Constitution and laws, had a perfect right to emigrate to Kansas or any other Territory; that the act of emigration was entirely voluntary on their part; and when they arrived in the Territory as actual settlers, they had as good a right as any other citizens to vote at the elections, and participate in the control of the government of the Territory. This would undoubtedly be true in a case of ordinary emigration, such as has filled up our new States and Territories, where each individual has gone, on his own account, to improve his condition and that of his family. But it is a very different thing where a State creates a vast moneyed corporation for the purpose of controlling the domestic institutions of a distinct political community fifteen hundred miles distant, and sends out the emigrants only as a means of accomplishing its paramount political objects. When a powerful corporation, with a capital of five millions of dollars invested in houses and lands, in merchandise and mills, in cannon and rifles, in powder and lead—in all the implements of art, agriculture, and war, and employing a corresponding number of men, all under the management and control of non-resident directors and stockholders, who are authorized by their charter to vote by proxy to the extent of fifty votes each, enters a distant and sparsely settled Territory with the fixed purpose of wielding all its power to control the domestic institutions and political destinies of the Territory, it becomes a question of fearful import, how far the operations of the company are compatible with the rights and liberties of the people. Whatever may be the extent or limit of congressional authority over the Territories, it is clear that no individual State has the right to pass any law or authorize any act concerning or affecting the Territories, which it might not enact in reference to any other State.

If the people of any State should become so much enamored with their own peculiar institutions as to conceive the philanthropic scheme of forcing so great a blessing on their unwilling neighbors, and with that view should create a mammoth moneyed corporation, for the avowed purpose of sending a sufficient number of their young men into the neighboring State, to remain long enough to acquire the right of voting, with the fixed and paramount object of reversing the settled policy and changing the domestic institutions of such State, would it not be deemed an act of aggression, as offensive and flagrant as if attempted by direct and open violence? It is a well-settled principle of constitutional law, in this country, that while all the States of the Union are united in one, for certain purposes, yet each State, in respect to everything which affects its domestic policy and internal concerns, stands in the relation of a foreign power to every other State.

Hence, no State has a right to pass any law, or do or authorize any act, with the view to influence or change the domestic policy of any other State or Territory of the Union, more than it would with reference to France or England, or any other foreign State with which we are at peace. Indeed, every State of this Union is under higher obligations to observe a friendly forbearance and generous comity towards each other member of the Confederacy, than the laws of nations can impose on foreign States. While foreign States are restrained from all acts of aggression and unkindness only by that spirit of comity which the laws of nations enjoin upon all friendly powers, we have assumed the additional obligation to obey the Constitution, which secures to every State the right to control its own internal affairs. If repugnance to domestic Slavery can justify Massachusetts in incorporating a mammoth company to influence and control that question in any State or Territory of this Union, the same principle of action would authorize France or England to use the same means to accomplish the same end in Brazil or Cuba, or in fifteen States of this Union; while it would license the United States to interfere with serfdom in Russia, or polygamy in Turkey, or any other obnoxious institution in any part of the world. The same principle of action, when sanctioned by our example, would authorize all the kingdoms, and empires, and despotisms in the world, to engage in a common crusade against republicanism in America, as an institution quite as obnoxious to them as domestic Slavery is to any portion of the people of the United States.

If our obligations arising under the laws of nations are so imperative as to make it our duty to enact neutrality laws, and to exert the whole power and authority of the executive branch of the government, including the army and navy, to enforce them, in restraining our citizens from interfering with the internal concerns of foreign States, can the obligations of each State and Territory of this Union be less imperative, under the Federal Constitution, to observe entire neutrality in respect to the domestic institutions of the several States and Territories? Non-interference with the internal concerns of other States is recognized by all civilized countries as a fundamental principle of the laws of nations, for the reason that the peace of the world could not be maintained for a single day without it. How, then, can we hope to preserve peace and fraternal feelings among the different portions of this republic, unless we yield implicit obedience to a principle which has all the sanction of patriotic duty as well as constitutional obligation?

When the emigrants sent out by the Massachusetts Emigrant Aid Company, and their affiliated societies, passed through the State of Missouri in large numbers on their way to Kansas, the violence of their language, and the unmistakable indications of their determined hostility to the domestic institutions of that State, created apprehensions that the object of the company was to abolitionize Kansas as a means of prosecuting a relentless warefare upon the institutions of Slavery within the limits of Missouri. These apprehensions increased and spread with the progress of events, until they became the settled convictions of the people of that portion of the State most exposed to the danger by their proximity to the Kansas border. The natural consequence was, that immediate steps were taken by the people of the western counties of Missouri to stimulate, organize, and carry into effect a system of emigration similar to that of the Massachusetts Emigrant Aid Company, for the avowed purpose of counteracting the effects, and protecting themselves and their domestic institutions from the consequences of that company's operations.

The material difference in the character of the two rival and conflicting movements consists in the fact that the one had its origin in an aggressive, and the other in a defensive policy. The one was organized in pursuance of the provisions and claiming to act under the authority of a legislative enactment of a distant State, whose internal prosperity and domestic security did not depend upon the success of the movement, while the other was the spontaneous action of the people living in the immediate vicinity of the theatre of operations, excited by a sense of common danger to the necessity of protecting their own firesides from the apprehended horrors of servile insurrection and intestine war. Both parties, conceiving it to be essential to the success of their respective plans that they should be upon the field of operations prior to the first election in the Territory, selected principally young men, persons unencumbered by families, and whose conditions in life enabled them to leave at a moment's warning, and move with great celerity, to go at once, and select and occupy the most eligible sites and favored locations in the Territory, to be held by themselves and their associates who should follow them. For the successful prosecution of such a scheme, the Missourians who lived in the immediate vicinity, possessed peculiar advantages over their rivals from the more remote portions of the Union. Each family could send one of its members across the line to mark out his claim, erect a cabin, and put in a small crop, sufficient to give him as valid a right to be deemed an actual settler and qualified voter as those who were being imported by the Emigrant Aid Societies. In an unoccupied Territory, where the lands have not been surveyed, and where there were no marks or lines to indicate the boundaries of sections and quarter-sections, and where no legal title could be had until after the surveys should be made, disputes, quarrels, violence, and bloodshed might have been expected as the natural and inevitable consequences of such extraordinary systems of emigration, which divided and arrayed the settlers into two great hostile parties, each having an inducement to claim more than was his right, in order to hold it for some new comer of his own party, and at the same time prevent persons belonging to the opposite party from settling in the neighborhood. As a result of this state of things, the great mass of emigrants from the northwest and from other States who went there on their own account, with no other object and influence, by no other motives than to improve their condition and secure good homes for their families, were compelled to array themselves under the banner of one of these hostile parties, in order to insure protection to themselves and their claims against the aggressions and violence of the other.

At the first election held in the Territory, on the 29th day of November, 1854, for a delegate to Congress, J. W. Whitfield was chosen by an overwhelming majority, having received the votes of men of all parties who were in favor of the principles of the Kansas-Nebraska act, and opposed to placing the political destinies of the Territory in the keeping of the Abolition party of the northern States, to be managed through the machinery of their emigrant Aid Companies. No sooner was the result of the election known, than the defeated party proclaimed throughout the length and breadth of the republic, that it had been produced by the invasion of the Territory by a Missouri mob, which had overawed and outnumbered and outvoted the *bona fide* settlers of the Territory. By reference to the executive journal of the Territory, which will be found in the papers furnished by the President of the United States in response to a call of the Senate, it will be found that Governor Reeder, in obedience to what he considered to be a duty enjoined on him by the act of Congress organizing the Territory, on the 10th day of November, 1854, issued a proclamation, prescribing the time, place, and mode of holding the election, and appointing by name three citizens of the Territory, residing in each election district, to conduct the election, in such district, together with the following oath, which was taken by the judges before entering on their duties, to wit:

"We do severally swear that we will perform our duties as judges of the election, to be held this day, in the —— district of the Territory of Kansas, to the best of our judgment and ability; that we will keep a correct and faithful record or list of persons who shall vote at said election; that we will poll no tickets from any person who is not an actual *bona fide* resident and inhabitant of said Territory on the day of election, and whom we shall not honestly believe to be a qualified voter according to the act of Congress organizing said Territory; that we will reject the votes of all and every non-resident whom we shall believe to have come into the Territory for the mere purpose of voting; that in all cases where we are ignorant of the voter's right, we will require legal evidence thereof, by his own oath or otherwise; that we will make a true and faithful return of the votes which shall be polled to the governor of the said Territory."

The same proclamation pointed out in detail the mode in which the election should be conducted; and, among other things, that the polls will be opened for reception of votes between eight and ten o'clock, a. m., and kept open continually until six o'clock, p. m.; that the judges will keep two corresponding lists of persons who shall vote, numbering each name; that when a dispute arises as to the qualifications of a voter, the judges shall examine the voter or any other persons, under oath, upon the subject, and the decision of a majority of the board will be conclusive; that when the election shall close, the judges shall open and count the votes, and keep two corresponding tally-lists, and if the tally-lists shall agree, the judges shall then publicly proclaim the result, and shall make up and sign duplicate certificates in the form prescribed; and shall certify, under their oaths, that the certificate is a true and correct return of the votes polled by lawful resident voters.

The proclamation also provides that the tickets or votes polled shall, after being counted, be again deposited in the box, together with one copy of the oath, and one list of the voters, and one tally-list, and one certificate of return; and that the judges shall seal them up in the box, and carefully preserve the same until called for by the governor of said Territory, in the event of its correctness being contested; and that the remaining copy of the oath, list of voters, tally-list, and return, will be taken by one of the judges, who shall deliver the same in person to the governor.

The proclamation also provides that, "In case any person or persons shall dispute the fairness or correctness of the return of any election-district, they shall make a written statement, directed to the governor, and setting forth the specific cause of complaint or errors in the conducting or returning of the election in said district, signed by not less than ten qualified voters of the Territory, and with an affidavit of one or more qualified voters to the truth of the fact therein stated; and the said complaint and affidavit shall be presented to the governor on or before the fourth day of December next, when the proper proceedings will be taken to hear and decide such complaint."

By reference to the executive journal of the Territory, we find the following entry:

"*December* 4, 1854.—The judges of the several election districts made return of the votes polled at the election held on the 29th day of November last, for a delegate to the House of Representatives of the United States; from which it appeared that the votes in the said several districts were as follows, to wit:"

Here follows a list of the votes cast for each candidate in each of the seventeen districts of the Territory, showing that

J. W. Whitfield had received 2,258 votes.
All other persons received 575 "

And on the same page is the following entry:

"*December* 5, 1854.—On examining and collating the returns, J. W. Whitfield is declared by the governor to be duly elected delegate to the House of Representatives of the United States, and the same day the certificate of the governor, under the seal of the Territory, issued to said J. W. Whitfield of his election."

It nowhere appears that Gen. Whitfield's right to a seat by virtue of that election was ever contested. It does not appear that "ten qualified voters of the Territory" were ever found who were willing to make the "written statement directed to the governor, with an affidavit" of one or more qualified voters to the "truth of the facts therein stated," to "dispute the fairness or correctness of the returns," or to "set forth specific cause of complaint or errors in the conducting or returning of the election," in any one of the seventeen districts of the Territory. Certain it is, that there could not have been a system of fraud and violence such as has been charged by the agents and supporters of the emigrant aid societies, unless the governor and judges of election were parties to it; and your committee are not prepared to assume a fact so disreputable to them, and so improbable upon the state of facts presented, without specific charges and direct proof. In the absence of all proof and probable truth, the charge that the Missourians had invaded the Territory and controlled the congressional election by fraud and violence, was circulated throughout the Free States, and made the basis of the most inflammatory appeals to all men opposed to the principles of the Kansas-Nebraska act to emigrate or send emigrants to Kansas, for the purpose of repelling the invaders, and assisting their friends who were then in the Territory in putting down the slave power, and prohibiting Slavery in Kansas, with the view of making it a Free State. Exaggerated accounts of the large number of emigrants on their way under the auspices of the emigrant aid companies, with the view of controlling the election for members of the territorial legislature, which was to take place on the 30th of March, 1855, were published and circulated. These accounts being republished and believed in Missouri, where the excitement had already been inflamed to a fearful intensity, induced a corresponding effort to send at least an equal number, to counteract the apprehended result of this new importation. Your committee have not been able to obtain definite and satisfactory information in regard to the alleged irregularities in conducting the election, and the number of illegal votes on the 30th of March; but, from the most reliable sources of information accessible to your committee, including various papers, documents, and statements, kindly furnished by Messrs. Whitfield and Reeder, rival claimants of the delegate's seat in Congress for Kansas Territory, it would seem that the facts are substantially as follows:

The election was held in obedience to the proclamation of the governor of the Territory, which prescribed the mode of proceeding, the form of the oath and returns, the precautionary safeguards against illegal voting, and the mode of contesting the election, which were, in substance, the same as those already referred to in connection with the congressional election. When the period arrived for the governor to canvass the returns, and issue certificates to the persons elected, it appeared that protests had been filed against the fairness of the proceedings and the correctness of the returns, in seven out of the eighteen election-districts into which the Territory had been divided for election purposes, alleging fraudulent and illegal voting by persons who were not actual settlers and qualified voters of the Territory. It also appears, that in some of these contested cases, the form of the oath administered to the judges, and of the returns made by them, were not in conformity to the proclamation of the governor. After a careful investigation of the facts of each case, as presented by the returns of the judges, and the protests and allegations of all persons who disputed the fairness of the election and the correctness of the returns, the governor came to the conclusion that it was his duty to set aside the election in these seven disputed districts; the effect of which was, to create two vacancies in the council, and nine in the House of Representatives of the Territory, to be filled by a new election; and to change the result so far as to cause the certificate for one councilman and one representative to issue to different persons than those returned as elected by the judges. Accordingly the governor issued his writs for special elections, to be held on the 24th of May, to fill those vacancies, and, at the same time, granted certificates of election to eleven councilmen and seventeen representatives, whose election had not been contested, and whom he adjudged to have been fairly elected. At the special election to fill these vacancies, three of the persons whose election on the 30th of March had been set aside for the reasons already stated, were re-elected, and in the other districts different persons were returned; and the governor having adjudged them to have been duly elected, accordingly granted them certificates of election, thus making the full complement of thirteen councilmen and twenty-six representatives, of whom, by the organic law of the Territory, the legislature was to be composed. On the 17th day of April the governor issued his proclamation, summoning these thirteen councilmen and twenty-six representatives, whom he had commissioned as having been fairly elected, to assemble at Pawnee City on the 2nd day of July, and organize as the legislature of the Territory of Kansas.

It appears from the journal that the two Houses did assemble, in obedience to the Governor's proclamation, at the time and place appointed by him; and, after the oath of office had been duly administered by one of the judges of the supreme court of the Territory, to each of the members who held the Governor's certificate, proceeded to organize their respective houses by the election of their officers; and each notified the other, by resolution, that they were thus duly organized. Also, by joint resolution, appointed a committee who waited on the Governor, and informed him that "the two houses of the *Kansas Legislature* are organized, and are now ready to proceed to business, and to receive" such communication as he may deem necessary.

In response to this joint resolution, "a message from the Governor, by Mr. Higgins, his private secretary, transmitting his message, was received, and ordered to be read."

The message commences thus:

"*To the Honorable the Council and House of Representatives of the Territory of Kansas:*

"Having been duly notified that your respective bodies have organized for the performance of your official functions, I herewith submit to you the usual executive communication relative to subjects of legislation, which universal and long-continued usage in analogous cases would seem to demand, although no express requirement of it is to be found in the act of Congress which has brought us into official existence, and prescribed our official duties.

"The position which we occupy, and the solemn trust which is confided to us for originating the laws and institutions, and moulding the destinies of a new republic in the very geographical centre of our vast and magnificent confederation, cannot but impress us with a deep and solemn sense of the heavy responsibility which we have assumed, and admonish us to lay aside all selfish and equivocal motives, to discard all unworthy ends, and, in the spirit of justice and charity to each other, with pure hearts, tempered feelings, and sober judgments, to address ourselves to our task, and so perform it in the fear and reverence of that God who oversees our work, that the star that we expect to add to the national banner shall be dimmed by no taint or tarnish of dishonor, and be subject to no reproach save that which springs from the inevitable fallibility of just and upright men."

The Governor, with the view to the "ascertainment of the existing law" in the Territory, proceeds to trace the history of all legislation affecting it since the country was acquired from France, and advises the legislature to pass such laws as the public interest might require upon all appropriate subjects of legislation, and particularly the Slavery question, the division of the Territory into counties, the organization of county courts, the election of judicial and ministerial officers, education, taxes, revenues, the location of the permanent seat of government, and the organization of the militia, as subjects worthy of their immediate attention.

From this message, as well as from all the official acts of the Governor preceding it, having reference to the election and return of the members and the convening of the two houses for legislative business, the conclusion is irresistible, that up to this period of time the Governor had never conceived the idea—if, indeed, he has since entertained it—that the two houses were spurious and fraudulent assemblies, having no rightful authority to pass laws which would be binding upon the people of Kansas. On the first day of the session, and immediately after the organization of the house was effected, the following Resolution was adopted:

"*Resolved*, That all persons who may desire to contest the seats of any persons now holding certificates of election as members of this house. may present their protests to the committee on credentials, and that notice thereof shall be given to the persons holding such certificates."

On the 4th day of July, (being the third day of the session,) the majority of the committee, including four of the five members, reported that, "HAVING HEARD AND EXAMINED ALL THE EVIDENCE TOUCHING THE MATTER OF INQUIRY BEFORE THEM, and taking the organic law of Congress, passed on the 20th day of May, in the year 1854, organizing the Territories of Kansas and Nebraska," as their guiding star, they have arrived at the conclusions which they proceed to elucidate and enforce in a lengthy report. From this report, it appears that fifteen out of twenty-two members present were permitted to retain their seats by unanimous consent, no one appearing to contest or dispute the fairness of the election, or regularity or truthfulness of the return, in either of their cases. Hence the contest was reduced to the claims of one member who received the certificate under the general election of the 30th of March, and the six members present who received certificates under the special election of the 24th of May. In the first case the decision of the Governor was reversed, and the seat awarded to the candidate who received the highest number of votes at the election of the 30th of March, and from whom the certificate had been withheld by the Governor, upon the ground of irregularity in the election and returns from one precinct, the exclusion of which poll gave the majority to the opposing candidate. In the other six cases, the sitting members were deprived of their seats; and the candidates receiving the highest number of votes at the general election on the 30th of March, were awarded their places, upon the ground that the special election on the 24th of May was illegal and void, the Governor not being authorized, by the organic law of the Territory, to go behind the returns, and set aside the election held on the 30th of March.

The minority report dissents from the reasoning, and protests against the conclusions of the majority, and affirms the right of the sitting members to retain their seats, upon the ground that the governor's certificate was not merely *prima facie* evidence, but was conclusive, in respect to the rights of all claimants and contestants; and hence the house could not go behind the certificates of election to inquire whether there had been a previous election in those districts on the 30th of March, and who had received the highest number of legal votes at that election. The proposition is thus stated in the minority report: "I cannot agree that this body has the right to go behind the decisions of the governor, who, by virtue of his office, is the organizing federal arm of the general government, to evolve and manage a new government for this Territory, for the obvious reason that Congress makes him the sole judge of the qualifications for membership." It is true that the minority report, alludes to "evidence before the committee of great deficiencies, not in the form of conducting the elections, but in the manner of holding them, both as to the qualifications of the judges who presided, and the returns made out by them," and says there is "no doubt that these illegal proceedings on the one hand induced the governor to withhold certificates from some who, from the number of votes returned in their favor, might at the same time appear to have been properly elected, and on the other, to have been the ground on which he presented a certificate in one instance, and in another ordered a new election in reference to other districts." But while the minority report affirms the right of the governor to go behind the returns and investigate irregularities and illegal voting at the election, as well as deficiencies in the forms of the returns, and asserts that he did exercise this right in each case in which he granted or withheld a certificate, it maintains that the governor's decision, as evinced by his certificate, was final and conclusive and could not be reviewed, much less reversed, by either branch of the Territorial legislature. So far as the question involves the legality of the Kansas legislature, and the validity of its acts, it is entirely immaterial whether we adopt the reasoning and conclusions of the minority or majority reports; for each proves that the legislature was legally and duly constituted. The minority report establishes the fact, by the position that the governor's certificate was conclusive, and that he granted certificates to ten out of the thirteen councilmen, and to seventeen out of the twenty-six representatives who finally held their seats, which was largely more than a quorum of each branch of the legislature. The majority report establishes the same fact, by the position tha after going behind the governor's certificate and carefully examining the facts, they confirmed these same ten councilmen and seventeen representatives in their seats, and then awarded the seats of the other three councilmen and nine representatives to the candidates whom they believed to have been legally elected at the general election on the 30th of March.

The house, by eighteen votes in the affirmative to one vote in the negative, passed a resolution adopting the majority report, and declaring that the contestants "having been duly elected on the 30th of March, 1855, are entitled to their seats as members of this house." Whereupon four of the sitting members, whose seats were vacated by the adoption of the majority report, signed a protest, and asked that it be spread on the journal of the house, which was accordingly done in the following words:

"*Protest.*

"We, the undersigned, members of the House of Representatives of Kansas Territory, believe the organic act organizing the said Territory gives this house no power to oust any member from this house who has received a certificate from the governor; that this house cannot go behind an election called by the governor, and consider any claims based on a prior election. We would therefore protest against such a proceeding, and ask this protest to be spread upon the journal of this house.

"JOHN HUTCHINSON,
WILLIAM JESSEE,
AUGUSTUS WATTLES,
E. D. LADD."

Under date of July 6, the journal contains a message from the governor to the "house of representatives of the Territory of Kansas," returning "house bill entitled 'An act to remove the seat of government temporarily to the Shawnee Manual Labor School, in the Territory of Kansas,' together with his objections." While the governor, in assigning his reasons for returning the bill, labors to prove that the legislature had transcended its authority under the organic act, in adopting this particular measure, and argues against its expediency, on the score of the loss of time and money in removing to a different place during the session, he clearly and distinctly recognizes the council and house of representatives as constituting the legislature of the Territory of Kansas, elected and organized in conformity to the act of Congress creating the Territory.

The reasons of the governor for returning the

bill, was spread upon the journal, and upon reconsideration, it was passed by a two-thirds' vote in each branch of the legislature, and thus became the law of the land, "the objections of the governor to the contrary notwithstanding."

On the same day the following resolution was adopted by both houses:

"*Resolved by the House of Representatives of the Territory of Kansas, (the Council concurring therein,)* That the legislature of said Territory do adjourn on the 6th day of July, A. D. 1855, to meet again on Monday, the 16th day of July, 1855, at 2 o'clock, P. M., at the Shawnee Manual-labor School, in the said Territory."

And on the same day the following resolution was also adopted by both houses:

"*Resolved*, That a Committee of three be appointed on the part of the Council, to act in conjunction with a Committee on the part of the House of Representatives, to inform his excellency the Governor that the Legislative Assembly will adjourn this afternoon, to meet on Monday, the 16th instant, at the Shawnee Manual-labor School, in the Territory of Kansas."

On the 16th of July, the two houses assembled, in pursuance of the adjournment, at the Shawnee Manual-labor School, known as Shawnee Mission, and proceeded to the discharge of their legislative duties. In the mean time the Governor had also repaired to Shawnee Mission, it being the place of his residence in the Territory, and the seat of the executive offices as established and continued by himself, during the whole period he exercised the executive functions.

On the 21st of July, a message was received from the Governor, by his private secretary, Mr. Lowry, directed "To the House of Representatives of the Territory of Kansas," in which he says: "I return to your House, in which they originated, the bill entitled 'An act to prevent the sale of intoxicating liquors, and games of chance, within one mile of the Shawnee Manual-labor School, in the Territory of Kansas,' and the bill entitled 'An act to establish a ferry at the town of Atchison, in Kansas Territory,' without my approval. I see nothing in the bills themselves to prevent my sanction of them, and my reasons for disapproval have been, doubtless, anticipated by you, as necessarily resulting from the opinion expressed in my message of the 6th instant."

The Governor then proceeds to argue the question at great length, *whether the legislature is now in session at a place which can be recognized as a seat of government, where the business of legislation can be legally or legitimately carried on.*

He does not question the fairness and legality of the election of the members composing the legislature; nor the regularity and validity of their organization; nor their competency as a legislature to pass all laws which they may deem necessary and proper for the best interests of the people of Kansas, *provided it shall be done at the right place.* Upon this point he says:

"It seems to be plain that the legislature now in session, so far as the place is concerned, is in contravention of the act of Congress, and where they have no right to sit, and can make no valid legislation. Entertaining these views, I can give no sanction to any bill that may be passed; and if my reasons are not satisfactory to the Legislative Assembly, it follows that we must act independently of each other."

In conclusion the Governor says:

"If I am right in these opinions, and our Territory shall derive no fruits from the meeting of the present Legislative Assembly, I shall at least have the satisfaction of recollecting that I called the attention of the Assembly to the point before they removed, and that the responsibility, therefore, rests not on the Executive."

The Governor having thus suspended all official intercourse with the two branches of the legislature, refusing to examine their acts with a view of either approving or disapproving them, they appointed a joint committee of the two houses to draught a memorial to the President of the United States, asking his removal from the office of governor; which memorial was signed by the presiding officers and members in joint session. The memorialists, after reviewing the causes which had led to such serious difficulties, and vindicating the right of the legislature, under the organic act, to remove the seat of government from Pawnee City to Shawnee Mission, concluded as follows:

"In conclusion, we charge the Governor, A. H. Reeder, with willful neglect of the interests of the Territory; with endeavoring, by all means in his power, to subvert the ends and objects intended to be accomplished by the 'Kansas and Nebraska bill,' by neglecting the public interests and making them subservient to private speculation; by aiding and encouraging persons in factious and treasonable opposition to the wishes of the majority of the citizens of the Territory, and the laws of the United States in force in said Territory; by encouraging persons to violate the laws of the United States, and set at defiance the commands of the general Government; by inciting persons to resist the laws which may be passed by the present Legislative Assembly of this Territory. For these, and many other reasons, we respectfully pray your excellency to remove the said A. H. Reeder from the exercise of the functions now held by him in said Territory; and represent that a continuance of the same will be prejudicial to the best interests of the said Territory. And, as in duty bound, we will ever pray," etc., etc.

[*Signed by the officers and members of both houses.*]

On the 15th of August, Governor Reeder addressed a note to the Department of State, acknowledging the receipt of a communication from the acting Secretary, under date of the 28th July, in which he was notified that "in consequence of your [Governor Reeder's] purchase of Kansas half-breed lands," and "more especially the undertaking of sundry persons, yourself included, to lay out new cities on military or other reservations in the Territory of Kansas," and "more particularly, as you have summoned the Legislative Assembly of the Territory to meet at one of the places referred to, denominated in your official proclamation 'Pawnee City,' I have, therefore, by the direction of the President, to notify you that your functions and authority as Governor of the Territory of Kansas are hereby terminated."

On the 16th of August, the journal of the House of Representatives says:

"The following message was received from Governor A. H. Reeder, by Mr. Lowry, his private secretary:

"*To the honorable the members of the Council and House of Representatives of the Territory of Kansas:*

"GENTLEMEN: Although, in my message to your bodies under date of the 21st instant, (ult.) I stated that I was unable to convince myself of the legality of your session at this place, for reasons then given; and although that opinion still remains unchanged, yet, inasmuch as my reasons were not satisfactory to your body, and the bills passed by your houses have been up to this time sent to me for approval, it is proper that I should inform you that after your adjournment of yesterday I received official notification that my functions as governor of the Territory of Kansas were terminated. No successor having arrived, Secretary Woodson will of course perform the duties of the office as acting governor.

"A. H. REEDER."

Inasmuch as Governor Reeder dissolved his official relations with the legislature, and denied the validity of their acts, solely upon the ground that they were enacted *in the wrong place*, it becomes material to inquire whether it was competent for them, under the organic act, to remove the seat of government temporarily from "Pawnee City" to the Shawnee Mission. The 24th section of the organic act provides "that the legislative power of the Territory shall extend to all rightful subjects of legislation consistent with the Constitution of the United States and the provisions of this act."

That the location of the seat of government, and the changing of the same whenever the public interests and convenience may require it, is a "rightful subject of legislation," is too plain to admit of argument; hence the power is clearly included in this general grant, and may be exercised at pleasure by the legislature, unless it shall be made to appear that Congress, by some other provision, has imposed restrictions or conditions upon its exercise.

The thirty-first section of the organic act provides "that the temporary seat of government of said Territory is hereby located at Fort Leavenworth; and that such portions of the public buildings as may not be actually used and needed for military purposes may be occupied and used, under the direction of the governor and legislative assembly, for such public purposes as may be required under the provisions of this act;" and the twenty-second section of the same act provides that "the persons thus elected to the legislative assembly shall meet at such place and on such day as the governor shall appoint" for the first meeting. These two provisions, being parts of the same act, and having reference to the same subject-matter, must be taken together, and receive such a construction as will give full effect to each, and not render either nugatory. While, therefore, the governor was authorized to convene the legislature, in the first instance, at such place as he should appoint, still he was required, by that provision which made Fort Leavenworth the temporary seat of government, with the view of using some of the public buildings, to designate as the place some one of the public buildings within the military reservation of Fort Leavenworth. Had not Congress, in the mean time, interposed and changed the law, as here presented, the governor would not have been authorized to have convened the legislature at "Pawnee City," nor at any other place in the Territory than some one of the public buildings at Fort Leavenworth, as provided in the organic act.

In view of the fact that the Secretary of War had intimated an opinion that all of the public buildings at Fort Leavenworth were needed for military purposes, and that the location of the seat of government, even temporarily, within the lines of a military reservation, where the military law must necessarily prevail, would be inconvenient, if not injurious to the public service, the following provision was adopted in the appropriation bill of the 5th of August, 1854, for the purpose of enabling the governor to erect buildings for the temporary seat of government at some more suitable and convenient point in the Territory: "That, in the event that the Secretary of War shall deem it inconsistent with the interest of the military service to furnish a sufficient portion of the military buildings at Fort Leavenworth for the use of the Territorial government of Kansas, the sum of twenty-five thousand dollars shall be, and in that contingency is hereby, appropriated, for the erection of public buildings for the use of the legislature of the Territory of Kansas, to be expended under the direction of the governor of said Territory."

Under this provision, taken in connection with that clause of the organic act which authorized the governor to convene the legislature at such place as he should appoint, he would have had the right to establish the temporary seat of government and erect the public buildings at Pawnee City, or any other place he might have selected in the Territory, instead of Fort Leavenworth, but for the fact that on the 3d of March, 1855, and before any portion of the money had been expended, or even the site selected, Congress made a further appropriation of twenty-five thousand dollars for public buildings, with the proviso "that said money, or any part thereof, or any portion of the money heretofore appropriated for this purpose shall not be expended until the legislature of said Territory shall have fixed by law the permanent seat of government." This provision did not confer upon the legislature any power in respect to the location of the seat of government, either temporarily or permanently, which it did not previously possess; for the general grant, extending to all "rightful subjects of legislation," necessarily included the right to determine the place of holding its sessions. The object, as well as legal effect, of this provision, was, to restrain the governor from expending the appropriation until the voice of the people of Kansas should be expressed, through their legislature, in the selection of the place; leaving the governor to perform his whole duty under the 22d section of the organic act, by appointing the place and day of the first meeting of the legislature, and of expending the money appropriated by Congress for the erection of public buildings, at such place as the legislature should designate for the permanent seat of government of the Territory.

Under this view of the subject, it is evident that the legislature was clothed with legitimate authority to enact the law in obedience to which its session was adjourned from Pawnee City to Shawnee Mission; and that its enactments, made at the latter place, must have the same force and validity that they would have possessed had not the removal taken place.

Those who seek to find some tenable ground upon which to destroy the validity of the legislative acts of Kansas, seeing that they cannot safely rely upon the alleged irregularity of the elections, nor upon the absence of legal authority in the legislature to remove the seat of Government, flatter themselves that they have recently discovered a new fact which will extricate them from their difficulty, and enable them to accomplish their purpose. It is, that by the treaties of November 7, 1825, and of August 8, 1831, with the Shawnees of Missouri and Ohio, a large tract of land, including the Shawnee Mission, where the legislature held its session, and the governor established the executive offices, was secured to those Indians, with the guaranty on the part of the United States "that said lands shall never be within the bounds of any State or Territory, nor subject to the laws thereof;" and that the 19th section of the Kansas-Nebraska act provides that "nothing in this act contained shall be construed to include any territory which, by treaty with any Indian tribe, is not, without the consent of said tribe, to be included within the territorial limits or jurisdiction of any State or Territory; but all such territory shall be excepted out of the boundaries, and constitute no part of the Territory of Kansas." Upon the authority of these clauses of the treaties, and of the act of Congress organizing the Territory, it is assumed that the Shawnee Mission, where the legislature enacted those laws, was not within the limits or jurisdiction of the Territory of Kansas, and hence they were null and void. Without admitting, even by implication, that the place where the legislature should enact its laws would to any extent impair their validity, it is proper to call the attention of the Senate to the fact recorded on its journal, that on the 10th of May, 1854, (only a few days before the passage of the Kansas-Nebraska act,) a treaty was made with these same Indians, by the first article of which all the lands granted to them by the said treaties of 1825 and 1831 were ceded to the United States, and, being thus exempted from the operation of the guaranties in those treaties, were, by the terms of the organic act of Kansas, included within the limits, and rendered subject to the jurisdiction of said Territory.

The second article granted the house in which the legislature afterwards held its sessions, and the land upon which the house stood, to the missionary society of the Methodist Episcopal Church South, in these words: "Of the lands lying east of the parallel line aforesaid, there shall first be set apart to the missionary society of the Methodist Episcopal Church South, to include the improvements of the Indian Manual-labor School, three sections of land; to the Friends' Shawnee Labor-school, including the improvements there, three hundred and twenty acres of land; and to the American Baptist Union, to include the improvements where the superintendent of the school now resides, one hundred and sixty acres of land; and also five acres of land to the Shawnee Methodist Church, including the meeting-house and grave-yard; and two acres of land to the Shawnee Baptist Church, including the meeting-house and grave-yard."

The other articles of the treaty provide for the survey of those lands, and for granting two hundred acres to each Shawnee Indian, to be held as private property, subject to such conditions as Congress should impose, and recognize the right of the legislature to lay out roads and public highways across the Indian lands, on the same terms as the law provides for their location through the lands of citizens of the United States. The Rev. Thomas Johnson, who was president of the Kansas legislative council, and also agent of the Missionary society of the Methodist Episcopal Church, to which the lands and improvements belonged, authorized the legislature to use and occupy such portions of the buildings of which he held the lawful possession as they should find convenient in the exercise of their legislative functions.

Upon a careful review and examination of all the facts, laws, and treaties, bearing upon the point, your committee are clearly of the opinion that the Shawnee Manual-labor School was a place to which the legislature might lawfully adjourn and enact valid laws in pursuance of the organic act of the Territory.

We do not deem it necessary to inquire into the expediency of the removal of the seat of government, for the reason that it cannot affect the validity of the legislative proceedings. It is sufficient to state, that the reasons assigned by the Governor against the expediency of the measure were: first, "the loss of time (more valuable because limited) which our organic law allots to the legislative session;" and secondly, "because it will involve a pecuniary loss, in view of the arrangements which have been made at this place for our accommodation." As an offset to the unfortunate circumstance that the people of Kansas would be deprived, for the period of ten days, of all the advantages and protection which were expected to result from the wholesome laws which the governor had recommended them to enact upon all rightful subjects of legislation, and to the pecuniary loss which would be sustained in consequence of the removal from Pawnee City, the members of the legislature, in their memorial to the President of the United States, asking him to remove the governor, state their reasons as follows, for the allegation that there was an unnecessary loss of three months' time after the election in convening the legislature, and that Pawnee was not a suitable place for them to meet:

"After the contest was over, and the result known, he delayed the assembling of the body until the 2d day of July—more than three months afterwards—and that, too, when the whole Union was convulsed on account of alleged outrages in Kansas Territory, and yet no law for the punishment or prevention of them. When at last they did meet, upon the call of the governor, at a point where they had previously, in an informal manner, protested against being called, with an avowal of their intention to adjourn to the point at which they are now assembled, for the reasons that the requisite accommodations could not be had; where there were no facilities for communication with their families or constituents; where they could not even find the commonest food to eat, unless at an enormous expense, there being no gardens yet made by the squatters; where the house in which we were expected to assemble had no roof or floor on the Saturday preceding the Monday of our assembling, and for the completion of which the entire Sabbath day and night was desecrated by the continual labor of the mechanics; where, at least, one-half of the members, employés, and almost all others who had assembled there for business or otherwise, had to camp out in wagons and tents during a rainy, hot season, and where cholera broke out, as a consequence of the inadequate food and shelter; and when, under all of these circumstances of annoyance, they finally passed an act adjourning to this point—Shawnee Manual-labor School—where ample accommodations are provided, and where the governor himself had previously made it the seat of government, they were met by his veto, which is herewith transmitted."

Your committee have not considered it any part of their duty to examine and review each enactment and provision of the large volume of laws adopted by the legislature of Kansas upon almost every rightful subject of legislation, and affecting nearly every relation and interest in life, with a view either to their approval or disapproval by Congress, for the reason that they are local laws, confined in their operation to the internal concerns of the Territory, the control and management of which, by the principles of the Federal Constitution, as well as by the very terms of the Kansas-Nebraska act, are confided to the people of the Territory, to be determined by themselves through their representatives in their local legislature, and not by the Congress, in which they have no representatives to give or withhold their assent to the laws upon which their rights and liberties may all depend. Under these laws marriages have taken place, children have been born, deaths have occurred, estates have been distributed, contracts have been made, and rights have accrued which it is not competent for Congress to divest. If there can be a doubt in respect to the validity of these laws, growing out of the alleged irregularity of the election of the members of the legislature, or the lawfulness of the place where its sessions were held, which it is competent for any tribunal to inquire into with a view to its decision at this day, and after the series of events which have ensued, it must be a judicial question, over which Congress can have no control, and which can be determined only by the courts of justice, under the protection and sanction of the Constitution.

When it was proposed in the last Congress to annul the acts of the legislative assembly of Minnesota, incorporating certain railroad companies, this committee reported against the proposition, and, instead of annulling the local legislation of the Territory, recommended the repeal of that clause of the organic act of Minnesota which reserves to Congress the right to disapprove its laws. That recommendation was based on the theory that the people of the Territory, being citizens of the United States, were entitled to the privilege of self-government in obedience to the Constitution; and if, in the exercise of this right, they had made wise and just laws, they ought to be permitted to enjoy all the advantages resulting from them; while, on the contrary, if they had made unwise and unjust laws, they should abide the consequences of their own acts until they discovered, acknowledged, and corrected their errors.

It has been alleged that gross misrepresentations have been made in respect to the character of the laws enacted by the legislature of Kansas, calculated, if not designed, to prejudice the public mind at a distance against those who enacted them, and to create the impression that it was the duty of Congress to interfere and annul them. In view of the violent and insurrectionary measures which were being taken to resist the laws of the Territory, a convention of delegates, representing almost every portion of the Territory of Kansas, was held at the city of Leavenworth on the 14th of November, 1855, at which men of all shades of political opinions, "Whigs, Democrats, Pro-slavery men, and Free-state men, all met and harmonized together, and forgot their former differences in the common danger that seemed to threaten the peace, good order, and prosperity of this community." This convention was presided over by the governor of the Territory, assisted by a majority of the judges of the supreme court; and the address to the citizens of the United States, among other distinguished names, bears the signatures of the United States district attorney and marshal for the Territory.

It is but reasonable to assume that the interpretation which these functionaries have given to the acts of the Kansas legislature in this address will be observed in their official exposition and execution of the same. In reference to the wide-spread perversions and misrepresentations of those laws, this address says:

"The laws passed by the legislature have been most grossly misrepresented, with the view of prejudicing the public against that body, and as an excuse for the revolutionary movements in this Territory. The limits of this address will not permit a correction of all these misrepresentations; but we will notice some of them, that have had the most wide-spread circulation.

"It has been charged and widely circulated that the legislature, in order to perpetuate their rule, had passed a law prescribing the qualification of voters, by which it is declared 'that any one may vote who will swear allegiance to the fugitive-slave law, the Kansas and Nebraska bill, and pay one dollar.' Such is declared to be the evidence of citizenship, such the qualification of voters. In reply to this, we say that no such law was ever passed by the legislature. The law prescribing the qualification of voters expressly provides that, to entitle a person to vote, he must be twenty-one years of age, an actual inhabitant of this Territory, and of the county or district in which he offers to vote, and shall have paid a territorial tax. There is no law requiring him to pay a dollar-tax as a qualification to vote. He must pay a tax it is true, [and this is by no means an unusual requirement in the States;] but whether this tax is levied on his personal or real property, his money at interest, or is a poll-tax, makes no difference; the payment of any territorial tax entitles the person to vote, provided he has the other qualifications provided by law. The act seems to be carefully drawn with the view of excluding all illegal and foreign votes. The voter must be an inhabitant of the Territory, and of the county or district in which he offers to vote, and he must have paid a territorial tax. The judges and clerks are required to be sworn, and to keep duplicate poll-boxes; and ample provision is made for contesting elections, and purging the polls of all illegal votes. It is difficult to see how a more guarded law could be framed, for the purpose of protecting the purity of elections and the sanctity of the ballot-box. The law does not require the voter to swear to support the fugitive-slave law, or the Kansas and Nebraska bill, unless he is challenged; in that case, he is required to take an oath to support each of these laws. As to the dollar law, [so called,] it is merely a poll-tax, and has no more connection with the right of suffrage than any other tax levied by the territorial authority, and is to be paid whether the party votes or not. It is a mere temporary measure, having no force beyond this year, and was resorted to as such to supply the territorial treasury with the necessary means to carry on the government.

"It has also been charged against the legislature that they elected all of the officers of the Territory for six years. This is without any foundation. They elected no officer for six years; and the only civil officers they retain the election of, that occurs to us at present, are the auditor and treasurer of state, and the district attorneys, who hold their offices for four, and not six years. By the organic act, the commissions issued by the governor to the civil officers of the Territory all expired on the adjournment of the legislature. To prevent a failure in the local administration, and from necessity, the legislature made a number of temporary appointments, such as probate judge, and two county commissioners, and a sheriff of each county.* The probate judge and county commissioners constitute the tribunal for the transaction of county business, and are invested with the power to appoint justices of the peace, constables, county surveyor, recorder, and clerk, etc. Probate judges, county commissioners, sheriffs, etc., are all temporary appointments, and are made elective by the people at the first annual election in 1857. The legislature could not have avoided making some temporary appointments. No election could have been held without them. There were no judges, justices of the peace, or other officers to conduct an election of any kind, until appointed by the legislature. It was the exercise of a power which the first legislative assembly in every Territory must, of necessity, exercise, in order to put the local government in motion. We see nothing in this to justify revolution or a resort to force. The law for the protection of slave property has also been much misunderstood. The right to pass such a law is expressly stated by Governor Reeder in his inaugural message, in which he says: 'A territorial legislature may undoubtedly act upon the question to a limited and partial extent, and may temporarily prohibit, tolerate or regulate slavery in the Territory, and in an absolute or modified form, with all the force and effect of any other legislative act, binding until repealed by the same power that enacted it.' There is nothing in the act itself, as has been charged, to prevent a free discussion of the subject of slavery. Its bearing on society, its morality or expediency, or whether it would be politic or impolitic to make this a slave State, can be discussed here as freely as in any State in this Union, without infringing any of the provisions of the law. To deny the right of a person to hold slaves under the law in this Territory is made penal; but beyond this, there is no restriction to the discussion of the Slavery question, in any aspect in which it is capable of being considered. We do not wish to be understood as approving of all the laws passed by the legislature; on the contrary, we would state that there are some that we do not approve of, and which are condemned by public opinion here, and which will, no doubt, be repealed or modified at the meeting of the next legislature. But this is nothing more than what frequently occurs, both in the legislation of Congress and of the various State legislatures. The remedy for such evils is to be found in public opinion, to which, sooner or later, in a government like ours, all laws must conform."

A few days after Governor Reeder dissolved his official relations with the legislature, on account of the removal of the seat of government, and while that body was still in session, a meeting was called by "many voters," to assemble at Lawrence on the 14th or 15th of August, 1855, "to take into consideration the propriety of calling a Territorial convention, preliminary to the formation of a State government, and other subjects of public interest." At that meeting the following preamble and resolutions were adopted with but one dissenting voice:

"Whereas the people of Kansas Territory have been since its settlement, and now are, without any law-making power: therefore,

"*Be it resolved*, That we, the people of Kansas Territory, in mass meeting assembled, irrespective of party distinctions, influenced by a common necessity, and greatly desirous of promoting the common good, do hereby call upon and request all *bona fide* citizens of Kansas Territory, of whatever political views and predilections, to consult together in their respective election districts, and in mass convention or otherwise, elect three delegates for each representative of the legislative assembly, by proclamation of Governor Reeder of date 10th March, 1855; said delegates to assemble in convention at the town of Topeka, on the 19th day of September, 1855, then and there to consider and determine upon all subjects of public interest, and particularly upon that having reference to the speedy formation of a State constitution, with an intention of an immediate application to be admitted as a State into the Union of the United States of America."

This meeting, so far as your committee have been able to ascertain was the first step in that series of proceedings which resulted in the adoption of a constitution and State government, to be put in operation on the 4th of the present month, in subversion of the Territorial government established under the authority of Congress. The right to set up the State government in defiance of the constituted authorities of the Territory, is based on the assumption "that the people of Kansas Territory have been since its settlement, and now are, without any law-making power;" in the face of the well-known fact, that the Territorial legislature were then in session, in pursuance of the proclamation of Governor Reeder, and the organic law of the Territory. On the 5th of September, a "Territorial delegate convention" assembled at the Big Springs "to take into consideration the present exigencies of political affairs," at which, among others, the following resolutions were adopted:

"*Resolved*, That this Convention, in view of its recent repudiation of the acts of the so-called Kansas legislative assembly, respond most heartily to the call made by the people's convention of the 14th ultimo, for a delegate convention of the people of Kansas, to be held at Topeka, on the 19th instant, to consider the propriety of the formation of a State Constitution, and such matters as may legitimately come before it.

"*Resolved*, That we owe no allegiance or obedience to the tyrannical enactments of this spurious legislature; that their laws have no validity or binding force upon the people of Kansas; and that every freeman among us is at full liberty, consistently with his obligations as a citizen and a man, to defy and resist them if he choose so to do.

"*Resolved*, That we will endure and submit to these laws no longer than the best interests of the Territory require, as the least of two evils, and will resist them to a bloody issue as soon as we ascertain that peaceable remedies shall fail, and forcible resistance shall furnish any reasonable prospect of success; and that in the mean time we recommend to our friends througout the Territory, the organization and discipline of volunteer companies, and the procurement and preparation of arms."

With the view to a distinct understanding of the meaning of so much of this resolution as relates to the "organization and discipline of volunteer companies, and the procurement and preparation of arms," it may be necessary to state, that there was at that time existing in the Territory a secret military organization, which had been formed for political objects prior to the alleged invasion, at the election on the 30th of March, and which held its first "Grand Encampment at Lawrence, February 8th, 1855." Your Committee have been put in possession of a small printed pamphlet, containing the "constitution and ritual of the grand encampment and regiments of the Kansas legion of Kansas Territory, adopted April 4th, 1855," which, during the recent disturbances in that Territory, was taken on the person of one George F. Warren, who attempted to conceal and destroy the same by thrusting it into his mouth, and biting and chewing it. Although somewhat mutilated by the "tooth prints," it bears internal evidence of being a genuine document, authenticated by the original signatures of "G. W. Hutchinson, grand general," and "J. K. Goodwin, grand quartermaster." On the last page was a charter of the Kansas legion, authorizing the said George F. Warren, from whose mouth the document was taken, to form a new regiment, as follows:

"*Charter of the Kansas Legion.*

"UNITED STATES OF AMERICA,
Territory of Kansas.

"Know all men by these presents, that we, the Grand Encampment of the Kansas Legion of Kansas Territory, have created, chartered, and empowered, and by these presents do create, charter, and empower George F. Warren to be regiment ——, No. ——, of the Kansas Legion; and, as such, they are hereby invested with all and singular the authority and privileges with which each and every regiment is invested, working under a charter from the Grand Encampment.

"In witness whereof, we have hereunto set our hands, this sixteenth day of August, one thousand eight hundred and fifty-five.

"G. W. HUTCHINSON,
Grand General.
"J. K. GOODWIN,
Grand Quartermaster."

The constitution consists of six articles, regulating the organization of the "Grand Encampment," which is "composed of representatives elected from each subordinate regiment existing in the Territory, as hereafter provided. The officers of the Grand Encampment shall consist of a Grand General, Grand Vice-General, Grand Quartermaster, Grand Paymaster, Grand Aid two Grand Sentinels, and Grand Chaplain.

"The Grand Encampment shall make all nominations for Territorial officers at large, and immediately after such nominations shall have been made, the Grand General shall communicate the result to every regiment in the Territory."

The officers of the "GRAND ENCAMPMENT" are, Grand General Rev. G. W. Hutchinson, Lawrence, K. T.

Grand Vice-General, C. K. Holliday, Topeka, K. T.

Grand Quartermaster, J. K. Goodwin, Lawrence, K. T.

Grand Paymaster, Charles Leib, M. D., Leavenworth city, K. T.

By "the constitution of the subordinate encampment," "the officers of each subordinate regiment shall consist of a colonel, a lieutenant-colonel, a quartermaster, aid, and two sentinels. The regiment located in each and every election district, shall make nominations for all candidates for offices in their respective districts; but where there shall be two or more regiments in any one election district, of whatever kind, these nominations shall be made by delegates from the respective encampments within said district."

The "ritual" continues the order of business and modes of proceeding in the subordinate encampment, under the following heads:

1st. Reading the minutes by the quartermaster.
2d. Proposals for new recruits.
3d. Voting for same.
4th. Initiation of recruits.
5th. Reports of committees.
6th. Unfinished business appearing on the minutes.
7th. Miscellaneous business.
8th. Adjournment.

The "opening ceremony" of the subordinate encampments is as follows:

"The colonel, lieutenant-colonel, quartermaster, paymaster, aid, and sentinels, being in their respective places, the regiment shall be called and thus addressed by the colonel:

"*Colonel.* Fellow-soldiers in the Free-State army: The hour has arrived when we must resume the duties devolving upon us. Let us each, with a heart devoted to justice, patriotism, and liberty, attend closely to all the regulations laid down for our government and action; each laboring to make this review pleasant and profitable to ourselves, and a blessing to our country. Aid, are the sentinels at their post, with closed doors?

"*Aid.* They are.

"*Colonel.* Aid, you will now review the troops in the regiment's pass-words.

"*Aid.* (After examination.) I have examined them personally, and find each correct.

"*Colonel.* I pronounce this regiment arrayed and ready for service."

Then follows the process of initiating new recruits, who are properly vouched for by members of the order, the preliminary obligations to observe secrecy, the catechism to which the candidate is subjected, and the explanations of the colonel in respect to the objects of the order, which are thus stated:

"First, to secure to Kansas the blessing and prosperity of being a free State; and, secondly, to protect the ballot-box from the LEPROUS TOUCH OF UNPRINCIPLED MEN."

These and all other questions being satisfactorily answered, the final oath is thus administered:

"With these explanations upon our part, we shall ask of you that you take with us an obligation placing yourself in the same attitude as before.

"OBLIGATION.

"I, ——— ———, in the most solemn manner, here in the presence of Heaven and these witnesses, bind myself that I will never reveal, nor cause to be revealed, either by word, look, or sign, by writing, printing, engraving, painting, or in any manner whatsoever, anything pertaining to this institution, save to persons duly qualified to receive the same. I will never reveal the nature of the organization, the place of meeting, the fact that any person is a member of the same, or even the existence of the organization, except to persons legally qualified to receive the same. Should I at any time withdraw, or be suspended or expelled from this organization, I will keep this obligation to the end of life. If any books, papers, or moneys belonging to this organization be intrusted to my care or keeping, I will faithfully and completely deliver up the same to my successor in office, or any one legally authorized to receive them. I will never knowingly propose a person for membership in this order who is not in favor of making *Kansas a free State*, and whom I feel satisfied will exert his entire influence to bring about this result. I will support, maintain, and abide by any honorable movement made by the organization to secure this great end, which will not conflict with the laws of the country and the Constitution of the United States. I will unflinchingly vote for and support the candidates nominated by this organization in preference to any and all others.

"To all of this obligation I do most solemnly promise and affirm, binding myself under the penalty of being expelled from this organization, of having my name published to the several Territorial encampments as a perjurer before Heaven, and a traitor to my country, of passing through life scorned and reviled by man, frowned on by devils, forsaken by angels, and abandoned by God."

The "closing ceremony" is as follows:

"*Colonel.* Fellow-soldiers: I trust this review has been both pleasant and profitable to all. We met as friends; let us part as brothers, remembering that we seek no wrong to any; and our bond of union in battling for the right must tend to make us better men, better neighbors, and better citizens. We thank you for your kindness and attention, and invite you all to be present at our next review, to be holden at ———, on ——— next, at ——— o'clock P. M. Sentinels, you will open the doors, that our soldiers may retire pleasantly and in order."

Your committee have deemed it important to give this outline of the "constitution and ritual of the grand encampment and regiments of the Kansas legion," as constituting the secret organization, political and military, in obedience to which the public demonstrations have been made to subvert the authority of the Territorial government established by Congress, by setting up a State government, either with or without the assent of Congress, as circumstances should determine. The endorsement of this military organization, and the recommendation by the Big Springs convention for "the procurement and preparation of arms," accompanied with the distinct declaration that "we will resist them [the laws enacted by the Kansas legislature] to a bloody issue, as soon as we ascertain that peaceable remedies shall fail, and forcible resistance shall furnish any reasonable prospect of success," would seem to admit of no other interpretation than that, in the event that the courts of justice shall sustain the validity of those laws, and Congress shall refuse to admit Kansas as a State with the constitution to be formed at Topeka, they will set up an independent government in defiance of the federal authority.

The same purpose is clearly indicated by the other proceedings of this convention, in which it is declared that "we with scorn repudiate the election-law, so called," and nominate Governor Reeder for Congress, to be voted for on a different day from that authorized by law, at an election to be held by judges and clerks not appointed in pursuance of any legal authority, and not to be sworn by any person authorized by law to administer oaths; and the returns to be made, and result proclaimed, and certificate granted, in a mode and by persons not permitted to perform these acts by any law, in or out of the Territory.

In accepting the nomination, Governor Reeder addressed the convention as follows; and, among other things, said:

"In giving him this nomination in this manner, they had strengthened his arms to do their work, and, in return, he would now pledge to them a steady, unflinching pertinacity of purpose, never-tiring industry, dogged perseverance, and, in all the abilities with which God had endowed him, to the righting of their wrongs, and the final triumph of their cause. He believed, from the circumstances which had for the last eight months surrounded him, and which had, at the same time, placed in his possession many facts, and bound him, heart and soul, to the oppressed voters of Kansas, that he could do much towards obtaining a redress of their grievances.

"He said that, day by day a crisis was coming upon us; that, in after-times, this would be to posterity a turning point, a marked period, as are to us the opening of the Revolution, the adoption of the Declaration of Independence, and the era of the alien and sedition laws; that we should take each carefully, so that each be a step of progress, and so that no violence be done to the tie which binds the American people together. He alluded to the unprecedented tyranny under which we are and have been; and said that, if any one supposed that institutions were to be imposed by force upon a free and enlightened people, they never knew, or had forgotten, the history of our fathers. American citizens bear in their breasts too much of the spirit of other and trying days, and have lived too long amid the blessings of liberty, to submit to oppression from any quarter: and the man who having once been free, could tamely submit to tyranny, was fit to be a Slave.

"He urged the Free-State men of Kansas to forget all minor issues, and pursue determinedly the one great object, never swerving, but steadily pressing on, as did the wise men who followed the star to the manger, looking back only for fresh encouragement. He counseled that peaceful resistance be made to the tyrannical and unjust laws of the spurious legislature;

that appeals to the courts, to the ballot-box, and to Congress, be made for relief from this oppressive load; that violence should be deprecated as long as a single hope of peaceable redress remained; but if, at last, all these should fail—if, in the proper tribunals, there is no hope for our dearest rights, outraged and profaned—if we are still to suffer, that corrupt men may reap harvests watered by our tears—then there is one more chance for justice. God has provided, in the eternal frame of things, redress for every wrong; and there remains to us still the steady eye and the strong arm, and we must conquer, or mingle the bodies of the oppressors with those of the oppressed upon the soil which the Declaration of Independence no longer protects. But he was not at all apprehensive that such a crisis would ever arrive. He believed that justice might be found far short of so dreadful an extremity; and, even should an appeal to arms come, it was his opinion, that if we are well prepared, that moment the victory is won."

In pursuance of the recommendation of the mass meeting held at Lawrence on the 14th of August, and endorsed by the convention held at the Big Springs on the 5th and 6th of September, a convention was held at Topeka on the 19th and 20th of September, at which it was determined to hold another convention at the same place on the fourth Tuesday of October, for the purpose of forming a constitution and State government; and to this end such proceedings were had as were deemed necessary for giving the notices, conducting the election of delegates, making the returns, and assembling the convention. With regard to the regularity of these proceedings, your committee see no necessity for further criticism than is to be found in the fact that it was the movement of a political party instead of the whole body of the people of Kansas, conducted without the sanction of law, and in defiance of the constituted authorities, for the avowed purpose of overthrowing the territorial government established by Congress.

The constitutional convention met at Topeka on the fourth Tuesday of October, and organized by electing Col. J. H. Lane president, who, in returning his acknowledgments for the honor, repudiated the validity of the territorial legislature and its acts in these words:

"Gentlemen of the convention: For the position assigned me, accept my thanks. You have met, gentlemen, on no ordinary occasion, to accomplish no ordinary purpose. You are the first legal representatives the real settlers of Kansas have ever had. You comprise the first legally-elected representative body ever assembled in the Territory," etc.

"*Friday, October 26.*—Mr Smith offered the following resolution, instructing the standing committees:

"*Resolved*, That the various committees of this convention be, and they are hereby, instructed to frame their work, having in view an immediate organization of a State government."

"*October 30.*—In the evening session the debates ran high upon Mr. Smith's resolution in reference to an immediate State organization. The mover of the resolution was in favor of electing State officers at once. He would advise no hesitation, he would present a bold front, and waver not at all. The Territory was without laws; life and property were unprotected. The territorial government had broken down. He would not leave it an hour for the action of Congress, after an application for admission, but would set up an independent form of government," etc.

Mr. Emery said:

"Now, Mr. Chairman, what does this resolution contemplate? What is proposed to be done? It first proposes to supersede the present weak and inefficient territorial government, and hence it enunciates the fundamental idea of the constitutional movement. Ay, it does more. It proposes to prove into a fact the leading idea of the Declaration of Independence, the highest human authority in American politics, which is this: whenever any form of government becomes destructive of the ends for which it was instituted, it is the right of the people to alter or abolish it, and to institute a new government. It proposes to force theories of human rights into facts, to practically apply this great principle to the wants and the necessities of the down-trodden people of Kansas. I do not question this right of the people, and certainly no gentleman on this floor will disagree with me. If he does, he occupies a most extraordinary position, and consistency would suggest that he withdraw from this body. No, when we say that we will take measures to supersede and render unnecessary that *thing* now extended over us called a territorial government—when we say and maintain that we have a right guaranteed by the Constitution, to have a form of government resting on our own consent and free will, we are only doing what, as American citizens, we have a right to do; we only propose to carry out the doctrine, much abused and grossly misrepresented as it has been—I mean the doctrine of squatter sovereignty, under which we are assembled here to-day, and in pursuance of the principles of which we hope to extricate ourselves from our present unhappy condition."

It is but just to state, that in another part of this same speech, Mr. Emery declared himself opposed to an immediate election "under the new constitution, and an immediate session of the general assembly, when all the wheels of State government shall be put in motion, irrespective of the action of Congress, upon due application for admission. Mr. E. presented his objections to the position of Mr. Smith, and maintained the views above indicated. He contended that, inasmuch as the Territorial form of government was recognized by the Supreme Court of the United States, and hence a legal form of government, no other government could be substituted so long as that was in existence, without risking the most serious consequences, to say the least."

In reply to the advocates of immediate State organization, Mr. Delahay, of Leavenworth, said:

"Under the defined rights of squatter sovereignty as enunciated by the Kansas-Nebraska act, it seems reasonable that the people have the right to take upon themselves the burdens of a government, but I question the right of the people of Kansas to organize a new government if its authority is to come in conflict with that of the government created by Congress. The gentleman from Lawrence [Colonel Lane] has assumed as a fundamental position, in advocating an immediate State organization, that neither government nor local law exists in this Territory. Sir, I must dissent from that position. I deny, Mr. Chairman, that a Territorial government can be legally abolished by the election of another government. I hold, on the contrary, and I think that my position would be supported by our highest legal authorities, that the power of a Territorial government ceases only by the enactment of the body which created it; in other words, that the government and laws of Kansas can be abolished by Congress alone, and are beyond the reach of this Territory, or any other power. I do not pretend to deny that, as all civil power is derived from the people, they have the moral right to abolish unjust laws, or to overthrow obnoxious governments by force; but I do question the expediency of effecting a reform in Kansas by any overt act of rebellion. For I must confess, Mr. Chairman, while I cast not the shadow of suspicion on the motives of the advocates of this measure, that from the point of view from which I regard this question, it appears to me to be an act of rebellion."

Your committee have made these voluminous extracts from the best authenticated reports which they have been able to obtain of the proceedings of the convention, for the purpose of showing that it was distinctly understood on all sides that the adoption of the proposition for organizing the State government, before the assent of Congress for the admission of the State should be obtained, was a decision in favor of repudiating the laws, and overthrowing the Territorial government in defiance of the authority of Congress. By this decision as incorporated into the schedule to the constitution, the vote on the ratification to the constitution was to be held on the 15th of December, 1855, and the election for all State officers on the third Tuesday of January, 1856. The third section of the schedule is as follows:

"The general assembly shall meet on the 4th day of March, A. D. 1856, at the city of Topeka, at 12 m., at which time and place the governor, lieutenant-governor, secretary of state, judges of supreme court, treasurer, auditor, state printer, reporter, and clerk of supreme court, and attorney-general, shall appear, take the oath of office, and enter upon the discharge of the duties of their respective offices under this constitution; and shall continue in office in the same manner, and during the same period, they would have done had they been elected on the first Monday in August, A. D. 1856."

The elections for all these officers were held at the time specified; and on the fourth day of the present month, the new government was to have been put in operation, in conflict with the Territorial government established by Congress, and for the avowed purpose of subverting and overthrowing the same, without reference to the action of Congress upon their application for admission into the Union.

Your committee are not aware of any case in the history of our own country, which can be fairly cited as an example, much less a justification, for these extraordinary proceedings. Cases have occurred in which the inhabitants of particular Territories have been permitted to form constitutions, and take the initiatory steps for the organization of State governments, preparatory to their admission into the Union, without obtaining the previous assent of Congress; BUT IN EVERY INSTANCE THE PROCEEDING HAS ORIGINATED WITH, AND BEEN CONDUCTED IN SUBORDINATION TO, THE AUTHORITY OF THE LOCAL GOVERNMENTS ESTABLISHED OR RECOGNIZED BY THE GOVERNMENT OF THE UNITED STATES. Michigan, Arkansas, Florida, and California, are sometimes cited as cases in point. Michigan was erected into a Territory in pursuance of the ordinance of the 13th of July, 1787, as recognized and carried into effect by acts of Congress subsequent to the adoption of the Federal Constitution. In that ordinance it was provided that the Territory northwest of the Ohio river should be divided into not less than three nor more than five States; "and, whenever any of said States shall have sixty thousand free inhabitants therein, such State shall be admitted, by its delegates, into the Congress of the United States on an equal footing with the original States in all respects whatever, and shall be at liberty to form a permanent constitution and State government."

In pursuance of this provision of their organic law, the legislature of the Territory of Michigan passed an act providing for a convention of the people to form a constitution and State government, which was accordingly done in obedience to the laws and constituted authorities of the Territory. The legislature of the Territory of Arkansas, having ascertained by a census that the Territory contained about fifty-one thousand eight hundred inhabitants, at a time when the ratio of representation in Congress awarded one representative to each forty-seven thousand seven hundred inhabitants, passed an act authorizing the people to form a constitution and ask for admission into the Union, as they supposed they had a right to do under the treaty acquiring the Territory from France, which guarantied their admission as soon as may be consistent with the Federal Constitution. Upon this point your committee adopt the legal opinion of the Attorney-General of the United States, (B. F. Butler,) as expressed in the following extract:

"But I am not prepared to say that all proceedings on this subject, on the part of the citizens of Arkansas, will be illegal. They, undoubtedly, possess the ordinary privileges and immunities of citizens of the United States. Among these, is the right to assemble and to petition the government for the redress of grievances; in the exercise of this right, the inhabitants of Arkansas may peaceably meet together in primary assemblies, or in conventions chosen by such assemblies, for the purpose of petitioning Congress to abrogate the Territorial government, and to admit them into the Union as an independent State. The particular form which they may give to their petition cannot be material, so long as they confine themselves to the mere right of petitioning, and conduct all their proceedings in a peaceable manner. And as the power of Congress over the whole subject is plenary and unlimited, they may accept any constitution, however framed, which in their judgment meets the sense of the people to be affected by it. If, therefore, the citizens of Arkansas think proper to accompany their petition with a written constitution, framed and agreed on by their primary assemblies, or by a convention of delegates chosen by such assemblies, I perceive no legal objection to their power to do so, nor to any measure which may be taken to collect the sense of the people in respect to it; provided, always, that such measures be commenced and prosecuted in a peaceable manner, in strict subordination to the existing Territorial government, and in entire subserviency to the power of Congress to adopt, reject, or disregard them at their pleasure.

"It is, however, very obvious, that all measures commenced and prosecuted with a design to subvert the Territorial government, and to establish and put in force in its place a new government, without the consent of Congress, will be unlawful. The laws establishing the Territorial government must continue in force until abrogated by Congress; and, in the mean time, it will be the duty of the governor, and of all the Territorial officers, as well as of the President, to take care that they are faithfully executed."

On the 11th day of January, 1839, a committee of the constitutional convention of Florida addressed a memorial to Congress, in which they state that, in 1837, the Territorial council passed a law submitting to the people the question of "State" or "Territory," to be decided at the election of delegates to Congress in the month of May of that year; that a decided majority of the suffrages given at that election was in favor of "State;" that the legislative council of 1838, in obedience to the expressed wishes of the people, enacted a law authorizing the holding of a convention to form and adopt a State constitution; that the convention assembled on the 3d of December, 1838, and continued in session until the 11th of January, 1839: and that, on behalf of the people of Florida, they transmit the "constitution, or form of government," and ask for admission into the Union. It is also stated in the memorial that in 1838 a census of the Territory was taken, in obedience to a law passed by the Territorial council, and that this census, although taken during the ravages of Indian hostilities, when a large portion of the inhabitants could not be found at home, showed an aggregate population of forty-eight thousand two hundred and twenty-three persons, which the memorialists insisted furnished satisfactory assurance of a sufficient population to entitle them to admission, according to the treaty acquiring the country from Spain, and the then ratio of representation, which awarded a member of Congress to each 47,700 inhabitants. Congress failing to yield its assent to the admission of Florida for more than six years after this constitution was formed and application made, the people of Florida, during all that period, remained loyal to the Territorial government, and obedient to its laws, and did not assume the right to supersede the existing government by putting into operation a State government until the assent of Congress was obtained in 1845.

The circumstances connected with the formation of the constitution and State government of California are peculiar. During the Mexican war the country was conquered and occupied by our troops, and the civil government administered by the military authorities under the war-power. According to an official communication of General Persifer F. Smith, acting governor of California, to a committee of citizens of San Francisco, under date of March 27, 1849, withholding his "recognition and concurrence" in their proposition "to organize a legislative assembly, and to appoint judges and other ministerial officers, and to enact suitable laws to establish principles of justice and equity, and to give protection to life, liberty, and property," it appears that the President of the United States (Mr. Polk) and his cabinet officially promulgated the following opinions as the decision of the Executive on the points stated:

1st. That at the conclusion of the treaty with Mexico, on the 30th of May, 1848, the military government existing in California was a government *de facto*.

2nd. That it, of necessity, continue until Congress provide another; because, if it cease, anarchy must ensue: thus inferring that no power but Congress can establish any government.

It also appears, from the proclamation of General Riley, acting governor, to the people of California, dated June 3d, 1849, that a government *de facto* was constituted as follows:

"A brief summary of the organization of the present government may not be uninteresting. It consists—First, of a governor appointed by the supreme government; in default of such appointment, the office is temporarily vested in the commanding military officer of the department. The powers and duties of the governor are of a limited character, but fully defined and pointed out by the laws. Second, a secretary, whose duties and powers are also properly defined. Third, a territorial or departmental legislature, with limited powers to pass laws of a local character. Fourth, a superior court (tribunal superior) of the Territory, consisting of four judges and a fiscal. Fifth, a prefect and sub-prefect for each district, who are charged with the preservation of the public order and the execution of the laws; their duties correspond, in a great measure, with those of district marshals and sheriffs. Sixth, a judge of first instance, for each district. This office is, by a custom, not inconsistent with the laws, vested in the first alcalde of the district. Seventh, alcaldes, who have concurrent jurisdiction among themselves in the same district, but are subordinate to the higher judicial tribunals. Eighth, local justices of the peace. Ninth, ayuntamientos, or town councils. The powers and functions of all these officers are fully defined in the laws of the country, and are almost identical with those of the corresponding officers in the Atlantic and Western States."

On the 3d of April, 1849, President Taylor appointed Thomas Butler King agent, for the purpose of conveying important instructions to our military and naval commanders who were intrusted with the administration of the civil government *de facto* in California, and to make known to the people his opinions and wishes in respect to the formation of a constitution and State government preparatory to their admission into the Union. What these opinions and wishes were, are distinctly stated by the President in the following extract from his special message to Congress on the 23d of January, 1850:

"I did not hesitate to express to the people of those Territories my desire that each Territory should, if prepared to comply with the requisitions of the Constitution of the United States, form a plan of a State Constitution, and submit the same to Congress, with a prayer for admission into the Union as a State; but I did not anticipate, suggest, or authorize the establishment of any such government without the assent of Congress; nor did I authorize any government-agent or officer to interfere with, or exercise any influence or control over the election of delegates, or over any convention, in making or modifying their domestic institutions, or any of the provisions of their proposed Constitution. On the contrary, the instructions by my orders were, that all measures of domestic policy, adopted by the people of California, must originate solely with themselves; that, while the Executive of the United States was desirous to protect them in the formation of any government republican in its character, to be, at the proper time, submitted to Congress, yet it was to be distinctly understood that the plan of such a government must, at the same time, be the result of their own deliberate choice, and originate with themselves, without the interference of the Executive."

On the 30th of June, 1850, General Riley, in his capacity as civil governor of California, reports to the government at Washington that:

"On the 3rd instant, I issued my proclamation to the people of California, defining what was understood to be the legal position of affairs here; and pointing out the course it was deemed advisable to pursue in order to procure a new political organization, better adapted to the character and present condition of the country. The course indicated in my proclamation will be adopted by the people, almost unanimously; and there is now little or no doubt that the convention will meet on the first of September next, and form a State Constitution, to be submitted to Congress in the early part of the coming session.

"A few prefer a Territorial organization; but I think a majority will be in favor of a State government, so as to avoid all further difficulties respecting the question of Slavery. This question will probably be submitted, together with the Constitution, to a direct vote of the people, in order that the wishes of the people of California may be clearly and fully expressed. Of course, the Constitution or plan of a Territorial government formed by this convention, can have no legal force till approved by Congress."

On the 12th day of October, General Riley, acting governor, issued the following proclamation:

"*To the People of California.*

"The delegates of the people, assembled in convention, have formed a constitution which is now presented for your ratification. The time and manner of voting on this constitution, and of holding the first general election, are clearly set forth in the schedule. The whole subject is, therefore, left for your unbiased and deliberate consideration.

"The prefect (or person exercising the functions of that office), of each district will designate the places for opening the polls, and give due notice of the election, in accordance with the provisions of the constitution and schedule.

"The people are now called upon to form a government for themselves, and to designate such officers as they desire to make and execute the laws. That their choice may be wisely made, and that the government so organized may secure the permanent welfare and happiness of the people of the new State, is the sincere and earnest wish of the present executive, who, if the constitution be ratified, will with pleasure surrender his powers to whomsoever the people may designate as his successor.

"Given at Monterey, California, this twelfth day of October, in the year of our Lord eighteen hundred and forty-nine.

"B. RILEY,
Brevet Brig. Gen. U. S. A., and Governor of California.

"Official: H. W. HALLECK,
Brevet Captain, and Secretary of State."

These facts and official papers prove conclusively that the proposition to the people of California, to hold a convention and organize a State government, originated with, and that all the proceedings were had in subordination to, the authority and supremacy of the existing local government of the Territory, under the advice, and with the approval, of the executive government of the United States. Hence the action of the people of California in forming their constitution and State government, and of Congress in admitting the State into the Union, cannot be cited, with the least show of justice or fairness, in justification or palliation of the revolutionary movements to subvert the government which Congress has established in Kansas.

Nor can the insurgents derive aid or comfort

from the position assumed by either party to the unfortunate controversy which arose in the State of Rhode Island, a few years ago, when an effort was made to change the organic law, and set up a State government in opposition to the one then in existence, under the charter granted by Charles the Second of England. Those who were engaged in that unsuccessful struggle assumed, as fundamental truths in our system of government, that Rhode Island was a Sovereign State in all that pertained to her internal affairs; that the right to change their organic law was an essential attribute of sovereignty; that, inasmuch as the charter under which the existing government was organized contained no provision for changing or amending the same, and the people had not delegated that right to the legislature or any other tribunal, it followed, as a matter of course, that they had retained it, and were at liberty to exercise it in such manner as to them should seem wise, just, and proper.

Without deeming it necessary to express any opinion on this occasion, in reference to the merits of that controversy, it is evident that the principles upon which it was conducted are not involved in the revolutionary struggle now going on in Kansas; for the reason, that the sovereignty of a Territory remains in abeyance, suspended in the United States, in trust for the people, until they shall be admitted into the Union as a State. In the mean time, they are entitled to enjoy and exercise all the privileges and rights of self-government, in subordination to the Constitution of the United States, and in obedience to their organic law passed by Congress in pursuance of that instrument. These rights and privileges are all derived from the Constitution, through the act of Congress, and must be exercised and enjoyed in subjection to all the limitations and restrictions which that Constitution imposes. Hence, it is clear that the people of the Territory have no inherent sovereign right, under the Constitution of the United States, to annul the laws and resist the authority of the territorial government which Congress has established in obedience to the Constitution.

In tracing, step by step, the origin and history of these Kansas difficulties, your Committee have been profoundly impressed with the significant fact, that each one has resulted from an attempt to violate or circumvent the principles and provisions of the act of Congress for the organization of Kansas and Nebraska. The leading idea and fundamental principle of the Kansas-Nebraska act, as expressed in the law itself, was *to leave the actual settlers and bona-fide inhabitants of each Territory "perfectly free to form and regulate their domestic institutions in their own way, subject only to the Constitution of the United States."* While this is declared to be "the true intent and meaning of the act," those who were opposed to allowing the people of the Territory, preparatory to their admission into the Union as a State, to decide the Slavery question for themselves, failing to accomplish their purpose in the halls of Congress, and under the authority of the Constitution, immediately resorted, in their respective States, to unusual and extraordinary means to control the political destinies and shape the domestic institutions of Kansas, in defiance of the wishes, and regardless of the rights, of the people of that Territory, as guaranteed by their organic law. Combinations, in one section of the Union, to stimulate an unnatural and false system of emigration, with the view of controlling the elections, and forcing the domestic institutions of the Territory to assimilate to those of the non-slaveholding States, were followed, as might have been foreseen, by the use of similar means in the slaveholding States, to produce directly the opposite result. To these causes, and to these alone, in the opinion of your Committee, may be traced the origin and progress of all the controversies and disturbances with which Kansas is now convulsed.

If these unfortunate troubles have resulted, as natural consequences, from unauthorized and improper schemes of foreign interference with the internal affairs and domestic concerns of the Territory, it is apparent that the remedy must be sought in a strict adherence to the principles, and rigid enforcement of the provisions, of the organic law. In this connection, your Committee feel sincere satisfaction in commending the messages and proclamation of the President of the United States, in which we have the gratifying assurance that the supremacy of the laws will be maintained; that rebellion will be crushed; that insurrection will be suppressed; that aggressive intrusion for the purpose of deciding elections, or any other purpose, will be repelled; that unauthorized intermeddling in the local concerns of the Territory, both from adjoining and distant States, will be prevented; that the federal and local laws will be vindicated against all attempts of organized resistance; and that the people of the Territory will be protected in the establishment of their own institutions, undisturbed by encroachments from without, and in the full enjoyment of the rights of self-government assured to them by the Constitution and the organic law.

In view of these assurances, given under the conviction that the existing laws confer all the authority necessary to the performance of these important duties, and that the whole available force of the United States will be exerted to the extent required for their performance, your Committee repose in entire confidence that peace, and security, and law, will prevail in Kansas. If any further evidence were necessary to prove that all the collisions and difficulties in Kansas have been produced by the schemes of foreign interference which have been developed in this report, in violation of the principles and in evasion of the provisions of the Kansas-Nebraska act, it may be found in the fact that in Nebraska, to which the emigrant-aid societies did not extend their operations, and into which the stream of emigration was permitted to flow in its usual and natural channels, nothing has occurred to disturb the peace and harmony of the Territory, while the principle of self-government, in obedience to the Constitution, has had fair play, and is quietly working out its legitimate results.

It now only remains for your Committee to respond to the two specific recommendations of the President, in his special message. They are as follows:

"This, it seems to me, can be best accomplished by providing that, when the inhabitants of Kansas may desire it, and shall be of sufficient numbers to constitute a State, a convention of delegates, duly elected by the qualified voters, shall assemble to frame a constitution, and thus prepare, through regular and lawful means, for its admission into the Union as a State. I respectfully recommend the enactment of a law to that effect.

"I recommend, also, that a special appropriation be made to defray any expense which may become requisite in the execution of the laws, or the maintenance of public order in the Territory of Kansas."

In compliance with the first recommendation, your committee ask leave to report a bill authorizing the legislature of the Territory to provide by law for the election of delegates by the people, and the assembling of a convention to form a constitution and State government preparatory to their admission into the Union on an equal footing with the original States, so soon as it shall appear, by a census to be taken under the direction of the governor, by the authority of the legislature, that the Territory contains ninety-three thousand four hundred and twenty inhabitants—that being the number required by the present ratio of representation for a member of Congress.

In compliance with the other recommendation, your committee propose to offer to the appropriation bill an amendment appropriating such sum as shall be found necessary, by the estimates to be obtained, for the purpose indicated in the recommendation of the President.

All of which is respectfully submitted to the Senate by your committee.

Mr. Collamer of Vermont, the minority member of said Committee, submitted the following

MINORITY REPORT.

Views of the minority of the Committee on Territories, to whom was referred so much of the annual message of the President as relates to Territorial affairs, the message of the President of 24th January in relation to Kansas Territory, and the message of the President of the 18th February, in answer to the resolution of the Senate of the 4th February, relative to affairs in Kansas.

Thirteen of the present prosperous States of this Union passed through the period of apprenticeship or pupilage of territorial training, under the guardianship of Congress, preparatory to assuming their proud rank of manhood as sovereign and independent States. This period of their pupilage was, in every case, a period of the good offices of parent and child, in the kind relationship sustained between the national and the Territorial government, and may be remembered with feelings of gratitude and pride. We have fallen on different times. A Territory of our government is now convulsed with violence and discord, and the whole family of our nation is in a state of exitement and anxiety. The national executive power is put in motion, the army in requisition, and Congress is invoked for interference.

In this case, as in all others of difficulty, it becomes necessary to inquire what is the true *cause* of existing trouble, in order to apply effectual cure. It is but temporary palliatives to deal with the external and more obvious manifestations and developments, while the real, procuring cause lies unattended to, and uncorrected, and unremoved.

It is said that organized opposition to law exists in Kansas. That, if existing, may probably be suppressed by the President, by the use of the army; and so, too, may invasions by armed bodies from Missouri, if the Executive be sincere in its efforts; but when this is done, while the cause of trouble remains, the results will continue with renewed and increased developments of danger.

Let us, then, look fairly and undisguisedly at this subject, in its true character and history. Wherein does this Kansas Territory differ from all our other Territories, which have been so peacefully and successfully carried through, and been developed into the manhood of independent States? Can that difference account for existing troubles? Can that difference, as a cause of trouble, be removed?

The first and great point of difference between the Territorial government of Kansas and that of the thirteen Territorial governments before mentioned, consists in the subject of Slavery—the undoubted cause of present trouble.

The action of Congress in relation to all those thirteen Territories was conducted on a uniform and prudent principle, to wit: To settle, by a clear provision, the law in relation to the subject of slavery to be operative in the Territory, while it remained such; not leaving it in any one of those cases to be a subject of controversy within the same, while in the plastic gristle of its youth. This was done by Congress in the exercise of the same power which moulded the form of their organic laws, and appointed their executive and judiciary, and sometimes their legislative officers; It was the power provided in the Constitution, in these words: "Congress shall have power to dispose of and make all needful rules and regulations respecting the Territory or other property belonging to the United States." Settling the subject of Slavery while the country remained a Territory, was no higher exercise of power in Congress than the regulation of the functions of the Territorial government, and actually appointing its principal functionaries. This practice commenced with this national government, and was continued, with uninterrupted uniformity, for more than *sixty* years. This practical contemporaneous construction of the constitutional *power* of this government is too clear to leave room for doubt, or opportunity for skepticism. The peace, prosperity, and success which attended this course, and the results which have ensued, in the formation and admission of the thirteen States therefrom, are most conclusive and satisfactory evidence, also, of the wisdom and prudence with which this *power* was *exercised*. Deluded must be that people who, in the pursuit of plausible theories, become deaf to the lessons, and blind to the results, of their own experience.

Let us next inquire by what rule of uniformity Congress was governed, in the exercise of this power of determining the condition of each Territory as to Slavery, while remaining a Territory, as manifested in those thirteen instances. An examination of our history will show that this was not done from time to time by agitation and local or party triumphs in Congress. The rule pursued was uniform and clear; and whoever may have lost by it, peace and prosperity have been gained. That rule was this:

Where Slavery was actually existing in a country to any considerable or general extent, it was (though somewhat modified as to further importation in some instances, as in Mississippi and Orleans Territories) suffered to remain. The fact that it had been taken and existed there, was taken as an indication of its adaptation and local utility. Where Slavery did not in fact exist to any appreciable extent, the same was, by Congress, expressly prohibited; so that in either case the country settled up without difficulty or doubt as to the character of its institutions. In no instance was this difficult and disturbing subject left to the people who had and who might settle in the Territory, to be there an everlasting bone of contention, so long as the Territorial government should continue. It was ever regarded, too, as a subject in which the whole country had an interest, and, therefore, improper for local legislation.

And though whenever the people of a Territory come to form their own organic law, as an indedependent State, they would, either before or after their admission as a State, form and mould their institutions, as a sovereign State, in their own way, yet it must be expected, and has always proved true, that the State has taken the character her pupilage has prepared her for, as well in respect to Slavery as in other respects. Hence, six of the thirteen States are free States, because Slavery was prohibited in them by Congress while Territories, to wit: Ohio, Indiana, Illinois, Michigan, Wisconsin, and Iowa. Seven of the thirteen are slaveholding States, because Slavery was allowed in them by Congress while they were Territories, to wit: Tennessee, Alabama, Mississippi, Florida, Louisiana, Arkansas and Missouri.

On the 6th of March, A. D. 1820, was passed by Congress the act preparatory to the admission of the State of Missouri into the Union. Much controversy and discussion arose on the question whether a prohibition of Slavery within said State should be inserted, and it resulted in this: that said State should be admitted without such prohibition, but that Slavery should be *forever prohibited* in the rest of that country ceded to us by France lying north 36° 30′ north latitude, and it was so done. This contract is known as the *Missouri Compromise.* Under this arrangement, Missouri was admitted as a slaveholding State, the same having been a slaveholding Territory. Arkansas, south of the line, was formed into a Territory, and Slavery allowed therein, and afterwards admitted as a slaveholding State. Iowa was made a Territory, north of the line, and, under the operation of the law, was settled up without slaves, and admitted as a free State. The country now making the Territories of Kansas and Nebraska, in 1820, was almost or entirely uninhabited, and lay north of said line, and whatever settlers entered the same before 1854 did so under that law, forever forbidding Slavery therein.

In 1854 Congress passed an act establishing two new Territories—Nebraska and Kansas—in this region of country, where Slavery had been prohibited for more than thirty years; and, instead of leaving said law against Slavery in operation, or prohibiting or expressly allowing or establishing Slavery, Congress left the subject in said Territories, to be discussed, agitated, and legislated on, from time to time, and the elections in said Territories to be conducted with reference to that subject, from year to year, so long as they should remain Territories; for, whatever laws might be passed by the Territorial legislatures on this subject, must be subject to change or repeal by those of the succeeding years. In most former Territorial governments, it was provided by law that their laws were subject to the revision of Congress, so that they would be made with caution. In these Territories that was omitted.

The provision in relation to Slavery in Nebraska and Kansas is as follows: "The eighth section of the act preparatory to the admission of Missouri into the Union (which being inconsistent with the *principle* of non-intervention by Congress with Slavery in the States and Territories, as required by the legislation of 1850, commonly called the compromise measures) is hereby declared *inoperative and void;* it being the true intent and meaning of this act not to legislate Slavery into said Territory or State, nor to exclude it therefrom, but to leave the people thereof *perfectly free* to form and regulate their domestic institutions in their own way, subject only to the Constitution of the United States: *Provided*, That nothing herein contained shall be construed to revive or put in force any law or regulation which may have existed prior to the act of 6th March, 1820, either protecting, establishing, prohibiting, or abolishing Slavery."

Thus it was promulgated to the people of this whole country that here was a clear field for competition—an open course for the race of rivalship; the goal of which was, the ultimate establishment of a sovereign State; and the prize, the reward of everlasting liberty and its institutions on the one hand, or the perpetuity of Slavery and its concomitants on the other. It is the obvious duty of this government, while this law continues, to see this manifesto faithfully, and honorably, and honestly performed, even though its particular supporters may see cause of a result unfavorable to their hopes.

It is further to be observed, that in the performance of this novel experiment, it was provided that all white men who became inhabitants in Kansas were entitled to vote without regard to their *time of residence*, usually provided in other Territories. Nor was this right of voting confined to American citizens, but included all such aliens as had declared, or would declare, on oath their intention to become citizens. Thus was the proclamation to the world to become inhabitants of Kansas, and enlist in this great enterprise, by the force of numbers, by vote, to decide for it the great question. Was it to be expected that this great proclamation for the political tournament would be listened to with indifference and apathy? Was it prepared and presented in that spirit? Did it relate to a subject on which the people were cool or indifferent? A large part of the people of this country look on domestic Slavery as "only evil, and that continually," alike to master and to slave, and to the community; to be left alone to the management or enjoyment of the people of the States where it exists, but not to be extended, more especially as it gives, or may give, political supremacy to a minority of the people of this country in the United States government. On the other hand, many of the people of another part of the United States regard Slavery, if not in the abstract a blessing, at least as now existing, a condition of society best for both white and black, while they exist together; while others regard it as no evil, but as the highest state of social condition. These consider that they cannot, with safety to their interests, permit political ascendancy to be largely in the hands of those unfriendly to this *peculiar institution.* From these conflicting views, long and violent has been the controversy, and experience seems to show it interminable.

Many, and probably a large majority of this nation, lovers of quiet, entertained the hope, that, after 1850, the so-called Compromise Measures, even though not satisfactory to the Free States, would be kept by their supporters, and made by them what they were professed to be, a finality on the subject of the extent and limitations of slave territory; more especially after the assurances contained in the Inaugural Address of President Pierce. This hope was fortified with the consideration that at that time Congress had, by different provisions, settled by law the condition of Freedom or Slavery for all the territory of the United States. These hopes have been disappointed, and from this very provision for repose has been extracted a *principle* for disturbing the condition of things on which its foundation of finality rested—that is, the permanence and continuance of the then existing condition of legal provisions. The establishment of the territorial governments for Utah and New-Mexico, without a prohibition of Slavery, was sustained by many on the ground that no such provision was required for its exclusion, as the condition of the country and its laws were a sufficient barrier; and therefore they sustained them, because it would complete the series, and finish the provisions as to Slavery in all our territory, and make an end of controversy on that subject: yet, in 1854, it was insisted by the friends and supporters of the laws of 1850, and it is actually asserted in the law establishing the territorial government of Kansas, that the laws for New-Mexico and Utah, being of the Compromise Measures, adopt and contain a *principle* utterly at war with their great and professed object of finality; and that, instead of completing and ending the provisions of congressional action for the Territories as to Slavery, it really declared a *principle* which *unsettled* all those where Slavery had been prohibited, and rendered it proper, and only proper, to declare such prohibitions all "*inoperative and void.*" The spirit and feeling which thus perverted those *Compromise laws*, and made them the direct instrument of renewed disturbance, could not be expected then to leave the result to the decision of the people of Kansas with entire inactivity and indifference.

The slaveholding States, in 1820, secured the admission of Missouri as a slaveholding State, and all the region south of 36° 30′ to the same purpose, by agreeing and enacting that all north of that line should be *forever free*; and by this they obtained only a sufficient number of votes from the Free States, as counted with theirs, to adopt it. In 1850, they agreed that if New-Mexico and Utah were made Territories, without a prohibition of Slavery, it would, with the laws already made for the rest of our territory, settle forever the whole subject. This proposition, for such a termination, also secured votes from the Free States, enough, with their own from the slaveholding States, to adopt it. In 1854, in utter disregard of these repeated contracts, both these arrangements were broken, and both these compromises disregarded, and all their provisions for freedom declared inoperative and void, by the vote of the slaveholding States, with a very few honorable exceptions, and a minority of the votes of the Free States. After this extraordinary and inexcusable proceeding, it was not to be expected that the people of the slaveholding States would take no active measures to secure a favorable result by votes in the Territory of Kansas. Neither could it be expected that the people of the Free States, who regarded the act of 1854 as a double breach of faith, would sit down and make no effort, by legal means, to correct it.

It has been said that the repeal of this provision of the Missouri Compromise, and breach of the Compromise of 1850, should not be regarded as a measure of the slaveholding States, because it was presented by a Senator from a Free State.

The actions or votes of one or more individual men cannot give character to, or be regarded as fixing a measure on, their section or party. The only true or honest mode of determining whether any measure is that of any section or party is, to ascertain whether the *majority* of that section or party voted for it. Now, a large majority—indeed, the whole, with a few rare exceptions—of the representatives from the slaveholding States voted for that repeal. On the other hand, a majority of the representatives from the Free States voted against it.

This subject of Slavery in the Territories, which has violently agitated the country for many years, and which has been attempted to be settled twice by compromise, as before stated, does not remain settled. The Missouri Compromise and the supposed finality by the acts of 1850, are scattered and dissolved by the vote of the slaveholding States; and it is not to be disguised that this uncalled for and disturbing measure has produced a spirit of resentment, from a feeling of its injustice, which, while the cause continues, will be difficult to allay.

This subject, then, which Congress has been unable to settle in any such way as the Slave States will sustain, is now turned over to those who have or shall become inhabitants of Kansas to arrange; and all men are invited to participate in the experiment, regardless of their character, political or religious views, or place of nativity.

Now, what is the *right* and the *duty* of the people of this country in relation to this matter? Is it not the right of all who believe in the blessings of slaveholding, and regard it as the best condition of society, either to go to Kansas *as inhabitants*, and by their votes to help settle this good condition of that Territory; or if they cannot so go and settle, is it not their duty, by all lawful means in their power, to promote this object by inducing others like-minded to go? This *right* becomes a *duty* to all who follow their convictions. All who regard an establishment of Slavery in Kansas as best for that Territory, or as necessary to their own safety by the political weight it gives in the national government, should use all lawful means to secure that result; and clearly, the inducing men to go there to become permanent inhabitants and voters, and to vote as often as the elections occur in favor of the establishment of Slavery, and thus *control* the elections, and preserve it a Slave State forever, is neither unlawful nor censurable. It is, and would be highly praiseworthy and commendable, because it is using lawful means to carry forward honest convictions of public good. All lawfully-associated effort to that end is equally commendable. Nor will the application of opprobrious epithets, and calling it *propagandism*, change its moral or legal character from whatever quarter or source, official or otherwise, such epithets may come. Neither should they deter any man from peaceably performing his duty by following his honest convictions.

On the other hand, all those who have seen and realized the blessings of universal liberty, and believe that it can only be secured and promoted by the prohibition of domestic Slavery, and that the elevation of honest industry can never succeed where servitude makes labor degrading, should, as in duty bound, put forth all reasonable exertions to advance this great object, by lawful means, whenever permitted by laws of their country. When, therefore, Kansas was presented, by law, as an open field for this experiment, and all were invited to enter, it became the right and duty of all such as desired, to go there as inhabitants for the purpose, by their numbers and by their votes lawfully cast, from time to time, to carry or *control*, in a legal way, the elections there for this object. This could only be lawfully effected by permanent residence, and continued and repeated effort, during the continuance of the Territorial government, and permanently remaining there to form and preserve a Free-State constitution. All those who entertained the same sentiments, but were not disposed themselves to go, had the right and duty to use all lawful means to encourage and promote the object. If the purpose could be best effected by united efforts, by voluntary associations or corporations, or by State assistance, as proposed in some Southern States, it was all equally lawful and laudable. This was not the officious intermeddling with the internal affairs of another nation, or State, or the Territory of another people. The Territory is the property of the nation, and is, professedly, open to the settlement and the institutions of every part of the United States. If lawful means, so extensive as to be effectual, were used to people it with a majority of inhabitants opposed to Slavery, is now considered as a violation of, or an opposition to, the law establishing the Territory, then the declarations and provisions of that law were but a premeditated delusion, which not only allowed such measures, but actually invited them, by enacting that the largest number of the settlers should determine the condition of the country; thus inviting efforts for numbers. Such an invitation must have been expected to produce such efforts on both sides.

It now becomes necessary to inquire what has in fact taken place. If violence has taken place as the natural, and, perhaps, unavoidable, consequences of the nature of the experiment, bringing into dangerous contact and collision inflammable elements, it was the vice of a mistaken law, and immediate measures should be taken by Congress to correct such law. If force and violence have been substituted for peaceful measures there, legal provisions should be made and executed to correct all the wrong such violence has produced, and to prevent their recurrence, and thus secure a fair fulfillment of the experiment by peaceful means, as originally professed and presented in the law.

A succinct statement of the exercise and progress of the material events in Kansas is this: After the passage of this law, establishing the Territory of Kansas, a large body of settlers rapidly entered into said Territory with a view to permanent inhabitancy therein. Most of these were from the Free-States of the West and North, who probably intended by their votes and influence to establish there a Free State, agreeable to the law which invited them. Some part of those from the Northern States had been encouraged and aided in this enterprise by the Emigrant Aid Society formed in Massachusetts, which put forth some exertions in this laudable object, by open and public measures, in providing facilities for transportation to all peaceable citizens who desired to become permanent settlers in said Territory, and providing therein hotels, mills, etc., for the public accommodation of that new country.

The governor of Kansas, having, in pursuance of law, divided the Territory into districts, and procured a census thereof, issued his proclamation for the election of a legislative assembly therein, to take place on the 30th day of March, 1855, and directed how the same should be conducted, and the returns made to him agreeable to the law establishing said Territory. On the day of election, large bodies of armed men from the State of Missouri appeared at the polls in most of the districts, and by most violent and tumultuous carriage and demeanor overawed the defenseless inhabitants, and by their own votes elected a large majority of the members of both houses of said assembly. On the returns of said election being made to the governor, protests and objections were made to him in relation to a part of said districts; and as to them, he set aside such, and such only, as by the returns appeared to be bad. In relation to others, covering, in all, a majority of the two houses, equally vicious in fact, but apparently good by formal returns, the inhabitants thereof, borne down by said violence and intimidation, scattered and discouraged, and laboring under apprehensions of personal violence, refrained and desisted from presenting any protest to the governor in relation thereto; and he, then uninformed in relation thereto, issued certificates to the members who appeared by said formal returns to have been elected.

In relation to those districts which the governor so set aside, orders were by him issued for new elections. In one of these districts the same proceedings were repeated by men from Missouri, and in others not, and certificates were issued to the persons elected.

This legislative assembly, so elected, assembled at Pawnee, on the second day of July, 1855, that being the time and place for holding said meeting, as fixed by the governor, by authority of law. On assembling, the said houses proceeded to set aside and reject those members so elected on said second election, except in the district where the men from Missouri had, at said election, chosen the same persons they had elected at the said first election, and they admitted all of the said first-elected members.

A legislative assembly, so created by military force, by a foreign invasion, in violation of the organic law, was but a usurpation. No act of its own, no act or neglect of the governor, could legalize or sanctify it. Its own decisions as to its own legality are like its laws, but the fruits of its own usurpation, which no governor could legitimate.

They passed an act altering the place of the temporary seat of government to the Shawnee Mission, on the border of, and in near proximity to, Missouri. This act the governor regarded as a violation of the organic law establishing the Territory, which fixed the temporary seat of government, and prohibited the legislative assembly from doing anything inconsistent with said act. He, therefore, and for that cause, vetoed said bill; but said assembly repassed the same by a two-thirds majority, notwithstanding said veto, and removed to said Shawnee Mission. They then proceeded to pass laws, and the governor, in writing, declined further to recognize them as a legitimate assembly, sitting at that place. They continued passing laws there, from the 16th day of July to the 31st day of August, 1855.

On the 15th day of August last, the governor of said Territory was dismissed from office, and the duties devolved upon the secretary of the Territory; and how many of the laws passed with his official approbation does not appear, the laws as now presented being without date or authentication.

As by the law of Congress organizing said Territory it was expressly provided, that the people of the Territory were to be "left perfectly free to form and regulate their domestic institutions in their own way," and among these institutions Slavery is included, it was, of course, implied that that subject was to be open and free to public and private discussion in all its bearings, rights, and relationships. Among these must, of course, be the question, What was the state of *the existing laws*, and the modifications that might be required on that subject? The law had declared that its "true intent and meaning was not to legislate Slavery into the Territory, or exclude it therefrom." This would, of course, leave to that people the inquiry, What, then, are the existing rights under the Constitution? Can slaves be holden in the absence of any law on the subject? This question, about which so much difference of opinion exists, and which Congress and the courts have never settled, was thus turned over to the people there, to discuss and settle for themselves.

This territorial legislature, so created by force from Missouri, utterly refused to permit discussion on the subject; but, assuming that Slavery already existed there, and that neither Congress nor the people in the Territory, under the authority of Congress, had or could prohibit it, passed a law which, if enforced, utterly prohibits all *discussion* of the question. The eleventh and twelfth sections of that act are as follows:

"Sec. 11. If any person print, write, introduce into, publish or circulate, or cause to be brought into, printed, written, published or circulated, or shall knowingly aid or assist in bringing into, printing, publishing or circulating within this Territory, any book, paper, pamphlet, magazine, hand-bill or circular, containing any statements, arguments, opinions, sentiments, doctrines, advice or innuendo, calculated to promote a disorderly, dangerous or rebellious disaffection among the slaves in this Territory, or to induce such slaves to escape from the service of their masters or to resist their authority, he shall be guilty of a felony, and be punished by imprisonment and hard labor for a term not less than five years.

"Sec. 12. If any free person, by speaking or by writing, assert or maintain that persons have not the right to hold slaves in this Territory, or shall introduce into this Territory, print, publish, write, circulate, or cause to be introduced into this Territory, written, printed, published or circulated in this Territory, any book, paper, magazine, pamphlet or circular, containing any denial of the right of persons to hold slaves in this Territory, such person shall be deemed guilty of felony, and punished by imprisonment at hard labor for a term of not less than two years."

And further providing, that no person "conscientiously opposed to holding slaves" shall sit as a juror in the trial of any cause founded on a breach of the foregoing law. They further provided, that all officers and attorneys should be sworn not only to support the Constitution of the United States, but also to support and sustain the organic law of the Territory, and the fugitive-slave laws; and that any person offering to vote shall be presumed to be entitled to vote until the contrary is shown, and if any one, when required, shall refuse to take oath to sustain the fugitive-slave laws, he shall not be permitted to vote. Although they passed a law that none but an inhabitant, who had paid a tax, should vote, yet they required no *time of residence* necessary, and provided for the immediate payment of a poll-tax; so providing, in effect, that on the eve of an election the people of a neighboring State could come in, in unlimited numbers, and, by taking up a residence of a day or an hour, pay a poll-tax, and thus become legal voters, and then, after voting, return to their own State. They thus, in practical effect, provided for the people of Missouri to control elections at their pleasure, and permitted such only of the real inhabitants of the Territory to vote as are friendly to the holding of slaves.

They permitted no election of any of the officers in the Territory to be made by the people thereof, but created the offices and filled them, or appointed officers to fill them for long periods, and provided that the next annual election should be holden in October, 1856, and the assembly to meet in January, 1857; so that none of these laws could be changed until the lower house might be changed, in 1856; but the council, which is elected for two years, could not be changed so as to allow a change of the laws or officers until the session of 1858, however much the inhabitants of the Territory might desire it.

These laws, made by an assembly created by a foreign force, are but a manifestation of the spirit of oppression which was the parent of the whole transaction. No excuse can be found for it in the pretense that the inhabitants had carried with them into said Territory a quantity of Sharp's rifles—first, because that, if true, formed no excuse; secondly, it is untrue, as their Sharp's rifles were only obtained afterwards, and entirely for the purpose of self-defense, the necessity for which, this invasion and other acts of violence and threats clearly demonstrated. These laws were obviously made to oppress and drive out all who were inclined to the exclusion of Slavery; and if they remained, to silence them on this subject, and subject them to the will and control of the people of Missouri. These are the laws which the President says must be enforced by the army and the whole power of this nation.

The people of Kansas, thus invaded, subdued, oppressed, and insulted, seeing their territorial government (such only in form) perverted into an engine to crush them in the dust, and to defeat and destroy the professed object of their organic law, by depriving them of the "*perfect freedom*" therein provided; and finding no ground to hope for rights in that organization, they proceeded, under the guaranty of the United States Constitution, "peaceably to assemble to petition the government for the redress of (their) grievances." They saw no earthly source of relief but in the formation of a State government by the people, and the acceptance and ratification thereof by Congress.

It is true that in several instances in our political history, the people of a Territory have been authorized by an act of Congress to form a State constitution, and after so doing, were admitted by Congress. It is quite obvious that no such authority could be given by the act of the territorial government. *That* clearly has no power to create another government, paramount to itself. It is equally true, that, in numerous instances in our history, the people of a Territory have, without any previous act of Congress, proceeded to call a convention of the people by their delegates; have formed a State constitution, which has been adopted by the people, and a State legislature assembled under it, and chosen Senators to Congress, and then have presented said constitution to Congress, who has approved the same, and received the senators and members of Congress who were chosen under it before Congress had approved the same. Such was the case of Tennessee; such was the case of Michigan, where the people not only formed a State constitution without an act of Congress, but they actually put their State government into full operation and passed laws, and it was approved by Congress by receiving it as a State. The people of Florida formed their constitution without any act of Congress therefor, six years before they were admitted into the Union. When the people of Arkansas were about forming a State constitution without a previous act of Congress, in 1835, the territorial governor applied to the President on the subject, who referred the matter to the Attorney-General, and his opinion, as then expressed and published, contained the following:

"It is not in the power of the general assembly of Arkansas to pass any law for the purpose of electing members to a convention to form a Constitution and State government, nor to do any other act, directly or indirectly, to create such government. Every such law, even though it were approved by the governor of the Territory, would be null and void; if passed by them notwithstanding his veto, by a vote of two-thirds of each branch, it would still be equally void."

He further decided that it was not rebellious or insurrectionary, or even unlawful, for the people peaceably to proceed, even without an act of Congress, in forming a constitution, and that the so forming a State constitution, and so far organizing under the same as to choose the officers necessary for its representation in Congress, with a view to present the same to Congress for admission, was a power which fell clearly within the right of the people to assemble and petition for redress. The people of Arkansas proceeded without an act of Congress, and were received into the Union accordingly. If any rights were derived to the people of Arkansas from the terms of the French treaty of cession, they equally extended to the people of Kansas, it being a part of the same cession.

In this view of the subject, in the first part of August, 1855, a call was published in the public papers for a meeting of the citizens of Kansas, irrespective of party, to meet at Lawrence, in said Territory, on the 15th of said August, to take into consideration the propriety of calling a convention of the people of the whole Territory, to consider that subject. That meeting was held on the 15th day of August last, and it proceeded to call such convention of delegates to be elected, and to assemble at Topeka, in said Territory, on the 19th day of September, 1855, not to form a constitution, but to consider the propriety of calling, formally, a convention for that purpose. The proceedings of this meeting of the 15th of August were as follows:*

State Constitution.

"LAWRENCE, KANSAS TERRITORY,
August 15, 1855.

"Pursuant to a published call, signed 'Many Citizens,' 'to take into consideration the propriety of calling a Territorial convention, preliminary to the formation of a State government, and other subjects of public interest,' a convention of the citizens of Kansas Territory, *irrespective* of party, met, and upon motion of C. K. Holliday, Dr. A. Hunting was called to the chair, G. W. Brown, E. D. Ladd, C. E. Blood, L P. Lincoln, James Christian, and Dr. J. D. Barnes elected vice-presidents, and J. K. Goodin, and J. P. Fox, secretaries.

"On motion of J. Hutchinson, esq., a committee of five were appointed to prepare business for the convention. Messrs. G. W. Smith, C. K. Holliday, C. Robinson, John Brown, jr., and A. F. Powell were chosen that committee.

"During the absence of the committee, the convention was addressed by Rev. — Lovejoy, G. W. Brown, J. Hutchinson, and M. F. Conway. After which, Mr. G. W. Smith, chairman, submitted the following as the report of the committee:

"Whereas the people of Kansas Territory have been, since its settlement, and now are, without any law-making power; threfore, be it

Resolved, That we, the people of Kansas Territory in mass meeting assembled, irrespective of party distinctions, influenced by a common necessity, and greatly desirous of promoting the common good, do hereby call upon and request all *bona fide* citizens of Kansas Territory, of whatever political views or predilections, to consult together in their respective election-districts, and in mass convention, or otherwise, elect three delegates for each representative to which such district is entitled in the House of Representatives of the the legislative assembly, by proclamation of Governor Reeder of date 10th March, 1855; said delegates to assemble in convention at the town of Topeka, on the 19th day of September, 1855, then and there to consider and determine upon all subjects of public interest, and *particularly* upon that having reference to the speedy formation of a State constitution, with an intention of an immediate application to be admitted as a State into the Union of the 'United States of America.'

"After the discussion of the resolution by Mr. Stearns and others, the report of the committee was adopted with but *one* dissenting voice.

"On motion, it was ordered that the proceedings of this convention be published in the newspapers of the Territory, and Messrs. J. Speer, R. G. Elliot, and G. W. Brown, were appointed a committee to publish and circulate the call for the convention to be holden at Topeka.

"On motion, the convention adjourned *sine die*.

"A. HUNTING, *President*.

"G. W. Brown,
E. D. Ladd,
C. E. Blood,
L. P. Lincoln,
Jas. Christian,
J. D. Barnes,
Vice-Presidents,

"J. K. Goodin,
J. P. Fox,
Secretaries."

Agreeable to these proceedings, the people of the different districts did, as therein recommended, proceed to appoint delegates to this meeting at Topeka, to be holden on said 19th day of September, 1855. The delegates so appointed did assemble at Topeka on said day, and proceeded to consider said subject, and they took the following proceedings:

"*Proceedings of the State Constitutional Convention, held at Topeka, Kansas Territory, September* 19-20, 1855.

"Whereas the Constitution of the United States guarantees to the people of this republic the right of assembling together in a peaceable manner for the common good, to 'establish justice, insure domestic tranquillity, provide for the common defense, promote the general welfare, and secure the blessings of liberty to themselves and their posterity,' and whereas the citizens of Kansas Territory were prevented from electing members of a legislative sembly, in pursuance of the proclamation of Governor Reeder, on the 30th of March last, by invading forces from foreign States coming into the Territory and forcing upon the people a legislature of non-residents and others, inimical to the interests of the people of Kansas Territory, defeating the object of the organic act, in consequence of which the Territorial government became a perfect failure, and the people were left without any legal government until their patience has become exhausted, and 'endurance ceases to be a virtue;' and they are compelled to resort to the only remedy left—that of forming a government for themselves; therefore,

"*Resolved by the people of Kansas Territory in delegate convention assembled*, That an election shall be held in the several election precincts of this Territory on the second Tuesday of October next, under the regulations and restrictions hereinafter imposed, for members of a convention to form a constitution, adopt a bill of rights for the people of Kansas, and take all needful measures for organizing a State government preparatory to the admission of Kansas into the Union as a State.

"*Resolved*, That the apportionment of delegates to said convention shall be as follows: two delegates for each representative to which the people were entitled in the legislative assembly by proclamation of Governor Reeder, of date 10th March, 1855.

"*Resolved*, That a committee of seven be appointed by the chair, who shall organize by the appointment of a chairman and secretary. They shall keep a record of their proceedings, and shall have the general superintendence of the affairs of the Territory so far as regards the organization of a State government, which committee shall be styled 'the executive committee of Kansas Territory.'

"*Resolved*, That it shall be the duty of the executive committee of Kansas Territory to advertise said election at least fifteen days before the second Tuesday of October next; and to appoint three judges thereof for each precinct, and the said judges of each precinct shall appoint two clerks, all of whom shall be duly sworn or affirmed to discharge the duties of their respective offices impartially, and with fidelity; and they shall have power to administer the oath or affirmation to each other, and the said judges shall open said election at 10 o'clock A. M., at the place designated in each precinct by the said executive committee, and close the same at 4 o'clock P. M. And in case any of the officers appointed fail to attend, the officer or officers in attendance shall supply the vacancy or vacancies; and in the event of all of them failing to attend, ten qualified voters shall supply their places. And the said judges shall make out duplicate returns of said election, seal up, and transmit one copy of the same within five days, to the chairman of the executive committee, to be laid before the convention, and they shall, within ten days, seal up and hand the other to some member of the executive committee.

"*Resolved*, That the chairman of the executive committee of Kansas Territory shall announce, by proclamation, the names of the persons elected delegates to the said convention; and in case the returns from any precinct should not be completed by that day, as soon thereafter as practicable; and in case of a tie, a new election shall be ordered by the executive committee, giving five days' notice thereof, by the same officers who officiated at the first election.

"*Resolved*, That all white male inhabitants, citizens of the United States, above the age of twenty-one years, who have had a *bona fide* residence in the Territory of Kansas for the space of thirty days immediately preceding the day of said election, shall be entitled to vote for delegates to said convention; and all white male inhabitants, citizens of the United States, above the age of twenty-one years, who have resided in the Territory of Kansas for the space of three months immediately preceding the day of election, shall be eligible as delegates to said convention.

"*Resolved*, That if at the time of holding said election it shall be inconvenient, on account of Indian hostilities or any other cause whatever that would disturb or prevent the voters of any election-precinct in the Territory from the free and peaceable exercise of the elective franchise, the officers are hereby authorized to adjourn said election into any other precinct in the Territory, and to any other day they may see proper, of the necessity of which they shall be the exclusive judges, at which time and place the qualified voters may cast their votes.

"*Resolved*, That said convention shall be held at Topeka on the fourth Tuesday of October next, at 12 o'clock, A. M., of that day.

"*Resolved*, That a majority of said convention shall constitute a quorum, and that the said convention shall determine upon the returns and qualifications of its members, and shall have and exercise all the rights, privileges, and immunities incident to such bodies, and may adopt such rules and regulations for its government as a majority thereof may direct. If a majority of said convention do not assemble on the day appointed therefor, a less number is hereby authorized to adjourn from day to day.

"*Resolved*, That in case of the death, resignation, or non-attendance of any delegate chosen from any district of the Territory, the president of the convention shall issue his writ ordering a new election, on five days' notice, to be conducted as heretofore directed.

"*Resolved*, That no person shall be entitled to a seat in the convention at its organization except the members whose names are contained in the proclamation of the chairman of the executive committee. But after the convention is organized, seats may be contested in the usual way.

"*Resolved*, That the members of the convention shall receive, as a compensation for their services, the sum of three dollars per day, and three dollars for every twenty miles' travel to and from the same, and that Congress be respectfully requested to appropriate a sufficient sum to defray the necessary expenses of said convention.

"*Resolved*, That on the adoption of a Constitution for the State of Kansas, the president of the convention shall transmit an authenticated copy thereof to the President of the United States, to the President of the Senate, and to the Speaker of the House of Representatives; to each member of Congress, and to the governor of each of the several States in the Union; and adopt such other measures as will secure to the people of Kansas the rights and privilege of a sovereign State.

"On motion, the committee on address was vested with authority to notify the people of the several districts of the Territory of the coming election, by handbills, public addresses, and otherwise as they may think proper.

"The Territorial executive committee was appointed by the chair, consisting of the following persons: J. H. Lane, C. K. Holliday, M. J. Parrott, P. C. Schuyler, G. W. Smith, G. W. Brown, and J. K. Goodin.

"On motion, the proceedings of this convention were ordered to be published in all the papers of the Territory.

"A vote of thanks was passed to the president and officers of the convention.

"Adjourned, with three enthusiastic cheers for the new government of Kansas.

"WM. Y. ROBERTS, *President*.

"E. D. LADD,
J. H. NESBITT,
M. W. DELAHAY,
Secretaries."

"CONSTITUTIONAL PROCLAMATION.

"*To the Legal Voters of Kansas*:

"Whereas the Territorial government, as now constituted for Kansas, has proved a failure—squatter sovereignty under its workings a miserable delusion, in proof of which it is only necessary to refer to our past history and our present deplorable condition, our ballot-boxes have been taken possession of by bands of armed men from foreign States—our people forcibly driven therefrom—persons attempting to be foisted upon us as members of a so-called legislature, unacquainted with our wants, and hostile to our best interests—some of them never residents of our Territory—misnamed *laws* passed, and now attempting to be enforced by the aid of citizens of foreign States of the most oppressive, tyrannical, and insulting character—the right of suffrage taken from us—debarred from the privilege of a voice in the election of even the most insignificant officers—the right of free speech stifled—the muzzling of the press attempted; and whereas longer forbearance with such oppression and tyranny has ceased to be a virtue; and whereas the people of this country have heretofore exercised the right of changing their form of government when it became oppressive, and have at all times conceded this right to the people in this and all other governments; and whereas a Territorial form of government is unknown to the Constitution, and is the mere creature of necessity awaiting the action of the people; and whereas the debasing character of the slavery which now involves us impels to action, and leaves us as the only legal and peaceful alternative the immediate establishment of a State government; and whereas the organic act fails in pointing out the course to be adopted in an emergency like ours Therefore you are requested to meet at your several precincts in said Territory, hereinafter mentioned, on the second Tuesday of October next, it being the ninth day of said month, and then and there cast your ballots for members of a convention, to meet at Topeka on the fourth Tuesday in October next, to form a Constitution, adopt a bill of rights for the people of Kansas, and take all needful measures for organizing a State government preparatory to the admission of Kansas into the Union as a State.

"*Places for Polls.*

"*First election-district.*—Lawrence precinct, at the office of John Hutchinson, in Lawrence. Blanton precinct, at the house of J. B. Abbott, in Blanton. Palmyra precinct, at the house of H. Barricklow, in Palmyra—Wakarusa river the dividing line between the two precincts.

"*Second election-district.*—Bloomington precinct, house of Harrison Burson, on the Wakarusa. Benicia precinct, house of J. J. Cranmer, East Douglas.

"*Third election-district.*—Topeka precinct, house of F. W. Giles, Topeka. Big Springs precinct, at the house of Wesley Frost, in Washington. Tecumseh precinct, at the house of Mr. Hoagland, in Tecumseh.

"*Fourth election-district.*—Willow Springs precinct, at the house of Dr. Chapman, on the Santa Fe road, Springfield.

"*Fifth election-district.*—Bull-Creek precinct, at the house of Baptiste Peoria, on Pottawatomie-Creek. Pottawatomie precinct, at the house of Henry Sherman. Osawattamie precinct, at the house of Wm. Hughes, in Osawattamie. Big Sugar-Creek precinct, at the house of Elijah Tucker, at old Pottawatomie Mission. Little Sugar-Creek precinct, at the house of Isaac Stockton. Neosho precinct, at the store of Hamilton Smith, in Neosho. Hampden precinct, at the house of W. A. Ela, in Hampden.

"*Sixth election-district.*—Fort Scott precinct, at the house of Mr. Johnson, or a suitable building in Fort Scott. Scott's Town precinct, at the house of Mr. Vandever.

"*Seventh election-district.*—Titus precinct, at the house of J. B. Titus, on the Santa Fe road.

"*Eighth election-district.*—Council Grove precinct, at Council Grove Mission House. Waubonsa precinct, at some suitable building in Waubonsa. Mill-Creek precinct, at the house of G. E. Hoheneck, on Mill-Creek. Ashland precinct, at the house of Mr. Adams, in Ashland.

"*Ninth election-district.*—Pawnee precinct, at Loden and Shaw's store, in Pawnee.

"*Tenth election-district.*—Big Blue precinct, at the house of S. D. Dyer, in Juniatta. Rock-Creek precinct, at the house of Robert Wilson.

"*Eleventh election district.*—Vermillion precinct, at the house of John Schmidt, on Vermillion branch of Blue river.

"*Twelfth election-district.*—St. Mary's precinct, at the house of B. F. Bertrand. Silver Lake precinct, at the house of Joseph Leframbois.

"*Thirteenth election-district.*—Hickory Point precinct, at the house of Charles Hardt. Falls precinct, at the house of 'Mill Company,' at Grass-hopper Falls.

"*Fourteenth election-district.*—Bur-Oak precinct, at the house of Benjamin Harding. Doniphan precinct, (including part of the 15th district to Walnut-Creek), at the house of Dr. G. A. Cutler, in Doniphan. Wolf river precinct, at the house of Aaron Lewis.

"*Fifteenth election-district.* — Walnut-Creek precinct (south Walnut-Creek), at the house of Charles Hays, on Military road.

"*Sixteenth election-district.*—Leavenworth precinct, at the store of Thomas Doyle, in Leavenworth City. Easton precinct, at the house of Thomas A. Maynard, on Stranger-Creek. Wyandot precinct, at the council-house, in Wyandot City. Ridge precinct, at the house of Wm. Pennock.

"*Seventeenth election-district.*—Mission precinct, at the Baptist Mission-building. Wakarusa precinct, at the store of Paschal Fish.

"*Eighteenth election-district.*—California precinct, at the house of W. W. Moore, on the St. Joseph and California road.

"INSTRUCTION TO JUDGES OF ELECTION.

"The three judges will provide for each poll, ballot-boxes for depositing the ballots cast by electors; shall appoint two clerks, all of whom shall be sworn or affirm to discharge the duties of their respective offices impartially and with fidelity · and the judges and clerks shall have power to administer the oath or affirmation to each other; and the said judges shall open said election at 10 o'clock a.m., at the place designated in each precinct by the executive committee of Kansas Territory, and close the same at 4 o'clock p. m. In case any of the officers appointed fail to attend, the officer or officers in attendance shall supply their places. And the said judges shall make out duplicate returns of said election, seal up and transmit one copy ef the same within five days to the chairman of the executive committee to be laid before the convention, and they shall within ten days seal up and hand the other to some member of the said executive committtee. If at the time of holding said election it shall be inconvenient on account of Indian hostilities, or any other cause whatever, that would disturb or prevent the voters of any election-precinct in the Territory from the free and peaceable exercise of the elective franchise, the officers are hereby authorized to adjourn said election into any other precinct in the Territory, and to any other day they may see proper, of the necessity of which they shall be the exclusive judges, at which time and place the qualified voters may cast their votes.

"QUALIFICATION OF VOTERS, ETC.

"All white male inhabitants, citizens of the United States, or who have declared their intentions, before the proper authorities, to become such, above the age of twenty-one years, who have had a *bona fide* residence in the Territory for the space of thirty days immediately preceding the day of the said election, shall be entitled to vote for delegates to said convention; and all white male inhabitants, citizens of the United States, above the age of twenty-one years, who have had a *bona fide* residence in the Territory of Kansas for the space of three months immediately preceding the day of election, shall be eligible as delegates to said convention.

"APPORTIONMENT.

"The apportionment of delegates to said convention shall be as follows: Two delegates for each representative to which the people were entitled in the legislative assembly, by proclamation of Governor Reeder of date March 10, 1855

"It is confidently believed that the people of Kansas are fully alive to the importance of the step they are about to take in disenthralling themselves from the slavery which is now fettering them; and the *squatters of Kansas* are earnestly requested to be at their several polls on the day above designated. See that there be no illegal votes cast, and that every ballot received be in accordance with your choice for delegate to the constitutional convention, and have all the regulations and restrictions carried out.

"The plan proposed in the proclamation, to govern you in the election, has been adopted after mature deliberation, and, if adhered to by you, will result in establishing in Kansas an independent government that will be admitted into our beloved Union as a sovereign State, securing to our people the liberty they have heretofore enjoyed, and which has been so ruthlessly wrested from them by reckless invaders.

"By order of the executive committee of Kansas Territory,

"J. H. LANE, *Chairman*.

"J. K. GOODIN, *Secretary*."

Delegates were elected agreeably to the proclamation so issued, and they met at Topeka on the fourth Tuesday in October, 1855, and formed a constitution, which was submitted to the people, and was ratified by them by vote in the districts. An election of State officers and members of the State legislature has been had, and a representative to Congress elected, and it is intended to proceed to the election of senators, with the view to present the same, with the constitution, to Congress for admission into the Union.

Whatever views individuals may at times, or in meetings, have expressed, and whatever ultimate determination may have been entertained in the result of being spurned by Congress, and refused redress, is now entirely immaterial. That cannot condemn or give character to the proceedings thus far pursued.

Many may have honestly believed usurpation could make no law, and that if Congress made no further provisions they were well justified in forming a law for themselves; but it is not now necessary to consider that matter, as it is to be hoped that Congress will not leave them to such a necessity.

Thus far, this effort of the people for redress is peaceful, constitutional, and right. Whether it will succeed, rests with Congress to determine; but clear it is that it should not be met and denounced as revolutionary, rebellious, insurrectionary, or unlawful, nor does it call for or justify the exercise of any force by any department of this government to check or control it.

It now becomes proper to inquire what should be done by Congress; for we are informed by the President, in substance, that he has no power to correct a usurpation, and that the laws, even though made by usurped authority, must be by him enforced and executed, even with military force. The measures of redress should be applied to the true cause of the difficulty. This obviously lies in the repeal of the clause for freedom in the act of 1820, and therefore the true remedy lies in the entire repeal of the act of 1854, which effected it. Let this be done with frankness and magnanimity, and Kansas be organized anew, as a Free Territory, and all will be put right.

But, if Congress insist on proceeding with the experiment, then declare all the action by this spurious, foreign legislative assembly utterly inoperative and void, and direct a reorganization, providing proper safeguard for legal voting and against foreign force.

There is, however, another way to put an end to all this trouble there, and in the nation, without retracing steps or continuing violence, or by force compelling obedience to tyrannical laws made by foreign force; and that is, by admitting that Territory as a State, with her free constitution. True, indeed, her numbers are not such as gives her a right to demand admission, being, as the President informs us, probably only about twenty-five thousand. The Constitution fixes no number as necessary, and the importance of *now* settling this question may well justify Congress in admitting this as a State, *at this time*, especially as we have good reason to believe that, if admitted as a State, and controversy ended, it will immediately fill up with a numerous and successful population.

At any rate, it seems impossible to believe that Congress is to leave that people without redress, to have enforced upon them by the army of the nation these measures and laws of violence and oppression. Are they to be dragooned into submission? Is that an experiment pleasant to execute on our own free people?

The true character of this transaction is matter of extensive notoriety. Its essential features are too obvious to allow of any successful disguise or palliation, however complicated or ingenious may be the statements, or however special the pleadings, for that purpose. The case requires some quieting, kind, and prudent treatment by the hand of Congress to do justice and satisfy the nation. The people of this country are peacefully relying on Congress to provide the competent measures of redress which they have the undoubted power to administer.

The Attorney-General, in the case of Arkansas, says: "Congress may at pleasure repeal or modify the laws passed by the territorial legislature, and may at any time abrogate and remodel the legislature itself, and all the other departments of the territorial government."

Treating this grievance in Kansas with ingenious excuses, with neglect or contempt, or riding over the oppressed with an army, and dragooning them into submission, will make no satisfactory termination. Party success may at times be temporarily secured by adroit devices, plausible pretenses, and partisan address; but the permanent preservation of this Union can be maintained only by frankness and integrity. Justice may be denied where it ought to be granted; power may perpetuate that vassalage which violence and usurpation have produced; the subjugation of white freemen may be necessary, that African Slavery may succeed; but such a course must not be expected to produce peace and satisfaction in our country, so long as the people retain any proper sentiment of justice, liberty, and law.

J. COLLAMER.

It is not possible, within the limits prescribed for this volume, to give a full account of the debates and proceedings in the present Congress with relation to Kansas. Suffice it that, on the 19th of March, the House was brought to a vote on the proposition of the Committee of Elections, to empower said Committee to send to Kansas for persons and papers, modified, on motion of Mr. Dunn of Indiana, with the assent of said Committee, so as to read as follows:

"*Resolved*, That a Committee of three of the members of this House, to be appointed by the Speaker, shall proceed to inquire into and collect evidence in regard to the troubles in Kansas generally, and particularly in regard to any fraud or force attempted or practiced in reference to any of the elections which have taken place in said Territory, either under the law organizing said Territory, or under any pretended law which may be alleged to have taken effect there since. That they shall fully investigate and take proof of all violent and tumultuous proceedings in said Territory, at any time since the passage of the Kansas-Nebraska act, whether engaged in by the residents of said Territory, or by any person or persons from elsewhere going into said Territory, and doing, or encouraging others to do, any act of violence or public disturbance against the laws of the United States, or the rights, peace, and safety of the residents of said Territory; and, for that purpose, said Committee shall have full power to send for, and examine, and take copies of, all such papers, public records, and proceedings, as in their judgment will be useful in the premises; and also, to send for persons and examine them on oath, or affirmation, as to matters within their knowledge, touching the matters of said investigation; and said Committee, by their Chairman, shall have power to administer all necessary oaths or affirmations connected with their aforesaid duties.

"*Resolved further*, That said Committee may hold their investigations at such places and times as to them may seem advisable, and that they have leave of absence from the duties of this House until they shall have completed such investigation. That they be authorized to employ one or more clerks, and one or more assistant sergeants-at-arms, to aid them in their investigation; and may administer to them an oath, or affirmation, faithfully to perform the duties assigned to them, respectively, and to keep secret all matters which may come to their knowledge touching such investigation, as said Committee may direct, until the Report of the same shall be submitted to this House; and said Committee may discharge any such clerk, or assistant sergeant-at-arms, for neglect of duty or disregard of instructions in the premises, and employ others under like regulations.

"*Resolved further*, That if any person shall, in any manner, obstruct or hinder said Committee, or attempt to do so, in their said investigation or shall refuse to attend on said Committee, and to give evidence, when summoned for that purpose, or shall refuse to produce any paper, book public record, or proceeding, in their possession or control, to said Committee, when so required, or shall make any disturbance where said Committee is [are] holding their sittings, said Committee may, if they see fit, cause any such person to be arrested by said assistant sergeant-at-arms, and brought before this House, to be dealt with as for contempt.

"*Resolved further*, That, for the purpose of defraying the expenses of said Commission, there be, and hereby is, appropriated the sum of ten thousand dollars, to be paid out of the contingent fund of this House.

"*Resolved further*, That the President of the United States be, and is hereby, requested to furnish to said Committee, should they be met with any serious opposition by bodies of lawless men in the discharge of their duties aforesaid, such aid from any military force as may at the time be convenient to them, as may be necessary to remove such opposition, and enable said Committee, without molestation, to proceed with their labors.

"*Resolved further*, That when said Committee shall have completed said investigation, they report all the evidence so collected to this House."

This proposition the House adopted—Yeas 101; Nays 93—as follows:

YEAS—For the proposed Investigation:

MAINE—Samuel P. Benson, Ebenezer Knowlton, Israel Washburn, Jr.—3.

NEW-HAMPSHIRE—Aaron H. Cragin, James Pike—2.

MASSACHUSETTS—James Buffinton, Anson Burlingame, Calvin C. Chaffee, Linus B. Comins, William S. Damrell, Timothy Davis, Robert B. Hall, Chauncey L. Knapp, Mark Trafton—9.

RHODE ISLAND—Nathaniel B. Durfee—1.

CONNECTICUT—Ezra Clark, Jr., Sidney Dean, William W. Welch, John Woodruff—4.

VERMONT—James Meacham, Justin S. Morrill—2.

NEW-YORK—Henry Bennett, Bayard Clarke, Samuel Dickson, Edward Dodd, Francis S. Edwards, Thomas T. Flagler, William A. Gilbert, Amos P. Granger, *Solomon G. Haven*, Thomas R. Horton, Jonas A. Hughston, William H. Kelsey, Rufus H. King, Orsamus B. Matteson, Andrew Z. McCarty, Killian Miller, Edwin B. Morgan, Ambrose S. Murray, Andrew Oliver, John M. Parker, Benjamin Pringle, Russell Sage, George A. Simmons, Francis E. Spinner, James S. T. Stranahan, Abram Wakeman—26.

NEW-JERSEY—Isaiah D. Clawson, James Bishop, George R. Robbins—3.

PENNSYLVANIA—John Allison, DAVID BARCLAY, Samuel C. Bradshaw, James H. Campbell, John Covode, John Dick, John R. Edie, Galusha A. Grow, JOHN HICKMAN, Jonathan Knight, David Ritchie, Anthony E. Roberts, Job R. Tyson, Lemuel Todd—14.

OHIO—Edward Ball, Philemon Bliss, Lewis D. Campbell, Timothy C. Day, Jonas R. Emrie, Samuel Galloway, Joshua R. Giddings, Aaron Harlan, *John Scott Harrison*, Valentine B. Horton, Benjamin F. Leiter, *Oscar F. Moore*, Richard Mott, Matthias H. Nichols, William R. Sapp, John Sherman, Edward Wade, Cooper K. Watson—18.

INDIANA—Lucien Barbour, Samuel Brenton, Schuyler Colfax, William Cumback, *George G. Dunn*, Daniel Mace, John U. Pettit, *Harvey D Scott*—8.

ILLINOIS—James Knox, Jesse O. Norton,

Elihu B. Washburne, James H. Woodworth—4.

MICHIGAN—William A. Howard, David S. Walbridge, Henry Waldron—3.

WISCONSIN—Charles Billinghurst, Cadwallader C. Washburne—2.

IOWA—AUGUSTUS C. HALL, James Thorington—2.

Total Yeas, 101.

NAYS—Against the Investigation:

MAINE—Thomas J. D. Fuller—1.

OTHER NEW-ENGLAND STATES—*None.*

NEW-YORK—John Kelly, *William W. Valk*, John Wheeler, *Thomas R. Whitney*—4.

NEW-JERSEY—George Vail—1.

PENNSYLVANIA—John Cadwalader, Thomas B. Florence, J. Glancy Jones—3.

OHIO—*None.* WISCONSIN—*None.*

INDIANA—William H. English, Smith Miller 2.

MICHIGAN—George W. Peck—1.

ILLINOIS—James C. Allen, Thomas L. Harris, Samuel S. Marshall, William A. Richardson—4.

CALIFORNIA—Philemon T. Herbert—1.

IOWA—*None.*

Total from Free States, 17.

DELAWARE—*None.*

MARYLAND—Thomas F. Bowie, *Henry W. Davis, Henry W. Hoffman, J. Morrison Harris, James B. Ricaud*, James A. Stewart—6.

VIRGINIA—Thomas S. Bocock, *John S. Carlisle*, John S. Caskie, Henry A. Edmundson, Charles J. Faulkner, William O. Goode, Zedekiah Kidwell, John Letcher, Fayette McMullen, John S. Millson, Paulus Powell, William Smith—12.

NORTH CAROLINA—Louis O'B. Branch, Thomas L. Clingman, Burton Craige, *Robert T. Paine*, Thomas Ruffin, Warren Winslow—6.

SOUTH CAROLINA—William Aiken, William W. Boyce, Preston S. Brooks, John McQueen, James L. Orr—5.

GEORGIA—Howell Cobb, Martin J. Crawford, John H. Lumpkin, James L. Seward, Alex. H. Stephens, *Robert P. Trippe*, Hiram Warner—7.

ALABAMA—W. R. W. Cobb, James F. Dowdell, Sampson W. Harris, George S. Houston, Eli S. Shorter, *William R. Smith, Percy Walker*—7.

MISSISSIPPI—Hendley S. Bennett, *William A. Lake*, John A. Quitman—3.

LOUISIANA—Thos. G. Davidson, *George Eustis, Jr.*, John M. Sandidge, Miles Taylor—4.

FLORIDA—Augustus E. Maxwell—1.

TEXAS—Peter H. Bell, *Lemuel D. Evans*—2.

KENTUCKY—Henry C. Burnett, *John P. Campbell, Leander M. Cox*, John M. Elliot, *Alex. K. Marshall, Humphrey Marshall, Samuel F. Swope*, Albert G. Talbott, *William L. Underwood*—9.

TENNESSEE—George W. Jones, *Charles Ready*, John H. Savage, Samuel A. Smith, *William H. Sneed*, Albert G. Watkins, John V. Wright, *Felix K. Zollicoffer*—8.

MISSOURI—Samuel Caruthers, *Luther M. Kennett, James J. Lindley*, Mordecai Oliver, John S. Phelps, Gilchrist Porter—6.

ARKANSAS—*None.*

[Fillmore men in *Italics*; Buchanan men voting Yea in SMALL CAPITALS; Anti-Nebraska Yeas and Buchanan Nays in Roman.]

So the resolution prevailed, and Messrs. WILLIAM A. HOWARD of Michigan, JOHN SHERMAN of Ohio, and MORDECAI OLIVER of Missouri, were appointed the Committee of Investigation thereby required.

These gentlemen proceeded to Kansas, and spent several weeks there in taking testimony as to the elections, etc., which had taken place in that Territory. The testimony thus taken forms a volume of nearly twelve hundred large and closely-printed pages, the substance of which was summed up on their return by the majority (Messrs. Howard and Sherman), in the following

REPORT ON THE OUTRAGES IN KANSAS.

A journal of proceedings, including sundry communications made to and by the Committee was kept, a copy of which is herewith submitted. The testimony also is herewith submitted; a copy of it has been made and arranged, not according to the order in which it was taken, but so as to present, as clearly as possible, a consecutive history of events in the Territory, from its organization to the 19th day of March, A. D. 1856.

Your Committee deem it their duty to state, as briefly as possible, the principal facts proven before them. When the act to organize the Territory of Kansas was passed on —— day of May, 1854,, the greater portion of its eastern border was included in Indian reservations not open for settlement, and there were but few white settlers in any portion of the Territory. Its Indian population was rapidly decreasing, while many emigrants from different parts of our country were anxiously waiting the extinction of the Indian title, and the establishment of a Territorial Government, to seek new homes in its fertile prairies. It cannot be doubted that if its condition as a free Territory had been left undisturbed by Congress its settlement would have been rapid, peaceful, and prosperous. Its climate, soil, and its easy access to the older settlements would have made it the favored course for the tide of emigration constantly flowing to the West, and by this time it would have been admitted into the Union as a Free State, without the least sectional excitement. If so organized, none but the kindest feeling could have existed between it and the adjoining State. Their mutual interests and intercourse, instead of, as now, endangering the harmony of the Union, would have strengthened the ties of national brotherhood. The testimony clearly shows, that before the proposition to repeal the Missouri Compromise was introduced into Congress, the people of western Missouri appeared indifferent to the prohibition of Slavery in the Territory, and neither asked nor desired its repeal.

When, however, the prohibition was removed by the action of Congress, the aspect of affairs entirely changed. The whole country was agitated, by the reopening of a controversy which conservative men in different sections hoped had been settled, in every State and Territory, by some law beyond the danger of repeal. The excitement which has always accompanied the discussion of the Slavery question was greatly increased, by the hope on the one hand of extending Slavery into a region from which it had been excluded by law, and on the other by a sense of wrong done by what was regarded as a dishonor of a national compact. This excitement was naturally transferred into the border counties of Missouri and the Territory as settlers favoring free or Slave institutions moved into it. A new difficulty soon occurred. Different constructions were put upon the organic law. It was contended by the one party that the right to hold Slaves in the Territory existed, and that neither the people nor the Territorial Legislature could prohibit Slavery—that that power was alone possessed by the people when they were authorized to form a State government. It was contended that the removal of the restriction virtually established Slavery in the Territory. This claim was urged by many prominent men in western Missouri, who actively engaged in the affairs of the Territory. Every movement, of whatever character, which tended to establish free institutions, was regarded as an interference with their rights.

Within a few days after the organic law passed, and as soon as its passage could be known on the border, leading citizens of Missouri crossed into the Territory, held squatter meetings and then returned to their homes. Among their resolutions are the following:

"That we will afford protection to no Abolitionist as a settler of this Territory."

"That we recognize the institution of Slavery as already existing in this Territory, and advise slaveholders to introduce their property as early as possible."

Similar resolutions were passed in various parts of the Territory, and by meetings in several counties of Missouri. Thus the first effect of the repeal of the restriction against Slavery was to substitute the resolves of squatter meetings, composed almost exclusively of citizens of a single State, for the deliberate action of Congress, acquiesced in for thirty-five years.

This unlawful interference has been continued in every important event in the history of the Territory; *every election* has been controlled not by the actual settlers, but by citizens of Missouri, and as a consequence every officer in the Territory, from constables to legislators, except those appointed by the President, owe their positions to non-resident voters. None have been elected by the settlers, and your Committee have been unable to find that any political power whatever, however unimportant, has been exercised by the people of the Territory.

In October, A. D. 1854, Gov. A. H. Reeder and the other officers appointed by the President arrived in the Territory. Settlers from all parts of the country were moving in in great numbers, making their claims and building their cabins. About the same time, and before any election was or could be held in the Territory, a secret political society was formed in the State of Missouri (1). It was known by different names, such as "Social Band," "Friends' Society," "Blue Lodge," "The Sons of the South." Its members were bound together by secret oaths, and they had passwords, signs, and grips by which they were known to each other. Penalties were imposed for violating the rules and secrets of the Order. Written minutes were kept of the proceedings of the Lodges, and the different Lodges were connected together by an effective organization. It embraced great numbers of the citizens of Missouri, and was extended into other Slave States and into the Territory. Its avowed purpose was not only to extend Slavery into Kansas, but also into other Territory of the United States, and to form a union of all the friends of that institution. Its plan of operating was to organize and send men to vote at the elections in the Territory, to collect money to pay their expenses, and, if necessary, to protect them in voting. It also proposed to induce Pro-Slavery men to emigrate into the Territory, to aid and sustain them while there, and to elect none to office but those friendly to their views. This dangerous society was controlled by men who avowed their purpose to extend Slavery into the Territory at all hazards, and was altogether the most effective instrument in organizing the subsequent armed invasions and forays. In its Lodges in Missouri the affairs of Kansas were discussed, the force necessary to control the election was divided into bands, and leaders selected, means were collected, and signs and badges were agreed upon. While the great body of the actual settlers of the Territory were relying upon the rights secured to them by the organic law, and had formed no organization or combination whatever even of a party character, this conspiracy against their rights was gathering strength in a neighboring State, and would have been sufficient at their first election to have overpowered them, if they had been united to a man.

Your Committee had great difficulty in eliciting the proof of the details in regard to this secret society. One witness, member of the legislative council, refused to answer questions in reference to it (2). Another declined to answer fully, because to do so would result to his injury (3). Others could or would only answer as to the general purposes of the Society, but sufficient is disclosed in the testimony to show the influence it had in controlling the elections in the Territory.

The first election was for a Delegate to Congress. It was appointed for the 29th of November, 1854. The Governor divided the Territory into seventeen Election-Districts; appointed Judges and prescribed proper rules for the election. In the Ist, IIId, VIIIth, IXth, Xth, XIIth, XIIIth, and XVIIth Districts there appears to have been but little if any fraudulent voting.

The election in the IId District was held at the village of Douglas, nearly fifty miles from the Missouri line. On the day before the election, large companies of men came into the district in wagons and on horseback, and declared that they were from the State of Missouri, and were going to Douglas to vote. On the morning of the election they gathered around the house where the election was to be held. Two of the Judges appointed by the Governor did not appear, and other Judges were elected by the crowd. All then voted. In order to make a pretense of right to vote, some persons of the company kept a pretended register of squatter claims, on which any one could enter his name and then assert he had a claim in the Territory. A citizen of the district who was himself a candidate for Delegate to Congress, was told by one of the strangers, that he would be abused and probably killed if he challenged a vote (4). He was seized by the collar, called a d—d Abolitionist, and was compelled to seek protection in the room with the Judges. About the time the polls were closed, these strangers mounted their horses and got into their wagons and cried out—

"All aboard for Westport and Kansas City."

A number were recognized as residents of Missouri, and among them was Samuel H. Woodson, a leading lawyer of Independence. Of those whose names are on the poll-books, 35 were resident settlers and 226 were non-residents.

The election in the IVth District was held at Dr. Chapman's, over 40 miles from the Missouri State line. It was a thinly-settled region, containing but 47 voters in February, 1855, when the census was taken. On the day before the election, from 100 to 150 citizens of Cass and Jackson Counties, Mo., came into this district, declaring their purpose to vote, and that they were bound to make Kansas a Slave State, if they did it at the point of the sword (5). Persons of the party on the way drove each a stake in the ground and called it a claim—and in one case several names were put on one stake. The party of strangers camped all night near where the

(1) Jordan Davidson, J. C. Prince, John Scott, J. H. Stringfellow.

(2) W. P. Richardson. (3) O. C. Prince. (4) John A. Wakefield. (5) Peter Bassinger.

election was to be held, and in the morning were at the election-polls and voted. One of their party got drunk, and to get rid of Dr. Chapman, a judge of the election, they sent for him to come and see a sick man, and in his absence filled his place with another judge, who was not sworn. They did not deny or conceal that they were residents of Missouri, and many of them were recognized as such by others. They declared that they were bound to make Kansas a Slave State. They insisted upon their right to vote in the Territory if they were in it one hour. After the election they again returned to their homes in Missouri, camping over night on the way.

We find upon the poll-books 161 names; of these not over 30 resided in the Territory, 131 were non-residents (6).

But few settlers attended the election in the Vth District, the District being large and the settlement scattered. 82 votes were cast; of these between 20 and 30 were settlers (7), and the residue were citizens of Missouri. They passed into the Territory (8) by way of the Santa Fe road and by the residence of Dr. Westfall, who then lived on the western line of Missouri (9). Some little excitement arose at the polls as to the legality of their voting, but they did vote for Gen. Whitfield, and said they intended to make Kansas a Slave State—and that they had claims in the Territory. Judge Teazle, judge of the Court in Jackson County, Missouri, was present, but did not vote (9). He said he did not intend to vote, but came to see that others voted. After the election, the Missourians returned the way they came.

The election in the VIth District was held at Fort Scott, in the southeast part of the Territory and near the Missouri line. A party of about one hundred men, from Cass and the counties in Missouri south of it, went into the Territory, traveling about 45 miles, most of them with their wagons and tents, and camping out. They appeared at the place of election. Some attempts were made to swear them, but two of the Judges were prevailed upon not to do so, and none were sworn, and as many as chose voted. There were but few resident voters at the polls. The settlement was sparse—about 25 actual settlers voted out of 105 votes cast, leaving 80 illegal votes (10). After the voting was over the Missourians went to their wagons and commenced leaving for home.

The most shameless fraud practiced upon the rights of the settlers at this election was in the VIIth District. It is a remote settlement about 75 miles from the Missouri line, and contained in February, A. D. 1855, three months afterwards, when the census was taken, but 53 voters; and yet the poll-books show that 604 votes were cast. The election was held at the house of Frey McGee, at a place called "110." But few of the actual settlers were present at the polls (11). A witness who formerly resided in Jackson County, Mo., and was well acquainted with the citizens of that county (12), says that he saw a great many wagons and tents at the place of election, and many individuals he knew from Jackson County. He was in their tents and conversed with some of them, and they told him they had come with the intention of voting. He went to the polls intending to vote for Flennekin, and his ticket being of a different color from the rest, his vote was challenged by Frey McGee, who had been appointed one of the Judges but did not serve. Lemuel Ralstone, a citizen of Missouri, was acting in his place. The witness then challenged the vote of a young man by the name of Nolan, whom he knew to reside in Jackson County. Finally the thing was hushed up as the witness had a good many friends there from that county, and it might lead to a fight if he challenged any more votes. Both voted and he then went down to their camp. He there saw many of his old acquaintances whom he knew had voted at the election in August previous in Missouri, and who still resided in that State. By a careful comparison of the poll-lists with the census rolls, we find but 12 names on the poll-book who were voters when the census was taken three months afterwards, and we are satisfied that not more than 20 legal votes could have been polled at that election. The only residents who are known to have voted are named by the witness, and are 13 in number—thus leaving 584 illegal votes cast in a remote district, where the settlers within many miles were acquainted with each other.

The total number of white inhabitants in the XIth District in the month of February, A. D. 1855, including men, women, and children, was 36, of whom 24 were voters—yet the poll-lists in this District show that 245 votes were cast at this election. For reasons stated hereafter in regard to the election on the 30th of March, your Committee were unable to procure the attendance of witnesses from this District. From the records it clearly appears that the votes cast could not have been by lawful resident voters. The best test, in the absence of direct proof, by which to ascertain the number of legal votes cast, is by a comparison of the census-roll with the poll-book—by which it appears that but 7 resident settlers voted, and 238 votes were illegally and fraudulently given.

The election in the XIVth District was held at the house of Benjamin Harding, a few miles from the town of St. Joseph, Missouri. Before the polls were opened, a large number of citizens of Buchanan County, Missouri, and among them many of the leading citizens of St. Joseph, were at the place of voting, and made a majority of the company present. At the time appointed by the Governor for opening the polls, two of the Judges were not there, and it became the duty of the legal voters present to select other Judges. The Judge who was present (13) suggested the name of Mr. Waterson as one of the Judges—but the crowd voted down the proposition. Some discussion then arose as to the right of non-residents to vote for Judges, during which Mr. Bryant was nominated and elected by the crowd. Some one nominated Col. John Scott as the other Judge, who was then and is now a resident of St. Joseph. At that time he was the City Attorney of that place, and so continued until this Spring, but he claimed that the night before he had come to the house of Mr. Bryant, and had engaged boarding for a month, and considered himself a resident of Kansas on that ground. The Judges appointed by the Governor refused to put the nomination of Col. Scott to vote, because he was not a resident. After some discussion, Judge Leonard, a citizen of Missouri, stepped forward and put the vote himself; and Mr. Scott was declared by him as elected by the crowd, and served as a Judge of Election that day. After the election was over he returned to St. Joseph, and never since has *resided* in the Territory. It is manifest that this election of a non-resident lawyer as a Judge was imposed upon the settlers by the citizens of the State. When the board of Judges was thus completed, the voting proceeded, but the effect of the rule adopted by the Judges allowed many, if not a majority of the non-residents, to vote. They claimed that their presence on the ground, es-

(6) Thomas Hopkins, Rubin Hacket, Perry Fuller, John F. Lucas. (7) James W. Wilson. (8) Dr. B. C. Westfall. (9) J. W. Wilson. (10) S. C. Prince. (11) Matthias A. Reed. (12) Wm. F. Johnstone.

(13) Benjamin Harding.

pecially when they had a *claim* in the Territory, gave them a right to vote—under that construction of the law they readily, when required, swore they were "residents" and then voted. By this evasion, as near as your Committee can ascertain from the testimony, as many as 50 illegal votes were cast in this District out of 153, the whole number polled.

The election in the XVth District was held at Penseman's, on Stranger Creek, a few miles from Weston, Missouri. On the day of the election a large number of citizens of Platte County, but chiefly from Weston and Platte City, came in small parties, in wagons and on horseback, to the polls. Among them were several leading citizens of that town, and the names of many of them are given by the witnesses (14). They generally insisted upon their right to vote, on the ground that every man having a claim in the Territory could vote, no matter where he lived (15). All voted who chose. No man was challenged or sworn. Some of the residents did not vote. The purpose of the strangers in voting was declared to be to make Kansas a Slave State (16). We find by the poll-books that 306 votes were cast—of these we find but 57 are on the census-rolls as legal voters in February following. Your Committee is satisfied from the testimony that not over 100 of those who voted had any right so to do, leaving at least 206 illegal votes cast.

The election in the XVIth District was held at Leavenworth. It was then a small village of three or four houses, located on the Delaware Reservation (17). There were but comparatively few settlers then in the district, but the number rapidly increased afterward. On the day before and on the day of the election, a great many citizens of Platte, Clay, and Ray counties crossed the river—most of them camping in tents and wagons about the town, "like a camp meeting" (18). They were in companies or messes of ten to fifteen in each, and numbered in all several hundred. They brought their own provisions and cooked it themselves, and were generally armed. Many of them were known by the witnesses, and their names given, and their names are found upon the poll-books. Among them were several persons of influence where they resided in Missouri, who held, or had held, high official positions in that State. They claimed to be residents of the Territory, from the fact that they were then present, and insisted upon the right to vote, and did vote. Their avowed purpose in doing so was to make Kansas a Slave State. These strangers crowded around the polls, and it was with great difficulty that the settlers could get to the polls (19). One resident attempted to get to the polls in the afternoon, but was crowded and pulled back. He then went outside of the crowd and hurrahed for Gen. Whitfield, and some of those who did not know him said, "that's a good Pro-Slavery man," and lifted him up over their heads so that he crawled on their heads and put in his vote. A person who saw from the color of his ticket that it was not for Gen. Whitfield, cried out, "He is a damned Abolitionist—let him down;" and they dropped him (20). Others were passed to the polls in the same way, and others crowded up in the best way they could. After this mockery of an election was over, the non-residents returned to their homes in Missouri. Of the 312 votes cast, not over 150 were by legal voters.

The following abstract exhibits the whole number of votes at this election, for each candidate; the number of legal and illegal votes cast in each district; and the number of legal votes in each district in February following:

ABSTRACT OF CENSUS AND ELECTION OF NOV. 29, 1854.

Districts	PLACE OF VOTING.	Whitfield	Wakefield	Flenniken	Scattering	Total	Number Votes by Census	Legal Votes	Illegal Votes
I	Lawrence	46	188	51	15	300	869	300	—
II	Douglas	235	20	6	—	261	199	35	226
III	Stinson's	40	—	7	—	47	101	47	—
IV	Dr. Chapman's	140	21	—	—	161	47	30	131
V	H. Sherman's	63	4	15	—	82	442	30	52
VI	Fort Scott	105	—	—	—	105	253	25	80
VII	"116"	597	—	7	—	604	53	2[illegible]	584
VIII	Council Grove	16	—	—	—	16	39	16	—
IX	Reynold's	9	—	31	—	40	36	40	—
X	Big Blue Cross	2	6	29	—	37	63	37	—
XI	Marvsville	237	—	3	5	245	24	7	233
XII	Warton's Store	31	9	—	1	41	78	41	—
XIII	Osawkie	69	1	1	—	71	96	71	—
XIV	Harding's	130	—	23	—	153	334	103	50
XV	Penseno	267	—	39	—	306	308	100	206
XVI	Leavenworth	232	—	80	—	312	385	150	162
XVII	Shawnee Agency	49	—	13	—	62	50	62	—
XVIII	———	—	—	—	—	28	—	—	—
	Total	2268	249	305	21	2871	—	1114	1729

Thus your Committee find that in this the first election in the Territory, a very large majority of the votes were cast by citizens of the State of Missouri, in violation of the organic law of the Territory. Of the legal votes cast, General Whitfield received a plurality. The settlers took but little interest in the election, not one-half of

(14) J. B. Crane, Francis M. Peter, John W. How, Phineas Skinner, H. B. Gale. (15) J. B. Crane. (16) H. B. Gale. (17) George H. Keller, and John A. Lunday.

(18) Geo. H. Keller. (19) John A. Lunday, L. L Easdreau. (20) John A. Lunday.

them voting. This may be accounted for, from the fact that the settlements were scattered over a great extent—that the term of the Delegate to be elected was short—and that the question of Free and Slave institutions was not generally regarded by them as distinctly at issue. Under these circumstances a systematic invasion from an adjoining State, by which large numbers of illegal votes were cast in remote and sparse settlements for the avowed purpose of extending Slavery into the Territory, even though it did not change the result of the election, was a crime of great magnitude. Its immediate effect was to further excite the people of the Northern States—induce acts of retaliation, and exasperate the actual settlers against their neighbors in Missouri.

In January and February, A. D. 1855, the Governor caused an enumeration to be taken of the inhabitants and qualified voters in the Territory, an abstract of which is here given:

ABSTRACT OF CENSUS RETURNS.

By	Districts	Males	Females	Voters	Minors	Natives of the United States	Foreign Birth	Negroes	Slaves	Total
C. W. Babcock	I	628	339	369	459	887	75	—	—	962
O. H. Brown	II	316	203	199	237	506	19	1	7	519
T. W. Hayes	III	161	91	101	112	215	12	—	6	252
E. B. Donaldson	IV	106	71	47	97	169	2	1	1	177
William Barbee	V	824	583	442	724	1385	22	27	26	1407
William Barbee	VI	492	318	253	418	791	12	11	11	810
J. R. McClure	VII	82	36	53	50	117	1	1	1	118
J. R. McClure	VIII	56	27	39	28	76	7	13	10	83
M. F. Conway	IX	61	25	36	31	66	12	14	3	86
M. F. Conway	X	97	54	63	61	108	23	—	—	151
B. H. Twombly	XI	33	3	24	5	30	6	—	—	36
B. H. Twombly	XII	104	40	78	35	109	37	1	7	144
H. B. Jolly	XIII	168	116	96	145	273	9	14	14	284
Albert Heed	XIV	655	512	334	—	301	46	1	35	1167
H. B. Jolly	XV	492	381	308	448	846	16	15	15	873
Charles Leib	XVI	708	475	385	514	1042	104	48	33	1183
Alex. S. Johnson	XVII	91	59	50	54	143	5	4	23	150
B. H. Twombly	XVIII	59	40	28	51	97	1	—	—	99
Total		5128	3373	2905	3469	7161	409	151	242	8501

On the same day the census was completed, the Governor issued his Proclamation for an election to be held on the 30th of March, A. D. 1855, for Members of the Legislative Assembly of the Territory. It prescribed the boundaries of Districts; the places for polls; the names of Judges; the appointment of members; and recited the qualification of voters. If it had been observed, a just and fair election would have reflected the will of the people of the Territory. Before the election, false and inflammatory rumors were busily circulated among the people of Western Missouri. The number and character of the emigration then passing into the Territory were grossly exaggerated and misrepresented. Through the active exertions of many of its leading citizens, aided by the secret societies before referred to, the passions and prejudices of the people of that State were greatly excited. Several residents there have testified to the character of the reports circulated among, and credited by, the people. These efforts were successful. By an organized movement, which extended from Andrew County in the north to Jasper County in the south, and as far eastward as Boone and Cole Counties, companies of men were arranged in regular parties and sent *into every Council-District in the Territory, and into every Representative District* but one. The numbers were so distributed as to control the election in each district. They went to vote and with the avowed design to make Kansas a Slave State. They were generally armed and equipped, carried with them their own provisions and tents, and so marched into the Territory. The details of this invasion from the mass of the testimony taken by your Committee, are so voluminous that we can here state but the leading facts elicited.

1st District—March 30, 1855.—Lawrence.

The company of persons who marched into this District, collected in Ray, Howard, Carroll, Boone, La Fayette, Randolph, Saline, and Cass Counties, in the state of Missouri. Their expenses were paid—those who could not come contributing provisions, wagons, etc. (21). Provisions were deposited, for those who were expected to come to Lawrence, in the house of William Lykins, and were distributed among the Missourians after they arrived there (22). The evening before and the morning of the day of election, about 1,000 men from the above counties arrived at Lawrence, and encamped in a ravine a short distance from town, near the place of voting. They came in wagons—of which there were over one hundred—and on horseback, under the command of Col. Samuel Young, of Boone County, Missouri, and Clayborne F. Jackson, of Missouri. They were armed with guns, rifles, pistols, and bowie-knives, and had tents, music, and flags with them (23). They brought with them two pieces of artillery (24).

(21) F. P. Vaughan, Jourdan Davidson. (22) Wm. Tates, O. W. Babcock, Dr. John Day. (23) E. D. Ladd, Norman Allen, Wm. Yates, Wm. B. Hornsby, G. W. Dietzler, C. W. Babcock, Lyman Allen, S. N., Wood, E. Chapman, Robert Elliott, N. W. Blanton. Jourdan Davidson, Wm. Lyon, J. B. Abbott, Ira. W, Ackley, Dr. John Day, A. B. Wade, John M. Banks. H. W. Buckley. (24) E. Chapman, Jourdan Davidson.

loaded with musket-balls (25). On their way to Lawrence some of them met Mr. N. B. Blanton, who had been appointed one of the Judges of Election by Gov. Reeder, and after learning from him that he considered it his duty to demand an oath from them as to their place of residence, first attempted to bribe, and then threatened him with hanging, in order to induce him to dispense with that oath. In consequence of these threats, he did not appear at the polls the next morning to act as Judge (26).

The evening before the election, while in camp, the Missourians were called together at the tent of Captain Claiborne F. Jackson, and speeches were made to them by Col. Young and others, calling for volunteers to go to other districts where there were not Missourians enough to control the election, and there were more at Lawrence than were needed there (27). Many volunteered to go, and the morning of the election, several companies, from 150 to 200 men each, went off to Tecumseh, Hickory Point, Bloomington, and other places (28). On the morning of the election, the Missourians came over to the place of voting from their camp, in bodies of one hundred at a time (29). Mr. Blanton not appearing, another Judge was appointed in his place—Col. Young claiming that, as the people of the Territory had two Judges, it was nothing more than right that the Missourians should have the other one, to look after their interests (30); and Robert E. Cummins was elected in Blanton's stead, because he considered that every man had a right to vote if he had been in the Territory but an hour (31). The Missourians brought their tickets with them, (32); but not having enough, they had three hundred more printed in Lawrence on the evening before and the day of election (33). They had white ribbons in their button-holes to distinguish themselves from the settlers (34).

When the voting commenced, the question of the legality of the vote of a Mr. Page was raised. Before it was decided, Col. Samuel Young stepped up to the window where the votes were received, and said he would settle the matter. The vote of Mr. Page was withdrawn, and Col. Young offered to vote. He refused to take the oath prescribed by the Governor, but swore he was a resident of the Territory, upon which his vote was received (35). He told Mr. Abbott, one of the Judges, when asked if he intended to make Kansas his future home, that it was none of his business; that if he were a resident then, he should ask no more (36). After his vote was received, Col. Young got up in the window-sill and announced to the crowd that he had been permitted to vote, and they could all come up and vote (37). He told the Judges that there was no use in swearing the others, as they would all swear as he had done (38). After the other Judges concluded to receive Col. Young's vote, Mr. Abbott resigned as Judge of Election, and Mr. Benjamin was elected in his place (39).

The polls were so much crowded until late in the evening, that, for a time, when the men had voted, they were obliged to get out by being hoisted up on the roof of the building where the election was being held, and pass out over the house (40). Afterward a passage-way through the crowd was made, by two lines of men being formed, through which the voters could get up to the polls (41). Col. Young asked that the old men be allowed to go up first and vote, as they were tired with the traveling, and wanted to get back to camp (42).

The Missourians sometimes came up to the polls in procession, two by two, and voted (43).

During the day the Missourians drove off the ground some of the citizens, Mr. Stevens, Mr. Bond, and Mr. Willis (44). They threatened to shoot Mr. Bond, and a crowd rushed after him threatening him, and as he ran from them some shots were fired at him as he jumped off the bank of the river and made his escape (45). The citizens of the town went over in a body, late in the afternoon, when the polls had become comparatively clear, and voted (46).

Before the voting had commenced, the Missourians said, if the Judges appointed by the Governor did not receive their votes, they would choose other Judges (47). Some of them voted several times, changing their hats or coats and coming up to the window again (48). They said they intended to vote first, and after they had got through then the others could vote (49). Some of them claimed a right to vote under the organic act, from the fact that their mere presence in the Territory constituted them residents, though they were from Wisconsin, and had homes in Missouri (50). Others said they had a right to vote, because Kansas belonged to Missouri, and people from the east had no right to settle in the Territory and vote there (51). They said they came to the Territory to elect a legislature to suit themselves, as the people of the Territory and persons from the east and north wanted to elect a legislature that would not suit them (52). They said they had a right to make Kansas a Slave State, because the people of the north had sent persons out to make it a Free State (53). Some claimed that they had heard that the Emigrant Aid Society had sent men out to be at the election, and they came to offset their votes; but the most of them made no such claim. Col. Young said he wanted the citizens to vote in order to give the election some show of fairness (54). The Missourians said there would be no difficulty if the citizens did not interfere with their voting, but they were determined to vote—peaceably, if they could, but vote any how (55). They said each one of them was prepared for eight rounds without loading, and would go the ninth round with the butcher knife (56). Some of them said that by voting in the Territory, they would deprive themselves of the right to vote in Missouri for twelve months afterward (57).

The Missourians began to leave the afternoon of the day of election, though some did not go home until the next morning (58).

In many cases, when a wagon-load had voted,

(25) E. Chapman. (26) N. B. Blanton. (27) Norman Allen, J Davidson. (28) Norman Allen, Wm. Yates, W. B. Hornsby, C. W. Babcock, S. N. Wood, J. Davidson, A. B. Wade. (29) E. D. Ladd. (30) S. N. Wood. (31) R. A. Cummins, Norman Allen, S. N. Wood, C. S. Pratt, J. B. Abbott. (32) C. W. Babcock, Robert Elliott. (33) Robert Elliott. (34) E. W. Dietzler. (35) E. D Ladd, Norman Allen, S. N. Wood, C. S. Pratt, J. B. Abbott. (36) Norman Allen, J. B. Abbott. (37) E. D. Ladd, Norman Allen, S. N. Wood, C. S. Pratt, J. B. Abbott. (38) C. W. Babcock, J. B. Abbott. (39) C. W. Babcock, S. N. Wood, C. S. Pratt, J. B. Abbott.

(40) E. D. Ladd, Norman Allen, C. W. Babcock, Lyman Allen, J. M. Banks. (41) E. D. Ladd, Norman Allen, Lyman Allen. (42) Lyman Allen, E. D. Ladd. (43) E. D. Ladd, Ira W. Ackley. (44) E. D. Ladd, C. W. Babcock, Lyman Allen, S. N. Wood. N. B. Blanton, John Dey, J Davidson, Charles Robinson. (45) E. D. Ladd, C. W. Babcock, Lyman Allen, S. N. Wood. N. B. Blanton, J. Davidson, Dr. John Dey. (46) E. D. Ladd, C. Robinson, A. B. Wade, J. Whitlock, J. M. Banks, H. W. Buckley. (47) G. W. Deitzler. (48) S. N. Wood, Ira W. Ackley. (49) J. Davidson. (50) E. D. Ladd. Norman Allen, Lyman Allen. (51) W. B. Hornsby, C. W. Babcock, C. Robinson. (52) Wm. Yates, Thos. Hopkins, Ira W. Ackley. (53) Lyman Allen, J. Davidson. (54) Norman Allen. (55) Norman Allen, Lyman Allen, C. W. Babcock, S. N. Wood, F. Chapman, Thos. Hopkins. (56) Jourdan Davidson. (57) J. B. Abbott. (58) E. D. Ladd, Norman Allen, Wm. Yates, W. B. Hornsby. G. W. Dietzler, C. W. Babcock, C. Robinson, E. Chapman, Lyman Allen, J. Davidson.

they immediately started for home (59). On their way home they said that if Governor Reeder did not sanction the election, they would hang him (60).

The citizens of the town of Lawrence, as a general thing, were not armed on the day of election, though some had revolvers, but not exposed, as were the arms of the Missourians (61). They kept a guard about the town the night after the election, in consequence of the threats of the Missourians, in order to protect it (62).

The Pro-Slavery men of the District attended the nominating Conventions of the Free-State men, and voted for, and secured the nominations of, the men they considered the most obnoxious to the Free-State party, in order to cause dissension in that party (63).

Quite a number of settlers came into the District before the day of election, and after the census was taken (64). According to the census returns, there were then in the District 369 legal voters. Of those whose names are on the census returns, 177 are to be found on the poll-books of the 30th of March, 1855. Messrs. Ladd, Babcock, and Pratt, testify to 55 names on the poll-books of persons they knew to have settled in the District after the census was taken and before the election. A number of persons came into the Territory in March, before the election, from the northern and eastern States, intending to settle, who were in Lawrence on the day of election. At that time, many of them had selected no claims, and had no fixed place of residence. Such were not entitled to vote. Many of them became dissatisfied with the country. Others were disappointed in its political condition, and at the price and demand for labor, and returned. Whether any such voted at the election, is not clearly shown, but from the proof, it is probable that in the latter part of the day, after the great body of the Missourians had voted, some did go to the polls. The number was not over 50. These voted the Free-State ticket. The whole number of names appearing upon the poll-lists is 1,034. After full examination, we are satisfied that not over 232 of these were legal voters, and 802 were non-resident and illegal voters. This District is strongly in favor of making Kansas a Free State, and there is no doubt that the Free-State candidates for the legislature would have been elected by large majorities, if none but the actual settlers had voted. At the preceding election in November, 1854, where none but legal voters were polled, General Whitfield, who received the full strength of the Pro-Slavery party (65), got but 46 votes.

II. District—Bloomington.

On the morning of election, the Judges appointed by the Governor appeared and opened the polls. Their names were Harrison Burson, Nathaniel Ramsay, and Mr. Ellison. The Missourians began to come in early in the morning, some 500 or 600 of them, in wagons and carriages, and on horseback, under the lead of Samuel J. Jones, then Postmaster of Westport, Missouri, Claiborne F. Jackson, and Mr. Steely, of Independence, Mo. They were armed with double-barreled guns, rifles, bowie-knives and pistols, and had flags hoisted (66). They held a sort of informal election, off at one side, at first for Governor of Kansas, and shortly afterward announced Thomas Johnson of Shawnee Missions, elected Governor (67). The polls had been opened but a short time, when Mr. Jones marched with the crowd up to the window, and demanded that they should be allowed to vote without swearing as to their residence (68). After some noisy and threatening talk Claiborne F. Jackson addressed the crowd, saying they had come there to vote, that they had a right to vote if they had been there but five minutes, and he was not willing to go home without voting; which was received with cheers (69). Jackson then called upon them to form into little bands of fifteen or twenty, which they did (70), and went to an ox-wagon filled with guns, which were distributed among them (71), and proceeded to load some of them on the ground (72). In pursuance of Jackson's request, they tied white tape or ribbons in their buttonholes, so as to distinguish them from the "Abolitionists" (73). They again demanded that the Judges should resign, and upon their refusing to do so, smashed in the window, sash and all, and presented their pistols and guns to them, threatening to shoot them (74). Some one on the outside cried out to them not to shoot, as there were Pro-Slavery men in the room with the Judges (75). They then put a pry under the corner of the house, which was a log house, and lifted it up a few inches and let it fall again (76), but desisted upon being told there were Pro-Slavery men in the house. During this time the crowd repeatedly demanded to be allowed to vote without being sworn, and Mr. Ellison, one of the Judges, expressed himself willing, but the other two Judges refused (77); thereupon a body of men, headed by "Sheriff Jones," rushed into the Judges' room with cocked pistols and drawn bowie-knives in their hands, and approached Burson and Ramsay (78). Jones pulled out his watch, and said he would give them five minutes to resign in, or die (79). When the five minutes had expired and the Judges *did not* resign, Jones said he would give them another minute, and no more (80). Ellison told his associates that if they did not resign, there would be one hundred shots fired in the room in less than fifteen minutes (81); and then, snatching up the ballot-box, ran out into the crowd, holding up the ballot-box and hurrahing for Missouri (82). About that time Burson and Ramsay were called out by their friends, and not suffered to return (83). As Mr. Burson went out, he put the ballot poll-books in his pocket, and took them with him (84); and as he was going out, Jones snatched some papers away from him (85), and shortly afterward came out himself holding them up, crying "hurrah for Missouri" (86). After he discovered they were not the poll-books, he took a party of men with him and started off to take the poll-books from Burson (87). Mr. Burson saw them coming, and he gave the books to Mr. Umberger, and told him to start off in another direction, so as to mislead Jones and his party (88). Jones and his party caught Mr. Umberger, took the poll-books away from him, and Jones

(59) S. N. Wood. (60) Gaius Jenkins. (61) E. D. Ladd. (62) E. D. Ladd. (63) A. B. Wade. (64) E. D. Ladd, Norman Allen, C. W. Babcock, Charles Robinson, Lyman Allen, J. M. Banks. (65) James Whitlock. (66) H. Burson, N. Ramsay, James M. Dunn, Andrew White, Dr. E. G. Macey, H. Muzzy, Wm. Jessee, John A. Wakefield. (67) E. G. Macey.

(68) H. Burson, N. Ramsay, J. M. Dunn, A. White, E. G. Macey, H. Muzzy, Wm. Jessee, John A. Wakefield. (69) J. M. Dunn, A. White, E. G. Macey, J. S. Wakefield. (70) E. G. Macey, J. A. Wakefield. (71) J. M. Dunn, J. C. Dunn, A. White. (72) E. G. Macey. (73) J. M. Dunn, J. N. Mace, A. White, E. G. Macey, J. A. Wakefield. (74) H. Burson, N. Ramsay. (75) J. C. Dunn. (76) H. Burson, N. Ramsay, J. W. Mace, J. C. Dunn, A. White, E. G. Macey, H. Muzzy, S. Jones, J. A. Wakefield. (77) J. C. Dun, (78) H. Burson, N. Ramsay. (79) H. Burson, N. Ramsay, J. C. Dunn, H. Muzzy, W. Jessee. (80) H. Burson, N. Ramsay, H. Muzzy. (81) H. Burson, N. Ramsay, J. N. Macey, H. Muzzy, W. Jessee, S. Jones, J. A. Wakefield. (82) H Burson, J. C. Dunn. (83) H. Burson, N. Ramsay, J. C. Dunn, A. White, H. Muzzy, Wm. Jessee. (84) H. Burson, Wm. Jessee. (85) H. Burson. (86) H. Burson, J. M. Dunn, E. G. Macey, Wm. Jessee. (87) H. Burson, N. Ramsay. (88) H. Burson, A. White, G. W. Umberger, Wm. Jessee.

took him up behind him on a horse, and carried him back a prisoner (89). After Jones and his party had taken Umberger back, they went to the house of Mr. Ramsay and took Judge John A. Wakefield prisoner, and carried him to the place of election (90), and made him get up on a wagon and make them a speech; after which they put a white ribbon in his button-hole and let him go (91). They then chose two new Judges, and proceeded with the election (92).

They also threatened to kill the Judges if they did not receive their votes without swearing them, or else resign (92). They said no man should vote who would submit to be sworn—that they would kill any one who would offer to do so—"shoot him," "cut his guts out," etc. (93). They said no man should vote this day unless he voted an open ticket, and was "all right on the goose," (94), and that if they could not vote by fair means, they would by foul means (95). They said they had as much right to vote, if they had been in the Territory two minutes, as if they had been there for two years, and they would vote (96). Some of the citizens who were about the window, but had not voted when the crowd of Missourians marched up there, upon attempting to vote, were driven back by the mob, or driven off (97). One of them, Mr. J. M. Macey, was asked if he would take the oath, and upon his replying that he would if the judges required it, he was dragged through the crowd away from the polls, amid cries of "Kill the d—d nigger thief," "Cut his throat," "Tear his heart out," etc. After they got him to the outside of the crowd, they stood around him with cocked revolvers and drawn bowie-knives, one man putting a knife to his heart, so that it touched him, another holding a cocked pistol to his ear, while another struck at him with a club (98). The Missourians said they had a right to vote if they had been in the Territory but five minutes (99). Some said they had been hired to come there and vote, and get a dollar a day, and, by G—d, they would vote or die there (100).

They said the 30th day of March was an important day, as Kansas would be made a Slave State on that day (101). They began to leave in the direction of Missouri in the afternoon, after they had voted (102), leaving some thirty or forty around the house where the election was held, to guard the polls until after the election was over (103). The citizens of the Territory were not around, except those who took part in the mob (104), and a large portion of them did not vote (105); 341 votes were polled there that day, of which but some thirty were citizens (106). A protest against the election was made to the Governor (107). The returns of the election made to the Governor were lost by the Committee of Elections of the Legislature at Pawnee (108). The duplicate returns left in the ballot-box were taken by F. E. Laley, one of the Judges elected by the Missourians, and were either lost or destroyed in his house (109), so that your Committee have been unable to institute a comparison between the poll-lists and census returns of this district. The testimony, however, is uniform, that not even thirty of those who voted there that day were entitled to vote, leaving 311 illegal votes. We are satisfied from the testimony that, had the actual settlers alone voted, the Free State candidates would have been elected by a handsome majority.

IIId District—Tecumseh.

On the 28th of March, persons from Clay, Jackson, and Howard Counties, Mo., began to come into Tecumseh, in wagons, carriages and on horseback, armed with guns, bowie-knives, and revolvers; and, with threats, encamped close by the town, and continued coming until the day of election (110). The night before the election 200 men were sent for from the camp of Missourians at Lawrence (111). On the morning of the election, before the polls were opened, some 300 or 400 Missourians and others were collected in the yard about the house of Thomas Stinson, where the election was to be held, armed with bowie-knives, revolvers, and clubs (112). They said they came to vote, and whip the damned Yankees, and would vote without being sworn (113). Some said they came to have a fight and wanted one (114). Col. Samuel H. Woodson of Independence, Mo., was in the room of the Judges when they arrived, preparing poll-books and tally-lists, and remained there during their attempts to organize (114). The room of the Judges was also filled by many of the strangers (115). The Judges could not agree concerning the oath to be taken by themselves and the oath to be administered to the voters, Mr. Burgess desiring to administer the oath prescribed by the Governor and the other two Judges opposing it (116). During this discussion between the Judges, which lasted some time, the crowd outside became excited and noisy, threatening and cursing Mr. Burgess, the Free-State Judge (117). Persons were sent at different times, by the crowd outside, into the room where the Judges were, with threatening messages, especially against Mr. Burgess, and at last ten minutes were given them to organize in or leave; and as the time passed, persons outside would call out the number of minutes left, with threats against Burgess, if he did not agree to organize (118). At the end of that time, the Judges not being able to organize, left the room and the crowd proceeded to elect nine Judges and carry on the election (119). The Free-State men generally left the ground without voting, stating that there was no use in their voting there (120). The polls were so crowded during the first part of the day that the citizens could not get up to the window to vote (121). Threats were made against the Free-State men (122). In the afternoon the Rev. Mr. Gispatrick was attacked and driven off by the mob. A man, by some called "Texas," made a speech to the crowd urging them to vote and to remain on the ground until the polls were closed, for fear the abolitionists would come there in the afternoon and overpower them, and thus they would lose all their trouble.

For making an affidavit in a protest against this

(89) H. Burson, N. Ramsay, A. White, G. W. Umberger, E. C. Macey, Wm. Jessee, J. A. Wakefield. (90) N. Ramsay, J. M. Dunn, A. White, E. G. Macey, G. W. Umberger, Wm. Jessee, J. A. Wakefield. (91) E. G. Macey, G. W. Umberger, J. A. Wakefield. (92) F. Lahey. (92) J. C. Dunn, Wm. Jessee, J. Jones. (93) H. Burson, N. Ramsay, J. M. Dunn, J. N. Mace, A. White, E. G. Macey, W. Jessee. (94) N. Ramsay. (95) H. Burson, N. Ramsay, J. M. Dunn. (96) J. M. Dunn. (97) H. Burson, N. Ramsay, Wm. Jessee, J. N. Macey. (98) J. N. Macey, H. Muzzy. (99) J. M. Dunn, A. White, E. G. Macey, J. A. Wakefield. (100) J. M. Dunn, J. C. Dunn, A. White. (101) N. Ramsay. (102) J. C. Dunn, A. White. (103) A. White. (104) H. Burson. (105) H. Burson, J. N. Mace, H. Muzzy, Wm. Jessee, J. A. Wakefield (106) H. Burson. (107) S. Jones, J. A. Wakefield. (108) Daniel Woodman.

(109) F. E. Laley. (110) W. A. M. Vaughan, M. J. J. Mitchell, John Long. (111) H. B. Burgess. (112) The Rev. H. B. Burgess, Charles Jordan, James Hickey, L. O. Wilworth, D. H. Howe, J. M. Merrian, W. R. Baggs, W. A M. Vaughn. (113) John Long, L. O. Wilworth, George Holmes. (114) L. O. Wilworth. (115) A. W. Burgess. (116) H. B. Burgess, George Holmes. (117) H. B. Burgess, John Long, D. H. Horne. (118) H. B. Burgess, Charles Jordan, H. D. Horne. (119) H. B. Burgess, Charles Jordan, J. M. Merrian, Geo. Holmes. (120) H. B Burgess, C. Jordan, J. M. Merrian. (121) L. O. Wilworth. (122) C. Jordan.

election, setting forth the facts, Mr. Burgess was indicted by the Grand Jury for perjury, which indictment was found more than fifteen months ago, and is still pending, Mr. Burgess never having been informed who his accuser was or what was the testimony against him (123). A large majority, four to one, of the actual settlers of that district were Free-State men (124), and there cannot be the least doubt, if none but the actual settlers of the district had voted at that election, that the Free-State candidate would have been elected. The number of legal votes in the district, according to the census returns, was 101. The total number of votes cast was 372, and of these but thirty-two are on the returns, and from the testimony and records, we are satisfied that not over forty legal votes were cast at that election. A body of armed Missourians came into the district previous to the election, and encamped there (125). Before the time arrived for opening the polls, the Missourians went to another than the town appointed for the election; and one of the Judges appointed by the Governor, and two chosen by the Missourians, proceeded to open the polls and carry on the election (126). The Missourians said none but Pro-Slavery men should vote, and threatened to shoot any Free-State man who should come up to vote (127). Mr. Mockbee, one of the judges elected by the Missourians, had a store near the boundary fixed by the proclamation of the Governor, while he cultivated a farm in Missouri, where his family lived (128), and where his legal residence was then and is now. The Missourians also held a side-election for governor of the Territory, voting for Thomas Johnson of Shawnee Mission (129). The Free-State men finding the polls under the control of the non-residents, refused to, and did not, vote (130). They constituted a decided majority of the actual settlers (131). A petition signed by a majority of the residents of the district was sent to the Governor (132). The whole number of voters in this district, according to the census returns, was forty-seven; the number of votes cast was eighty, of whom but fifteen were residents, the number of residents whose names are on the census-rolls, who did not vote, was thirty-two.

For some days prior to the election, companies of men were organized in Jackson, Cass, and Clay counties, Mo., for the purpose of coming to the Territory and voting in this Vth district (133). The day previous to the election, some 400 or 500 Missourians, armed with guns, pistols, and knives, came into the Territory and camped, some at Bull Creek, and others at Potawatamie Creek (134.) Their camps were about sixteen miles apart. On the evening before the election, Judge Hamilton of the Cass County Court, Mo., came from the Potawatamie Creek camp to Bull Creek for sixty more Missourians, as they had not enough there to render the election certain, and about that number went down there with him (135). On the evening before the election, Dr. B. C. Westfall was elected to act as one of the Judges of Election in the Bull Creek precinct, in place of one of the Judges appointed by the Governor, who, it was said, would not be there the next day (136). Dr. Westfall was at that time a citizen of Jackson county, Mo. (137). On the morning of the election, the polls for Bull Creek precinct were opened, and, without swearing the Judges, they proceeded to receive the votes of all who offered to vote. For the sake of appearance they would get some one to come to the window and offer to vote, and when asked to be sworn he would pretend to grow angry at the Judges and would go away, and his name would be put down as having offered to vote, but "rejected, refusing to be sworn." This arrangement was made previously and perfectly understood by the Judges (138). But few of the residents of the district were present at the election, and only thirteen voted (139). The number of votes cast in the precinct was 393.

One Missourian voted for himself and then voted for his little son, but 10 or 11 years old (140). Col. Coffer, Henry Younger and Mr. Lykins, who were voted for and elected to the Legislature, were residents of Missouri at the time (141). Col. Coffer subsequently married in the Territory. After the polls were closed the returns were made, and a man, claiming to be a magistrate, certified on them that he had sworn the Judges of Election before opening the polls (142). In the Potawatamie precinct the Missourians attended the election, and after threatening Mr. Chesnut, the only Judge present appointed by the Governor, to induce him to resign, they proceeded to elect two other Judges—one a Missourian and the other a resident of another precinct of that District. The polls were then opened, and all the Missourians were allowed to vote without being sworn.

After the polls were closed, and the returns made out for the signature of the Judges, Mr. Chesnut refused to sign them, as he did not consider them correct returns of legal voters.

Col. Coffer, a resident of Missouri, but elected to the Kansas Legislature from that District at that election, endeavored with others to induce Mr. Chesnut by threats to sign the returns, which he refused to do, and left the House. On his way home he was fired at by some Missourians, though not injured (143). There were three illegal to one legal vote given there that day (144). At the Big Layer precinct, the Judges appointed by the Governor met at the time appointed, and proceeded to open the polls, after being duly sworn. After a few votes had been received, a party of Missourians came into the yard of the house where the election was held, and, unloading a wagon filled with arms, stacked their guns in the yard, and came up to the window and demanded to be admitted to vote. Two of the Judges decided to receive their votes, whereupon the third Judge, Mr. J. M. Arthur, resigned, and another was chosen in his place. Col. Young, a citizen of Missouri, but a candidate for, and elected to, the Territorial Legislative Council, was present and voted in the precinct. He claimed that all Missourians who were present on the day of election were entitled to vote. But thirty or forty of the citizens of the precinct were present, and many of them did not vote (145). At the Little Sugar precinct, the election seemed to have been conducted fairly, and there a Free-State majority was polled (146). From the testimony, the whole District appears to have been largely Free-State, and had none but actual settlers voted, the Free-State candidates would have been elected by a large majority. From a careful examination of the testimony and the records, we find that from 200 to 225 legal votes were polled out of 885,

(123) H. B. Burgess. (124) H. B. Burgess. (125) Perry Fuller, Peter Bassinger. (126) Perry Fuller, Wm. Moore, J. F. Javens. (127) J. F. Javens. (128) Wm. Moore, J. F. Javens, Thomas Mockbee. (129) Perry Fuller, William Moore. (130) Perry Fuller, Wm. Moore, J. F. Javens, T. Mockbee. (131) Perry Fuller, Wm. Moore, J. F. Javens. (132) Perry Fuller, J. F. Javens. (133) Dr. B. C. Westfall, Joseph M. Gearhart. (134) Dr. B. C. Westfall, Jessee W. Wilson, J. M. Gearhart. (135) Dr. B. C. Westfall. (136) Dr. B. C. Westfall. (137) Dr. B. Westfall, J. W. Wilson.

(138) Dr. B. C. Westfall. (139) J. W. Wilson. (140) Dr. B. C. Westfall, J. W. Wilson. (141) Dr. B. C. Westfall, J. M. Gearhart. (142) Dr. B. C. Westfall. (143) William Chestnut. (144) William Chestnut. (145) James M. Arthur. (146) S. W. Bouton.

the total number given in the precincts of the Vth District. Of the legal votes cast, the Free-State candidates received 152.

VITH DISTRICT—FORT SCOTT.

A company of citizens from Missouri, mostly from Bates County, came into this District the day before the election, some camping and others putting up at the public-house (147). They numbered from 100 to 200 (148), and came in wagons and on horseback, carrying their provisions and tents with them, and were generally armed with pistols. They declared their purpose to vote, and claimed the right to do so. They went to the polls generally in small bodies, with tickets in their hands, and many, if not all, voted. In some cases they declared that they had voted, and gave their reasons for so doing. Mr. Anderson, a Pro-Slavery candidate for the Legislature, endeavored to dissuade the non-residents from voting, because he did not wish the election contested (149). This person, however, insisted upon voting, and upon his right to vote, and did so. No one was challenged or sworn, and all voted who desired to. Out of 350 votes cast, not over 100 were legal, and but 64 of these named in the census taken one month before by Mr. Barber, the candidate for Council, voted. Many of the Free-State men did not vote, but your Committee is satisfied that, of the legal votes cast, the Pro-Slavery candidates received a majority. Mr. Anderson, one of these candidates, was an unmarried man, who came into the District from Missouri a few days before the election, and boarded at the public-house until the day after the election. He then took with him the poll-lists, and did not return to Fort Scott until the occasion of a barbecue the week before the election of October 1, 1855. He voted at that election, and after it left, and has not since been in the District. S. A. Williams, the other Pro-Slavery candidate, at the time of the election had a claim in the Territory, but his legal residence was not there until after the election.

VIITH DISTRICT.

From two to three hundred men, from the State of Missouri, came in wagons or on horseback to the election ground at Switzer's Creek, in the VIIth District, and encamped near the polls, on the day preceding the election. They were armed with pistols and other weapons, and declared their purpose to vote, in order to secure the election of Pro-Slavery members. They said they were disappointed in not finding more Yankees there, and that they had brought more men than were necessary to counterbalance their vote. A number of them wore badges of blue ribbon, with a motto, and the company were under the direction of leaders. They declared their intention to conduct themselves peacefully, unless the residents of the Territory atempted to stop them from voting. Two of the Judges of Election appointed by Governor Reeder, refused to serve, whereupon two others were appointed in their stead by the crowd of Missourians who surrounded the polls. The newly-appointed Judges refused to take the oath prescribed by Governor Reeder, but made one to suit themselves. Andrew Johnson requested each voter to swear if he had a claim in the Territory, and if he had voted in another District. The Judges did not take the oath prescribed, but were sworn to receive all legal votes. The Missourians voted without being sworn. They supported H. J. Stickler for Council, and M. W. McGee for Representative. They left the evening of the election. Some of them started on horseback for Lawrence, as they said they could be there before night, and all went the way they came. The census-list shows 53 legal voters in the District. 253 votes were cast; of these 25 were residents, 17 of whom were in the District when the census was taken (150). Some of the residents present at the polls did not vote, declaring it useless. Candidates declined to run on the Free-State ticket because they were unwilling to run the risk of so unequal a contest—it being known that a great many were coming up from Missouri to vote (151). Nearly all the settlers were Free-State men, and 23 of the 25 legal votes given were cast for the only Free-State candidate running. Mobiller McGee, who was declared elected Representative, had a claim—a saw-mill and a house in the Territory—and he was there part of the time. But his legal residence is now, and was then, near Westport, in Missouri, where he owns and conducts a valuable farm, and where his family resides.

VIIITH DISTRICT.

This was attached to the VIIth District for a member of the Council and a representative, and its vote was controlled by the illegal vote cast there. The census shows 39 votes in it—37 votes were cast, of whom a majority voted the Free-State ticket.

IXTH DISTRICT.

Fort Riley and Pawnee are in this District. The latter place was selected by the Governor as the temporary capital, and he designed there to expend the sums appropriated by Congress in the construction of suitable houses for the Legislature. A good deal of building was then being done at the fort near by. For these reasons a number of mechanics, mostly from Pennsylvania came into this district in March, 1855, to seek employment. Some of these voted at the election. The construction of the capital was first postponed, then abandoned, and finally the site of the town was declared by the Secretary of War to be within the military reservation of Fort Riley. Some of the inhabitants returned to the States, and some went to other parts of the Territory. Your Committee find that they came as settlers, intending to remain as such, and were entitled to vote (152).

XTH DISTRICT.

In this district ten persons belonging to the Wyandot tribe of Indians voted. They were of that class who under the law were entitled to vote, but their residence was in Wyandot Village, at the mouth of Kansas River, and they had no right to vote in this district. They voted the Pro-Slavery ticket (153). Eleven men recently from Pennsylvania voted the Free-State Ticket. From the testimony, they had not, at the time of the election, so established their residence as to have entitled them to vote (154). In both these classes of cases the judges examined the voters under oath and allowed them to vote, and in all respects the election seems to have been conducted fairly. The rejection of both would not have changed the result. This and the VIIIth Election-District formed one representative district, and was the only one to which the invasion from Missouri did not extend.

XITH DISTRICT.

The IXth, Xth, and XIth and XIIth Election-Districts, being all sparsely settled, were attached

(147) John Hamilton. (148) John Hamilton, E. B. Cook, F B. Arnett. (149) J. C. Anderson.

(150) James A. Stewart, Mr. H. Rose. (151) Wm. F. Johnstone. (152) Andrew McConnell, R. W. Wilson, A. H. Reeder. (153) M. A. Garrett, Joseph Stewart. (154) N. J. Osborn, Isaac Hascall.

together as a Council-District, and the XIth and XIIth as a Representative District. This Election-District is 60 miles north from Pawnee, and 150 miles from Kansas City. It is the northwest settlement in the Territory, and contained, when the census was taken, but 36 inhabitants, of whom 24 were voters. There was on the day of election no white settlement about Marysville, the place of voting, for 40 miles, except that Marshall and Bishop kept a store and ferry at the crossing of the Big Blue and the California road (155). Your Committee were unable to procure witnesses from this district. Persons who were present at the election were duly summoned by an officer, and among them was F. J. Marshall, the member of the House from that district. On his return the officer was arrested and detained, and persons bearing the names of some of the witnesses summoned were stopped near Lecompton, and did not appear before the Committee. The returns show that, in defiance of the Governor's proclamation, the voting was *viva voce*, instead of by ballot. 328 names appear upon the poll-books, as voting, and by comparing these names with those on the census-rolls, we find that but seven of the latter voted. The person voted for as Representative, F. J. Marshall, was chief owner of the store at Marysville, and was there sometimes (156), but his family lived in Weston. John Donaldson, the candidate voted for for the Council, then lived in Jackson County, Missouri (157).

On the day after the election, Mr. Marshall, with 25 or 30 men from Weston, Mo., was on the way from Marysville, to the State. Some of the party told a witness who had formerly resided at Weston, that they were up at Marysville and carried the day for Missouri, and that they had voted about 150 votes. Mr. Marshall paid the bill at that point for the party.

There does not appear to have been any emigration into that district in March, 1855, after the census was taken, and judging from the best test in the power of your Committee, there were but seven legal votes cast in the district, and 321 illegal.

XIITH DISTRICT.

The election in this district was conducted fairly. No complaint was made that illegal votes were cast.

XIIITH DISTRICT.

Previous to the day of election, several hundreds of Missourians from Platte, Clay, Boone, Clinton, and Howard counties, came into the district in wagons and on horseback, and camped there (158). They were armed with guns, revolvers, and bowie-knives, and had badges of hemp in their button-holes and elsewhere about their persons (159). They claimed to have a right to vote, from the fact that they were there on the ground, and had, or intended to make, claims in the Territory, although their families were in Missouri (160).

The judges appointed by the governor opened the polls, and some persons offered to vote, and when their votes were rejected on the ground that they were not residents of the district, the crowd threatened to tear the house down if the judges did not leave (161). The judges then withdrew, taking the poll-books with them (162). The crowd then proceeded to select other persons to act as judges, and the election went on (163). Those persons voting who were sworn were asked if they considered themselves residents of the district, and if they said they did, they were allowed to vote (164). But few of the residents were present and voted (165), and the Free-State men, as a general thing, did not vote (166). After the Missourians got through voting, they returned home (167). A formal return was made by the judges of election setting out the facts, but it was not verified. The number of legal voters in this district was 96, of whom a majority were Free-State men. Of these — voted. The total number of votes cast was 296.

XIVTH DISTRICT.

It was generally rumored in this district, for some days before the election, that the Missourians were coming over to vote (168). Previous to the election, men from Missouri came into the district, and electioneered for the Pro-Slavery candidates (169). Gen. David R. Atchison and a party controlled the nominations in one of the primary elections (170).

BURR OAK PRECINCT.

Several hundred Missourians from Buchanan, Platte, and Andrew Counties, Mo., including a great many of the prominent citizens of St. Joseph, came into this precinct the day before, and on the day of election, in wagons and on horse, and encamped there (171). Arrangements were made for them to cross the ferry at St. Joseph free of expense to themselves (172). They were armed with bowie-knives and pistols, guns and rifles (173). On the morning of the election, the Free-State candidates resigned in a body, on account of the presence of the large number of armed Missourians, at which the crowd cheered and hurrahed (174). Gen. B. F. Stringfellow was present, and was prominent in promoting the election of the Pro-Slavery ticket, as was also the Hon. Willard P. Hall, and others of the most prominent citizens of St. Joseph, Mo. (175). But one of the judges of election, appointed by the governor, served on that day, and the crowd chose two others to supply the vacancies (176).

The Missourians said they came there to vote for, and secure the election of, Major Wm. P. Richardson (177). Major Richardson, elected to the Council, had had a farm in Missouri, where his wife and daughter lived with his son-in-law, Willard P. Hall, he himself generally going home to Missouri every Saturday night. The farm was generally known as the Richardson farm. He had a claim in the Territory upon which was a saw-mill, and where he generally remained during the week (178).

Some of the Missourians gave as their reason for voting that they had heard that eastern emigrants were to be at that election (179), though no eastern emigrants were there (180). Others

---

(155) Augustus Baker. (156) Augustus Baker. (157) J. E. D'Aris. (158) J. B. Ross, W. H. Godwin, Dr. James Noble, T. A. Minard, Chas. Hardh. (159) J. B. Ross, W. H. Godwin. (160) J. B. Ross, Dr. J. Noble. (161) J. B. Ross, Charles Hardh, A. B. Sharp. (162) J. B. Ross, C. Hardh. (163) J. B. Ross, W. H. Godwin, Dr. J. Noble, R. Chandler, T. A. Minard, C. Hardh, G. M. Dyer, O. B. Tebbs.

(164) R. Chandler. (165) J. B. Ross, Dr. J. Noble. (166) J. B. Ross, Dr. J. Noble, R. Chandler, C. Hardh, O. B. Tebbs. (167) J. B. Ross, Dr. J. Noble. (168) B. Harding, John H. Whitehead, A. Larzelier. (169) Benj. Harding, Willard P. Hall, Dr. G. A. Cutler. (170) Dr. G. A. Cutler. (171) A. A. Jamieson, W. R. Richardson, Benj. Harding, J. H. Whitehead, J. R. Carter, A. Larzelier, Willard P. Hall, B. H. Brock, C. W. Stewart, A. M. Mitchell, H S. Creel, G. W. Gillespie. (172) L. Dillon, G. W. Gillespie. (173) A. A. Jamieson, Willard P. Hall, C. W. Stewart. (174) A. A. Jamieson, W. P. Richardson, Benj. Harding, J. H. Whitehead, A. Larzelier, Willard P. Hall, J. P. Blair. (175) A. A. Jamieson, W. P. Richardson, J. H. Whitehead. Willard P. Hall (176) A. A. Jamieson, Benjamin Harding, J. H. Witehead, A. Larzelier, O. Hulan. (177) A. A. Jamieson, W. P. Hall. (178) A. A. Jamieson, W. P. Richardson, W. P. Hall. (179) W. P. Richardson, J. H. Whitehead, J. R. Carter, W. P. Hall, A. M. Mitchell, H S. Creel. (180) B. Harding, J. H. Whitehead, J. R. Carter, W. P. Hall.

said they were going to vote for the purpose of making Kansas a Slave State (181).

Some claimed that they had a right to vote, under the provisions of the Kansas-Nebraska bill, from the fact that they were present on the ground on the day of election (182).

The Free-State men generally did not vote (183), and those who did vote, voted generally for John H. Whitehead, Pro-Slavery, for Council, against Major Wm. P. Richardson, and did not vote at all for members of the Lower House (184).

The parties were pretty nearly equally divided in the district, some being of opinion that the Free-State party had a small majority (185), and others that the Pro-Slavery party had a small majority (186). After the election was over, and the polls were closed, the Missourians returned home. During the day they had provisions and liquor served out, free of expense to all (187).

Doniphan Precinct.

The evening before the election some 200 or more Missourians from Platte, Buchanan, Saline, and Clay counties, Missouri, came into this precinct, with tents, music, wagons, and provisions, and armed with guns, rifles, pistols, and bowie-knives, and encamped about two miles from the place of voting (188). They said they came to vote, to make Kansas a Slave State, and intended to return to Missouri after they had voted (189).

On the morning of the election the Judges appointed by the Governor would not serve, and others were appointed by the crowd (190). The Missourians were allowed to vote without being sworn (191)—some of them voting as many as eight or nine times; changing their hats and coats and giving in different names each time (192). After they had voted they returned to Missouri (193). The Free-State men generally did not vote (194), though constituting a majority in the precinct (195). Upon counting the ballots in the box and the names on the poll-lists, it was found that there were too many ballots (196), and one of the judges of election took out ballots enough to make the two numbers correspond (197).

Wolf River Precinct.

But few Missourians were present in this precinct, though some of them threatened one of the judges, because he refused to receive their votes, and when he resigned another was chosen in his place, who consented to receive their votes (198).

Protests were drawn up against the elections in the various precincts in the XIVth District, but on account of threats that greater numbers of Missourians would be at a new election should it be called, and of personal violence to those who should take part in the protest, it was not presented to the Governor (199). Major Richardson, the Pro-Slavery candidate for Council, threatened Dr. Cutler, the Free-State candidate, that if he contested the election he and his office should be put in the Missouri River (200).

The number of votes in the district by the census was 334—of these 124 voted. The testimony shows that quite a number of persons whose legal residence was in the populous county of Buchanan, Mo., on the opposite side of the river, had claims in the Territory. Some ranged cattle, and others marked out their claim and built a cabin, and sold this incipient title where they could. They were not residents of the Territory in any just or legal sense. A number of settlers moved into the district in the month of March. Your Committee are satisfied, after a careful analysis of the records and testimony, that the number of legal votes cast did not exceed 200—out of 727.

XVth District.

The election in this district was held in the house of a Mr. Hayes. On the day of election a crowd of from 400 to 500 men (201) collected around the polls, of which the great body were citizens of Missouri. One of the Judges of Election, in his testimony (202), states that the strangers commenced crowding around the polls, and that then the residents left. Threats were made before and during the election day that there should be no Free-State candidates, although there were nearly or quite as many Free-State as Pro-Slavery men resident in the district. Most of the crowd were drinking and carousing, cursing the Abolitionists and threatening the only Free-State Judge of Election. A majority of those who voted wore hemp in their buttonholes (203) and their pass-word was, "all right on the hemp." Many of the Missourians were known and are named by the witnesses. Several speeches were made by them at the polls, and among those who spoke were Major Oliver, one of your Committee, Col. Burns, and Lalan Williams of Platte County. Major Oliver urged upon all present to use no harsh words, and expressed the hope that nothing would be said or done to harm the feelings of the most sensitive on the other side. He gave some grounds, based on the Missouri Compromise, in regard to the right of voting, and was understood to excuse the Missourians for voting. Your Committee are satisfied that he did not vote. Col. Burns recommended all to vote, and he hoped none would go home without voting. Some of the Pro-Slavery residents were much dissatisfied at the interference with their rights by the Missourians, and for that reason—because reflection convinced them that it would be better to have Kansas a Free-State—they "fell over the fence" (204). The judges requested the voters to take an oath that they were actual residents. They objected at first, some saying they had a claim, or "I am here." But the Free-State Judge insisted upon the oath, and his associates, who at first were disposed to waive it, coincided with him, and the voters all took it after some grumbling. One said he cut him some poles and laid them in the shape of a square, and that made him a claim; and another said that he had cut him a few sticks of wood, and that made him a claim. The Free-State men did not vote, although they believed their numbers to be equal to the Pro-Slavery settlers, and some claimed that they had the majority. They were deterred by threats throughout by the Missourians, before and on the day of election, from putting up candidates, and no candidates were run, for this reason—that there was

(181) W. P. Hall, H. S. Creel. (182) B. H. Brock, C. W. Stewart, H. S. Creel. (183) A. A. Jamieson, W. P. Richardson, J. H. Whitehead, A. Larzelier, C. W. Stewart, H. S. Creel. (184) W. P. Richardson, C. B. Whitehead. (185) A. A. Jamieson, B. Harding, A. Larzelier, C. W. Stewart. (186) S. P. Richardson, J. H. Whitehead, W. P. Hall, Thos. W. Watterson, J. P. Blair. (187) W. P. Richardson, G. W. Gillespie. (188) Richard Tuck, Eli Hamilton, John Landis, Luther Dickerson, J. W. Beattie, David Fizer. (189) R. Tuck, L. Dickerson, J. W. Beattie. (190) R. Tuck, E. Hamilton, J. Landis. (191) R. Tuck, E. Hamilton, David Fizer. (192) R. Tuck. (193) R. Tuck, E. Hamilton, J. Landis, L. Dickerson. (194) John Landis. (195) R. Tuck, John Landis. (196) E. Hamilton, J. F. Foreman. (197 E. Hamilton. (198) Dr. G. A. Cutler. (199) Dr. G. A. Cutler, John Landis, A. A. Jamieson.

(200) Dr. G. A. Cutler. (201) J. B. Crane. (202) E. R. Zimmerman. (203) E. R. Zimmerman, Joseph Potter. (204) E. R. Zimmerman.

a credited rumor previously that the Missourians would control the election. The Free-State Judge was threatened with expulsion from the polls, and a young man thrust a pistol into the window through which the votes were received. The whole number of votes cast was 417; of the names on the poll-book but 62 are in the census-rolls, and the testimony shows that a small portion, estimated by one witness at one-quarter of the legal voters, voted. Your Committee estimate the number of legal voters at 80. One of the judges referred to, certified to the Governor that the election was fairly conducted. It was not contested because no one would take the responsibility of doing it, as it was not considered safe, and that if another election was had, the residents would fare no better.

XVIth District.

For some time previous to the election, meetings were held and arrangements made in Missouri to get up companies to come over to the Territory and vote (205), and the day before and on the day of election, large bodies of Missourians from Platte, Clay, Ray, Charlton, Carrol, Clinton, and Saline Counties, Mo., came into this district and camped there (206). They were armed with pistols and bowie-knives, and some with guns and rifles (207), and had badges of hemp in their button-holes and elsewhere about their persons (208).

On the morning of the election there were from 1,000 to 1,400 persons present on the ground (209). Previous to the election, Missourians endeavored to persuade the two Free-State judges to resign by making threats of personal violence to them (210), one of whom resigned on the morning of election, and the crowd chose another to fill his place (211). But one of the judges, the Free-State judge, would take the oath prescribed by the Governor, the other two deciding that they had no right to swear any one who offered to vote, but that all on the ground were entitled to vote (212). The only votes refused were some Delaware Indians, some 30 Wyandot Indians being allowed to vote (213).

One of the Free-State candidates withdrew in consequence of the presence of the Missourians, amid cheering and acclamations by the Missourians (214). During the day, the steamboat New Lucy came down from Western Missouri, with a large number of Missourians on board, who voted and then returned on the boat (215).

The Missourians gave as a reason for their coming over to vote, that the North had tried to force emigration into the Territory, and they wanted to counteract that movement (216). Some of the candidates and many of the Missourians took the ground that, under the Kansas-Nebraska act, all who were on the ground on the day of election were entitled to vote (217), and others, that laying out a town, staking a lot, or driving down stakes, even on another man's claim, gave them a right to vote.

And one of the members (218) of the Council, R. R. Rees, declared in his testimony that he who should put a different construction upon the law must be either a knave or a fool.

The Free-State men generally did not vote at that election (219); and no newly-arrived Eastern emigrants were there (220). The Free-State Judge of Election refused to sign the returns until the words "by lawful resident voters" were stricken out, which was done, and the returns made in that way (221). The election was contested, and a new election ordered by Gov. Reeder for the 22d of May.

The testimony is divided as to the relative strength of parties in this district. The whole number of voters in the district, according to the census returns, was 385; and, according to a very carefully-prepared list of voters, prepared for the Pro-Slavery candidates and other Pro-Slavery men, a few days previous to the election, there were 305 voters in the district, including those who had claims but did not live on them (222). The whole number of votes cast was 964. Of these named in the census 106 voted. Your Committee, upon careful examination, are satisfied that there were not over 150 legal votes cast, leaving 814 illegal votes.

XVIIth District.

The election in this district seems to have been fairly conducted, and not contested at all. In this district the Pro-Slavery party had the majority.

XVIIIth District.

Previous to the election, Gen. David R. Atchison of Platte City, Mo., got up a company of Missourians, and passing through Weston, Mo., (223) went over into the Territory. He remained all night at the house of ———, and then exhibited his arms, of which he had an abundance. He proceeded to the Nemohaer (XVIIIth) District (224). On his way, he and his party attended a Nominating Convention in the XIVth District, and proposed and caused to be nominated a set of candidates in opposition to the wishes of the Pro-Slavery residents of the district (225). At that Convention he said that there were 1,100 men coming over from Platte County, and if that wasn't enough they could send 5,000 more—that they came to vote, and would vote or kill every G—d d—d Abolitionist in the Territory (226).

On the day of election, the Missourians under Atchison, who were encamped there, came up to the polls in the XVIIIth District, taking the oath that they were residents of the district. The Missourians were all armed with pistols or bowie-knives, and said there were 60 in their company (227). But 17 votes given on that day were given by residents of the district (228). The whole number of votes was 62.

R. L. Kirk, one of the candidates, came into the district from Missouri about a week before the election, and boarded there (229). He left after the election, and was not at the time a legal resident of the district in which he was elected. No protest was sent to the Governor on account of threats made against any who should dare to contest the election (230). The following tables embody the result of the examination of your Committee in regard to this election. In some of the districts it was impossible to ascertain

(205) H. Miles Moore, A. McAuley, L. Kerr. (206) David Brown, T. A. Hart, G. F. Warren, R. R. Rees, A. Russell, P. R. Orr, L. J. Eastin, A. Fisher, M. France, H. M. Moore. (207) D. Brown, E. A. Hart, G. F. Warren, A. Fisher, H. M. Moore, W. G. Matthias. (208) F. A. Hart, L. J. Eastin, M. France, W. H. Adams, H. M. Moore. (209) F. A. Hart, T. A. Minard, G. F. Warren, R. R. Rees, A. J. Pattie, W. G. Matthias. (210) D. Brown, M. France. (211) D. Brown, F. A. Hart, M. France. (212) M. France. (213) M. France. (214) F. A. Hart, L. J. Farin, W. H. Adams. (215) D. Brown, F. A. Hart, T. A. Minard, G. F. Warren, R. R. Rees, S. J. Bastin, A. T. Kyle, D. J. Johnson, M. France, A. T. Pattie, H. M. Moore. (216) H. R. Rees, L. J. Eastin, W H. Adams, H. M. Moore. (217) D. Brown, T. A. Minard, G. F. Warren, R. R. Rees, H. M. Moore.

(218) D. Brown. T. A. Hart. (219) D. Brown, E. A. Minard, G. F Warren, F. A. Hart, M. France, H. M. Moore. (220) L. J. Eastin, M. France, W. H. Adams. (221) L. J. Eastin. M. France, W. H. Adams. (222) L. J. Eastin, A. McAuley. (223) H. Niles Moore. (224) Dr. G. A. Cutler, Amer Groom. (225) Dr. G. A. Cutler. (226) Dr. G. A. Cutler. (227) D. H. Baker, John Belew. (228) D. H. Baker, John Belew. (229) John Belew. (230) Dr. G. A. Cutler.

the precise number of the legal votes cast, and especially in the XIVth, XVth and XVIth Districts. In such cases the number of legal and illegal votes cast is stated, after a careful re-examination of all the testimony and records concerning the election:

ABSTRACT OF ELECTION OF MARCH 30, 1855, BY COUNCIL DISTRICTS.

No. of Council District.	No. of Election District	Precincts.	Voters in Election Dists	No. of Voters by Census in Council Districts	No. of Councilmen	Pro-Slavery Candidates.	No. of Voters for them in Election District	Total Voters in Council Districts for them	Free State Candidates.	No. of Votes for them in Election District	Total Votes in Council District for them	Scattering	Total Votes cast in Election District	Total Votes cast in Council District	No. of Legal Votes in Election District	No. of Illegal Votes in Election District	No. of Legal Votes in Council District	No. of Illegal Votes in Council District	No. Councilmen elected by Illegal Votes	*Probable Result if no Invasion.*
1	1	Lawrence	369	466	2	Thos. Johnson	780		Joel K. Goodwin	254		1	1024		232	802			2	Free-State.
						Ed. Chapman	783		S. N. Wood	255										
	4	Chapman's	47			Thos. Johnson	78		Joel K. Goodwin	2			80		15	65				
						Ed. Chapman	78		S. N. Wood	2										
	17		50			Thos. Johnson	42		Joel K. Goodwin	16			59		59		356	827		
						Ed Chapman	43	900	S. N. Wood	16	273	10		1183						
2	2		212	212	1	A. McDonald	318	318	J. A. Wakefield	12	12		330	330	25	316	25	316	1	
3	3		101	193	1	H. J. Strickler	370		A. McDonald	4			374		32	338				
	7	Titus's	53			H. J. Strickler	211		Wm. F. Johnson	23			234		25	209				
	8		39			H. J. Strickler	17	598	—— Rice	17	44	3	37	612	37		94	547		
4	5	Bull Creek	412	442	2	A. M. Coffee	377		M. G. Morris	9										
						David Lykins	376		James P. Fox	9			393		13	330				
		Pottawatamie				A. M. Coffee	199		M. G. Morris	65										
						David Lykins	199		James P. Fox	63			266		75	191				
		Big Sugar Creek				A. M. Coffee	74		M. G. Morris	17										
						David Lykins	74		James P. Fox	16			91		32	59				
		Little Sugar Creek				A. M. Coffee	31		M. G. Morris	62										
						David Lykins	34	680	James P. Fox	70	156	17	855	855	105		225	630	2	Free-State.
5	6		253	253	1	Wm. Barbee	343	343					343	343	100	243	100	243		Pro-Slavery.
6	9		36	201	1	John Donaldson	23		M. F. Conway	50		2	75		75					
	10	Big Blue	63			John Donaldson	27		M. F. Conway	42			69		48	21				
		Rock Creek				John Donaldson	2		M. F. Conway	21			23		23					
	11	Marysville	24			John Donaldson	328		M. F. Conway	3			331		7	324				
	12	Silver Lake	78			John Donaldson	12		M. F. Conway	19			31		31					
		St. Mary's				John Donaldson	4	396	M. F. Conway	7	140		11	568	11		195	345	1	Free-State.
7	14	Wolf River	219	247	1	John W. Foreman	74								72	2				
		Doniphan				John W. Foreman	343								186	160				
	18		28			John W. Foreman	61	478						478	17	45	275	207		Pro-Slavery.
8	14	Burr Oak	215	215	1	Wm. P. Richardson	234	234	Jno. W. Whitehead	68	68		302	302	140	166	140	166		Doubtful.
9	15		208	208	1	D. A. M. Grover	411	411				1	412	412	80	332	80	332		Pro-Slavery.
10	13		83	468	2	R. R. Reese	233		B. H. Twombly	6										
						L. J. Eastin	233		A. J. Whitney	6			242		12	230				Doubtful.
	16		385			R. R. Reese	896		B. H. Twombly	60										
						L. J. Eastin	893	1129	A. J. Whitney	59	66		964	1206	150	814	162	1044		
				2905	13			5487			861	35		6289						

ABSTRACT OF ELECTION OF MARCH 30, 1855, BY REPRESENTATIVE DISTRICTS.

of Rep. Dist.	of Elec. Dist.	Precincts and Places of Voting.	oters by cen- in Election rict	oters by cen- n Represent- District	Represent'vs	Pro-Slavery Candidates.	of Votes for m in Election rict	Votes for n in Repre- ative District	Free-State Candidates.	of Votes for m in Election trict	al Votes for m in Repre- tative District	ttering	al Votes cast Election Dist.	al Votes cast Representative trict	Legal Votes Election Dist.	Illegal Votes Election Dist.	Legal Votes Represent'tive trict	Illegal Votes Represent'tive trict	Represent'es ed by Ille- Votes
1	4	Dr. Chapman's	47	97	1	A. S. Johnson	77		A. F. Powell	3			80		15	65			
	17	Shawnee Mission	50			A. S. Johnson	43	120	A. F. Powell	18	19	3	59	139	59		74	65	
2	1	Lawrence	369	389	3	James Whitlock	780		J. Hutchinson	252									
						J. M. Banks	781		E. D. Ladd	253									
3	2	Bloomington	212	212	2	A. B. Wade	781	781	P. P. Fowler	254	253	10	1034	1034	232	302	232	802	3
						G. W. Ward	318		Isaac Davis	12									
4	3	Tecumseh	101	101	1	O. H. Brown	318	318	E. G. Macy	12	12	11	341	341	25	316	25	316	2
5	7	J. B. Titus's	53	92	1	D. L. Croysdale	366	366	C. K. Holliday	4	4	1	370	370	32	338	32	338	1
						M. W. McGee	210		A. J. Baker	1									
	8	Council Grove	39						H. Rice	23			234						
6	6	Fort Scott	253	253	2	M. W. McGee	12	222	A. J. Baker	25	49		37	271	25	209			
						Joseph C. Anderson	315		John Hamilton	35					37		62	209	1
7	5	Bull Creek	442	442	4	S. A. Williams	313	315	W. Margraves	16	35		350	350					
						W. A. Haskell	377		John Serpell	9							100	250	
						Allen Wilkinson	375		Adam Pore	9									
						Henry Younger	375		S. H. Houser	9									
		Potawatamie Creek				Samuel Scott	377	(377)	Wm. Jennings	9		7	(393)		13	380			
						Wm. A. Haskell	198		John Serpell	61									
						Allen Wilkinson	198		Adam Pore	54									
						Henry Younger	198		S. H. Houser	64									
		Big Sugar Creek				Samuel Scott	198	(198)	Wm. Jennings	62		6	(266)		75	191			
						W. A. Haskell	74		John Serpell	17									
						Allen Wilkinson	74		Adam Poee	16									
						Henry Younger	74		S. H. Houser	17									
		Little Sugar Creek				Samuel Scott	74	(74)	Wm. Jennings	17			(91)		32	59			
						W. A. Haskell	33		John Serpell	62									
						Allen Wilkinson	32	(35)	Adam Pore	62			(105)						
						Henry Younger	35		S. H. Houser	64									
8	9	Pawnee	36	99	1	Samuel Scott	35	684	Wm. Jennings	66	152	4	855	855	104		224	630	4
	10	Big Blue	63			Russell Garrett	18		S. D. Houston	56			75		75				
		Rock Creek				Russell Garrett	21		S. D. Houston	43			69		59	10			
9	11		24	102	1	Russell Garrett	2	41	S. D. Houston	21	120	6	23	167	23		156	10	1
	12	Silver Lake	78			Fr. J. Marshall	328						328		7	321			
		St. Mary's				Fr. J. Marshall	12		H. McCartney	19			31						
10	13	Hickory Point	83	83	1	Fr. J. Marshall	11	344	P. McCartney	7	26	4	11	270	46		58	321	1
11	14	Wolf River	219	247	2	Wm. H. Tibbs	237	237	C. Hart (Hard?)	3			242	242	12	230	12	230	1
						J. H. Stringfellow	57		G. A. Cutler	15									
						R. L. Kirk	52		Jno. Landis	8									
		Doniphan							J. Ryan	8		1	78		76	2			
						J. H. Stringfellow	313		G. A. Cutler	30									
						R. L. Kirk	292		John Landis	25									
	18	Nemaha	28						Joel Ryan	18		6	346		186	160			
						J. H. Stringfellow	48		G. A. Cutler	14									
12	14	Burr Oak	215	215	2	R. L. Kirk	50	420	John Landis	13	54	1	62	486	17	45	279	206	
						Joel P. Blair	256		John Fee	2									
13	15		208	208	2	T. W. Waterson	258	258					303		140	166	140	166	
						H. B. C. Harris	412												
14	16	Leavenworth	385	385	3	J. Weddell	412	412					417	417	80	332	80	332	
						Wm G. Matthias	899		Felix G. Bradin	59									
						H. D. McMeekin	897		Samuel France	59									
						Archy Paine	895	897	F. Browning	59	59		964	964	150	814	150	814	

ABSTRACT OF CENSUS, AND RETURNS OF ELECTION OF MARCH 30, 1855, BY ELECTION DISTRICTS.

Number of District	Place of Voting.	Pro-Slavery Votes	Free-State Votes	Scattering	Total	Total of Legal Votes	Total of Illegal Votes	Census. No. persons resd'ts	Census. No. of Voters	C'cl. No. of District	C'cl. No. of Members	H'se. No. of District	H'se. No. of Members
1	Lawrence	781	253	—	1034	232	802	962	369	1	2	2	3
2	Bloomington	318	12	11	341	30	316	519	199	2	1	3	2
3	Stinson's, or Tecumseh	366	4	2	372	32	338	252	101	3	1	4	1
4	Dr. Chapman's	78	2	—	80	15	65	177	47	1	—	1	1
5	Bull Creek	377	9	—	386	13	380	—	—	—	—	—	—
	Potawatamie	199	65	—	264	75	191	—	—	—	—	—	—
	Big Sugar Creek	74	17	7	98	32	59	1407	442	4	2	7	4
	Little Sugar Creek	34	70	—	104	104	—	—	—	—	—	—	—
6	Fort Scott	315	35	—	350	100	250	810	253	5	1	6	2
7	Isaac B. Titus	211	23	—	234	25	209	118	58	3	—	5	1
8	Council Grove	17	17	3	37	37	—	83	39	3	—	5	
9	Pawnee	23	52	—	75	75	—	86	36	6	1	8	1
10	Big Blue	27	42	—	69	48	21	151	63	10	—	8	—
	Rock Creek	2	21	—	23	23	—	—	—	8	—	8	—
11	Marysville	328	—	—	328	7	321	36	24	9	—	9	1
12	St. Mary's	4	7	—	11	11	—	—	—	10	—	9	—
	Silver Lake	12	19	2	33	33	—	144	78	1	—	9	—
13	Hickory Point	233	6	—	239	12	230	284	96	10	—	10	1
14	Doniphan	313	30	3	346	—	—	—	—	7	—	11	—
	Wolf Creek	57	15	6	78	200	530	1167	334	7	1	11	2
	Burr-Oak, Hodge's	256	2	48	306	—	—	—	—	8	—	12	2
15	Hayes	412	—	5	417	80	337	873	208	9	1	13	2
16	Leavenworth	899	60	5	964	150	814	1183	385	10	2	14	3
17	Gum Springs	43	16	—	59	59	—	150	50	1	—	—	—
18	Moonestown	48	14	—	62	17	45	99	28	7	1	—	—
	Total	5427	791	92	6320	1310	4968	3501	2892	—	13	—	26

Your Committee report the following facts not shown by the tables:

Of the twenty-nine hundred and five voters named in the census-rolls, eight hundred and thirty-one are found on the poll-books. Some of the settlers were prevented from attending the election by the distance of their homes from the polls; but the great majority were deterred by the open avowal that large bodies of armed Missourians would be at the polls to vote, and by the fact that they did so appear and control the election. The same causes deterred the Free-State settlers from running candidates in several districts, and in others induced the candidates to withdraw.

The poll-books of the IId and VIIIth districts were lost; but the proof is quite clear that, in the IId district, there were thirty, and in the VIIIth district thirty-eight legal votes, making a total of eight hundred and ninety-eight legal voters of the Territory, whose names are on the census-returns, and yet the proof, in the state in which we are obliged to present it, after excluding illegal votes, leaves the total vote of 1,310, showing a discrepancy of 412. The discrepancy is accounted for in two ways: First, the coming in of settlers before the March election, and after the census was taken, or settlers who were omitted in the census; or secondly, the disturbed state of the Territory while we were investigating the elections in some of the districts, thereby preventing us from getting testimony in relation to the names of legal voters at the time of election.

If the election had been confined to the actual settlers undeterred by the presence of non-residents, or the knowledge that they would be present in numbers sufficient to out-vote them, the testimony indicates that the council would have been composed of seven in favor of making Kansas a Free State, elected from the Ist, IId, IIId, IVth, and VIth, council-districts. The result in the VIIIth, and Xth, electing three members, would have been doubtful, and the Vth, VIIth, and IXth would have elected three Pro-Slavery members.

Under like circumstances the House of Representatives would have been composed of fourteen members in favor of making Kansas a Free State, elected from the IId, IIId, IVth, Vth, VIIth, VIIIth, IXth, and Xth representative-districts.

The result in the XIIth and XIVth representative-districts, electing five members, would have been doubtful, and the Ist, VIth, XIth, and XVth districts would have elected seven Pro-Slavery members.

By the election, as conducted, the Pro-Slavery candidates in every district but the VIIIth representative-district, received a majority of the votes; and several of them, in both the Council and the House, did not "reside in" and were not "inhabitants of" the district for which they were elected, as required by the organic law. By that act it was declared to be the true intent and meaning of this act to leave the people thereof perfectly free to form and regulate their domestic institutions in their own way, subject to the Constitution of the United States.

So careful was Congress of the right of popular sovereignty, that to secure it to the people, without a single petition from any portion of the country, they removed the restriction against Slavery imposed by the Missouri Compromise. And yet this right, so carefully secured, was thus by force and fraud overthrown by a portion of the people of an adjoining State.

The striking difference between this Republic and other Republics on this Continent, is not in the provisions of Constitutions and laws, but that here changes in the administration of those laws have been made peacefully and quietly through the ballot-box. This invasion is the first and only one in the history of our Government, by which an organized force from one State has elected a Legislature for another State or Territory, and as such it should have been resisted by the whole executive power of the National Government.

Your Committee are of the opinion that the Constitution and laws of the United States have invested the President and Governor of the Territory with ample power for this purpose. They could only act after receiving authentic information of the facts, but when received, whether before or after the certificates of election were granted, this power should have been exercised to its fullest extent. It is not to be tolerated that a legislative body thus selected should assume or exercise any legislative functions; and their enactments should be regarded as null and void; nor should the question of its legal existence as a legislative body be determined by itself, as that would be allowing the criminal to judge of his own crime. In section twenty-two of the organic act it is provided, that "the persons having the highest number of legal votes in each of said Council-districts for members of the Council, shall be declared by the Governor to be duly elected to the Council, and the persons having the highest number of legal votes for the House of Representatives, shall be declared by the Governor duly elected members of said House." The proclamation of the Governor required a verified notice of a contest when one was made, to be filed with him within four days after the election. Within that time he did not obtain information as to force or fraud in any except the following districts, and in these there were material defects in the returns of election. Without deciding upon his power to set aside elections for force and fraud, they were set aside for the following reasons:

In the Ist district, because the words "by lawful resident voters," were stricken from the return.

In the IId district, because the oath was administered by G. W. Taylor, who was not authorized to administer an oath.

In the IIId district, because material erasures from the printed form of the oath were purposely made.

In the IVth district for the same reason.

In the VIIth district, because the Judges were not sworn at all.

In the XIth district, because the returns show the election to have been held *viva voce* instead of by ballot.

In the XVIth district, because the words "by lawful residence" were stricken from the returns.

ABSTRACT OF THE RETURNS OF ELECTION OF MAY 22, 1855.

No. of District	Places of Voting.	Pro-Slavery Votes	Free-State Votes	Scattering	Total
1	Lawrence	—	288	18	306
2	Douglas	—	127	—	127
3	Stinson's	—	148	1	149
7	"110"	—	66	13	79
8	Council Grove	—	33	—	33
16	Leavenworth	560	140	15	715
	Total	560	802	47	1409

Although the fraud and force in other districts were equally great as in these, yet as the Governor had no information in regard to them, he issued certificates according to the returns.

Your Committee here felt it to be their duty not only to inquire into and collect evidence in regard to force and fraud attempted and practiced at the elections in the Territory, but also into the facts and pretexts by which this force and fraud has been excused and justified; and for this purpose, your Committee have allowed the declarations of non-resident voters to be given as evidence in their own behalf, also the declarations of all who came up the Missouri River as emigrants in March, 1855, whether they voted or not, and whether they came into the Territory at all or not; and also the rumors which were circulated among the people of Missouri previous to the election. The great body of the testimony taken at the instance of the sitting Delegate is of this character.

When the declarations of parties passing up the river were offered in evidence, your Committee received them upon the distinct statement that they would be excluded unless the persons making the declarations were by other proof shown to have been connected with the elections. This proof was not made, and therefore much of this class of testimony is incompetent by the rules of law, but is allowed to remain as tending to show the cause of the action of the citizens of Missouri.

The alleged causes of the invasion of March, 1855, are included in the following charges:

I. That the New-England Aid Society of Boston was then importing into the Territory large numbers of men merely for the purpose of controlling the elections. That they came without women, children, or baggage, went into the Territory, voted, and returned again.

II. That men were hired in the Eastern or Northern States, or induced to go into the Territory solely to vote, and not to settle, and by so doing to make it a Free State.

III. That the Governor of the Territory purposely postponed the day of election to allow this emigration to arrive, and notified the Emigrant Aid Society, and persons in the Eastern States, of the day of election, before he gave notice to the people of Missouri and the Territory.

That these charges were industriously circulated; that grossly exaggerated statements were made in regard to them; that the newspaper press and leading men in public meetings in western Missouri, aided in one case by a Chaplain of the United States Army, gave currency and credit to them, and thus excited the people, and induced many well-meaning citizens of Missouri to march into the Territory to meet and repel the alleged Eastern paupers and Abolitionists, is fully proven by many witnesses.

But these charges are not sustained by the proof.

In April, 1854, the General Assembly of Massachusetts passed an act entitled "An act to incorporate the Massachusetts Emigrant Aid Society." The object of the Society as declared in the first section of this act, was "for the purpose of assisting emigrants to settle in the West." The moneyed capital of the corporation was not to exceed five millions of dollars; but no more than four per cent. could be assessed during the year 1854, and no more than ten per cent. in any one year thereafter. No organization was perfected, or proceedings had, under this law.

On the 24th day of July, 1854, certain persons in Boston, Massachusetts, concluded articles of agreement and association for an Emigrant Aid Society. The purpose of this association was declared to be "assisting emigrants to settle in the West." Under these articles of association, each stockholder was individually liable. To avoid this difficulty, an application was made to the General Assembly of Massachusetts for an act of incorporation, which was granted. On the 21st day of February, 1855, an act was passed to incorporate the New England Emigrant Aid Company. The purposes of this act were declared to be "directing emigration westward, and aiding and providing accommodation for the emigrants after arriving at their place of destination." The capital stock of the corporation was not to exceed one million of dollars. Under this charter a company was organized.

Your Committee have examined some of its officers and a portion of its circulars and records to ascertain what has been done by it. The public attention, at that time, was directed to the Territory of Kansas, and emigration naturally tended in that direction. To ascertain its character and resources, this Company sent its agent into it, and the information thus obtained was published. The Company made arrangements with various lines of transportation to reduce the expense of emigration into the Territory, and procured tickets at the reduced rates. Applications were made to the Company by persons desiring to emigrate, and when they were numerous enough to form a party of convenient size, tickets were sold to them at the reduced rates. An agent acquainted with the route was selected to accompany them. Their baggage was checked, and all trouble and danger of loss to the emigrant in this way avoided.

Under these arrangements, companies went into the Territory in the Fall of 1854, under the articles of association referred to. The company did not pay any portion of the fare, or furnish any personal or real property to the emigrant. The company during 1855 sent into the Territory from eight to ten saw-mills, purchased one hotel in Kansas City, which they subsequently sold, built one hotel at Lawrence, and owned one other building in that place. In some cases, to induce them to make improvements, town lots were given to them by town associations in this Territory. They held no property of any other kind or description. They imposed no condition upon their emigrants and did not inquire into their political, religious, or social opinions. The total amount expended by them, including the salaries of their agents and officers, and the expenses incident to all organizations, was less than $100,000.

Their purposes, as far as your Committee can ascertain, were lawful, and contributed to supply those wants most experienced in the settlement of a new country.

The only persons or company who emigrated into the Territory under the auspices of the Emigrant Aid Society in 1855, prior to the election in March, was a party of 159 persons who came under the charge of Charles Robinson (231).

In this party there were 67 women and children (232). They came as actual settlers, intending to make their homes in the Territory, and for no other purpose (233). They had about their persons but little baggage; usually sufficient clothing in a carpet-sack for a short time. Their personal effects, such as clothing, furniture, etc., was put into trunks and boxes; and for convenience in selecting and cheapness in transporting, was marked "Kansas party baggage, care B. Slater, St. Louis." Generally this was consigned as freight, in the usual way, to the care of a commission merchant. This party had, in addition to the usual allowance of one hundred pounds to each passenger, a large quantity of baggage on which the respective owners paid the usual extra freight (234). Each passenger or party paid his or their own expenses; and the only benefit they derived from the Society, not shared by all the people of the Territory, was the reduction of about $7 in the price of the fare, the convenience of traveling in a company instead of alone, and the cheapness and facility of transporting their freight through regular agents. Subsequently, many emigrants, being either disappointed with the country or its political condition, or deceived by the statements made by the newspapers and by the agents of the Society, became dissatisfied, and returned, both before and after the election, to their old homes. Most of them are now settlers in the Territory (235). Some few voted at the election in Lawrence (235), but the number was small. The names of these emigrants have been ascertained, and ——— of them were found upon the poll-books. This company of peaceful emigrants, moving with their household goods, was distorted into an invading horde of pauper Abolitionists, who were, with others of a similar character, to control the domestic institutions of the Territory, and then overturn those of a neighboring powerful State.

In regard to the second charge: There is no proof that any man was either hired or induced to come into the Territory from any Free State, merely to vote. The entire emigration in March 1855, is estimated at 500 persons (236), including men, women, and children. They came on steamboats up the Missouri River, in the ordinary course of emigration. Many returned for causes similar to those before stated; but the body of them are now residents. The only persons of those who were connected by proof with the election, were some who voted at the Big Blue Precinct in the Xth District, and at Pawnee in the IXth District. Their purpose and character are stated in a former part of this report.

The third charge is entirely groundless. The organic law requires the Governor to cause an enumeration of the inhabitants and legal voters to be made, and that he apportion the members of the Council and House according to this enumeration. For reasons stated by persons engaged in taking the census, it was not completed until the early part of March, 1855 (237). At that time the day of holding the election had not been, and could not have been, named by the Governor. As soon as practicable after the returns were brought in, he issued his proclamation for an election, and named the earliest day consistent with due notice, as the day of election. The day on which the election was to be held, was a matter of conjecture all over the country; but it was generally known that it would be in the latter part of March. The precise day was not known by any one until the proclamation issued. It was not known to the agents of the Emigrant Aid Society in Boston on the 13th of March, 1855, when the party of emigrants, before referred to, left (238).

Your Committee are satisfied that these charges were made the mere pretext to induce an armed invasion into the Territory, as a means to control the election and establish Slavery there.

The real purpose is avowed and illustrated by the testimony and conduct of Col. John Scott, of St. Joseph's, Missouri, who acted as the attorney for the sitting delegate before your Committee. The following are extracts from his deposition:

"Prior to the election in Burr-Oak precinct, in the XIVth district on the 29th of November, 1854, I had been a resident of Missouri, and I then determined, if I found it necessary, to become a resident of Kansas

(231) Benj. Slater, Charles Robinson, F. A. Hunt (232) Charles Robinson. (233) Samuel C. Smith.

(234) B. Slater and F. A. Hunt. (235) Charles Robinson. Samuel C. Smith. (236) W. H. Chick; Mr. Ridderburger. (237) Wm. Barbour. (238) Charles Robinson.

Territory. On the day previous to that election, I settled up my board at my boarding-house, in St. Joseph's, Missouri, and went over to the Territory, and took boarding with Mr. Bryant. near whose house the polls were held the next day, for one month, so that I might have it in my power, by merely determining to do so, to become a resident of the Territory on the day of election.

"When my name was proposed as a Judge of Election, objections were made by two persons only. * * * * I then publicly informed those present, that I had a claim in the Territory; that I had taken board in the Territory for a month, and that I could, at any moment, become an actual resident and legal voter in the Territory, and that I would do so, if I concluded at any time during the day that my vote would be necessary to carry that precinct in favor of the Pro-Slavery candidate for delegate to Congress. * * * * * I did not during the day consider it necessary to become a resident of the Territory for the purpose mentioned, and did not vote or offer to vote at that election.

"I held the office of City-Attorney for St. Joseph's at that time, and had held it for two or three years previously, and continued to hold it until this spring. * * * I voted at an election in St. Joseph's, in the spring of 1855, and was re-appointed City-Attorney. The question of Slavery was put in issue at the election of November, 1854, to the same extent as in every election in this Territory. Gen. Whitfield was regarded as the Pro-Slavery candidate for the Pro-Slavery party. I regarded the question of Slavery as the primarily prominent issue at that election, and, so far as I know, all parties agreed in making that question the issue of that election.

"*It is my intention, and the intention of a great many other Missourians now resident in Missouri, whenever the Slavery issue is to be determined upon by the people of this Territory in the adoption of the State Constitution, to remove to this Territory in time to acquire the right to become legal voters upon that question. The leading purpose of our intended removal to the Territory is to determine the domestic institutions of this Territory, when it comes to be a State, and we would not come but for that purpose, and would never think of coming here but for that purpose. I believe there are a great many in Missouri who are so situated.*"

The invasion of March 30th left both parties in a state of excitement, tending directly to produce violence. The successful party was lawless and reckless, while assuming the name of the "Law and Order" party. The other party, at first surprised and confounded, was greatly irritated, and some resolved to prevent the success of the invasion. In some Districts, as before stated, protests were sent to the Governor; in others, this was prevented by threats; in others, by the want of time, only four days being allowed by the proclamation for this purpose; and in others, by the belief that a new election would bring a new invasion. About the same time, all classes of men commenced bearing deadly weapons about the person, a practice which has continued to this time. Under these circumstances, a slight or accidental quarrel produced unusual violence, and lawless acts became frequent. This evil condition of the public mind was further increased by acts of violence in Western Missouri, where, in April, a newspaper press called *The Parkville Luminary* was destroyed by a mob.

About the same time, Malcolm Clark assaulted Cole McCrea, at a squatter meeting in Leavenworth, and was shot by McCrea, in alleged self-defense.

On the 17th day of May, William Phillips, a lawyer of Leavenworth, was first notified to leave, and upon his refusal, was forcibly seized, taken across the river, and carried several miles into Missouri, and then tarred and feathered, and one side of his head shaved, and other gross indignities put upon his person.

Previous to the outrage a public meeting was held (239), at which resolutions were unanimously passed, looking to unlawful violence, and grossly intolerant in their character. The right of free speech upon the subject of Slavery was characterized as a disturbance of the peace and quiet of the community, and as "circulating incendiary sentiments." They say "to the peculiar friends of northern fanatics," "Go home and do your treason where you may find sympathy. Among other resolves, is the following:

"*Resolved*, That the institution of Slavery is known and recognized in this Territory; that we repel the doctrine that it is a moral and political evil, and we hurl back with scorn upon its slanderous authors the charge of inhumanity; and we warn all persons not to come to our peaceful firesides to slander us, and sow the seeds of discord between the master and the servant; for, as much as we deprecate the necessity to which we may be driven, we cannot be responsible for the consequences."

A Committee of Vigilance of 30 men was appointed, "to observe and report all such persons as shall, * * * * by the expression of Abolition sentiments, produce disturbance to the quiet of the citizens, or danger to their domestic relations; and all such persons so offending, shall be notified, and made to leave the Territory."

The meeting was "ably and eloquently addressed by Judge Lecompte, Col. J. N. Burns of Western Missouri, and others." Thus the head of the Judiciary in the Territory, not only assisted at a public and bitterly partisan meeting whose direct tendency was to produce violence and disorder, but before any law is passed in the Territory, he prejudges the character of the domestic institutions, which the people of the Territory were, by their organic law, "left perfectly free to form and regulate in their own way."

On this Committee were several of those who held certificates of election as members of the Legislature; some of the others were then and still are residents of Missouri; and many of the Committee have since been appointed to the leading offices in the Territory, one of which is the Sheriffalty of the County. Their first act was that of mobbing Phillips.

Subsequently, on the 25th of May, A. D. 1855, a public meeting was held, at which R. R. Rees, a member elect of the Council, presided (240). The following resolutions, offered by Judge Payne, a member elect of the House, were unanimously adopted:

"*Resolved*, That we heartily indorse the action of the committee of citizens that shaved, tarred, and feathered, rode on a rail, and had sold by a negro, Wm. Phillips, the moral perjurer.

"*Resolved*, That we return our thanks to the committee for faithfully performing the trust enjoined upon them by the Pro-Slavery party.

"*Resolved*, That the committee be now discharged.

"*Resolved*, That we severely condemn those Pro-Slavery men who, from mercenary motives, are calling upon the Pro-Slavery party to submit without further action.

"*Resolved*, That in order to secure peace and harmony to the community, we now solemnly declare that the Pro-Slavery party will stand firmly by and carry out the resolutions reported by the committee appointed for that purpose on the memorable 30th."

The act of moral perjury here referred to, is the swearing by Phillips to a truthful protest in regard to the election of March 30, in the XVIth District.

The members receiving their certificates of the Governor as members of the General Assembly of the Territory, met at Pawnee, the place appointed by the Governor, on the 2d of July, A. D. 1855. Their proceedings are stated in three printed books, herewith submitted, entitled respectively, "The Statutes of the Territory of Kansas;" "The Journal of the Council of the Territory of Kansas;" and "The Journal of the House of Representatives of the Territory of Kansas."

Your Committee do not regard their enactments as valid laws. A Legislature thus im

(239) A. Payne.

(240) R. R. Rees.

posed upon a people, cannot affect their political rights. Such an attempt to do so, if successful, is virtually an overthrow of the organic law, and reduces the people of the Territory to the condition of vassals to a neighboring State. To avoid the evils of anarchy, no armed or organized resistance to them should be made, but the citizens should appeal to the ballot-box at public elections, to the Federal Judiciary, and to Congress, for relief. Such, from the proof, would have been the course of the people, but for the nature of these enactments and the manner in which they are enforced. Their character and their execution have been so intimately connected with one branch of this investigation—that relating to "violent and tumultuous proceedings in the Territory"—that we were compelled to examine them.

The "laws" in the statute-books are general and special; the latter are strictly of a local character, relating to bridges, roads, and the like. The great body of the general laws are exact transcripts from the Missouri Code. To make them in some cases conform to the organic act, separate acts were passed, defining the meaning of words. Thus the word "State" is to be understood as meaning "Territory" (241); the word "County Court" shall be construed to mean the Board of Commissioners transacting county business, or the Probate Court, according to the intent thereof. The words "Circuit Court" to mean "District Court" (242).

The material differences in the Missouri and Kansas statutes are upon the following subjects: The qualifications of voters and of members of the legislative assembly; the official oath of all officers, attorneys, and voters; the mode of selecting officers and their qualifications; the slave code, and the qualifications of jurors.

Upon these subjects the provisions of the Missouri Code are such as are usual in many of the States. But by the "Kansas Statutes," every office in the Territory, executive and judicial, was to be appointed by the legislature, or by some officer appointed by it. These appointments were not merely to meet a temporary exigency, but were to hold over two regular elections, and until after the general election in October, 1857 (243), at which the members of the new Council were to be elected (244). The new Legislature is required to meet on the first Monday in January, 1858 (245). Thus, by the terms of these "laws," the people have no control whatever over either the Legislature, the executive, or the judicial departments of the territorial government until a time before which, by the natural progress of population, the territorial government will be superseded by a State government.

No session of the Legislature is to be held during 1856, but the members of the House are to be elected in October of that year (246). A candidate, to be eligible at this election, must swear to support the fugitive-slave law (247), and each judge of election, and each voter, if challenged, must take the same oath (248). The same oath is required of every officer elected or appointed in the Territory, and of every attorney admitted to practice in the courts (249).

A portion of the militia is required to muster on the day of election (250). "Every free white male citizen of the United States, and every free male Indian, who is made a citizen by treaty or otherwise, and over the age of twenty-one years, and who shall be an *inhabitant* of the Territory and of the county and district in which he offers to vote, and shall have paid a territorial tax, shall be a qualified elector for all elective offices (251)." Two classes of persons were thus excluded who by the organic act were allowed to vote, viz.: those who would not swear to the oath required, and those of foreign birth who had declared on oath their intention to become citizens (252). Any man of proper age who was in the Territory on the day of election, and who had paid one dollar as a tax to the Sheriff, who was required to be at the polls to receive it (253), could vote as an "inhabitant," although he had breakfasted in Missouri, and intended to return there for supper. There can be no doubt that this unusual and unconstitutional provision was inserted to prevent a full and fair expression of the popular will in the election of members of the House, or to control it by non-residents.

All jurors are required to be selected by the Sheriff, and "no person who is conscientiously opposed to the holding of slaves, or who does not admit the right to hold slaves in the Territory, shall be a juror in any cause" affecting the right to hold slaves, or relating to slave property.

The Slave Code, and every provision relating to slaves, are of a character intolerant and unusual even for that class of legislation. The character and conduct of the men appointed to hold office in the Territory contributed very much to produce the events which followed. Thus Samuel I. Jones was appointed Sheriff of the County of Douglas, which included within it the Ist and IId Election-Districts. He had made himself peculiarly obnoxious to the settlers by his conduct on the 30th of March in the IId District, and by his burning the cabins of Joseph Oakley and Samuel Smith (254).

An election for delegates to Congress, to be held on the 1st day of October, 1855, was provided for with the same rules and regulations as were applied to other elections. The Free-State men took no part in this election, having made arrangements for holding an election on the 9th of the same month. The citizens of Missouri attended at the election of the 1st of October, some paying the dollar tax, others not being required to pay it. They were present and voted at the voting-places of Atchison (255) and Doniphan (256), in Atchison County; at Green Springs, Johnson County (257); at Willow Springs (258); Franklin (259), and Lecompton (260), in Douglas County; at Fort Scott, Bourbon County (261); at Baptiste Paola, Lykins Co., where some Indians voted, some whites paying the $1 tax for them (262); at Leavenworth City (263), and at Kickapoo City, Leavenworth County; at the latter place under the lead of Gen. B. F. Stringfellow and Col. Lewis Barnes of Missouri (264). From two of the election precincts at which it was alleged there was illegal voting—viz.: Delaware and Wyandotte, your Committee failed to obtain the attendance of witnesses. Your Committee did not deem it necessary, in regard to this election, to enter into details, as it was manifest that, from there being but one candidate—Gen. Whitfield—he must have received a majority of the votes cast. This election, therefore, depends not on the number or character of the votes received, but upon the validity of the laws under which it was held. Sufficient testimony was taken to show that the voting of citizens of Missouri was practiced at this election, as at all former elections in the Territory. The following table will exhibit

(241) Statutes, page 718. (242) Statutes, page 766. (243) Statutes, pages 168, 227, 712. (244) 330. (245) 475. (246) Statutes, page 330. (247) p. 333. (248) p. 332. (249) pp. 152, 330, 5, 6. (250) p. 469.

(251) p. 332. (252) Statutes, p. 34. (253) p. 333. (254) Saml. Smith and Ed. Oakley. (255) D. W. Field. (256) John Landis. (257) Robert Morrow, E. Jenkins, B. C. Westfall. (258) A. White, T. Wolverton, J. Reid. (259) L. M. Cox, L. A. Prather. (260) B. C. Westfall. (261) E. B. Cook, J. Hamilton. (262) B. C. Westfall. (263) G. F. Warren, H. Niles Moore. (264) J. W. Stephens.

the result of the testimony as regards the number of legal and illegal votes at this election. The County of Marshall embraces the same territory as was included in the XIth District; and the reasons before stated indicate that the great majority of the votes then cast were either illegal or fictitious. In the counties to which our examination extended, there were —— illegal votes cast, as near as the proof will enable us to determine.

ABSTRACT OF POLL-BOOKS OF OCTOBER 1 1855.

COUNTIES.	TOWNSHIPS.	No. of Votes cast for J. W. Whitfield	Scattering	Total Votes cast	No. of Legal Votes	No. of Illegal Votes
Atchison	Grasshopper	7	—	—	—	—
	Shannon	131	4	219	—	—
Bourbon		242	—	242	50	192
Brown		4	—	4	4	—
Calhoun		29	—	29	29	—
Davis		8	4	12	12	—
Doniphan	Burr Oak	42	—	—	41	1
	Iowa	31	—	—	31	—
	Wayne	66	—	—	62	4
	Washington	59	—	—	59	—
	Wolf River	53	—	251	53	—
Douglas	Franklin	86	—	—	23	63
	Lawrence	42	—	—	42	—
	Lecompton	101	—	—	—	—
	Willow Springs	103	—	332	53	50
Franklin		15	—	15	15	—
Jefferson		42	3	45	—	—
Johnson		190	—	190	90	100
Leavenworth	Alexandria	42	—	—	—	—
	Delaware	239	—	—	—	—
	Kickapoo	150	1	—	—	50
	Leavenworth	212	—	—	—	100
	Wyandott	246	5	895	—	—
Lykins		220	—	220	70	150
Lynn		67	—	67	—	—
Madison	(See Wise Co.)					
Marshall		171	—	171	24	147
Nemaha		6	—	6	6	—
Riley		28	—	28	28	—
Shawnee	One Hundred and Ten	23	—	—	23	—
	Tecumseh	52	—	75	52	—
Wise	Council Grove	14	—	14	14	—

While these enactments of the alleged legislative assembly were being made, a movement was instituted to form a State government, and apply for admission into the Union as a State. The first step taken by the people of the Territory, in consequence of the invasion of March 30, 1855, was the circulation for signature of a graphic and truthful memorial to Congress. Your Committee find that every allegation in this memorial has been sustained by the testimony. No further step was taken, as it was hoped that some action by the general government would protect them in their rights. When the alleged legislative assembly proceeded to construct the series of enactments referred to, the settlers were of opinion that submission to them would result in depriving them of the rights secured to them by the organic law. Their political condition was freely discussed in the Territory during the summer of 1855. Several meetings were held in reference to holding a convention to form a State government, and to apply for admission into the Union as a State. Public opinion gradually settled in favor of such an application to the Congress to meet in December, 1855. The first general meeting was held in Lawrence on the 15th of August, 1855.

The following preamble and resolutions were then passed:

"*Whereas*, The people of Kansas have been, since its settlement, and now are, without any law-making power, therefore be it

"*Resolved*, That we, the people of Kansas Territory, in mass meeting assembled, irrespective of party distinctions, influenced by common necessity, and greatly desirous of promoting the common good, do hereby call upon and request all *bona fide* citizens of Kansas Territory, of whatever political views or predilections, to consult together in their respective Election-Districts, and in mass convention or otherwise, elect three delegates for each representative to which said Election-District is entitled in the House of Representatives of the Legislative Assembly, by proclamation of Governor Reeder, of date 19th of March, 1855; said delegates to assemble in convention, at the town of Topeka, on the 19th day of September, 1855, then and there to consider and determine upon all subjects of public interest, and particularly upon that having reference to the speedy formation of a State Constitution, with an intention of an immediate application to be admitted as a State into the Union of the United States of America."

Other meetings were held in various parts of the Territory, which indorsed the action of the Lawrence meeting, and delegates were selected in compliance with its recommendations.

They met at Topeka, on the 19th day of September, 1855. By their resolutions they provided for the appointment of an Executive Committee to consist of seven persons, who were required to "keep a record of their proceedings, and shall have a general superintendence of the affairs of the Territory so far as regards the organization of the State Government." They were required to take steps for an election to be held on the second Tuesday of the October following, under regulations imposed by that Committee, "for members of a Convention to form a Constitution, adopt a Bill of Rights for the people of Kansas, and take all needful measures for organizing a State Government, preparatory to the admission of Kansas into the Union as a State." The rules prescribed were such as usually govern elections in most of the States of the Union, and in most respects were similar to those contained in the proclamation of Gov. Reeder for the election of March 30, 1855.

The Executive Committee, appointed by that Convention, accepted their appointment, and entered upon the discharge of their duties by issuing a proclamation addressed to the legal voters of Kansas, requesting them to meet at their several precincts, at the time and places named in the proclamation, then and there to cast their ballots for members of a Constitutional Convention, to meet at Topeka on the 4th Tuesday of October then next.

The proclamation designated the places of elections, appointed judges, recited the qualifications of voters and the apportionment of members of the Convention.

After this proclamation was issued, public meetings were held in every district in the Territory, and in nearly every precinct. The State movement was a general topic of discussion throughout the Territory, and there was but little opposition exhibited to it. Elections were held at the time and places designated, and the returns were sent to the Executive Committee.

The result of the election was proclaimed by the Executive Committee, and the members-elect were required to meet on the 23d day of October, 1855, at Topeka. In pursuance of this proclamation and direction, the Constitutional Convention met at the time and place appointed, and formed a State Constitution. A memorial to Congress was also prepared, praying for the admission of Kansas into the Union under that Constitution. The Convention also provided that the question of the adoption of the Constitution and other questions be submitted to the people, and required the Executive Committee to take the necessary steps for that purpose.

Accordingly, an election was held for that pur pose on the 15th day of December, 1855, in compliance with the proclamation issued by the Executive Committee. The returns of this election were made by the Executive Committee, and an abstract of them is contained in the following table:

ABSTRACT OF THE ELECTION ON THE ADOPTION OF THE STATE CONSTITUTION, DEC. 15, 1855.

Districts.	Precincts.	Constitution.		General Banking Law.		Exclusion of Negroes and Mulattoes.		No. votes cast.
		Yes.	No.	Yes.	No.	Yes.	No.	
1	Lawrence	348	1	225	83	133	223	356
	Blanton	72	2	59	14	48	20	76
	Palmyra	11	1	9	3	12	—	12
	Franklin	48	4	31	15	48	2	53
2	Bloomington	137	—	122	11	113	15	137
	East Douglas	18	—	13	4	14	4	18
3	Topeka	135	—	125	9	69	64	136
	Washington	42	—	41	1	42	—	42
	Brownsville	24	—	22	2	22	2	24
	Tecumseh	35	—	23	11	35	—	35
4	Prairie City	72	—	39	38	69	3	72
5	Little Osage	21	7	16	12	23	7	31
	Big Sugar	18	2	5	16	20	—	21
	Neosho	12	—	6	6	12	—	12
	Potawatamie	39	3	21	19	25	18	43
	Little Sugar	42	18	33	13	42	2	60
	Stanton	32	—	4	33	33	5	37
	Ossawattamie	56	1	33	20	38	17	59
7	Titus	39	5	32	7	25	15	44
	Juniata	30	—	23	6	10	19	31
8	Ohio City	21	—	16	5	20	1	21
	Mill Creek	20	—	—	20	20	—	20
	St. Mary's	14	—	—	14	14	—	14
	Waubaunsee	19	—	17	1	7	11	19
9	Pawnee	45	—	15	29	40	5	45
	Grasshopper Falls	54	—	19	34	50	3	54
10	Doniphan	22	—	5	14	21	—	22
	Burr Oak	23	—	7	16	22	1	23
	Jesse Padur's	12	—	1	11	12	—	12
11	Ocena	28	—	8	20	28	—	28
	Kickepoo	20	—	7	13	16	4	20
13	Pleasant Hill	47	—	37	6	45	1	47
	Indiana	19	—	—	18	19	—	19
	Whitfield	7	—	3	4	6	—	7
14	Wolf River	24	—	11	12	18	6	24
	St. Joseph's Bottom	15	—	4	9	14	1	15
15	Mt. Pleasant	32	—	32	1	30	2	33
16	Easton	71	2	53	19	71	—	73
17	Mission	7	—	3	—	1	2	7
	Total	1731	46	1120	564	1287	453	1778

N. B. Poll-Book at Leavenworth was destroyed.

The Executive Committe then issued a proclamation reciting the results of the election of the 15th of December, and at the same time provided for an election to be held on the 15th day of January, 1856, for State officers and members of the General Assembly of the State of Kansas.

An election was accordingly held in the several election-precincts, the returns of which were sent to the Executive Committee. An abstract of them is contained in the following table:

ABSTRACT OF THE ELECTION OF JANUARY 15, 1856.

Precincts.	Gov. C. Robinson	Gov. W. Y. Roberts	Lieut. Gov. W. Y. Roberts	Lieut. Gov. M. J. Parrott	Sec. State. P. C. Schuyler	Sec. State. C. K. Holliday	Auditor. G. A. Cutler	Auditor. W. R. Griffith	Treasurer. J. A. Wakefield	Treasurer. E. C. K. Garvey	Att. Gen. H. Miles Moore	Rep. Con., M. W. Delahay
Washington	1	29	—	29	1	29	1	29	1	29	30	30
Doniphan	32	—	32	—	32	—	31	—	32	—	32	32
Ossawatamie	82	—	80	—	82	—	81	—	82	—	81	78
Osage	19	—	19	—	19	—	19	—	19	—	19	19
Easton	66	6	66	7	66	7	66	7	64	3	75	73
Burr Oak	24	—	24	—	24	—	24	—	24	—	24	24
St. Joseph's Bottom	49	1	49	—	50	—	49	—	50	—	50	50
Padon's House	27	—	27	—	27	—	27	—	27	—	27	27
Wolf River	36	—	86	—	36	—	36	—	36	—	36	36
East Douglas	28	3	28	8	28	3	28	3	28	3	31	31
Stanton	31	—	31	—	31	—	31	—	31	—	31	28
Potawatamie	39	—	39	—	39	—	39	—	38	—	39	38
Titus	28	4	28	4	28	4	28	4	28	4	32	32
Blanton	52	25	42	33	55	23	54	24	55	17	78	77
Prairie City	24	50	25	45	27	37	27	45	27	38	72	71
Pleasant Hill	42	2	43	2	43	2	43	2	43	2	45	44
Mission	10	—	1	9	10	—	10	—	10	—	10	10
Palmyra	25	—	25	—	25	—	25	—	25	—	25	25
Franklin	8	58	5	59	8	58	8	58	8	58	66	66
Little Sugar Creek	33	—	35	—	32	—	34	—	34	—	34	34
Little Osage	19	—	19	—	19	—	19	—	19	—	19	19
Topeka	83	61	61	64	77	68	83	62	89	48	145	135
Tecumseh	1	34	1	34	1	34	1	34	8	24	35	35
Brownsville	3	23	3	23	—	23	3	23	29	—	—	26
Kickapoo	14	51	6	59	14	51	14	51	14	51	65	65
Leavenworth	94	7	94	7	94	7	94	7	94	7	101	100
Lawrence	365	41	176	245	383	43	380	—	385	36	426	395
Neosho	—	—	13	—	—	—	13	—	13	—	13	13
Slough Creek	—	14	14	—	—	14	—	14	—	14	—	14
Wyandot	1	1	34	—	35	—	35	—	35	—	35	1

Precincts.	Supreme Judges. M. Hunt	Supreme Judges. S. N. Latta	Supreme Judges. M. F. Conway	Supreme Judges. G. W. Smith	Supreme Judges. S. W. Johnson	Supreme Judges. J. A. Wakefield	Rep. S. Court. S. B. McKenzie	Rep. S. Court. E. M. Thurston	Clerk Sup'me Court—S. B. Floyd	Printer. John Speer	Printer. R. G. Elliott
Washington	1	3	1	29	29	27	29	1	30	1	29
Doniphan	32	31	31	—	—	—	—	32	32	32	—
Ossawatamie	81	81	82	—	—	—	—	79	82	82	—
Osage	19	19	19	—	—	—	—	19	19	19	—
Easton	66	73	65	7	7	—	7	66	76	70	7
Burr Oak	24	24	24	—	—	—	—	24	24	24	—
St. Joseph's Bottom	50	50	50	—	—	—	—	50	50	50	—
Padon's House	27	27	27	—	—	—	—	27	27	27	—
Wolf River	36	36	36	—	—	—	—	36	39	36	—
East Douglas	29	27	28	4	4	—	3	28	31	28	3
Stanton	31	31	31	—	—	—	—	31	31	31	—
Potawatamie	39	39	39	—	—	—	—	39	39	39	—
Titus	28	32	28	4	4	—	4	28	32	28	4
Blanton	55	55	55	23	23	23	23	55	77	54	24
Prairie City	27	27	27	45	45	45	45	27	70	25	45
Pleasant Hill	43	43	43	2	2	2	2	43	45	43	2
Mission	10	10	10	—	—	—	—	10	*9	10	—
Palmyra	25	25	35	—	—	—	—	25	25	25	—
Franklin	8	8	8	57	57	48	58	8	66	8	58
Little Sugar Creek	34	34	34	—	—	—	—	34	36	33	—
Little Osage	19	19	19	—	—	—	—	19	19	19	84
Topeka	84	141	84	61	61	—	61	84	145	96	—
Tecumseh	1	25	1	34	34	—	34	—	35	1	34
Brownsville	—	—	—	—	—	—	—	—	—	18	8
Kickapoo	14	14	14	51	51	51	51	14	65	14	51
Leavenworth	94	101	94	7	7	—	7	94	101	94	7
Lawrence	383	379	371	62	48	33	46	380	427	373	53
Neosho	13	13	—	—	—	—	—	—	10	13	—
Slough Creek	14	4	—	14	14	10	14	—	14	—	14
Wyandot	35	35	35	—	—	—	—	35	35	35	—

* Anthony Floyd 1.

The result of this election was announced by a proclamation by the Executive Committee.

In accordance with the Constitution thus adopted, the members of the State Legislature and most of the State officers met on the day and at the place designated by the State Constitution, and took the oath therein prescribed.

After electing United States Senators, passing some preliminary laws, and appointing a Codifying Committee and preparing a Memorial to Congress, the General Assembly adjourned to meet on the 4th day of July, 1856.

The laws passed were all conditional upon the admission of Kansas as a State into the Union. These proceedings were regular, and, in the opinion of your Committee, the constitution thus adopted fairly expresses the will of the majority of the settlers. They now await the action of Congress upon their memorial.

These elections, whether they were conducted in pursuance of law or not, were not illegal.

Whether the result of them is sanctioned by the action of Congress, or they are regarded as the mere expression of a popular will, and Congress should refuse to grant the prayer of the memorial, that cannot affect their legality. The right of the people to assemble and express their political opinion in any form, whether by means of an election or a convention, is secured to them by the Constitution of the United States. Even if the elections are to be regarded as the act of a party, whether political or otherwise, they were proper, in accordance with examples, both in States and Territories.

The elections, however, were preceded and followed by acts of violence on the part of those who opposed them, and those persons who approved and sustained the invasion from Missouri were peculiarly hostile to these peaceful movements preliminary to the organization of a State government. Instances of this violence will be referred to hereafter.

To provide for the election of delegates to Congress, and at the same time do it in such a manner as to obtain the judgment of the House of Representatives upon the validity of the alleged legislative assembly sitting at Shawnee Mission, a convention was held at Big Springs on the 5th and 6th days of September, 1855. This was a party convention, and a party calling itself the Free-State party was then organized. It was in no way connected with the State movement, except that the election of a delegate to Congress was fixed by it on the same day as the election of members of a constitutional convention, instead of the day prescribed by the alleged legislative assembly. Andrew H. Reeder was put in nomination as territorial delegate to Congress, and an election was provided for under the regulations prescribed for the election of March 30, 1855, excepting as to the appointment of officers, and the persons to whom the returns of the elections should be made. The election was held in accordance with these regulations, an abstract of the returns of which is contained in the following table:

ABSTRACT OF THE ELECTION OF A. H. REEDER.

District ...	Voting Places.	No. Votes..
I	Lawrence	557
	Blanton	77
	Palmyra	16
II	Bloomington	116
	Benicia	27
III	Brownsville	24
	Topeka	131
	Tecumseh	31
	Big Springs	35
	Camp Creek	7
IV	Willow Springs	54
V	Hampden	33
	Neosho	16
	Stanton	44
	Ossawatamie	74
	Potawatamie	56
	Big Sugar Creek	28
	Little Sugar Creek	41
VI	Scott Town	27
	Columbia	20
	Fergnals	12
VII	Council City	62
VIII	Waubousa	26
	A. J. Baker	16
IX	Pawnee	76
X	Big Blue	77
	Rock Creek	30
XI	Black Vermilion	14
XII	St. Mary's	18
	Silver Lake	28
XIII	Pleasant Hill	43
	Falls Precinct	45
	Hickory Point	11
XIV	Burr Oak	33
	Doniphan	43
	Palermo	32
XV	Ocena	32
	Crosby's Store	38
	Jackson Crane's	38
XVI	Leavenworth	503
	Wyandotte	38
	Delaware	22
	Easton	63
	Ridge Point	48
XVII	Wakarusa	7
	Mission	13
XVIII	Iowa Point	40
	Total	2827

The resolutions passed by this convention indicate the state of feeling which existed in the Territory in consequence of the invasion from Missouri, and the enactments of the alleged legislative assembly. The language of some of the resolutions is violent, and can only be justified either in consequence of the attempt to enforce the grossest acts of tyranny, or for the purpose of guarding against a similar invasion in future.

In the fall of 1855, there sprang out of the existing discords and excitement in the Territory, two secret Free-State societies (265). They were defensive in their character, and were designed to form a protection to their members against unlawful acts of violence and assault. One of the societies was purely of a local character, and was confined to the town of Lawrence. Very shortly after its organization it produced its desired effect, and then went out of use and ceased to exist (266). Both societies were cumbersome, and of no utility except to give confidence to the Free-State men, and enable them to know and aid each other in contemplated danger. So far as the evidence shows, they led to no act of violence in resistance to either real or alleged laws (267).

On the 21st day of November, 1855, F. M. Coleman, a Pro-Slavery man, and Charles W. Dow, a Free-State man, had a dispute about the division line between their respective claims. Several hours afterward, as Dow was passing from a blacksmith's shop toward his claim, and by the cabin of Coleman, the latter shot Dow with a double-barreled gun loaded with slugs. Dow was unarmed. He fell across the road and died immediately. This was about 1 o'clock P. M. His dead body was allowed to lie where it fell until after sundown, when it was conveyed by Jacob Branson to his house, at which Dow

(265) Pat. Laughlin, Francis. (266) G. P. Lowry, A. H. Reeder. (267) Lowry, Reeder and M. F. Conway.

boarded. The testimony in regard to this homicide is voluminous (268), and shows clearly that it was a deliberate murder by Coleman, and that Harrison Bulkely and a Mr. Hargous were accessories to it. The excitement caused by it was very great among all classes of the settlers. On the 26th, a large meeting of citizens was held at the place were the murder was committed, and resolutions passed that Coleman should be brought to justice. In the mean time Coleman had gone to Missouri, and then to Gov. Shannon at Shawnee Mission, in Johnson County. He was there taken into custody by S. I. Jones, then acting as Sheriff. No warrant was issued or examination had. On the day of the meeting at Hickory Point, Harrison Bradley procured a peace warrant against Jacob Branson, which was placed in the hands of Jones. That same evening, after Branson had gone to bed, Jones came to his cabin with a party of about 25 persons, among whom were Hargous and Buckley—burst open the door, and saw Branson in bed. He then drew his pistol, cocked it, and presented it to Branson's breast, and said, "You are my prisoner, and if you move I will blow you through." The others cocked their guns and gathered round him, and took him prisoner. They all mounted and went to Buckley's house. After a time they went on a circuitous route towards Blanton's Bridge, stopping to "drink" on the way. As they approached the bridge, there were 13 in the party, several having stopped. Jones rode up to the prisoner and, among other things, told him that he had "heard there were 100 men at your house to-day," and "that he regretted they were not there, and that they were cheated out of their sport" (269). In the mean time, the alarm had been given in the neighborhood of Branson's arrest, and several of the settlers, among whom were some who had attended the meeting at Hickory Point that day, gathered together. They were greatly excited; the alleged injustice of such an arrest of a quiet settler, under a peace warrant by "Sheriff Jones," aided by two men believed to be accessory to a murder, and who were allowed to be at large, exasperated them, and they proceeded as rapidly as possible by a nearer route than that taken by Jones, and stopped near the house of J. S. Abbott, one of them. They were on foot as Jones's party approached on a canter. The rescuers suddenly formed across the road in front of Jones and his party. Jones halted, and asked, "What's up?" The reply was, "That's what we want to know. What's up?" Branson said, "They have got me a prisoner." Some one in the rescuing party told him to come over to their side. He did so, and dismounted, and the mule he rode was driven over to Jones's party; Jones then left (270). Of the persons engaged in this rescue, three were from Lawrence, and had attended the meeting. Your Committee have deemed it proper to detail the particulars of this rescue, as it was made the groundwork of what is known as the Wakerusa War. On the same night of the rescue the cabins of Coleman and Buckley were burned, but by whom, is left in doubt by the testimony.

On the morning of the rescue of Branson, Jones was at the village of Franklin, near Lawrence. The rescue was spoken of in the presence of Jones, and more conversation passed between two others in his presence, as to whether it was most proper to send for assistance to Col. Boone in Missouri, or to Gov. Shannon. Jones wrote a dispatch and handed it to a messenger. As soon as he started, Jones said: "That man is taking my dispatch to Missouri, and by G—d I'll have revenge before I see Missouri." A person present, who was examined as a witness (271), complained publicly that the dispatch was not sent to the governor; and within half an hour one was sent to the governor by Jones, through Hargous. Within a few days, large numbers of men from the State of Missouri gathered and encamped on the Wakerusa. They brought with them all the equipments of war. To obtain them, a party of men under the direction of Judge T. V. Thompson broke into the United States arsenal and armory at Liberty, Missouri, and after a forcible detention of Captain Leonard (then in charge) (272), they took the cannon, muskets, rifles, powder, harness, and indeed all the materials and munitions of war they desired, some of which have never been returned or accounted for.

The chief hostility of this military foray was against the town of Lawrence, and this was especially the case with the officers of the law. Your Committee can see in the testimony no reason, excuse, or palliation for this feeling. *Up to this time no warrant or proclamation of any kind had been in the hands of any officer against any citizen of Lawrence* (273). No arrest had been attempted, and no writ resisted in that town. The rescue of Branson sprang out of a murder committed thirteen miles from Lawrence, in a detached settlement, and neither the town nor its citizens extended any protection to Branson's rescuers (274). On the contrary, two or three days after the rescue, S. N. Wood, who claimed publicly to be one of the rescuing party, wished to be arrested for the purpose of testing the territorial laws, and walked up to Sheriff Jones and shook hands with him, and exchanged other courtesies. He could have been arrested without any difficulty, and it was his design, when he went to Mr. Jones, to be arrested, but no attempt was made to do so (275).

It is obvious that the only cause of this hostility is the known desire of the citizens of Lawrence to make Kansas a Free State, and their repugnance to laws imposed upon them by non-residents.

Your Committee do not propose to detail the incidents connected with this foray. Fortunately for the peace of the country, a direct conflict between the opposing forces was avoided by an amicable arrangement. The losses sustained by the settlers in property taken and time and money expended in their own defense, added much to the trials incident to a new settlement. Many persons were unlawfully taken and detained—in some cases, under circumstances of gross cruelty. This was especially so in the arrest and treatment of Dr. G. A. Cutter and G. F. Warren. They were taken, without cause or warrant, 60 miles from Lawrence, and when Dr. Cutter was quite sick. They were compelled to go to the camp at Lawrence, were put into the custody of "Sheriff Jones," who had no process to arrest them—they were taken into a small room kept as a liquor shop, which was open and very cold. That night Jones came in with others, and went to "playing poker at twenty-five cents ante." The prisoners were obliged to sit up all night, as there was no room to lie down, when the men were playing. Jones insulted them frequently, and told one of them he must either "tell or swing." The guard then objected to this treatment of prisoners, and Jones desisted. G. F. Warren thus describes their subsequent conduct:

They then carried us down to their camp; Kelly of *The Squatter Sovereign*, who lives in Atchison, came round and said he thirsted for

(268) Wm. and Nicholas McKinney, D. T. Jones and wife, Thomas Brown, F. M. Coleman and others. (269) Jacob Branson. (270) Jacob Branson.

(271) L. A. Prattier. (272) Luther Leonard. (273) William Shannon, Chas. Robinson. (274) G. P. Lowry and Charles Robinson. (275) Chas. Robinson.

blood, and said he should like to hang us on the first tree. Cutter was very weak, and that excited him so that he became delirious. They sent for three doctors, who came. Dr. Stringfellow was one of them. They remained there with Cutter until after midnight, and then took him up to the office, as it was very cold in camp.

During the foray, either George W. Clark, or Mr. Burns, murdered Thomas Barber, while the latter was on the highway on his road from Lawrence to his claim. Both fired at him, and it is impossible from the proof to tell whose shot was fatal. The details of this homicide are stated by eye-witnesses (276).

Among the many acts of lawless violence which it has been the duty of your Committee to investigate, this invasion of Lawrence is the most defenseless. A comparison of the facts proven, with the official statements of the officers of the Government, will show how groundless were the pretexts which gave rise to it. A community in which no crime had been committed by any of its members, against none of whom had a warrant been issued or a complaint made, who had resisted no process in the hands of a real or pretended officer, was threatened with destruction in the name of "law and order," and that, too, by men who marched from a neighboring State with arms obtained by force, and who, in every stage of their progress, violated many laws, and among others the Constitution of the United States (277).

The chief guilt of it must rest on Samuel J. Jones. His character is illustrated by his language at Lecompton, where peace was made: "The said Maj. Clark and Burns both claimed the credit of killing that d—d Abolitionist, and he didn't know which ought to have it. If Shannon hadn't been a d—d old fool, that peace would never have been declared. He would have wiped Lawrence out. He had men and means enough to do it" (278).

Shortly after the retreat of the forces from before Lawrence, the election upon the adoption of the State Constitution was held at Leavenworth City, on the 15th of December, 1855. While it was proceeding quietly, about noon, Charles Dunn, with a party of others, smashed in the window of the building in which the election was being held, and then jumped into the room where the Judges of election were sitting, and drove them off (279). One of the clerks of election snatched up the ballot-box and followed the Judges, throwing the box behind the counter of an adjoining room through which he passed on his way out. As he got to the street door, Dunn caught him by the throat, and pushed him up against the outside of the building, and demanded the ballot-box (280).

Then Dunn and another person struck him in the face, and he fell into the mud, the crowd rushed on him and kicked him on the head and in his sides (281). In this manner the election was broken up, Dunn and his party obtaining the ballot-box and carrying it off.

To avoid a similar outrage at the election for State officers, etc., to be held on the 15th of January, 1856, the election for Leavenworth District was appointed to be held at Easton, and the time postponed until the 17th day of January, 1856 (282). On the way to the election, persons were stopped by a party of men at a grocery, and their guns taken from them (283). During the afternoon, parties came up to the place of election and threatened to destroy the ballot-box and were guilty of other insolent and abusive conduct (283). After the polls were closed, many of the settlers being apprehensive of an attack, were armed in the house where the election had been held until the next morning. Late that night Stephen Spark, with his son and nephew, started for home, his route running by the store of a Mr. Dawson, where a large party of armed men had collected. As he approached, these men demanded that he should surrender, and gathered about him to enforce the demand (284). Information was carried by a man in the company of Mr. Sparks to the house where the election had been held. R. P. Brown and a company of men immediately went down to relieve Mr. Sparks, and did relieve him when he was in imminent danger (285). Mr. Sparks then started back with Mr. Brown and his party, and while on their way were fired upon by the other party. They returned the fire, and an irregular fight then ensued, in which a man by the name of Cook, of the Pro-Slavery party, received a mortal wound, and two of the Free-State party were slightly wounded.

Mr. Brown, with seven others who had accompanied him from Leavenworth, started on their return home. When they had proceeded a part of the way, they were stopped and taken prisoners by a party of men called the Kickapoo Rangers, under the command of Capt. John W. Martin. They were disarmed and taken back to Easton, and put in Dawson's store (286). Brown was separated from the rest of his party, and taken into the office of E. S. Trotter (287). By this time several of Martin's party and some of the citizens of the place had become intoxicated, and expressed a determination to kill Brown (288). Capt. Martin was desirous, and did all in his power to save him. Several hours were spent in discovering what should be done with Brown and his party. In the mean time, without the knowledge of his party, Capt. Martin liberated all of Brown's party but himself, and aided them in their escape (289). The crowd repeatedly tried to get in the room where Brown was, and at one time succeeded, but were put out by Martin and others. Martin, finding that further effort on his part to save Brown was useless, left and went home. The crowd then got possession of Brown, and finally butchered him in cold blood. The wound of which he died was inflicted with a hatchet by a man of the name of Gibson. After he had been mortally wounded, Brown was sent home with Charles Dunn, and died that night. No attempt was made to arrest or punish the murderers of Brown. Many of them were well-known citizens, and some of them were officers of the law. On the next Grand Jury which sat in Leavenworth County, the Sheriff summoned several of the persons inplicated in this murder (290). One of them was M. P. Rively, at that time Treasurer of the County. He has been examined as a witness before us. The reason he gives why no indictments were found is, "they killed one of the Pro-Slavery men, and the Pro-Slavery men killed one of the others, and I thought it was about mutual." The same Grand Jury, however, found bills of indictment against those who acted as Judges of the Free-State election. Rively says, "I know our utmost endeavors were made to find out who acted as Judges and Clerks on the 17th of January last, and at all the bogus elections held by the Abolitionists

(276) Robert T. Barber, Thomas W. Pierson, Jane W. Colborn and others. (277) Article 4 of the Amendments. (278) Harrison Nichols. (279) Geo. Wetherell. George H. Keller. (280) George Wetherell. (281) George Wetherell, George W. Hallis. (282) J. C. Green, Henry J. Adams, Joseph H. Bird. (283) Stephen Sparks.

(284) Stephen Sparks. (285) George A. Taylor, Stephen Sparks, J. H. Bird. (286) Henry J. Adams, George A. Taylor, W. P. Kirby, John H. Martin, Wiley Williams. (287) Henry J. Adams, J. W. Martin. (288) Wiley Williams, J. W. Martin, H. J. Adams. (289) H. J. Adams, G. A. Taylor, J. H. Bird, Wiley Williams. (290) M. P. Rively.

here. We were very anxious to find them out, as we thought them acting illegally."

Your Committee, in their examination, have found that in no case of crime or homicide, mentioned in the report or in the testimony, has any indictment been found against the guilty party, except in the homicide of Clark by McCrea, McCrea being a Free-State man.

Your Committee did not deem it within their power or duty to take testimony as to events which have transpired since the date of their appointment; but as some of the events tended seriously to embarrass, hinder and delay their investigations, they deem it proper here to refer to them. On their arrival in the Territory, the people were arrayed in two hostile parties. The hostility of them was continually increased during our stay in the Territory, by the arrival of armed bodies of men who, from their equipments, came not to follow the peaceful pursuits of life, but armed and organized into companies, apparently for war—by the unlawful detention of persons and property while passing through the State of Missouri, and by frequent forcible seizures of persons and property in the Territory without legal warrant. Your Committee regret that they were compelled to witness instances of each of these classes of outrages. While holding their session at Westport, Mo., at the request of the sitting Delegate, they saw several bodies of armed men, confessedly citizens of Missouri, march into the Territory on forays against its citizens, but under the pretense of enforcing the enactments before referred to. The wagons of emigrants were stopped in the highways, and searched without claim or legal powers, and in some instances all their property taken from them. In Leavenworth City, leading citizens were arrested at noonday in our presence, by an armed force, without any claim of authority, except that derived from a self-constituted Committee of Vigilance, many of whom were Legislative and Executive officers. Some were released on promising to leave the Territory, and others, after being detained for a time, were formally notified to leave, under the severest penalties. The only offense charged against them was their political opinions, and no one was thus arrested for alleged crime of any grade. There was no resistance to these lawless acts by the settlers, because, in their opinion, the persons engaged in them would be sustained and reinforced by the citizens of the populous border counties of Missouri, from whence they were only separated by the river. In one case witnessed by your Committee, an application for the writ of habeas corpus was prevented by the urgent solicitation of Pro-Slavery men, who insisted that it would endanger the life of the prisoner to be discharged under legal process.

While we remained in the Territory, repeated acts of outrage were committed upon the quiet, unoffending citizens, of which we received authentic intelligence. Men were attacked on the highway, robbed, and subsequently imprisoned. Men were seized and searched, and their weapons of defense taken from them without compensation. Horses were frequently taken and appropriated. Oxen were taken from the yoke while plowing, and butchered in the presence of their owners. One young man was seized in the streets of the town of Atchison, and under circumstances of gross barbarity was tarred and cottened, and in that condition was sent to his family. All the provisions of the Constitution of the United States, securing persons and property, are utterly disregarded. The officers of the law, instead of protecting the people, were in some instances engaged in these outrages, and in no instance did we learn that any man was arrested, indicted or punished for any of these crimes. While such offenses were committed with impunity the laws were used as a means of indicting men for holding elections, preliminary to framing a constitution and applying for admission into the Union as the State of Kansas. Charges of high treason were made against prominent citizens upon grounds which seem to your Committee absurd and ridiculous, and under these charges they are now held in custody and are refused the privilege of bail. In several cases men were arrested in the State of Missouri while passing on their lawful business through that State, and detained until indictments could be found in the Territory.

These proceedings were followed by an offense of still greater magnitude. Under color of legal process, a company of about 700 armed men, the great body of whom your Committee are satisfied were not citizens of the Territory, marched into the town of Lawrence under Marshal Donaldson and S. J. Jones, officers claiming to act under the law, and bombarded and then burned to the ground a valuable hotel and one private house; destroyed two printing-presses and material; and then, being released by the officers, whose posse they claim to be, proceeded to sack, pillage, and rob houses, stores, trunks, etc., even to the clothing of women and children. Some of the letters thus unlawfully taken were private ones, written by the contesting Delegate, and they were offered in evidence. Your Committee did not deem that the persons holding them had any right thus to use them, and refused to be made the instruments to report private letters thus obtained.

This force was not resisted, because it was collected and marshaled under the forms of law. But this act of barbarity, unexampled in the history of our Government, was followed by its natural consequences. All the restraints which American citizens are accustomed to pay even to the appearance of law, were thrown off; one act of violence led to another; homicides became frequent. A party under H. C. Pate, composed chiefly of citizens of Missouri, were taken prisoners by a party of settlers; and while your Committee were at Westport, a company chiefly of Missourians, accompanied by the acting Delegate, went to relieve Pate and his party, and a collision was prevented by the United States troops. Civil war has seemed impending in the Territory. Nothing can prevent so great a calamity but the presence of a large force of United States troops, under a commander who will with prudence and discretion quiet the excited passions of both parties, and expel with force the armed bands of lawless men coming from Missouri and elsewhere, who with criminal pertinacity infest that Territory.

In some cases, and as to one entire election-district, the condition of the country prevented the attendance of witnesses, who were either arrested or detained while obeying our process, or deterred from so doing. The Sergeant-at-Arms who served the processes upon them was himself arrested and detained for a short time by an armed force, claiming to be a part of the posse of the Marshal, but was allowed to proceed upon an examination of his papers, and was furnished with a pass, signed by "Warren D. Wilkes of South Carolina." John Upton, another officer of the Committee, was subsequently stopped by a lawless force on the borders of the Territory, and after being detained and treated with great indignity was released. He also was furnished with a pass signed by two citizens of Missouri, and addressed to "Pro-Slavery men." By reason of these disturbances we were delayed in Westport, so that while in session there, our time was but partially occupied.

But the obstruction which created the most serious embarrassment to your Committee was the attempted arrest of Gov. Reeder, the contesting Delegate, upon a writ of attachment issued against him by Judge Lecompte to compel his attendance as a witness before the Grand Jury of Douglas County. William Fane, recently from the State of Georgia, and claiming to be the Deputy Marshal, came into the room of the Committee while Gov. Reeder was examining a witness before us, and producing the writ required Gov. Reeder to attend him. Subsequent events have only strengthened the conviction of your Committee that this was a wanton and unlawful interference by the Judge who issued the writ, tending greatly to obstruct a full and fair investigation. Gov. Reeder and Gen. Whitfield alone were fully possessed of that local information which would enable us to elicit the whole truth, and it was obvious to every one that any event which would separate either of them from the Committee would necessarily hinder, delay, and embarrass it. Gov. Reeder claimed that, under the circumstances in which he was placed, he was privileged from arrest except for treason, felony, or breach of the peace. As this was a question of privilege, proper for the Courts, or for the privileged person alone to determine on his peril, we declined to give him any protection or take any action in the matter. He refused to obey the writ, believing it to be a mere pretense to get the custody of his person, and fearing, as he alleged, that he would be assassinated by lawless bands of men then gathering in and near Lecompton. He then left the Territory.

Subsequently H. Miles Moore, an attorney in Leavenworth City, but for several years a citizen of Weston, Mo., kindly furnished the Committee information as to the residence of persons voting at the elections, and in some cases examined witnesses before us. He was arrested on the streets of that town by an armed band of about thirty men, headed by W. D. Wilkes, without any color of authority, confined, with other citizens, under a military guard for twenty-four hours, and then notified to leave the Territory. His testimony was regarded as important, and upon his sworn statement that it would endanger his person to give it openly, the majority of your Committee deem it proper to examine him ex parte and did so.

By reason of these occurrences, the contestant, and the party with and for whom he acted, were unrepresented before us during a greater portion of the time, and your Committee were required to ascertain the truth in the best manner they could.

Your Committee report the following facts and conclusions as established by the testimony:

First: That each election in the Territory, held under the organic or alleged Territorial law, has been carried by organized invasions from the State of Missouri, by which the people of the Territory have been prevented from exercising the rights secured to them by the organic law.

Second: That the alleged Territorial Legislature was an illegally-constituted body, and had no power to pass valid laws, and their enactments are, therefore, null and void.

Third: That these alleged laws have not, as a general thing, been used to protect persons and property and to punish wrong, but for unlawful purposes.

Fourth: That the election under which the sitting Delegate, John W. Whitefield, holds his seat, was not held in pursuance of any valid law, and that it should be regarded only as the expression of the choice of those resident citizens who voted for him.

Fifth: That the election under which the contesting Delegate, Andrew H. Reeder, claims his seat, was not held in pursuance of law, and that it should be regarded only as the expression of the choice of the resident citizens who voted for him.

Sixth: That Andrew H. Reeder received a greater number of votes of resident citizens than John W. Whitfield, for Delegate.

Seventh: That in the present condition of the Territory a fair election cannot be held without a new census, a stringent and well-guarded election law, the selection of impartial Judges, and the presence of United States troops at every place of election.

Eighth: That the various elections held by the people of the Territory preliminary to the formation of the State Government have been as regular as the disturbed condition of the Territory would allow; and that the Constitution passed by the Convention, held in pursuance of said elections, embodies the will of a majority of the people.

As it is not the province of your Committee to suggest remedies for the existing troubles in the Territory of Kansas, they content themselves with the foregoing statement of facts.

All of which is respectfully submitted.

WM. A. HOWARD,
JOHN SHERMAN.

The Free-State Constitution framed at Topeka for Kansas, by the Convention called by the Free-State party, (as set forth in the foregoing documents,) was in due season submitted to Congress—Messrs. Andrew H. Reeder (the Free-State Territorial delegate) and James H. Lane having been chosen by the first Free-State Legislature Senators of the United States, and Mr. M. W. Delahay elected Representative in the House, by the Free-State men of Kansas. Of course, these were not entitled to their seats until the aforesaid instrument (known as "the Topeka Constitution") should be accepted by Congress, and the State thereupon admitted into the Union. This Constitution, being formally presented in either House, was received and referred to their respective Committees on Territories; but the accompanying Memorial from the Free-State Legislature, setting forth the grounds of the application, and praying for admission as a State, was, after having been received by the Senate, reconsidered, rejected, and returned to Col. Lane, on the allegation that material changes had been made in it since it left Kansas. The Senate, in like manner, rejected repeated motions to accept the Constitution, and thereupon admit Kansas as a Free State—there never being more than Messrs. Hamlin and Fessenden of Maine, Hale and Bell of New-Hampshire, Collamer and Foot of Vermont, Sumner and Wilson of Mass., Foster of Connecticut, Seward and Fish of New York, Wade of Ohio, Durkee and Dodge of Wisconsin, Trumbull of Illinois, and Harlan of Iowa, (16) Senators in favor of such admission, and these never all present at the same time.

In the House—the aforesaid Constitution and Memorial having been submitted to the

Committee on Territories, its Chairman, Mr. Grow of Penna., from a majority of said Committee, reported in favor of the admission of Kansas under such Constitution, as a Free State; and after debate the Previous Question thereon was ordered (June 28th) by a vote of 98 Ayes to 63 Noes. Previous to this, however, Mr. Stephens of Georgia had proposed, as an amendment or substitute, a radically different bill, contemplating the appointment by the President and Senate of five Commissioners, who should repair to Kansas, take a census of the inhabitants and legal voters, and thereupon proceed to apportion, during the month of September, 1856, the delegates (52) to form a constitutional convention, to be elected by the legal voters aforesaid; said delegates to be chosen on the day of the Presidential election (Tuesday, Nov. 4th, 1856), and to assemble in convention on the first Monday in December, 1856, to form a State Constitution. The bill proposed, also, penalties for illegal voting at said election.

To this substitute-bill, Mr. Dunn of Indiana proposed the following amendment, to come in at the end as an additional section:

SEC. 18. *And be it further enacted*, That so much of the fourteenth section and of the thirty-second section of the act passed at the first session of the Thirty-Third Congress, commonly called the Kansas and Nebraska act, as reads as follows: "Except the eighth section of the act preparatory to the admission of Missouri into the Union, approved March 6, 1820, which, being inconsistent with the principle of non-intervention by Congress with slavery in the States and Territories, as recognized by the legislation of 1850, commonly called the compromise measures, is hereby declared inoperative and void; it being the true intent and meaning of this act not to legislate slavery into any State or Territory, or to exclude it therefrom, but to leave the people thereof perfectly free to form and regulate their domestic institutions in their own way, subject only to the Constitution of the United States: *Provided*, That nothing herein contained shall be construed to revive or put in force any law or regulation which may have existed prior to the act of 6th March, 1820, either protecting, establishing, prohibiting, or abolishing slavery," be, and the same is thereby, repealed, provided that any person or persons lawfully held to service within either of the Territories named in said act shall be discharged from such service, if they shall not be removed and kept out of said Territories within twelve months from the passage of this act.

Mr. Dunn's amendment to the Stephens amendment or substitute, was carried: Yeas 109; Nays 102—as follows:

YEAS—Messrs. Albright, Allison, Ball, Barbour, Henry Bennett, Benson, Billinghurst, Bingham, Bishop, Bliss, Bradshaw, Brenton, Broom, Buffinton, Burlingame, James H. Campbell, Lewis D. Campbell, Bayard Clarke, Ezra Clark, Clawson, Colfax, Comins, Covode, Cragin, Cumback, Damrell, Timothy Davis, Dean, De Witt, Dick, Dickson, Dodd, Dunn, Durfee, Edie, Edwards, Emrie, Flagler, Galloway, Giddings, Gilbert, Granger, Grow, Robert B. Hall, Harlan, Harrison, Haven, Holloway, Thomas R. Horton, Valentine B. Horton, Howard, Hughston, Kelsey, King, Knapp, Knight, Knowlton, Knox, Kunkel, Leiter, Mace, Matteson, McCarty, Meacham, Killian Miller, Millward, Moore, Morgan, Morrill, Murray, Andrew Oliver, Parker, Pearce, Pelton, Pennington, Perry, Pettit, Pike, Pringle, Purviance, Robbins, Roberts, Robison, Sabin, Sage, Sapp, Scott, Sherman, Simmons, Stanton, Stranahan, Tappan, Thorington, Thurston, Todd, Trafton, Wade, Wakeman, Walbridge, Waldron, Cadwalader C. Washburne, Elihu B. Washburne, Israel Washburn, Watson, Welch, Whitney, Wood, Woodruff, and Woodworth—109.

NAYS—Messrs. Aiken, Allen, Barclay, Barksdale, Bell, Hendley S. Bennett, Bocock, Bowie, Boyce, Branch, Brooks, Burnett, Cadwalader, John P. Campbell, Carlile, Caruthers, Caskie, Clingman, Howell Cobb, Williamson R. W. Cobb, Cox, Craige, Crawford, Davidson, Day, Denver, Dowdell, Edmundson, Elliot, English, Eustis, Faulkner, Florence, Foster, Thomas J. D. Fuller, Goode, Greenwood, Augustus Hall, J. Morrison Harris, Sampson W. Harris, Hickman, Hoffman, Houston, Jewett, George W. Jones, J. Glancy Jones, Keitt, Kelly, Kennett, Kidwell, Lake, Letcher, Lumpkin, Alexander K. Marshall, Humphrey Marshall, Maxwell, McMullin, McQueen, Smith Miller, Millson, Nichols, Mordecai Oliver, Orr, Packer, Paine, Peck, Phelps, Porter, Powell, Puryear, Quitman, Ready, Ricaud, Richardson, Rivers, Ruffin, Rust, Sandidge, Savage, Seward, Shorter, Samuel A. Smith, William Smith, William R. Smith, Sneed, Spinner, Stephens, Stewart, Swope, Talbott, Taylor, Trippe, Underwood, Valk, Walker, Warner, Watkins, Wheeler, Williams, Daniel B. Wright, John V. Wright, and Zollicoffer—102.

Mr. Stephens's substitute, as thus amended by its adversaries, was abandoned by its original friends, and received but *two* votes—those of Messrs. Geo. G. Dunn of Indiana and John Scott Harrison of Ohio—Nays 210.

Mr. Dunn had previously moved a reference of the bill to the Committee of the Whole on the state of the Union. This was now defeated: Yeas 101; Nays 109.

Mr. Jones of Tenn. now moved that the bill do lie on the table, which was defeated Yeas 106; Nays 107 (Barclay of Penn., Dunn of Ind., Haven and Williams of N. Y.—*Yeas;* Bayard Clarke of New-York, Hickman and Millward of Pa., Moore of Ohio, and Scott of Ind.—*Nays;* Scott Harrison of Ohio not voting, Wells of Wisc. absent). The House now refused to adjourn by 106 to 102; and, after a long struggle, the final question was reached, and the bill *rejected:* Yeas, 106; Nays 107—as follows:

YEAS—Messrs. Albright, Allison, Ball, Barbour, Henry Bennett, Benson, Billinghurst, Bingham, Bishop, Bliss, Bradshaw, Brenton, Buffinton, Burlingame, J. H. Campbell, Lewis D. Campbell, *Bayard Clarke*, Ezra Clark, Clawson, Colfax, Comins, Covode, Cragin, Cumback, Damrell, Timothy Davis, Day, Dean, De Witt, Dick, Dickson, Dodd, Durfee, Edie, Edwards, Emrie, Flagler, Galloway, Giddings, Gilbert, Granger, Grow, Robert B. Hall, Harlan, *Hickman*, Holloway, Thomas R. Horton, Valentine B. Horton, Howard, Hughston, Kelsey, King, Knapp, Knight, Knowlton, Knox, Kunkel, Leiter, Matteson, McCarty, Meacham, Killian Miller, *Millward*, *Moore*, Morgan, Morrill, Murray,

Nichols, Andrew Oliver, Parker, Pearce, Pelton, Pennington, Perry, Pettit, Pike, Purviance, Robbins, Roberts, Robison, Sabin, Sage, Sapp, *Scott*, Sherman, Simmons, Spinner, Stanton, Stranahan, Tappan, Thorington, Thurston, Todd, Trafton, Wade, Wakeman, Walbridge, Waldron, Cadwalader C. Washburne, Elihu B. Washburne, Israel Washburn, Watson, Welch, Wood, Woodruff, and Woodworth—106.

NAYS—Messrs. Aiken, Allen, *Barclay*, Barksdale, Bell, Hendley S. Bennet, Bocock, Bowie, Boyce, Branch, Brooks, *Broom*, Burnett, Cadwalader, John P. Campbell, Carlile, Caruthers, Caskie, Howell Cobb, Williamson R. W. Cobb, Cox, Craige, Crawford, Cullen, Davidson, *Denver*, Dowdell, Dunn, Edmundson, Elliot, English, Etheridge, Eustis, Evans, Faulkner, Florence, Foster, Thomas J. D. Fuller, Goode, Greenwood, Augustus Hall, J. Morrison Harris, Sampson W. Harris, *Harrison*, *Haven*, Herbert, Hoffman, Houston, Jewett, George W. Jones, J. Glancy Jones, Keitt, Kelly, Kennett, Kidwell, Lake, Letcher, Lindley, Lumpkin, Alexander K. Marshall, Humphrey Marshall, Samuel S. Marshall, Maxwell, McMullin, McQueen, Smith Miller, Millson, Mordecai Oliver, Orr, Packer, Paine, Peck, Phelps, Porter, Powell, Puryear, Quitman, Ready, Ricaud, Rivers, Ruffin, Rust, Sandidge, Savage, Seward, Shorter, Samuel A. Smith, William Smith, William R. Smith, Sneed, Stephens, Stewart, Swope, Talbott, Taylor, Trippe, Underwood, Valk, Walker, Warner, Watkins, Wheeler, Whitney, *Williams*, Daniel B. Wright, John V. Wright, and Zollicoffer—107.

So the bill was lost.

Mr. Goode of Virginia now sought to move a reconsideration, and to have that motion laid on the table; but was cut off by a motion to adjourn already pending, which prevailed.

July 1*st*.—Mr. Barclay (Dem.) of Pa. rose to a privileged motion. He moved a reconsideration of the preceding vote, by which the Free-Kansas bill had been rejected. A stormy debate ensued, in the midst of which Mr. Howard of Mich. rose to a question of higher privilege (as affecting the right of a member[delegate] to his seat) and submitted the Report of the Kansas Investigating Committee (already given). The Speaker sustained the motion, and the House sustained the Speaker. The Report was thereupon presented and read, consuming a full day.

July 3*rd*.—The question of reconsidering the vote defeating the Free-Kansas bill was again reached. Mr. Houston of Ala. moved that it do lie on the table: Defeated: Yeas 97; Nays 102. The main question was then ordered: Yeas 101; Nays 98; and the reconsideration carried: Yeas 101; Nays 99. The previous question on the passage of the bill was now ordered: Yeas 99; Nays 96; a motion by Mr. McQueen of S.C. to lay the bill on the table was defeated: Yeas 97; Nays 100; and then the bill was finally *passed*: Yeas 99; Nays 97, as follows:

YEAS—Messrs. Albright, Allison, Ball, Barbour, Barclay, Henry Bennett, Benson, Billinghurst, Bingham, Bliss, Bradshaw, Brenton, Buffinton, James H. Campbell, Lewis D. Campbell, Bayard Clarke, Ezra Clark, Clawson, Colfax, Comins, Covode, Cragin, Cumback, Damrell, Timothy Davis, Day, Dean, De Witt, Dick, Dickson, Dodd, Durfee, Edie, Edwards, Emrie, Flagler, Galloway, Giddings, Gilbert, Granger, Grow, Robert B. Hall, Harlan, Hickman, Holloway, Thomas R. Horton, Valentine B. Horton, Howard, Hughston, Kelsey, King, Knapp, Knight, Knowlton, Knox, Kunkel, Leiter, Matteson, McCarty, Meacham, Killian Miller, Millward, Morgan, Morrill, Mott, Murray, Nichols, Andrew Oliver, Parker, Pearce, Pelton, Perry, Pike, Pringle, Purviance, Robbins, Roberts, Robison, Sabin, Sage, Sapp, Scott, Sherman, Spinner, Stranahan, Tappan, Thorington, Thurston, Todd, Trafton, Wade, Wakeman, Walbridge, Waldron, Cadwalader C. Washburne, Elihu B. Washburne, Israel Washburn, Welch, Woodruff, and Woodworth—99.

NAYS—Messrs. Aiken, Allen, Barksdale, Bell, Hendley S. Bennett, Bocock, Bowie, Branch, Brooks, Broom, Burnett, Cadwalader, Caruthers, Caskie, Clingman, Howell Cobb, Williamson R. W. Cobb, Cox, Craige, Crawford, Cullen, Henry Winter Davis, Denver, Dowdell, Dunn, Edmundson, English, Etheridge, Eustis, Evans, Faulkner, Florence, Henry M. Fuller, Thos. J. D. Fuller, Goode, Greenwood, Augustus Hall, J Morrison Harris, Sampson W. Harris, Thomas L. Harris, Harrison, Haven, Houston, Jewett, George W. Jones, J. Glancy Jones, Kelly, Kennett, Kidwell, Lake, Lindley, Lumpkin, Alexander K. Marshall, Humphrey Marshall, Samuel S. Marshall, McMullin, McQueen, Smith Miller, Milson, Mordecai Oliver, Orr, Packer, Peck, Phelps, Porter, Powell, Puryear, Ready, Ricaud, Rivers, Ruffin, Rust, Sandidge, Savage, Seward, Shorter, Samuel A. Smith, William Smith, William R. Smith, Sneed, Stephens, Stewart, Swope, Taylor, Trippe, Underwood, Valk, Walker, Warner, Watkins, Wheeler, Whitney, Williams, Winslow, Daniel B. Wright, John V Wright, and Zollicoffer—97.

Mr. Grow of Pa. moved the reconsideration of this vote, and that the motion to reconsider do lie on the table, which was permitted, without further division.

The following is the Free-Kansas or Topeka Constitution aforesaid:

CONSTITUTION OF THE STATE OF KANSAS.

PREAMBLE:

We, the People of the Territory of Kansas, by our delegates in Convention assembled at Topeka, on the 23d day of October, A. D. 1855, and of the Independence of the United States the eightieth year, having the right of admission into the Union as one of the United States of America, consistent with the Federal Constitution and by virtue of the treaty of cession by France to the United States of the Province of Louisiana, in order to secure to ourselves and our posterity the enjoyment of all the rights of life, liberty and property, and the free pursuit of happiness, do mutually agree with each other to form ourselves into a free and independent State, by the name and style of the State of Kansas, bounded as follows, to wit: Beginning at a point on the western boundary of the State of Missouri where the thirty-seventh parallel of north latitude crosses the same; thence west on said parallel to the eastern boundary of New-Mexico; thence north on said boundary to latitude thirty-eight; thence following said boundary westward to the eastern boundary of the Territory of Utah on the summit of the Rocky Mountains; thence northward on said summit to the fortieth parallel of said latitude; thence east on said parallel to the western boundary of the State of Missouri; thence south with the western boundary of said State to the place of beginning; and do ordain and establish the following CONSTITUTION and BILL OF RIGHTS for the government thereof:

ARTICLE I.—BILL OF RIGHTS.

SECTION 1. All men are by nature free and independent, and have certain inalienable rights, among which are those of enjoying and defending life and liberty, acquiring, possessing, and protecting property, and seeking and obtaining happiness and safety.

SEC. 2. All political power is inherent in the PEOPLE. Government is instituted for their equal protection and benefit; and they have the right to alter, reform or abolish the same whenever they may deem it necessary; and no special privileges or immunities shall ever be granted that may not be altered, revoked, or repealed by the General Assembly.

SEC. 3. The people have the right to assemble together, in a peaceable manner, to consult, for their common good, to instruct their Representatives, and to petition the General Assembly for the redress of grievances.

SEC. 4. The people have the right to bear arms for their defense and security, but standing armies in time of peace are dangerous to liberty, and shall not be kept up; and the military shall be kept in strict subordination to the civil power.

SEC. 5. The right of trial by jury shall be inviolate.

SEC. 6 There shall be no Slavery in this State, nor involuntary servitude, unless for the punishment of crime.

SEC. 7. All men have a natural and indefeasible right to worship Almighty God according to the dictates of their own conscience. No person shall be compelled to attend, erect or support any place of worship, or maintain any form of worship against his consent; and no preference shall be given by law to any religious society; nor shall any interference with the rights of conscience be permitted. No religious test shall be required as a qualification for office, nor shall any person be incompetent to be a witness on account of his religious belief; but nothing herein shall be construed to dispense with oaths and affirmations. Religion, morality, and knowledge, however, being essential to good government, it shall be the duty of the General Assembly to pass suitable laws to protect every religious denomination in the peaceable enjoyment of its own mode of public worship, and to encourage schools and the means of instruction.

SEC. 8. The privilege of the writ of *habeas corpus* shall not be suspended, unless in case of rebellion or invasion the public safety require it.

SEC. 9. All persons shall be bailable by sufficient sureties, unless for capital offenses where the proof is evident, or the presumption great. Excessive bail shall not be required, nor excessive fines imposed, nor cruel and unusual punishments inflicted.

SEC. 10. Except in cases of impeachment, and cases arising in the army and navy, or in the militia, when in actual service, in time of war or public danger, and in cases of petit larceny and other inferior offenses, no person shall be held to answer for a capital or otherwise infamous crime, unless on presentment or indictment of a Grand Jury. In any trial, in any court, the party accused shall be allowed to appear and defend in person, and with counsel, to demand the nature and cause of the accusation against him, and to have a copy thereof; to meet the witnesses face to face, and to have compulsory process to procure the attendance of witnesses in his behalf, and a speedy public trial by an impartial jury of the county or district in which the offense is alleged to have been committed; nor shall any person be compelled in any criminal case to be a witness against himself, or be twice put in jeopardy for the same offense.

SEC. 11. Every citizen may freely speak, write and publish his sentiments on all subjects, being responsible for the abuse of the right; and no law shall be passed to restrain or abridge the liberty of speech or of the press. In all criminal prosecutions or indictments for libel, the truth may be given in evidence to the jury, and if it shall appear to the jury that the matter charged as libelous is true, and was published with good motives, and for justifiable ends, the party shall be acquitted.

SEC. 12. No person shall be transported out of the State for any offense committed within the same; and no conviction shall work corruption of blood or forfeiture of estate.

SEC. 13. No soldier shall, in time of peace, be quartered in any house without the consent of the owner; nor in time of war, except in a manner prescribed by law.

SEC. 14. The right of the people to be secure in their persons, houses, papers, and possessions, against unreasonable searches and seizures, shall not be violated: and no warrant shall issue but upon probable cause, supported by oath or affirmation, particularly describing the place to be searched, and the persons and things to be seized.

SEC. 15. No person shall be imprisoned for debt in any civil action, or mesne or final process, unless in case of fraud.

SEC. 16. All courts shall be open; and every person for an injury done him in his land, goods, person, or reputation, shall have remedy by due course of law, and justice administered without denial or delay.

SEC. 17. No hereditary emoluments, honors, or privileges, shall ever be granted or conferred by this State.

SEC. 18. No power of suspending laws shall ever be exercised, except by the General Assembly.

SEC. 19. The payment of a tax shall not be a qualification for exercising the right of suffrage.

SEC. 20. Private property shall ever be held inviolate, but subservient to the public welfare. When taken in time of war, or other public exigency, imperatively requiring its immediate seizure, or for the purpose of making or repairing roads, which shall be open to the public use, without toll or other charge therefor, a compensation shall be made to the owner in money; and in all other cases, where private property shall be taken for public use, a compensation therefor shall first be made in money, first secured by a deposit of money, and such compensation shall be assessed by a jury, without deduction for benefits to any property of the owner.

SEC. 21. No indenture of any negro, or mulatto, made and executed out of the bounds of the State, shall be valid within the State.

SEC. 22. This enumeration of rights shall not be construed to impair or deny others retained by the people; and all powers not herein delegated shall remain with the people.

ARTICLE II.—ELECTIVE FRANCHISE.

SECTION 1. In all elections by the people, the vote shall be by ballot, and in all elections in the General Assembly, the vote shall be *viva voce.*

SEC. 2. Every white male person, and every civilized male Indian who has adopted the habits of the white man, of the age of twenty-one years and upward, who shall be at the time of offering to vote a citizen of the United States; who shall have resided, and had his habitation, domicile, home, and place of permanent abode in the State of Kansas for six months next preceding the election at which he offers his vote; who, at such time, and for thirty days immediately preceding said time, shall have had his actual habitation, domicile, home, and place of abode in the county in which he offers to vote; and who shall have resided in the precinct or election-district for at least ten days immediately preceding the election, shall be deemed a qualified elector at all elections under this Constitution, except at elections by general ticket in the State or district prescribed by law, in which case the elector must have the aforesaid qualifications, but a residence in said district for ten days will entitle him to vote: *Provided*, That no soldier, seaman, or marine of the regular army of the United States shall be considered a resident of the State in consequence of being stationed within the same.

SEC. 3. The General Assembly shall, at its first session, provide for the registration of all qualified electors in each county, and thereafter, from time to time, of all who may become qualified electors.

SEC. 4. The Legislature shall have power to exclude from every office of honor, trust or profit within the State, and from the right of suffrage, all persons convicted of any infamous crime.

SEC. 5. No person shall be deemed capable of holding or being elected to any post of honor, profit, trust, or emolument, civil or military, or exercise the right of suffrage under the government of this State, who shall hereafter fight a duel, send or accept a challenge to fight a duel, or who shall be a second to either party, or who shall in any manner aid or assist in such duel, or who shall be knowingly the bearer of such challenge or acceptance, whether the same occur or be committed in or out of the State.

SEC. 5. No person who may hereafter be collector or holder of public moneys shall be eligible to any office of trust or profit in the State until he shall have accounted for and paid into the proper public treasury all sums for which he may be accountable.

SEC. 7. No State officer or member of the General Assembly of this State shall receive a fee, be engaged as counsel, agent, or attorney, in any case or claim against the State.

SEC. 8. No Senator or Representative shall, during the term of office for which he shall have been elected, be appointed to any civil office of profit in this State which shall have been created, or the emoluments of which shall have been increased during such term, except such offices as may be filled by election by the people.

SEC. 9. All officers, civil and military, in this State, before they enter upon the duties of their respective offices, shall take the following oath or affirmation: "I ——— ———, do swear [or affirm] that I will support the Constitution of the United States, and of the State of Kansas; that I am duly qualified according to the Constitution to exercise the office to which I have been elected, [or appointed,] and will, to the best of my abilities, discharge the duties thereof faithfully and impartially, according to law."

SEC. 10. Every person shall be disqualified from holding any office of honor or profit in this State, who shall have been convicted of having given or offered any bribe to procure his election, or who shall have made use of any undue influence from power, tumult, or other improper practices.

SEC. 11. All civil officers of the State shall reside within the State, and all District and County officers within their respective Districts and Counties, and shall have their offices at such places as may be required by law.

SEC. 12. Returns of elections for members of Congress, the General Assembly, and all other officers not otherwise provided for, shall be made to the Secretary of State, in such manner as may be prescribed by law.

SEC. 13. Electors shall in all cases be privileged from arrest during their attendance on elections, and in going to and returning therefrom, except in case of felony, treason, and breach of the peace.

ARTICLE III.—DISTRIBUTION OF POWERS.

SECTION 1. The powers of the Government shall be divided into three separate departments—the Legislative, the Executive, including the Administrative, and the Judicial; and no person charged with official duties under one of these departments shall exercise any of the functions of another, except as in this Constitution expressly provided.

ARTICLE IV.—LEGISLATIVE.

SECTION 1. The Legislative power of this State shall be vested in the General Assembly, which shall consist of a Senate and House of Representatives.

SEC. 2. The Senators and Representatives shall be chosen annually by the qualified electors of the respective Counties or Districts for which they are chosen, on the first Monday of August, for one year, and their term of office shall commence on the first day of January next thereafter.

SEC. 3. There shall be elected at the first election twenty Senators, and sixty Representatives, and the number afterward shall be regulated by law.

SEC. 4. No person shall be eligible to the office of Senator, or Representative, who shall not possess the qualifications of an elector.

SEC. 5. No person holding office under the authority of the United States, or any lucrative office under the authority of this State, shall be eligible to or hold a seat in the General Assembly; but this provision shall not extend to township officers, justices of the peace, notaries public, postmasters, or officers of the militia.

SEC. 6. Each House, except as otherwise provided in this Constitution, shall choose its own officers, determine its own rule of proceeding, punish its members for disorderly conduct, and with the concurrence of two-thirds expel a member, but not the second time for the same cause; and shall judge of the qualification, election and return of its own members, and shall have all other powers necessary for its safety and the undisturbed transaction of business.

SEC. 7. Each House shall keep a journal of its proceedings and publish the same. The Yeas and Nays on any question shall, at the request of two members, be entered on the journal.

SEC. 8. Any member of either House shall have the right to protest against any act or resolution thereof; and such protest and reason therefor shall, without alteration, commitment or delay, be entered on the journal.

SEC. 9. All vacancies which may occur in either House shall, for the unexpired term, be filled by election as shall be prescribed by law.

SEC. 10. Senators and Representatives shall, in all cases except treason, felony or breach of the peace, be privileged from arrest during the session of the General Assembly, and in going to and returning from the same; and for words spoken in debate they shall not be questioned in any other place.

SEC. 11. A majority of all the members elected

to each House shall be necessary to pass every bill or joint resolution, and all bills and joint resolutions so passed shall be signed by the presiding officers of the respective Houses, and presented to the Governor for his approval.

SEC. 12. The doors of each House, and of Committees of the Whole, shall be kept open. Neither House shall, without the consent of the other, adjourn for more than two days, nor to any other place than that in which the two Houses shall be sitting, except for personal safety.

SEC. 13. Every bill shall be read by sections on three several days in each House unless in case of emergency. Two-thirds of the House where such bill is pending, may, if deemed expedient, suspend the rules on a call of the Yeas and Nays; but the reading of a bill by sections on its final passage shall in no case be dispensed with; and the vote on the passage of every bill or joint resolution shall be taken by Yeas and Nays.

SEC. 14. Every act shall contain but one subject, which shall be clearly expressed in its title. Bills may originate in either House, but may be altered, amended, or rejected by the other.

SEC. 15. In all cases when a general law can be made applicable, special laws shall not be enacted.

SEC. 16. No act shall ever be revived or amended by mere reference to its title; but the act revived, or the section amended, shall be set forth and published at full length.

SEC. 17. No act shall take effect until the same shall have been published and circulated in the counties of the State by authority, except in case of emergency, which emergency shall be declared in the preamble, or the body of the law.

SEC. 18. The election and appointment of all officers, and the filling of all vacancies not otherwise provided for by this Constitution, or the Constitution of the United States, shall be made in such manner as shall be prescribed by law; but no appointing power shall be exercised by the General Assembly, except as provided in this Constitution and in the election of the United States Senator, and in these cases the vote shall be taken viva voce.

SEC. 19. The General Assembly shall not have power to enact laws annulling the contract of marriage in any case where by law the courts of this State may have power to decree a divorce.

SEC. 20. The General Assembly shall not have power to pass retro-active laws, or laws impairing the obligation of contracts, but may by general laws authorize Courts to carry into effect, upon such terms as shall be just and equitable, the manifest intention of parties and officers, by curing omissions, defects, and errors in instruments, and proceedings arising out of a want of conformity with the laws of this State.

SEC. 21. The style of the laws of this State shall be: "*Be it enacted by the General Assembly of the State of Kansas.*"

SEC. 22. The House of Representatives shall have the sole power of impeachment. All impeachments shall be tried by the Senate, and when sitting for the purpose, the Senators shall be upon oath or affirmation to do justice according to law and evidence. No person shall be convicted without the concurrence of two-thirds of all the Senators present.

SEC. 23. The Governor and all other civil officers, under the laws of this State, shall be liable to impeachment for any misdemeanor in office, but judgment in such cases shall not extend further than to removal from office, and disqualification to hold any office of honor, profit, or trust, under this State. The party, whether convicted or acquitted, shall nevertheless be liable to indictment, trial, judgment and punishment, according to law.

SEC. 24. Within one year after the ratification of this Constitution, and within every subsequent two years thereafter, for the term of ten years, an enumeration of all the white inhabitants of this State shall be made in such manner as shall be directed by law.

SEC. 25. All regular sessions of the General Assembly shall be held at the capital of the State, and shall commence on the firs tTuesday of January annually.

SEC. 26. All bills for raising revenue shall originate in the House of Representatives, subject, however, to amendment or rejection as in other cases.

SEC. 27. The members of the General Assembly shall receive for their services the sum of four dollars per day for each and every day they are actually in attendance at any regular or special session, and four dollars for every twenty miles they shall travel in going to and returning from the place of meeting by the most usually traveled route; and no session of the General Assembly, except the first under this Constitution, shall extend beyond the term of sixty days, nor any special session more than forty days.

ARTICLE V.—EXECUTIVE.

SECTION 1. The Executive Department shall consist of a Governor, a Lieutenant-Governor, Secretary of State, Treasurer, Auditor, and Attorney-General, who shall be chosen by the electors of the State at the same time and place of voting for the members of the General Assembly.

SEC. 2. The Governor, Lieutenant-Governor, Secretary of State, Treasurer, Auditor, Attorney-General, and State Printer, shall hold their office for two years. Their terms of office shall commence on the first Tuesday of January next after their election, and continue until their successors are elected and qualified, neither of which officers shall be eligible for re-election more than two out of three consecutive terms: nor shall any person be eligible for the office of Governor who who shall not have attained the age of thirty years.

SEC. 3. The returns of every election for the officers named in the foregoing section, shall be sealed up and transmitted to the seat of government by the returning-officers, directed to the Secretary of State, who shall lay the same before the General Assembly at their first meeting thereafter, when they shall open, publish and declare the result thereof in the presence of a majority of the members of both Houses. The person having the highest number of votes shall be declared duly elected, and a certificate thereof given to such person, signed by the presiding officers of both bodies; but if any two or more shall be highest and equal in votes for the same office, one of them shall be chosen by the joint vote of both Houses.

SEC. 4. The supreme executive power shall be vested in a Governor.

SEC. 5. He may require information in writing from the officers in the Executive Department upon any subject relating to the duties of their respective offices, and shall see that the laws are faithfully executed.

SEC. 6. He shall communicate at every session, by message, to the General Assembly, the condition of the affairs of the State, and recommend such measures as he shall deem expedient for their action.

SEC. 7. He may on extraordinary occasions convene the General Assembly by proclamation, and shall state to both Houses when assembled the purposes for which they were convened.

SEC. 8. In case of disagreement between the two Houses, in respect to the time of adjournment, he shall have power to adjourn the General Assembly to such time as he may think proper, but not beyond the regular meetings thereof.

SEC. 9. He shall be commander-in-chief of the military in the State, except when they shall be called into the service of the United States.

SEC. 10. The pardoning power shall be vested in the Governor, under such regulations and restrictions as may be prescribed by law.

SEC. 11. There shall be a seal of the State, the device of which shall be fixed upon by the Governor and other State officers, be kept by the Governor and used by him officially, and shall be called "*The Great Seal of the State of Kansas.*"

SEC. 12. All grants and commissions shall be used in the name and by the authority of the State of Kansas, sealed with the great seal, signed by the Governor, and countersigned by the Secretary of State.

SEC. 13. No member of either House of Congress, or other persons holding office under the authority of this State, or of the United States, shall execute the office of Governor except as herein provided.

SEC. 14. In the case of death, impeachment, resignation, removal, or other disability of the Governor, the Lieutenant-Governor shall exercise the duties of the office of Governor, until another Governor shall be duly qualified; but in such case another Governor shall be chosen at the next annual election for members of the General Assembly, unless such death, resignation, impeachment, removal, or other disability shall occur within three calendar months immediately preceding such next annual election, in which case a Governor shall be chosen at the second succeeding annual election for members of the General Assembly, and in case of the death, impeachment, resignation, removal, or other disability of the Lieutenant-Governor, the President of the Senate *pro tem.* shall exercise the office of Governor until a Governor shall be duly qualified as aforesaid.

SEC. 15. The Lieut.-Governor shall be President of the Senate, but shall vote only when the Senate is equally divided, and shall be entitled to the same pay as the Speaker of the House of Representatives, and in case of his death, impeachment, resignation, removal from office, or when he shall exercise the office of Governor, the Senate shall choose a President *pro tem.*

SEC. 16. Should the office of Secretary of State, Treasurer, Auditor, or Attorney-General become vacant, for any of the causes specified in the fourteenth and fifteenth sections, the Governor shall fill the vacancy or vacancies until the disability is removed or a successor is elected and qualified. Every such vacancy shall be filled by election, at the first general election that occurs more than thirty days after such vacancy shall have occurred, and the person chosen shall hold the office for the full term fixed in the second section of this article.

SEC. 17. The officers mentioned in this article shall, at stated times, receive for their services compensation to be fixed by law, which shall neither be increased nor diminished during the period for which they shall have been elected.

SEC. 18. The officers of the Executive Department, and of the public State Institutions shall, at least ten days preceding each regular session of the General Assembly, severally report to the Governor, who shall transmit the same to the General Assembly.

SEC. 19. Every bill which shall have passed both Houses shall be presented to the Governor. If he approve he shall sign the same; but if he shall not approve, he shall return it with his objections to the House in which it shall have originated, who shall enter the objections at large upon the journal, and proceed to reconsider the same. If after such reconsideration two-thirds of that House shall agree to pass the bill, it shall be sent, with the objections, to the other House, by which, likewise, it shall be reconsidered, and if approved by two-thirds of that House, it shall be a law. But in such case the votes of both Houses shall be determined by Yeas and Nays, and the names of the persons voting for or against the bill shall be entered upon the journals of the House respectively. If any bill shall not be returned by the Governor within five days (Sunday excepted) after it shall have been presented to him, it shall be a law in like manner as if he had signed it, unless the General Assembly, by their adjournment, prevented its return, in which case it shall also be a law, unless sent back within two days after the next meeting.

SEC. 20. Contested elections for Governor, Lieutenant-Governor, Judges of the Supreme Court, and all other State officers, shall be determined by the General Assembly in such manner as may be prescribed by law.

SEC. 21. The General Assembly shall have power to provide by law for the election of a Surveyor-General, State Geologist, and Superintendent of Common Schools, whose duties shall be prescribed by law.

ARTICLE VI.—JUDICIAL.

SECTION 1. The Judicial power of the State shall be vested in a Supreme Court, Courts of Common Pleas, Justices of the Peace, and in such other Courts inferior to the Supreme Court as the General Assembly may establish.

SEC. 2. The Supreme Court shall consist of three Judges, a majority of whom shall form a quorum. It shall have such original and appellate jurisdiction as may be provided by law. It shall hold at least one term each year at the seat of Government, and such other Terms as may be provided by law. The Judges of the Supreme Court shall be elected by the electors of the State at large.

SEC. 3. The State shall be divided by the first General Assembly under this Constitution into three Common Pleas Districts of compact Territory, bounded by county lines, and as nearly equal in population as practicable; and a Judge for each District shall be chosen by the electors thereof, and their term of office shall be for three years.

SEC. 4. The Courts of Common Pleas shall consist of one Judge each, who shall reside within the district for which he is chosen during his continuance in office.

SEC. 5. The jurisdiction of the Court of Common Pleas and of the Judges thereof shall be fixed by law.

SEC. 6. A competent number of Justices of the Peace shall be elected by the electors in each township of several counties. The term of office shall be three years, and their powers and duties shall be fixed by law.

SEC. 7. All Judges, other than those provided for in the Constitution, shall be elected by the electors of the judicial district for which they may be created, but not for a longer term of office than three years.

SEC. 8. The Judges of the Supreme Court shall, immediately after the first election under this Constitution, be classified by lot, so that one shall hold for the term of one year, one for the term of three years; and all subsequent elections the term of each of said Judges shall be for three years.

SEC. 9. In case the office of any Judge shall become vacant before the expiration of the term for which he was elected, the vacancy shall be filled by appointment by the Governor, until a successor shall be elected and qualified; and such successor shall be elected for the residue of the unexpired term, at the first annual election that occurs more than thirty days after such vacancy shall have happened.

SEC. 10. The Judges of the Supreme Court and of the Court of Common Pleas shall, at stated times, receive such compensation as may be provided by law, which shall not be increased or diminished during their term of office; but they shall receive no fees or perquisites, nor hold any other office of profit and trust under the State, other than a judicial office.

SEC. 11. The General Assembly may increase or diminish the number of the Judges of the Supreme Court, the number of the districts of the Courts of Common Pleas, the number of Judges in any district, or establish other courts, whenever two-thirds of the members elected to each House shall concur therein; but no such change, addition, or diminution shall vacate the office of any Judge.

SEC. 12. There shall be elected in each county, by the electors thereof, one Clerk of the Court of Common Pleas, who shall hold his office for the term of three years, and until his successor shall be elected and qualified.

SEC. 13. The General Assembly shall provide by law for the speedy publication of the decisions of the Supreme Court made under this Constitution.

SEC. 14. The Supreme Court shall, upon the decision of every case, give an opinion in writing of each question arising in the record in such case and the decision of the Court thereon.

SEC. 15. There shall be elected by the voters of the State a Clerk and a Reporter for the Supreme Court, who shall hold their offices for three years, and whose duties shall be prescribed by law.

SEC. 16. Judges may be removed from office by concurrent resolution of both Houses of the General Assembly, if two-thirds of the members elected to each House concur therein; but no such removal shall be made except upon complaint, the substance of which shall be entered upon the journal, nor until the party thereof charged shall have had notice thereof, and an opportunity to be heard.

SEC. 17. The several Judges of the Supreme Court, of the Court of Common Pleas, and of such other courts as may be created by law, shall respectively have and exercise such power and jurisdiction, at chambers or otherwise, as may be provided by law.

SEC. 18. The style of all process shall be "The State of Kansas." All prosecutions shall be carried on in the name and by the authority of the State of Kansas, and all indictments shall conclude "Against the peace and dignity of the State of Kansas."

ARTICLE VII.—EDUCATION.

SECTION 1. The principal of all funds arising from the sale or other disposition of lands or other property granted or intrusted to this State for educational and religious purposes, shall forever be preserved inviolate and undiminished, and the income arising therefrom shall be faithfully applied to the specific objects of the original grants or appropriations.

SEC. 2. The General Assembly shall make such provision, by taxation or otherwise, as, with the income arising from the school-trust fund, will secure a thorough and efficient system of common schools throughout the State; but no religious or other sect or sects shall ever have any exclusive right to, or control of, any part of the school funds of this State.

SEC. 3. The General Assembly may take measures for the establishment of a University, with such branches as the public convenience may hereafter demand, for the promotion of literature, the arts, sciences, medical and agricultural instruction.

SEC. 4. Provision may be made by the law for the support of normal schools, with suitable libraries and scientific apparatus.

ARTICLE VIII.—PUBLIC INSTITUTIONS.

SECTION 1. It shall be the duty of the General Assembly, at as early a date as possible, to provide State Asylums for the benefit, treatment and instruction of the blind, deaf and dumb, and insane.

SEC. 2. The General Assembly shall make provision for the establishment of an Asylum for idiots, to be regulated by law.

SEC. 3. The respective counties of the State shall provide in some suitable manner for those inhabitants who, by reason of age, infirmity or other misfortune, may have claims upon the sympathy and aid of society; under provisions to be made by the laws of the General Assembly.

SEC. 4. The General Assembly shall make provision for the establishment of houses of refuge for the correction, reform, and instruction of juvenile offenders.

SEC. 5. It shall be the duty of the General Assembly to make provisions as soon as possible for a State General Hospital.

ARTICLE IX.—PUBLIC DEBT AND PUBLIC WORKS.

SECTION 1. No money shall be paid out of the treasury except in pursuance of an appropriation by law.

SEC. 2. The credit of the State shall never be given or loaned in aid of any individual association or corporation.

SEC. 3. For the purpose of defraying extraordinary expenditures, the State may contract public debts, but such debts shall never in the aggregate exceed one hundred thousand dollars, unless authorized by a direct vote of the people at a general election. Every such debt shall be authorized by law, and every such law shall provide for the payment of the annual interest of such debt, and the principal within ten years from the passage of such law, and such appropriation shall not be repealed until the principal and interest shall have been wholly paid.

SEC. 4. The Legislature may also borrow money to repel invasion, suppress insurrection, or defend the State in time of war; but the money thus raised shall be applied exclusively to the object for which the loan was authorized, or repayment of the debts thereby created.

SEC. 5. No scrip, certificate, or other evidence of State debt whatever, shall be issued, except for such debts as are authorized by the third and fourth sections of this article.

ARTICLE X.—MILITIA.

SECTION 1. The militia shall consist of all able-bodied white male persons between the ages of eighteen and forty years: except such as may be exempt by the laws of the United States or of this State, and shall be organized, officered, armed, equipped, and trained in such manner as may be provided by law.

SEC. 2. The Governor shall appoint the Adjutant, Quartermaster and Commissary Generals.

SEC. 3. All militia officers shall be commissioned by the Governor and shall hold their offices not longer than three years.

SEC. 4. The General Assembly shall determine the method of dividing the militia into divisions, brigades, regiments, battalions and companies, and fix the rank of all officers.

SEC. 5. The militia may be divided into classes, in such manner as shall be prescribed by law.

SEC. 6. No person conscientiously opposed to bearing arms shall be compelled to do militia duty; but such person shall pay an equivalent for such exemption, the amount to be prescribed by law.

SEC. 7. The first General Assembly shall offer inducements for the formation, uniforming and drilling of independent volunteer companies in the different cities and counties in this State.

ARTICLE XI.—FINANCE AND TAXATION.

SECTION 1. The General Assembly shall provide, by law, for uniform and equal rate of assessment and taxation; and taxes shall be levied upon all such property, real and personal, as the General Assembly may, from time to time, prescribe; but all property appropriated and used exclusively for municipal, literary, educational, scientific or charitable purposes, and personal property to an amount not exceeding one hundred dollars, for each head of a family, and all property appropriated and used exclusively for religious purposes to an amount not exceeding $200,000, may, by general laws, be exempted from taxation.

SEC. 2. The General Assembly shall provide by law for an annual tax sufficient to defray the estimated ordinary expenses of the State for each year.

SEC. 3. Every law imposing a tax shall state distinctly the object of the same, to which it shall be applied.

SEC. 4. On the passage, in either House of the General Assembly, of any law which imposes, continues or renews a tax; or makes, continues or renews an appropriation of public or trust money; or releases, discharges or commutes a claim or demand of the State, the question shall be taken by Yeas and Nays, which shall be duly entered on the journal; and three-fifths of all the members elected to such House shall, in all such cases, be required to constitute a quorum.

ARTICLE XII.—COUNTY AND TOWNSHIP OFFICERS.

SECTION 1. The General Assembly shall provide by law for the election of county, city, town and township officers.

SEC. 2. All officers whose election or appointment is not provided for by this Constitution shall be elected by the people, or appointed as the General Assembly may by law direct.

SEC. 3. Provision shall be made by law for the removal, for misconduct or malversation in office, of all officers whose powers and duties are not local or legislative, and who shall be elected at general elections, and also for supplying vacancies created by such removal.

SEC. 4. The Legislature may declare the cases in which any office shall be deemed vacant, where no provision is made for that purpose in this Constitution.

ARTICLE XIII.—CORPORATION.

SECTION 1. The General Assembly shall not create corporations by special act, except for municipal purposes.

SEC. 2. Corporations may be formed under general laws, but such laws may at any time be altered or repealed.

ARTICLE XIV.—JURISPRUDENCE.

SECTION 1. The General Assembly, at its first session, shall constitute three Commissioners, whose duty it shall be to revise, reform, simplify and abridge the rules of practice, pleadings, forms and proceedings of the Courts of Record of this State, and to provide, so far as practicable and expedient, that justice shall be administered by intelligent and uniform proceedings, without any distinction between law and equity.

SEC. 2. The proceedings of the Commissioners shall be reported to the General Assembly, and be subject to the action of that body.

ARTICLE XV.—MISCELLANEOUS.

SECTION 1. The first General Assembly shall locate the permanent seat of government.

SEC. 2. Lotteries and the sale of lottery tickets for any purpose whatever, shall forever be prohibited in the State.

SEC. 3. No person shall be elected or appointed to any office in this State unless they possess the qualifications of an elector.

SEC. 4. There may be established in the Secretary of State's office a Bureau of Statistics and Agriculture, under such regulations as may be prescribed by law, and provision shall be made by the General Assembly for the organization and encouragement of State and county Agricultural Associations.

SEC. 5. The first General Assembly shall provide by law for securing to the wife the separate property acquired by her before or after coveture, and the equal right with the husband to the custody of their children during their minority; and in case of death, insanity, intemperance, or gross impropriety of the husband, their exclusive custody.

ARTICLE XVI.—AMENDMENTS TO THE CONSTITUTION.

SECTION 1. All propositions for amendments to the Constitution shall be made by the General Assembly.

SEC. 2. A concurrence of two-thirds of the members elected to each House shall be necessary, after which such proposed amendments shall be entered upon the journals with the Yeas and Nays, and the Secretary of State shall cause the same to be published in at least one newspaper in each County in the State where a newspaper is published, for at least six months preceding the next election for Senators and Representatives, when such proposed amendments shall be again referred to the Legislature elected next succeeding said publication. If passed by the second Legislature, by a majority of two-thirds of the members elected to each House, such amendments shall be re-published as aforesaid for at least six months prior to the next general election, at which election such proposed amendments shall be submitted to the people for their approval or rejection, and if the majority of the electors voting at such election shall adopt such amendments, the same shall becon e a part of the Constitution.

SEC. 3. When more than one amendment is submitted at the same time, they shall be so submitted as to enable the electors to vote upon each amendment separately.

SEC. 4. No convention for the formation oı a new constitution shall be called, and no amendment to the Constitution shall be by the General Assembly made, before the year 1865, nor more than once in five years thereafter.

ARTICLE XVII.—BANKS AND CURRENCY.

SECTION 1. No banks shall be established otherwise than under a General Banking Law.

SEC. 2. If the General Assembly shall enact a General Banking Law, such law shall provide for the registry and countersigning by the Auditor of State of all paper credit designed to be circulated as money, with ample collateral security, readily convertible into specie for the redemption of the same in gold or silver, shall be required; which collateral security shall be under the control of the proper officer, or officers of State. Such law shall restrict the aggregate amount of all paper credit to be circulated as money, and the aggregate amount to be put in circulation in any one year; and no note issued under the provision of this section shall be of a less denomination than ten dollars.

SEC. 3. The stockholders in every bank or banking company shall be individually liable to an amount over and above their stock equal to their respective shares of stock for all debts and liabilities of said bank or banking company.

SEC. 4. All bills or notes issued as money shall be at all times redeemable in gold or silver; and no law shall be passed sanctioning, directly or indirectly, the suspension by any bank or banking company of specie payments.

SEC. 5. Holders of bank notes shall be entitled, in case of insolvency, to preference of specie payment over all other creditors.

SEC. 6. No bank shall receive, directly or indirectly, a greater rate of interest than shall be allowed by law to individuals loaning money.

SEC. 7. Every bank or banking company shall be required to cease all banking operations within twenty years from the time of its organization, and promptly thereafter to close its business.

SEC. 8. The State shall not be a stockholder in any bank or banking institution.

SEC. 9. All banks shall be required to keep offices and proper officers for the issue and redemption of their paper at some accessible and convenient point within the State.

SEC. 10. The said Banking law shall contain a provision reserving the power to alter, amend, or repeal said law.

SEC. 11. At the time of submitting this Constitution to the electors for their approval or disapproval, the articles numbered in relation to a General Banking Law shall be submitted as a distinct proposition in the following form: General Banking Law; Yes, or No; and if a majority of the votes cast shall be in favor of said article, then the same shall form a part of this Constitution; otherwise it shall be void and form no part thereof.

SCHEDULE.

In order that no inconvenience may arise from the organization and establishment of a State Government, and that the wishes of the people may be fully accomplished, it is declared:

First: That no existing rights, suits, prosecutions, claims, and contracts shall be affected by a change in the form of Government.

Second: That this Constitution shall be submitted to the people of Kansas for ratification on the 15th day of December next.

Third: That each qualified elector shall express his assent or dissent to the Constitution by voting a written or printed ticket labeled "Constitution" or "No Constitution," which election shall be held by the same Judges, and conducted under the same regulations and restrictions as is hereinafter provided for the election of Members of the General Assembly, and the Judges therein named shall, within ten days after said election, seal up and transmit to the Chairman of the Executive Committee of Kansas Territory the result of said election, who shall forthwith make proclamation of the same; and in case the Constitution be ratified by the people, the Chairman of the Executive Committee shall cause publication to be made by proclamation that an election will be held on the third Tuesday of January, A.D. 1856, for Governor, Lieutenant-Governor, Secretary of State, Treasurer, Auditor, Judges of the Supreme Court, State Printer, Attorney-General, Reporter of the Supreme Court, Clerk of the Supreme Court, and Members of the General Assembly, which said election shall be held by the same Judges, under the same restrictions, and conducted in the same manner as is hereinafter provided for the election of Members of the General Assembly; and the Judges herein named are hereby required, within ten days after said election, to seal up and transmit duplicate copies of the returns of said election to the Chairman of the Executive Committee, one of which shall be laid before the General Assembly at its first meeting.

Fourth: At the same time and place, the qualified voters shall, under the same regulations and restrictions, elect a Member of Congress to represent the State of Kansas in the XXXIVth Congress of the United States; the returns of said election to be made to the Chairman of the Executive Committee, who shall deposit the same in the office of the Secretary of State as soon as he shall enter upon the discharge of the duties of his office.

Fifth: The General Assembly shall meet on the fourth day of March, A. D. 1856, at the City of Topeka, at 12 M., at which time and place the Governor, Lieutenant-Governor, Secretary of State, Judge of the Supreme Court, Treasurer, Auditor, State Printer, Reporter and Clerk of the Supreme Court, and Attorney-General shall appear, take the oath of office, and enter upon the discharge of the duties of their respective offices under this Constitution, and shall continue in office in the same manner and during the same period they would have done had they been elected on the first Monday of August, A. D. 1856.

[The Constitution then goes on to give the boundaries of the Eighteen Election-Districts into which the State is to be divided, to apportion the Senators and Representatives, and to appoint the voting places and the Judges of election. We subjoin the concluding sections:]

INSTRUCTION TO JUDGES.

SEC. 7. The three Judges will provide for each poll ballot-boxes for depositing the ballots cast by electors; shall appoint two clerks, all of whom shall be sworn or affirmed to discharge the duties of their respective offices impartially and with fidelity; and the Judges and Clerks shall have power to administer the oath or affirmation to each other; and the said Judges shall open said election at 9 o'clock A. M., at the place designated in each precinct, and close the same at 6 o'clock P. M. In case any of the officers appointed fail to attend, the officer or officers in attendance shall supply their places, and in the event of all of them failing to attend the qualified voters shall supply their places, and the said Judges shall make out duplicate returns of said election, seal up and transmit the same within ten days to the Chairman of the Executive Committee, one copy of which is to be laid before the General Assembly. If at the time of holding said election it shall be inconvenient, from any cause whatever, that would disturb or prevent the voters of any election-precinct in the Territory from the free and peaceable exercise of the elective franchise, the officers are hereby authorized to adjourn said election into any other precinct in the Territory, and to any other day they may see proper, of the necessity of which they shall be the exclusive judges, at which time and place the qualified voters may cast their votes.

SEC. 8. Until otherwise provided by law, the Chairman of the Executive Commitee of Kansas Territory shall announce by proclamation the result of the elections and the names of persons elected to office.

SEC. 9. No person shall be entitled to a seat in the first General Assembly at its organization except the members whose names are contained in the proclamation of the Chairman of the Executive Committee; but after the General Assembly is organized seats may be contested in the usual way.

SEC. 10. Certificates of indebtedness may be issued by the Territorial Executive Committee, for all necessary expenses accruing in the formation of the State Government, not exceeding $25,000; provided no certificates shall be issued except for legitimate expenses. All claims shall be made in writing, and shall be numbered and kept on file in the Secretary's office, and all certificates of indebtedness shall be signed by the President and Secretary, and countersigned by the Treasur,er and numbered to correspond with the numbers of the claim or bill for which it was issued. The certificate shall bear ten per cent. interest per annum.

SEC. 11. The first General Assembly shall provide by law for the redemption of the certificates of indebtedness issued under the provisions of the foregoing section.

SEC. 12. Until the great seal of the State of Kansas is agreed upon and procured, as provided for in the eleventh section of the fifth article of this Constitution, the Governor shall use his own private seal as the Seal of State.

SEC. 13. At the election for the ratification of this Constitution, and the first election for State officers, a representation in the Congress of the United States and members of the General Assembly of this State, an actual residence in the Territory of thirty days immediately preceding said election shall be sufficient as a qualification for the elector; and an actual residence of ninety days for the candidates, provided said election and candidates possess all the other qualifications required by the provisions of this Constitution.

SEC. 14. The first Legislature shall provide by law for the enforcement of the provisions of the 6th section of the Bill of Rights on or before the 4th day of July, 1857, as to all persons in the Territory before the adoption of this Constitutin, and as to all others, the provisions of said section shall operate from and after the ratification of this Constitution by the people.

ROBERT KLOTZ,	W. GRAHAM,
M. J. PARROTT,	MORRIS HUNT,
M. W. DELAHAY,	J. H. NESBITT,
W. R. GRIFFITH,	C K HOLLIDAY,
G. S. HILLYER,	DAVID DODGE,
WM. HICKS,	J. A. WAKEFIELD,
S. N. LATTA,	W. Y. ROBERTS,
JOHN LANDIS,	G. W. SMITH,
H. BURSON,	J. G. THOMPSON,
C. W. STEWART,	G. A. CUTLER,
J. M. ARTHUR,	J. K. GOODIN,
J. L. SAYLE,	J. M. TUTON,
CALEB MAY,	THOMAS BELL,
S. MEWHINY,	R. H. CROSBY,
A. CURTISS,	P. C. SCHUYLER,
A. HUNTING,	C. ROBINSON,
R. KNIGHT,	M. F. CONWAY,
O. C. BROWN,	J. S. EMERY,

J. H. LANE, President.

SAM. C. SMITH, Secretary,
CHARLES A. FOSTER, Assistant Secretary.

June 30th.—Mr. Douglas reported to the Senate on several bills submitted by Messrs. Clayton, Toombs, and others, for the pacification of the Kansas troubles, as also decidedly against Gov. Seward's proposition to admit Kansas as a Free State, under her Topeka Constitution. Mr. Collamer, being the minority of the Territorial Committee, made a brief and pungent counter report. Mr. Douglas gave notice that he would ask for a final vote on the day after the next.

July 1st.—Bill debated by Messrs. Thompson of Ky., Hale of N. H., Bigler of Pa., Adams of Miss., and Crittenden of Ky.

July 2d.—Debate continued through the day and following night, the majority resisting all motions to adjourn. Messrs. Wade, Pugh, Biggs, Bigler, Toombs, Clayton, Crittenden, Bell, Seward, Hale, and nearly half the Senate participated. An amendment moved by Mr. Adams of Miss., the day before, striking out so much of the bill as secures the Right of Suffrage, in the proposed reorganization of Kansas, to alien residents who shall have declared their intention to become citizens, and renounced all allegiance to foreign governments, was adopted: Yeas 22; Nays 16, as follows:

YEAS—Messrs. Adams and Brown of Miss., Bayard and Clayton of Del., Biggs and Reid of N. C., John Bell of Tenn., Brodhead of Penn., C. C. Clay and Fitzpatrick of Ala., Collamer and Foot of Vt., Crittenden and J. B. Thompson of Ky., Fessenden of Maine, Foster of Conn., Geyer of Mo., Hunter and Mason of Va., Iverson of Ga., Mallory and Yulee of Fla.—22.

NAYS—Messrs. Allen of R. I., Bigler of Pa., Butler and Evans of S. C., Bright of Ind., Cass of Mich., Dodge of Wisc., Douglas of Ill., Jones of Iowa, Pugh of Ohio, Seward of N. Y., Slidell of La., Toombs of Ga., Weller of Cal., Wilson of Mass., Wright of N. J.—16.

Sometime in the morning of July 3rd, the following amendment, reduced to shape by Mr. Geyer of Mo., was added to the 18th section of the bill—only Brown of Miss., Fitzpatrick of Ala., and Mason of Va., voting against it: Yeas 40. It provides that

"No law shall be made or have force or effect in said Territory [of Kansas] which shall require any attestation or oath to support any act of Congress or other legislative act, as a qualification for any civil office, public trust, or for any employment or profession, or to serve as a juror, or vote at an election, or which shall impose any tax upon, or condition to, the exercise of the right of suffrage, by any qualified voter, or which shall restrain or prohibit the free discussion of any law or subject of legislation in the said Territory, or the free expression of opinion thereon by the people of said Territory."

An amendment proposed by Mr. Clayton, to the same effect as the above, but rather more comprehensive in its terms, was superseded by the adoption of the foregoing, by a party vote: Yeas 34; Nays 11 [Free-State men].

Mr. Trumbull of Ill. moved the following:

"*And be it further enacted*, That it was the true intent and meaning of the 'act to organize the Territories of Nebraska and Kansas,' not to legislate slavery into Kansas, nor to exclude it therefrom, but to leave the people thereof perfectly free through their Territorial Legislature to regulate the institution of slavery in their own way, subject only to the Constitution of the United States, and that, until the Territorial Legislature acts upon the subject, the owner of a slave in one of the States has no right or authority to take such slave into the Territory of Kansas, and there hold him as a slave; but every slave taken to the Territory of Kansas by his owner for purposes of settlement is hereby declared to be free, unless there is some valid act of a duly constituted Legislative Assembly of said Territory, under which he may be held as a slave."

The Yeas and Nays being ordered, the proposition was voted down—Yeas 9; Nays 34—as follows:

YEAS—Messrs Durkee, Fessenden, Foot, Foster, Hale, Seward, Trumbull, Wade, and Wilson—9.

NAYS—Messrs. Adams, Allen, Bayard, Bell of Tennessee, Benjamin, Biggs, Bigler, Bright, Brodhead, Brown, Cass, Clay, Crittenden, Dodge, Douglas, Evans, Fitzpatrick, Geyer, Hunter, Iverson, Johnson, Jones of Iowa. Mallory, Pratt, Pugh, Reid, Sebastian, Slidell, Thompson of Kentucky, Toombs, Toucey, Weller, Wright, and Yulee—34.

Mr. Trumbull then proposed the following:

"*And be it further enacted*, That the provision in the 'act to organize the Territories of Nebraska and Kansas,' which declares it to be 'the true intent and meaning' of said act 'not to legislate slavery into any Territory or State, nor to exclude it therefrom, but to leave the people thereof perfectly free to form and regulate their domestic institutions in their own way, subject only to the Constitution of the United States,' was intended to, and does, confer upon, or leave to, the people of the Territory of Kansas full power, at any time, through its Territorial Legislature, to exclude slavery from said Territory or to recognize and regulate it therein."

This, too, was voted down, as follows:

YEAS—Messrs. Allen, Bell of New-Hampshire, Collamer, Durkee, Fessenden, Foot, Foster, Hale, Seward, Trumbull, and Wade—11.

NAYS—Messrs. Adams, Bayard, Benjamin, Biggs, Bigler, Bright, Brodhead, Brown, Cass, Clay, Crittenden, Dodge, Douglas, Evans, Fitzpatrick, Geyer, Hunter, Iverson, Johnson, Jones of Iowa, Mallory, Mason, Pratt, Pugh, Reid, Sebastian, Slidell, Stuart, Thompson of Kentucky, Toombs, Toucey, Weller, Wright, and Yulee—34.

Mr. Trumbull then proposed the following:

And be it further enacted, That all the acts and proceedings of all and every body of men heretofore assembled in said Territory of Kansas, and claiming to be a Legislative Assembly thereof, with authority to pass laws for the government of said Territory, are hereby declared to be utterly null and void. And no person shall hold any office, or exercise any authority or jurisdiction in said Territory, under or by virtue of any power or authority derived from such Legislative Assembly; nor shall the members thereof exercise any power or authority as such.

This, too, was voted down, as follows:

YEAS—Messrs. Bell of New-Hampshire, Collamer, Durkee, Fessenden, Foot, Foster, Hale, Seward, Trumbull, Wade, and Wilson—11.

NAYS—Messrs. Adams, Allen, Bayard, Bell of Tennessee, Benjamin, Biggs, Bigler, Bright, Brodhead, Brown, Cass, Clay, Crittenden, Dodge, Douglas, Evans, Fitzpatrick, Geyer, Hunter, Iverson, Johnson, Jones of Iowa, Mallory, Mason, Pratt, Pugh, Reid, Sebastian, Slidell, Stuart, Thompson of Kentucky, Toombs, Toucey, Weller, Wright, and Yulee—36.

Mr. Foster of Conn. moved the following amendment:

"SEC. —. *And be it further enacted*, That, until the inhabitants of said Territory shall proceed to hold a convention to form a State constitution according to the provisions of this act, and so long as said Territory remains a Territory, the following sections contained in chapter one hundred and fifty-one, in the volume transmitted to the Senate by the President of the United States, as containing the laws of Kansas, be, and the same are hereby, declared to be utterly null and void, viz.:

"'SEC. 12. If any free person, by speaking or by writing, assert or maintain that persons have not the right to hold slaves in this Territory, or shall introduce into this Territory any book, paper, magazine, pamphlet, or circular, containing any denial of the right of persons to hold slaves in this Territory, such persons shall be deemed guilty of felony, and punished by imprisonment at hard labor for a term of not less than two years.

"'SEC. 13. No person who is conscientiously opposed to holding slaves, or who does not admit the right to hold slaves in this Territory, shall sit as a juror on the trial of any prosecution for the violation of any one of the sections of this act.'"

This was rejected [as superfluous, or covered by a former amendment,] as follows:

YEAS—Messrs. Allen, Bell of New-Hampshire, Clayton, Collamer, Durkee, Fessenden, Foot, Foster, Hale, Seward, Trumbull, Wade, and Wilson—13.

NAYS—Messrs. Bayard, Benjamin, Biggs, Bigler, Bright, Brodhead, Brown, Cass, Clay, Dodge, Douglas, Evans, Fitzpatrick, Geyer, Hunter, Iverson, Johnson, Jones of Iowa, Mallory, Mason, Pratt, Pugh, Reid, Sebastian, Slidell, Stuart, Thompson of Kentucky, Toombs, Toucey, Weller, Wright, and Yulee—32.

Mr. Collamer of Vt. proposed the following:

And be it further enacted, That until the people of said Territory shall form a constitution and State government, and be admitted into the Union under the provisions of this act, there shall be neither slavery nor involuntary servitude in said Territory, otherwise than in punishment of crimes whereof the party shall have been duly convicted: *Provided always*, That any person escaping into the same, from whom labor or service is lawfully claimed in any State, such fugitive may be lawfully reclaimed and conveyed to the person claiming his or her service or labor as aforesaid.

This was voted down as follows:

YEAS—Messrs. Bell of New-Hampshire, Collamer, Fessenden, Foot, Foster, Hale, Seward, Trumbull, Wade, and Wilson—10.

NAYS—Messrs. Bayard, Bell of Tennessee, Benjamin, Biggs, Bigler, Bright, Brodhead, Brown, Cass, Clay, Clayton, Crittenden, Dodge, Douglas, Evans, Fitzpatrick, Geyer, Hunter, Iverson, Johnson, Jones of Iowa, Mallory, Mason, Pratt, Pugh, Reid, Sebastian, Slidell, Stuart Thompson of Kentucky, Toombs, Toucey, Weller, Wright, and Yulee—35.

Mr. Wilson of Mass. moved that the whole bill be stricken out and another inserted instead, repealing all the Territorial laws of Kansas.

Rejected: Yeas 8, (Bell of N. H., Collamer, Durkee, Fessenden, Foster, Seward, Wade and Wilson;) Nays 35.

Mr. Seward moved to strike out the whole bill, and insert instead one admitting Kansas as a Free State, under the Topeka Constitution: Defeated—Yeas 11; Nays 36—as follows:

YEAS—Messrs. Bell of New Hampshire, Collamer, Durkee, Fessenden, Foot, Foster, Hale, Seward, Trumbull, Wade, and Wilson—11.

NAYS—Messrs. Allen, Bayard, Bell of Tennessee, Benjamin, Biggs, Bigler, Bright, Brodhead, Brown, Cass, Clay, Clayton, Crittenden, Dodge, Douglas, Evans, Fitzpatrick, Geyer, Hunter, Iverson, Johnson, Jones of Iowa, Mallory, Mason, Pratt, Pugh, Reid, Sebastian, Slidell, Stuart, Thompson of Kentucky, Toombs, Toucey, Weller, Wright, and Yulee—36.

The bill was now reported as amended, and the amendment made in Committee of the Whole concurred in. The bill was then (8 A. M.) ordered to be engrossed and read a third time; and, on the question of its final passage, the vote stood—Yeas 33; Nays 12—as follows:

YEAS—Messrs. Allen, Bayard, Bell of Tennessee, Benjamin, Biggs, Bigler, Bright, Brodhead, Brown, Cass, Clay, Crittenden, Douglas, Evans, Fitzpatrick, Geyer, Hunter, Iverson, Johnson, Jones of Iowa, Mallory, Pratt, Pugh, Reid, Sebastian, Slidell, Stuart, Thompson of Kentucky, Toombs, Toucey, Weller, Wright, and Yulee—33.

NAYS—Messrs. Bell of New-Hampshire, Collamer, Dodge, Durkee, Fessenden, Foot, Foster, Hale, Seward, Trumbull, Wade, and Wilson—12.

The bill was then sent to the House in the following shape:

AN ACT

To authorize the people of the Territory of Kansas to form a constitution and State government preparatory to their admission into the Union on an equal footing with the original States.

Be it enacted by the Senate and House of Representatives of the United States of America in Congress assembled, That, for the purpose of making an enumeration of the inhabitants, authorized to vote under the provisions of this act, an apportionment and an election of members of a convention to form a State constitution for Kansas, as hereinafter provided, five competent persons shall be appointed by the President, by and with the advice and consent of the Senate, to be commissioners, a majority of whom shall constitute a quorum for the purpose of carrying into effect the provisions of this act, each of whom, before entering upon the duties of his office, shall take and subscribe an oath or affirmation that he will support the Constitution of the United States, and faithfully and impartially exercise and discharge the duties enjoined on him by this act, according to the best of his skill and judgment, which oath or affirmation shall be administered to them severally, and be duly certified by a judge, clerk, or commissioner of a court of the United States, and filed and recorded in the office of the Secretary of the Territory of Kansas.

SEC. 2. *And be it further enacted*, That it shall be the duty of said commissioners, under such regulations as the Secretary of the Interior may prescribe, to cause to be made a full and faithful enumeration of the legal voters resident in each county in the said Territory on the fourth day of July, eighteen hundred and fifty-six, and make returns thereof during the month of August next, or as soon thereafter as practicable, one of which returns shall be made to the office of the Secretary of the Interior, and one to the secretary of the Territory of Kansas, and which shall also exhibit the names of all such legal voters, classed in such manner as shall be prescribed by the regulations of the Secretary of the interior.

SEC. 3. *And be it further enacted*, That it shall be the duty of the Secretary of the Interior, immediately after the passage of this act, to prescribe regulations and forms to be observed in making the enumeration aforesaid, and to furnish the same with all necessary blanks to each of the commissioners as soon as may be after their appointment; and the commissioners shall meet without delay at the seat of government of Kansas Territory, and proceed to the discharge of the duties herein imposed upon them, and appoint a secretary to the board and such other persons as shall be necessary to aid and assist them in taking the enumeration herein provided for, who must also be duly sworn faithfully, impartially, and truly to discharge the duties assigned them by the commissioners.

SEC. 4. *And be it further enacted*, That said board of commissioners shall, so soon as said census shall be completed and returns made, proceed to make an apportionment of the members for a convention, among the different counties in said Territory, in the following manner: The whole number of legal voters shall be divided by fifty-two, and the product of such division, rejecting any fraction of a unit, shall be the ratio or rule of apportionment of members among the several counties; and if any county shall not have a number of legal voters, thus ascertained, equal to the ratio, it shall be attached to some adjoining county, and thus form a representative district, the number of said voters in each county or district shall then be divided by the ratio, and the product shall be the number of representatives apportioned to such county or district: *Provided*, That the loss in the number of members caused by the fractions remaining in the several counties, in the division of the legal voters thereof, shall be compensated by assigning to so many counties as have the largest fractions an additional member for its fraction, as may be necessary to make the whole number of representatives fifty-two.

SEC. 5. *And be it further enacted*, That the said board, immediately after the apportionment of the members of said convention, shall cause a sufficient number of copies thereof and of the returns of the census (specifying the name of each legal voter in each county or district) to be published and distributed among the inhabitants of the several counties, and shall transmit one copy of the said apportionment and census, duly authenticated by them, to each clerk of a court of record within the Territory, who shall file the same, and keep open to the inspection of every inhabitant who shall desire to examine it, and shall also cause other copies to be posted up in at least three of the most public places in each voting precinct, to the end that every inhabitant may inspect the same, and apply to the board to correct any error he may find therein, in the manner hereinafter provided.

SEC. 6. *And be it further enacted*, That said board shall remain in session each day, Sundays excepted, from the time of making said apportionment until the twentieth day of October next, at such places as shall be most convenient to the inhabitants of said Territory, and shall proceed to the inspection of said returns, and hear, correct, and finally determine according to the facts, without unreasonable delay, under proper regulations to be made by the board, for the ascertainment of disputed facts concerning said enumeration, all questions concerning the omission of any person from said returns, or the improper insertion of any name on said returns, and any other question affecting the integrity or fidelity of said returns, and for this purpose the said board and each member thereof shall have power to administer oaths and examine witnesses, and compel their attendance in such manner as said board shall deem necessary.

SEC. 7. *And be it further enacted*, That as soon as the said lists of legal voters shall thus have been revised and corrected, it shall be the duty of said board to cause copies thereof to be printed and distributed generally among the inhabitants of the proposed State, and one copy shall be deposited with the clerk of each court of record within the limits of the proposed State, and one copy delivered to each judge of the election, and at least three copies shall be posted up at each place of voting.

SEC. 8. *And be it further enacted*, That an election shall be held for members of a convention to form a constitution for the State of Kansas, according to the apportionment to be made aforesaid, on the first Tuesday after the first Monday in November, eighteen hundred and fifty-six, to be held at such places and to be conducted in such manner, both as to persons who shall superintend such election and the returns thereof as the board of commissioners shall appoint and direct, except in cases by this act otherwise provided; and at such election no person shall be permitted to vote unless his name shall appear on said corrected lists.

SEC. 9. *And be it further enacted*, That the board of commissioners shall have power, and it shall be their duty, to make all needful rules and regulations for the conduct of the said election and the returns thereof. They shall appoint three suitable persons to be judges of the election at each place of voting, and prescribe the mode of supplying vacancies. They shall cause copies of the rules and regulations, with a notice of the places of holding elections and the names of the judges, to be published and distributed in every election-district or precinct ten days before the day of election, and shall transmit a copy thereof to the clerk of each court of record, and one copy to each judge of election.

SEC. 10. *And be it further enacted*, That the judges of election shall each, before entering on the discharge of his duties, make oath or affirmation that he will faithfully and impartially discharge the duties of judge of the election according to law, which oath may be administered by any officer authorized by law to administer oaths. The clerks of election shall be appointed by the judges, and shall take the like oath or affirmation, to be administered by one of the judges or by any of the officers aforesaid. Duplicate returns of election shall be made and certified by the judges and clerks, one of which shall be deposited in the office of the clerk of the tribunal transacting county business for the county in which the election is held, and the other shall be transmitted to the board of commissioners, whose duty it shall be to decide, under proper regulations to be made by themselves, who are entitled to certificates of election, and to issue such certificates accordingly, to the persons who, upon examination of he returns and of such proofs as shall be adduced in case of a contest, shall appear to have been duly elected in each county or district: *Provided*, In case of a tie or of a contest, in which it cannot be satisfactorily determined who was duly elected, said commissioners shall order a new election in like manner as is herein provided. Upon the completion of these duties the said commissioners shall return to Washington, and report their proceedings to the Secretary of the Interior, whereupon said commission shall cease and determine.

SEC. 11. *And be it further enacted*, That every white male citizen of the United States over twenty-one years of age, who may be a *bona fide* inhabitant of said Territory on the fourth day of July, eighteen hundred and fifty-six, and who shall have resided three months next before said election in the county in which he offers to vote, and no other persons whatever shall be entitled to vote at said election, and any person qualified as a voter may be a delegate to said convention, and no others; and all persons who shall possess the other qualifications for voters under this act, and who shall have been *bona fide* inhabitants of said Territory at any time since its organization, and who shall have absented themselves therefrom in consequence of the disturbances therein, and who shall return before the first day of October next and become *bona fide* inhabitants of the Territory with the intent of making it their permanent home, and shall present satisfactory evidence of these facts to the board of commissioners, shall be entitled to vote at said election, and to have their names placed on said corrected list of voters for that purpose and to avoid all conflict in the complete execution of this act, all other elections in said Territory are hereby postponed until such time as said convention shall appoint.

SEC. 12. *And be it further enacted*, That the said commissioners, and all persons appointed by them to assist in taking the census, shall have power to administer oaths and examine persons on oath in all cases where it shall be necessary to the full and faithful performance of their duties under this act; and the secretary shall keep a journal of the proceedings of said board, and transmit copies thereof from time to time to the Secretary of the Interior; and when said commissioners shall have completed the business of their appointment, the books and papers of the board shall be deposited in the office of the Secretary of the Territory and there kept as records of his office.

SEC. 13. *And be it further enacted*, That if any person by menaces, threats, or force, or by any other unlawful means, shall directly or indirectly attempt to influence any qualified voter in giving his vote, or deter him from going to the polls, or disturb or hinder him in the free exercise of his right of suffrage at said election, the person so offending shall be adjudged guilty of a misdemeanor, and punished by fine of not less than two hundred and fifty dollars, nor exceeding five hundred dollars, or by imprisonment of not less than three months, nor exceeding one year, or by both.

SEC. 14. *And be it further enacted*, That every person, not being a qualified voter according to the provisions of this act, who shall vote at any election within the said Territory, knowing that he is not entitled to vote, and every person who shall, at the same election, vote more than once, whether at the same or a different place, shall be adjudged guilty of a misdemeanor, and be punished by fine of not less than one hundred dollars, nor exceeding two hundred and fifty dollars, or by imprisonment not less than three months, nor exceeding six months, or both.

SEC. 15. *And be it further enacted*, That any person whatsoever who may be charged with holding the election herein authorized, who shall willfully and knowingly commit any fraud or irregularity whatever, with the intent it to hinder, or prevent, or defeat a fair expression of the popular will in the said election, shall be guilty of a misdemeanor, and punished by fine not less than five hundred dollars, nor exceeding one thousand dollars, and imprisonment not less than six months, nor exceeding two years, or both, at the discretion of the court.

SEC. 16. *And be it further enacted*, That the delegates thus elected shall assemble in convention at the capitol of said Territory on the first Monday in December next; and when so assembled, shall first determine by a majority of the whole number of members elected whether it be or be not expedient at that time to form a constitution and State government; and if deemed expedient, shall proceed to form a constitution and State government, which shall be republican in its form, for admission into the Union on an equal footing with the original States in all respects whatever, by the name of the State of Kansas, with the following boundaries, to wit: beginning on the western boundary of the State of Missouri, where the thirty-seventh parallel of north latitude crosses the same, then west on said parallel to the one hundred and third meridian of longitude, then north on said meridian to the fortieth parallel of latitude, then east on said parallel of latitude to the western boundary of the State of Missouri, then southward with said boundary to the beginning; and until the next congressional apportionment the said State shall have one representative in the House of Representatives of the United States.

SEC. 17. *And be it further enacted*, That said commissioners shall receive, as their compensation, ten dollars per day during their attendance on the business of said commission, beginning on the day they depart from home, and their actual expenses, and said secretary of the board the sum of eight dollars per day, computed in like manner, and his expenses, and the said assistants, for taking the census, shall receive such reasonable compensation as the board shall deem just and equitable.

SEC. 18. *And be it further enacted*, That inasmuch as the Constitution of the United States and the organic act of said Territory have secured to the inhabitants thereof certain inalienable rights of which they cannot be deprived by any legislative enactment, therefore no religious test shall ever be required as a qualification to any office or public trust; no law shall be in force or enforced in said Territory respecting an establishment of religion, or prohibiting the free exercise thereof; or abridging the freedom of speech, or of the press; or of the right of the people peaceably to assemble, and petition for the redress of grievances; the right of the people to be secure in their persons, houses, papers, and effects against unreasonable searches and seizures shall not be violated; and no warrant shall issue but upon probable cause, supported by oath or affirmation, and particularly describing the place to be searched, and the person or things to be seized; nor shall the rights of the people to keep and bear arms be infringed. No person shall be held to answer for a capital or otherwise infamous crime, unless on a presentment or indictment of a grand jury; nor shall any person be subject for the same offense to be twice put in jeopardy of life or limb; nor shall be compelled in any criminal case to be a witness against himself, nor be deprived of life, liberty, or property without due process of law; nor shall private property be taken for public use without just compensation. In all criminal prosecution, the accused shall enjoy the right to a speedy and public trial by an impartial jury of the district wherein the crime shall have been committed, which district shall have been previously ascertained by law, and to be informed of the nature and cause of the accusation; to be confronted with the witnesses against him; to have compulsory process of obtaining witnesses in his favor, and to have the assistance of counsel for his defense. The privilege of habeas corpus shall not be suspended, unless when in case of rebellion or invasion, the public safety may require it. In suits at common law, where the value in controversy shall exceed twenty dollars, the right of trial by jury shall be preserved, and no fact tried by jury shall be otherwise re-examined in any court of the United States than according to the rules of the common law. Excessive bail shall not be required, nor excessive fines imposed, nor cruel and unusual punishments inflicted. No law shall be made or have force or effect in said Territory which shall require a test oath or oath to support any act of Congress or other legislative act as a qualification for any civil office or public trust, or for any employment or profession, or to serve as a juror, or vote at an election, or which shall impose any tax upon or condition to the exercise of the right of suffrage by any qualified voter, or which shall restrain or prohibit the free discussion of any law or subject of legislation in the said Territory, or the free expression of opinion thereon by the people of said Territory.

SEC. 19. *And be it further enacted*, That the following propositions be, and the same are hereby, offered to the said convention of the people of Kansas for their free acceptance or rejection, which, if accepted by the convention, shall be obligatory on the United States and upon the said State of Kansas, to wit:

First. That sections numbered sixteen and thirty-six in every township of public lands in said State, and where either of said sections or any part thereof has been sold or otherwise been disposed of, other lands, equivalent thereto and as contiguous as may be, shall be granted in said State for the use of schools.

Second. That seventy-two sections of land shall be set apart and reserved for the use and support of a State university, to be selected by the Governor of said State, subject to the approval of the Commissioner of the General Land Office, and to be appropriated and applied in such manner as the legislature of said State may prescribe for the purpose aforesaid, but for no other purpose.

Third. That ten entire sections of land, to be selected by the governor of said State, in legal subdivisions, shall be granted to said State for the purpose of completing the public buildings, or for the erection of others at the seat of government, under the direction of the legislature thereof.

Fourth. That all salt springs within said State, not exceeding twelve in number, with six sections of land adjoining, or as contiguous as may be to each, shall be granted to said State for its use; the same to be selected by the governor thereof within one year after the admission of said State, and, when so selected, to be used or disposed of on such terms, conditions, and regulations as the legislature shall direct. *Provided*, That no salt spring or land, the right whereof is now vested in any individual or individuals, or which may be hereafter confirmed or adjudged to any individual or individuals, shall by this article be granted to said State.

Fifth. That five per centum of the net proceeds of sales of all public lands lying within said State, which shall be sold by Congress after the admission of said State into the Union, after deducting all the expenses incident to the same, shall be paid to said State, for the purpose of making public roads and internal improvements, as the legislature shall direct: *Provided*, The foregoing propositions herein offered are on the condition, that the said convention which shall form the constitution of said State shall provide, by a clause in said constitution, or an ordinance, irrevocable without the consent of the United States, that said State shall never interfere with the primary disposal of the soil within the same, by the United States, or with any regulations Congress may find necessary for securing the title in said soil to *bona fide* purchasers thereof, and that no tax shall be imposed on lands belonging to the United States, and that in no case shall non-resident proprietors be taxed higher than residents.

SEC. 20. *And be it further enacted*, That the President be, and is hereby, authorized and empowered, upon application of the said board of commissioners, to employ such military force, according to existing laws, as he shall deem necessary to secure the faithful execution of the provisions of this act.

Passed the Senate, July 2, 1856.

Attest: ASBURY DICKINS, *Secretary*.

The bill was never acted on in the House, but lay on the Speaker's table, untouched, when the session terminated by adjournment, Monday, Aug. 18th.

July 8th.—In Senate, Mr. Douglas reported back from the Committee on Territories the House bill to admit Kansas as a State, with an amendment striking out all after the enacting clause, and inserting instead the Senate bill (No. 356) just given.

Mr. Hale of N. H. moved to amend this substitute by providing that all who migrate to the Territory prior to July 4th, 1857, shall be entitled to a vote in determining the character of the institutions of Kansas: Lost; Yeas 13; Nays 32.

Mr. Trumbull, of Ill. moved that all the Territorial laws of Kansas be repealed and the Territorial officers dismissed: Rejected; Yeas 12; Nays 32.

Mr. Collamer of Vt. proposed an amendment, prohibiting Slavery in all that portion of the Louisiana purchase north of 36° 30′ not included in the Territory of Kansas: Rejected—Yeas 12; Nays 30—as follows:

YEAS — Messrs. Bell of N. H., Collamer, Dodge, Fessenden, Fish, Foot, Foster, Hale, Hamlin, Seward, Trumbull and Wade.

NAYS—Messrs. Adams, Bayard, Benjamin, Biggs, Bright, Brodhead, Butler, Cass, Clay, Crittenden, Douglas, Fitzpatrick, Geyer, Hunter, Iverson, Johnson, Jones of Iowa, Jones of Tenn., Mallory, Mason, Pearce, Pugh, Reid, Sebastian, Slidell, Stuart, Thompson of Ky., Toombs, Weller and Yulee.

The substitute reported by Mr. Douglas was then agreed to: Yeas 32; Nays 13—and the bill in this shape passed.

[This amendment was not concurred in nor ever acted on by the House.]

July 29th.—Mr. Dunn of Ind. called up a bill "To reorganize the Territory of Kansas and for other purposes," which he had originally (July 7th) proposed as a substitute for Senate bill (No. 356) aforesaid. Its length, and the substantial identity of many of its provisions with those of other bills organizing Territories contained in this volume, dissuade us from quoting it entire. It provides for a legislative election on the first Tuesday in November next; and section 7 proceeds:

But it shall not be competent for said Legislative Assembly to pass any *ex post facto* law, or law impairing the validity of contracts; nor any law in abridgment of the freedom of speech or of the press, or to deprive any one of the right of trial by jury, or of the writ of *habeas corpus*; nor any law requiring any property qualification, or religious test, for the right to vote, hold office, or practice law, or serve on juries, in any Court of Justice; neither shall any person, to be entitled to any of said privileges, be required to take an oath or affirmation to support any law other than the Constitution of the United States. Nor shall cruel or unusual punishments be allowed, nor reasonable bail be refused to any person accused of any crime except treason and murder, nor in the latter case unless the proof is evident or the presumption great.

* * * * *

SEC. 15. *And be it further enacted*, That all suits, processes, and proceedings, civil and criminal, at law and in chancery, and all indictments and informations which shall be pending and undetermined in the courts of the Territory of Kansas or of New-Mxeico, when this act shall take effect, shall remain in said courts where pending, to be heard, tried, prosecuted, and determined in such courts as though this act had not been passed: *Provided, nevertheless*, That all criminal prosecutions now pending in any of the courts of the Territory of Kansas imputing to any person or persons the crime of treason against the United States, and all criminal prosecutions, by information or indictment, against any person or persons for any alleged violation or disregard whatever of what are usually known as the laws of the Legislature of Kansas, shall be forthwith dismissed by the courts where such prosecutions may be pending, and every person who may be restrained of his liberty by reason of said prosecutions, shall be released therefrom without delay. Nor shall there hereafter be instituted any criminal prosecution, in any of the courts of the United States, or of said Territory, against any person or persons for any such charge of treason in said Territory prior to the passage of this act, or any violation or disregard of said Legislative enactments at any time.

SEC. 16. *And be it further enacted*, That all justices of the peace, constables, sheriffs, and all other judicial and ministerial officers, who shall be in office within the limits of said Territory when this act shall take effect, shall be, and they are hereby, authorized and required to continue to exercise and perform the duties of their respective offices as officers of the Territory of Kansas, temporarily, and until they, or others, shall be duly appointed and qualified to fill their places, in the manner herein directed, or until their offices shall be abolished.

SEC. 23 grants to every actual settler a right of preëmption to the quarter-section of public land improved and occupied by him in said Territory of Kansas, prior to Jan. 1st, 1858.

The two last and most important sections of Mr. Dunn's bill are *verbatim* as follows:

SEC. 24. *And be it further enacted*, That so much of the fourteenth section, and also so much of the thirty-second section, of the act passed at the first session of the thirty-third Congress, commonly known as the Kansas-Nebraska act, as reads as follows, to wit: "Except the eighth section of the act preparatory to the admission of Missouri into the Union, approved March 6, 1820, which being inconsistent with the principle of non-intervention by Congress with Slavery in the States and Territories as recognized by the legislation of 1850, commonly called the Compromise Measures, is hereby declared inoperative and void; it being the true intent and meaning of this act not to legislate Slavery into any Territory or State, nor to exclude it therefrom, but to leave the people thereof perfectly free to form and regulate their domestic institutions in their own way, subject only to the Constitution of the United States: *Provided*, That nothing herein contained shall be construed to revive or put in force any law or regulation which may have existed prior to the act of 6th March, 1820, either protecting, establishing, prohibiting, or abolishing Slavery"—be and the same is hereby repealed, and the said eighth section of said act of the 6th of March, 1820, is hereby revived and declared to be in full force and effect within the said Territories of Kansas and Nebraska: *Provided, however*, That any person lawfully held to service in either of said Territories shall not be discharged from such service by reason of such repeal and revival of said eighth section, if such person shall be permanently removed from such Territory or Territories prior to the 1st day of January, 1858; and any child or children born in either of said Territories, of any female lawfully held to service, if in like manner removed without said Territories before the expiration of that date, shall not be, by reason of anything in this act, emancipated from any service it might have owed had this act never been passed: *And provided further*, That any person lawfully held to service in any other State or Territory of the United States, and escaping into either the Territory of Kansas or Nebraska, may be reclaimed and removed to the person or place where such service is due, under any law of the United States which shall be in force upon the subject.

Sec. 25. *And be it further enacted*, That all other parts of the aforesaid Kansas-Nebraska act which relate to the said Territory of Kansas, and every other law or usage having, or which is pretended to have, any force or effect in said Territory in conflict with the provisions or the spirit of this act, except such laws of Congress and treaty stipulations as relate to the Indians, are hereby repealed, and declared void.

Mr. Dunn having carried a reference to the Committee of the Whole, of a bill introduced by Mr. Grow, repealing all the acts of the alleged Territorial Legislature of Kansas, now moved and carried a reconsideration of that vote, and proceeded to the striking out of Mr. Grow's bill and the insertion of his own as a substitute. This motion prevailed. Whereupon Mr. Dunn moved the previous question on ordering this bill to be engrossed and read a third time, which prevailed—Yeas 92; Nays 86—and then the bill passed —Yeas 88; Nays 74—as follows:

YEAS—Messrs. Albright, Allison, Ball, Barbour, Benson, Bishop, Bliss, Bradshaw, Brenton, Buffinton, Campbell of Pa., Campbell of Ohio, Chaffee, Clawson, Colfax, Comins, Covode, Cumback, Damrell, Dean, Dick, Dodd, Dunn, Durfee, Edie, Edwards, Emrie, Flagler, Giddings, Gilbert, Granger, Grow, Hall of Mass., Harlan, *Harrison*, *Haven*, Holloway, Horton of N. Y., Horton of Ohio, Hughston, Kelsey, King, Knapp, Knight, Knowlton, Knox, Kunkel, Matteson, M'Carty, Miller, *Moore*, Morgan, Morrill, Nichols, Norton, Oliver, Parker, Pelton, Perry, Pettit, Pringle, Purviance, Ritchie, Sabin, Sage, Sapp, Sherman, Simmons, Spinner, Stanton, Stranahan, Tappan, Thurston, Todd, Trafton, Wade, Wakeman, Walbridge, Waldron, Washburne of Ill., Washburn of Me., Watson, Welch, *Wells*, Wood, Woodruff, Woodworth—88.

NAYS—Messrs. Aiken, Barksdale, Bell, Bowie, Branch, *Broom*, Burnett, Campbell of Kentucky, Carlile, Caruthers, Caskie, Cobb of Ga., Cobb of Ala., Cox, Craige, Crawford, Cullen, Davidson, Davis of Md., Denver, Dowdell, Edmundson, English, Faulkner, Foster, Goode, Greenwood, Harris of Md., Harris of Ala., Harris of Illinois, Houston, Jewett, Jones of Tenn., Jones of Penn., Kennett, Kidwell, Lake, *Leiter*, Lumpkin, H. Marshall of Kentucky, Marshall of Illinois, Maxwell, Miller of Indiana, Millson, Packer, Peck, Phelps, Powell, Puryear, Quitman, Reade, Ready, Ricaud, Rivers, Ruffin, Savage, Shorter, Smith of Tenn., Smith of Va., Sneed, Stephens, Stewart, Swope, Taylor, Trippe, Underwood, Valk, Walker, Warner, Watkins, Winslow, Wright of Miss., Wright of Tenn., and Zollicoffer—74.

This bill was not acted on by the Senate.

The House in the course of its action on the several Annual Appropriation bills, affixed to several of them, respectively, provisos, abolishing, repealing, or suspending the various obnoxious acts of the Territorial Legislature; but all these were resisted by the Senate, and were ultimately given up by the House, save one appropriating $20,000 for the pay and expenses of the *next* Territorial Legislature, which the Senate gave up, on finding itself in serious disagreement with the House, and thus secured the passage of the Civil Appropriation bill. Finally the two Houses were at odds, on a proviso forbidding the employment of the Army to enforce the acts of the Shawnee Mission assemblage, claiming to be a Territorial Legislature of Kansas, when, at noon on the 18th of August, the Speaker's hammer fell, announcing the termination of the session, leaving the Army bill unpassed. But President Pierce immediately issued a proclamation convening an extra session on the 21st (Thursday), when the two Houses reconvened accordingly, and a full quorum of each was found to be present. The House promptly repassed the Army bill, again affixing a proviso forbidding the use of the army to enforce the disputed Territorial laws, which proviso the Senate as promptly struck out, and the House as promptly reinserted. The Senate insisted on its disagreement, but asked no conference, and the House (Aug. 22d) by a close vote decided to adhere to its proviso: Yeas 97; Nays 93; but one of the yeas (Bocock of Va.) was so given in order to be able to move a reconsideration; so that the true division was 96 to 94, which was the actual division on a motion by Mr. Cobb of Ga. that the House recede from its position. Finally, a motion to reconsider was made and laid on the table: Yeas 97; Nays 96; and the House thereupon adjourned.

Aug. 23d.—The Senate also voted to adhere: Yeas 35; Nays 9.

Mr. Clayton proposed a Committee of Conference, to which Mr. Seward objected. No action.

In the House, Mr. Campbell of Ohio proposed a similar Committee of Conference. Objected to.

Mr. Matteson of New-York submitted the following:

Whereas, By an act passed by the two Houses of Congress, and approved by the President, entitled "Joint resolution for annexing Texas to the United States, approved March 1, 1845," articles of compact were offered to Texas for her admission into the Union "*upon certain conditions and guarantees*," the third article of which tendered compact was in these words:

"New States of convenient size, not exceeding four in number, in addition to said State of Texas, and having sufficient population, may hereafter, by the consent of said State, be formed out of the Territory thereof, which shall be entitled to admission under the Federal Constitution; and such States as may be formed out of that portion of said Territory lying south of 36° 30' north latitude, commonly known as the Missouri Compromise line, shall be admitted into the Union, with or without Slavery, as the people of each State asking admission may desire; and in such State or States as shall be formed out of said Territory north of said Compromise line, Slavery or involuntary servitude (except for crime) shall be prohibited;"

And whereas, Texas, by a solemn public act, done in a convention of the people, according to the requirements of the said act of Congress, did accept the said articles of compact, and was admitted into the Union as one of the United States upon the "*conditions and guarantees*" mentioned in said joint resolution, and is now a State of this Union in virtue thereof;

And whereas, The said third article of compact as aforesaid, containing a limitation of Slavery in restricting the number of Slave States to be formed in Texas south of thirty-six degrees thirty minutes, to four States in addition to Texas itself, and also a prohibition of Slavery, except for crime, north of thirty-six degrees thirty minutes north latitude, is an independent and substantive motion, irrepealable by either of the contracting parties without the consent of the other, and is not repealed by the Kansas-Nebraska act, and could not be repealed by that act:

Therefore, be it resolved, That Slavery, except for crime, in all that part of the former province of Louisiana north of latitude thirty-six degrees thirty minutes is and remains prohibited, and that the President of the United States is under a double obligation to see that provision faithfully executed, both as a law of Congress and as a compact with a then foreign power, for a great and valuable consideration.

And whereas, Besides being a compact with Texas, the said third article was a compromise between the Free and Slave States of this Union with limitation of Slavery, both as to the number of Slave States which might be formed in Texas, and the prohibition of Slavery north of thirty-six degrees thirty minutes, by virtue of which Texas was admitted into the Union, and without which she could not have been admitted: Therefore,

Be it resolved, That any attempt to violate said third article of compromise, either by admitting a greater number of Slave States south of thirty-six degrees thirty minutes than allowed therein, or by extending Slavery north of that latitude, is a violation of said compromise and a direct attack upon the harmony and stability of the Union.

Mr. Dunn of Ind. moved that this do lie on the table: Carried: Yeas 101; Nays 83.

Mr. Cobb of Ga. moved that the House recede from its Kansas proviso: Defeated: Yeas 97; Nays 100. Adjourned.

The struggle for the passage of the bill with or without the proviso continued until Saturday, August 30th, when, several members, hostile to the proviso, and hitherto absent, unpaired, having returned, the House again passed the Army bill with the proviso modified as follows:

Provided, however, that no part of the military force of the United States, for the support of which appropriations are made by this act, shall be employed in aid of the enforcement of any enactments heretofore made by the body claiming to be the Territorial Legislature of Kansas.

The bill passed as reported (under the Previous Question:) Yeas 99; Nays 79; and was sent to the Senate, where the above Proviso was stricken out: Yeas 26; Nays 7; and the bill thus returned to the House, when the Senate's amendment was concurred in by the following vote:

YEAS—Messrs. Aiken, Akers, Barksdale, Bell, Bennett of Miss., Bocock, Bowie, Boyce, Branch, Burnett, Cadwalader, Campbell of Ky., Carlile, Caskie, Clingman, Cobb of Ga., Cobb of Ala., Cox, Craige, Crawford, Cullen, Davidson, Davis of Md., Denver, Dowdell, Edmundson, Elliott, Etheredge, Eustis, Evans, Faulkner, Florence, Fuller of Me., Goode, Greenwood, Hall of Iowa, Harris of Md., Harris of Ala., Harris of Ill., *Harrison*, *Haven*, HICKMAN, Hoffman, Houston, Jewett, Jones of Tenn., Jones of Penn., Keitt, Kelly, Kennett, Kidwell, Lake, Letcher, Lumpkin, A. K. Marshall of Ky., Humphrey Marshall of Ky., Marshall of Ill., Maxwell, McMullen McQueen, Miller of Ind., Millson, Oliver of Mo. Orr, Packer, Peck, Phelps, Porter, Powell Puryear, Quitman, Ricaud, Rivers, Ruffin, Rust Sandidge, Savage, Seward, Shorter, Smith of Tenn., Smith of Va., Smith of Ala., Sneed, Stephens, Stewart, Swope, Talbott, Taylor, *Tyson*, Underwood, Vail, Walker, Warner, Wells, Wheeler, *Whitney*, Williams, Winslow, Wright of Miss., Wright of Tenn., and Zollicoffer—101.

NAYS—Messrs. Albright, Allison, Barbour, BARCLAY, Bennett of N. Y., Benson, Billinghurst, Bingham, Bliss, Bradshaw, Brenton, Buffinton, Campbell of Penn., Campbell of Ohio Chaffee, E. Clark, Clawson, Colfax, Comins, Covode, Cragin, Cumback, Damrell, Davis of Mass., Dean, Dewitt, Dick, Dickson, Dodd, *Dunn*, Durfee, Edie, Edwards, Emrie, Flagler, Galloway, Giddings, Gilbert, Granger, Grow, Harlan, Holloway, Horton of N. Y., Howard, Hughston, Kelsey, King, Knapp, Knight, Knowlton, Knox, Kunkel, Leiter, Mace, Matteson, McCarty, Morgan, Mott, Murray, Norton, Oliver of N. Y., Parker, Pelton, Pennington, Pettit, Pike, Pringle, Purviance, Ritchie, Roberts, Robbins, Robison, Sabin, Sage, Sapp, Scott, Sherman, Simmons, Spinner, Stanton, Stranahan, Tappan, Thorington, Thurston, Todd, Trafton, Wade, Wakeman, Walbridge, Waldron, Washburne of Ill., Washburne of Wisc., Washburn of Me., Welch, Woodruff, and Woodworth—97.

So the Proviso was beaten at last, and the bill passed, with no restriction on the President's discretion in the use of the Army in Kansas; just as all attempts of the House, to direct the President to have a *nolle prosequi* entered in the case of the Free-State prisoners in Kansas charged with aiding the formation and adoption of the Free-State constitution as aforesaid, had been previously beaten, after prevailing in the House—the Senate striking them out and the House (by a union of nearly all the supporters of Fillmore with nearly or quite all those supporting Buchanan) finally acquiescing.

In conclusion, it may be said, generally, that nothing has been really done, or (owing to the triangular division of parties) *could* have been done, by this Congress with regard to Kansas, except to collect, authenticate, and present facts to be considered and acted on by the People in the ensuing Presidential and Congressional elections. By the result of these, in all human probability, the fate of Kansas is now to be decided.

www.ingramcontent.com/pod-product-compliance
Lightning Source LLC
LaVergne TN
LVHW021357110826
845150LV00007B/1685

9781425513368